내신 및 시·도 교육청 영어듣기평가 완벽 대비

Listening

올리고

Level **4**

중학영어듣기 모의고사

 **DARAKWON**

올리고

Listening Level 4

중학영어듣기 모의고사

지은이 정수진, 한길연, 박선화, 김호성
펴낸이 정규도
펴낸곳 (주)다락원

초판 1쇄 인쇄 2014년 8월 7일
초판 6쇄 발행 2023년 5월 8일

편집 콘텐츠온, 서정아
일러스트 노연지
디자인 김나경

다락원 경기도 파주시 문발로 211
내용문의: (02)736-2031 내선 503
구입문의: (02)736-2031 내선 250~252
Fax: (02)732-2037
출판등록 1977년 9월 16일 제406-2008-000007호

ISBN 978-89-277-0714-1 54740
      978-89-277-0710-3 54740 (set)

http://www.darakwon.co.kr

• 다락원 홈페이지를 방문하시면 상세한 출판정보와 함께 동영상강좌, MP3자료 등 다양한 어학 정보를 얻으실 수 있습니다.

내신 및 시·도 교육청 영어듣기평가 완벽 대비

Listening 올리고

Level 4

중학영어듣기 모의고사

DARAKWON

Structure & Features | 구성과 특징

Listening Test

전국 16개 시·도 교육청 주관 영어듣기능력평가 및 내신 교과서 반영!

최신 기출 유형을 철저히 분석, 반영하여 실제 시험과 유사하게 구성한 모의고사로 실전 감각을 키울 수 있습니다. 또한 영어 교과서의 주요 표현 및 소재들을 활용하여 내신까지 효과적으로 대비할 수 있습니다.

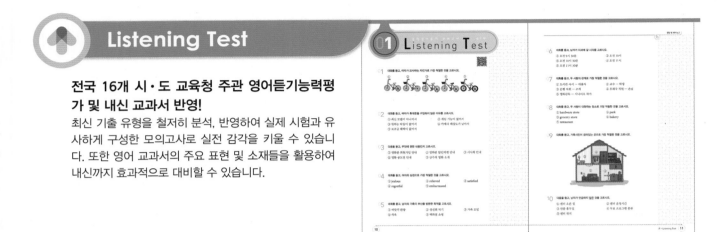

Further Study

주요 지문 심화학습으로 내신 서술형 완벽 대비!

Listening Test의 주요 지문만을 모아 서술형 문제로 다시 풀어볼 수 있도록 구성하였습니다. 보다 심화된 듣기 문제로 내신 서술형 평가에 철저히 대비하고, 듣기 실력을 강화할 수 있습니다.

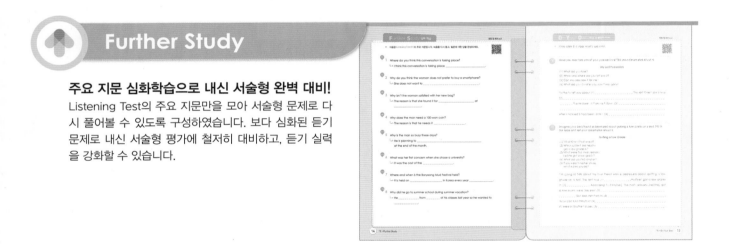

On Your Own

내신 말하기 수행평가 대비까지 한 번에!

Listening Test 및 기출 문제에서 출제된 주제와 소재를 응용한 다양한 연습 문제를 통해 별도로 준비하기 어려운 내신 말하기 수행평가까지 한 번에 대비할 수 있습니다.

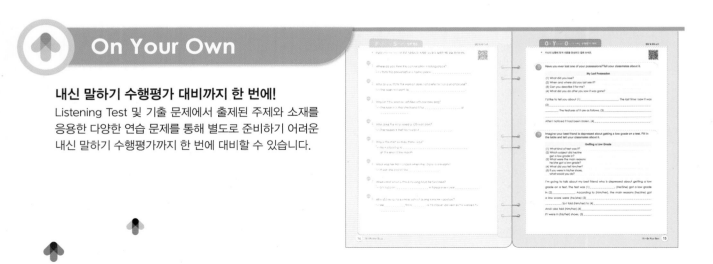

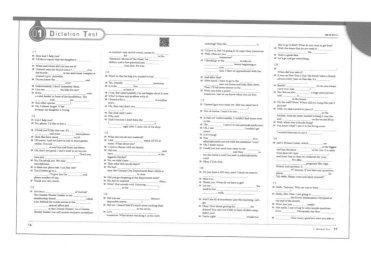

Dictation Test

전 지문 받아쓰기로 꼼꼼한 마무리 학습!

매회 전 지문 받아쓰기를 수록하여 놓친 부분을 빠짐없이 확인할 수 있습니다. 문제의 핵심이 되는 키워드, 중요 표현, 연음 등을 확인하며, 복습은 물론 자신의 취약점을 다시 한 번 확인할 수 있습니다.

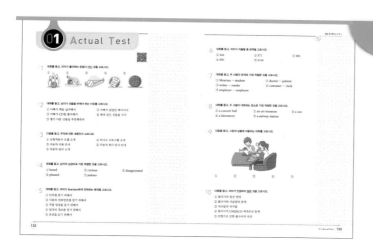

Actual Test

실전 모의고사로 최종 실력 점검!

실제 시험과 가장 유사한 모의고사로서 자신의 실력을 최종 점검해볼 수 있습니다. 시험에 자주 나오는 유형과 표현들을 100% 반영한 영어듣기능력평가 완벽 대비 모의고사입니다.

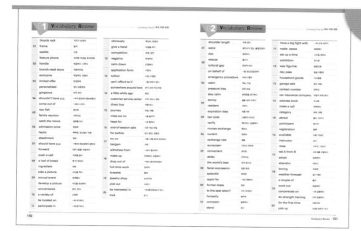

Vocabulary Review

중요 어휘 및 표현을 한눈에!

본문에 나오는 주요 어휘와 표현을 각 모의고사 회별로 한눈에 정리하여 단어 학습을 보다 효율적으로 할 수 있습니다.

Contents ㅣ 목차

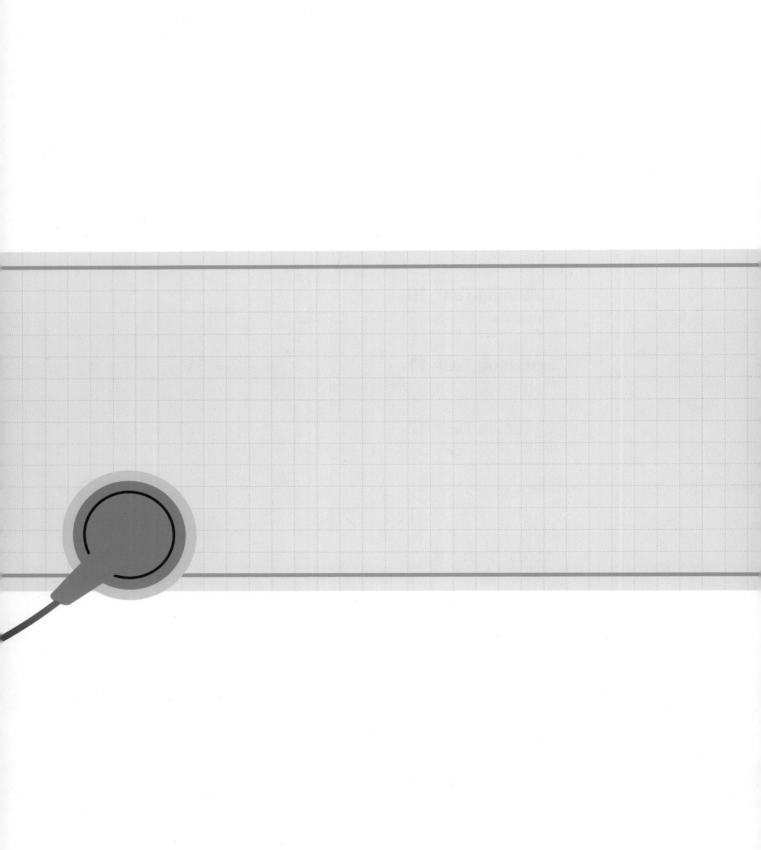

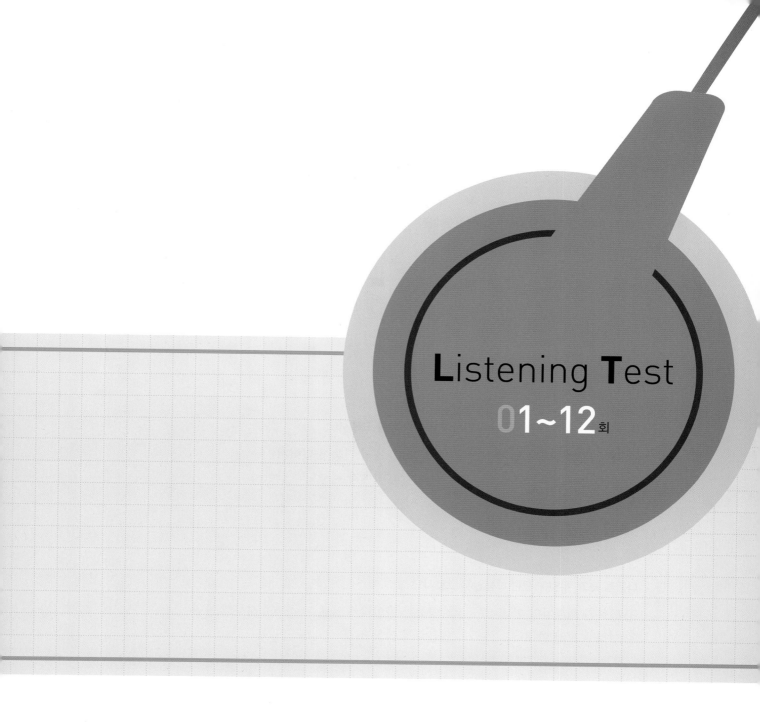

Listening Test
01~12회

01 대화를 듣고, 여자가 묘사하는 자전거로 가장 적절한 것을 고르시오.

02 대화를 듣고, 여자가 휴대폰을 구입하지 않은 이유를 고르시오.

① 최신 모델이 아니어서
② 게임 기능이 없어서
③ 원하는 타입이 없어서
④ 카메라 해상도가 낮아서
⑤ 보조금 혜택이 없어서

03 다음을 듣고, 무엇에 관한 내용인지 고르시오.

① 영화관 회원가입 안내
② 영화관 할인티켓 안내
③ 시사회 안내
④ 영화 공모전 안내
⑤ 금주의 영화 소개

04 대화를 듣고, 여자의 심경으로 가장 적절한 것을 고르시오.

① jealous
② relieved
③ satisfied
④ regretful
⑤ embarrassed

05 대화를 듣고, 남자의 가족이 부산을 방문한 목적을 고르시오.

① 바닷가 관광
② 생선회 먹기
③ 가족 모임
④ 족욕
⑤ 백화점 쇼핑

06 대화를 듣고, 남자가 치과에 갈 시각을 고르시오.

① 오전 9시 30분 ② 오전 10시
③ 오전 10시 30분 ④ 오전 11시
⑤ 오전 11시 30분

07 대화를 듣고, 두 사람의 관계로 가장 적절한 것을 고르시오.

① 도서관 사서 — 대출자 ② 교수 — 학생
③ 은행 직원 — 고객 ④ 우체국 직원 — 손님
⑤ 영화감독 — 시나리오 작가

08 대화를 듣고, 두 사람이 대화하는 장소로 가장 적절한 것을 고르시오.

① hardware store ② park
③ grocery store ④ bakery
⑤ restaurant

09 대화를 듣고, 가족사진이 걸려있는 곳으로 가장 적절한 것을 고르시오.

10 다음을 듣고, 남자가 언급하지 않은 것을 고르시오.

① 센터 오픈 일 ② 센터 운영시간
③ 연중 휴무일 ④ 무료 프로그램 종류
⑤ 센터 위치

11 대화를 듣고, 남자가 여자에게 부탁한 일로 가장 적절한 것을 고르시오.

① 수학 올림피아드 참가 신청해주기
② 수학 올림피아드 기출문제 뽑아주기
③ 수학 올림피아드 문제풀이 도와주기
④ 수학 올림피아드 문제 채점해주기
⑤ 수학 올림피아드에 같이 가기

12 대화를 듣고, 여자가 남자에게 해준 조언으로 옳지 <u>않은</u> 것을 고르시오.

① 잠을 푹 자기 ② 부정적으로 생각하지 않기
③ 자신을 믿기 ④ 따뜻한 우유 마시기
⑤ 클래식 음악 듣기

13 대화를 듣고, 여자가 진학하고 싶은 대학으로 가장 적절한 것을 고르시오.

University	Major	Yearly Tuition($)	Dormitory	Scholarship
①	Psychology	4,900	O	O
②	Psychology	4,400	X	O
③	Psychology	4,200	O	X
④	Education	5,400	X	O
⑤	Education	4,200	O	X

14 대화를 듣고, 대화 직후 두 사람이 할 일로 가장 적절한 것을 고르시오.

① 왔던 경로 다시 가보기 ② 주머니 속 확인해보기
③ 가방 속 확인해보기 ④ 여자 핸드폰에 전화하기
⑤ 고객 서비스 센터에 가기

15 다음을 듣고, Boryeong Mud Festival에 대해서 언급되지 <u>않은</u> 것을 고르시오.

① 개최 시기 ② 개최 장소 ③ 입장료
④ 폐막 시기 ⑤ 도착 소요 시간

[16-17] 대화를 듣고, 여자의 마지막 말에 이어질 남자의 응답으로 가장 적절한 것을 고르시오.

16　① I'm pleased to meet you.

② Great. I'll see you tomorrow.

③ Sounds good. Then see you there.

④ No, I can't. I have to take a rest today.

⑤ That's a good idea. I'll pick you up in an hour.

17　① Sure. How about this one?

② That's a big bargain. I'll take it.

③ I think I'd like to try on a few more.

④ Of course, it's a great deal. Go try it on.

⑤ That's right. However, it is worth trying it on.

[18-19] 대화를 듣고, 남자의 마지막 말에 이어질 여자의 응답으로 가장 적절한 것을 고르시오.

18　① She wanted to study as hard as possible.

② Her summer job turned into full-time work.

③ I advised her to concentrate on her academic work.

④ She worked to make enough money for her tuition, too.

⑤ It's because she got a scholarship from the government.

19　① He paid $100 for the bracelet.

② Yes, I bought him a neat neck tie.

③ No, he just wanted to buy me something.

④ Their wedding anniversary is on December 23th.

⑤ We went to Jeju Island to celebrate our engagement.

20　다음을 듣고, Pia가 Greg에게 할 말로 가장 적절한 것을 고르시오.

① Do you mind going to the library with me?

② What kind of book do you want to borrow?

③ Let's meet in front of the library in an hour.

④ I'm sorry, I have to go to the dental clinic now.

⑤ Let me think. OK. Let's go see a doctor together.

● 다음은 **Listening Test 01**의 주요 지문입니다. 녹음을 다시 듣고, 질문에 대한 답을 완성하세요.

Q1 **1** Where do you think this conversation is taking place?

↳ I think this conversation is taking place _____.

Q2 **2** Why do you think the woman does not prefer to buy a smartphone?

↳ She does not want to _____.

Q4 **3** Why isn't the woman satisfied with her new bag?

↳ The reason is that she found it for _____ at

_____.

Q8 **4** Why does the man need a 100-won coin?

↳ The reason is that he needs it _____.

Q11 **5** Why is the man so busy these days?

↳ He is planning to _____

at the end of the month.

Q13 **6** What was her first concern when she chose a university?

↳ It was the cost of the _____.

Q15 **7** Where and when is the Boryeong Mud Festival held?

↳ It is held on _____ in Korea every year _____.

Q18 **8** Why did he go to summer school during summer vacation?

↳ He _____ from _____ of his classes last year so he wanted to

_____.

자신의 상황에 맞게 내용을 완성하고 말해 보세요.

A

Have you ever lost one of your possessions? Tell your classmates about it.

My Lost Possession

(1) What did you lose?	
(2) When and where did you last see it?	
(3) Can you describe it for me?	
(4) What did you do after you saw it was gone?	

I'd like to tell you about (1)_____. The last time I saw it was

(2)_____

_____. The features of it are as follows. (3)_____

_____.

After I noticed it had been stolen, (4)_____.

B

Imagine your best friend is depressed about getting a low grade on a test. Fill in the table and tell your classmates about it.

Getting a Low Grade

(1) What kind of test was it?	
(2) Which subject did he/she get a low grade in?	
(3) What were the main reasons he/she got a low grade?	
(4) What did you tell him/her?	
(5) If you were in his/her shoes, what would you do?	

I'm going to talk about my best friend who is depressed about getting a low

grade on a test. The test was (1)_____. (He/She) got a low grade

in (2)_____. According to (him/her), the main reasons (he/she) got

a low score were (he/she) (3)_____

_____. So I told (him/her) to (4)_____.

And I also told (him/her) (4)_____.

If I were in (his/her) shoes, (5)_____.

01

M How may I help you?

W I'd like to report that my daughter's _____ _____ _____.

M When and where did you last see it?

W I haven't seen the bicycle since I _____ it to the bicycle _____ in my apartment complex at around 5 p.m. yesterday.

M Do you know the _____ _____ and _____ _____ of it?

W Unfortunately, I don't remember them.

M Can you _____ the bike for me?

W It has _____ _____ _____ with a violet basket in front of the handlebars. The _____ and _____ are _____.

M Any other special _____?

W Oh, I almost forgot. It has _____ _____ because my daughter is young.

02

M Can I help you?

W Yes, please. I'd like to buy a _____ _____.

M I think you'll like this one. It's _____ _____ and most _____ smartphone.

W Does this have many _____ on it?

M Of course. And you have access to more games online. You can _____ _____ _____ at anytime and from anywhere.

W Oh, that's not good. I don't want to let my son _____ _____ _____ _____. Don't you have any _____ _____?

M No, I'm afraid not. We only _____ smartphones.

W Is there any place that I can buy one?

M You'd better go to a _____ _____ _____. I'll give you the _____ and phone number of one.

W Thank you very much.

03

M Are you a _____ _____ of movies? The Cinema Theater Insider is our _____ membership-based _____ _____ which is for behind the scenes access to the _____ _____, special offers and _____ _____ at the Cinema Theater. As a Cinema Theater Insider you will receive exclusive invitations to member-only movie events, access to _____ _____ for _____ _____ to the 'Members' Movie of The Week' for _____ dollars, and a free personalized _____ _____. Join now. It's free.

04

M Wow! Is this the bag you wanted to buy _____ _____ _____?

W Yes, I finally _____ _____ yesterday.

M It looks _____. You _____ _____ _____ to have it.

W I was. But unfortunately, I'm not happy about it now.

M Why? Is there any problem with it?

W I found it for a _____ _____ at another store.

M Oh, then why don't you _____ _____ _____?

W The clerk said I can't.

M Why not?

W That's because I don't have the _____. I _____ _____ _____ it _____ right after I came out of the shop.

05

M What did you do last weekend?

W I did _____ _____ watch DVDs at home. What about you?

M I went to Busan with my family.

W Did you _____ _____ _____ and have _____ _____ _____ at the Jagalchi Market?

M No, we didn't have _____ _____.

W Then what did you do there?

M We had _____ _____ _____ near the Centum City Department Store which is _____ _____ in Asia.

W Did you go shopping at the department store?

M No, but we enjoyed _____ _____ there.

W Wow! That sounds cool. Enjoying _____ _____ at the _____ _____!

06

W Did you see _____ _____ *Mission Impossible* movie _____?

M Not yet. I heard that it's much more exciting than _____ _____ in the series.

W Let's _____ _____ _____ tomorrow. What about watching it in the early morning? Then the _____ _____ is _____.

M I'd love to, but I'm going to be super busy tomorrow.

W Well, what are you _____ _____ _____ tomorrow?

M I should go to the _____ to take an _____ _____ lesson beginning at _____ a.m. _____ _____ _____ that, I have an appointment with the _____.

W And after that?

M After lunch, I have to go to the _____ _____ near my house and help clean there. Then, I'll tell some stories to the _____.

W Wow, you have a pretty _____ _____ tomorrow. Just let me know when you are free.

07

M I haven't got your essay yet. Did you email me it _____ _____ _____?

W Yes, of course. I sent it to you _____ _____ _____ _____.

M Is that so? Unfortunately, I couldn't find yours even in the _____ _____.

W The _____ I sent it to was admin@cyjedu.com.

M Oh, I see. _____ _____ _____ I couldn't get yours.

W Is it wrong?

M You _____ _____ _____ it to admin@cyjedu.net not with the extension ".com"

W Oh, I didn't know.

M Could you just send your essay to me _____ _____ _____ and then _____ to me the initial e-mail you sent to admin@cyjedu.com?

W Okay, I'll do that.

08

M Do you have a 100-won coin? I think we need to _____ _____ _____.

W Here it is.

M Thank you. What do we have to get?

W Let me _____ _____ _____. We need to buy _____ _____ _____ _____, milk, _____, _____ _____.

M And I ate all of strawberry jam this morning. Let's get _____ _____.

W Okay. How about getting the _____ for dinner? You said you'd like to have chicken soup, didn't you?

M You're right. _____ _____ would you

like to go to first? What do you want to get first?

W Well, the items that do not need to _____ _____ _____ the _____.

M That's a great idea.

W Let's go and get everything.

09

W _____ _____ _____ _____ _____! When did you take it?

M It was on New Year's Day. My family takes a family picture every year on that day. It's _____ _____ _____.

W Really? _____ _____! So do you always carry it in your _____?

M Yes. But we also _____ a large sized picture and _____ it _____ _____ _____ in the house.

W On the wall? Wow! Where did you hang this year's picture?

M Well, my dad wanted to place it _____ _____ _____ _____ in the kitchen. And my mom wanted to hang it over her and _____ _____ on the second floor.

W Well, where was it finally hung?

M You know what? I put it in the living room _____ _____ _____ _____. I wanted everyone to see it _____.

10

M Jaeil's Fitness Center, which _____ on _____ _____, _____, is the biggest and has the latest _____ in the city. It is open from 6am till 11pm _____ _____, and from 7am to 9pm on weekends for your _____. We offer _____ _____ _____ _____ programs like yoga, Pilates, and aerobics. It _____ _____ _____ 5th Avenue. If you have any questions, please _____ _____ _____ _____ 02-702-9896. Please come and enjoy yourself!

11

W Hello, Taeyoon. Why are you so busy _____ _____?

M Hello, Mrs. Han. I am going to _____ _____ the Korea Mathematics Olympiad at the end of the month.

W Wow. Are you _____ ready?

M Not really. I am trying to solve sample questions from _____ Olympiads, but they _____ _____ _____ _____.

W _____. How many questions were you able to

solve?

M I guess _____% of them. Can you give me a hand to answer the _____ _____ _____?

W Hmm… I'll check my schedule and _____ _____ _____ in an hour.

M I'm really _____ for your help.

W Well, I'm _____ _____ if I have any time yet. So don't say that yet.

12

W What's the matter? You don't look fine.

M I'm so _____ _____ tomorrow's piano _____.

W Don't worry about that. You've been practicing so hard.

M I really hope I've _____ _____. But… could you give me some _____ _____ _____?

W Sure! Get enough sleep tonight. Never think in a _____ _____, and you should _____ _____.

M I will try to do those things.

W Then, tomorrow, on the day of the competition, _____ _____ _____ music. It will help you _____ _____.

M Thank you very much for your _____. I'm sure it will help me.

W I will _____ _____ _____ _____ for you!

13

M Are you done with _____ your university _____ _____?

W Yes, I finally have _____ to a _____. It was hard to pick one.

M How did you choose the university that you applied to?

W Well, first, the cost of the _____ _____. I _____ _____ _____ pay more than $4,500 a year, so I _____ those which are more expensive.

M What about your major? You were interested in _____, weren't you?

W Yes, I was. But recently, I have become more interested in _____, so I chose it.

M I didn't know about that. Is there anything else that is important?

W I think it would be good to choose one with a _____, but the availability of a _____ is more important.

M Wow! What good thinking! I'm sure you will be

accepted. Good luck!

14

M _____ _____, Dahee? You look worried.

W Oh, Hanul. I left my cell phone _____ _____ _____.

M How did that happen? Wasn't it in your hand?

W Right. I was holding it _____ _____ _____, but…

M I remember. I saw you holding it. Did you _____ _____ your _____ and _____?

W Of course I did. I didn't find it. What should I do?

M _____ _____ _____ call your cell phone? Someone might _____ _____.

W I already did that, too. _____ _____ answered it.

M Then, let's go to the _____ _____ _____. They might have it.

W Okay.

15

M The Boryeong Mud Festival in Korea is _____ on Daecheon Beach _____ _____ in _____. Direct buses do run from Seoul and it takes about _____ _____ to get to Daecheon Beach. If you are coming from one of the big _____ _____ _____ _____, be prepared for an even _____ _____, more than 4 hours. However, the festival is _____ and it's _____! Arrive _____ in the day or you will _____ _____ _____ some of the day's _____ _____. If you need more information, please visit our website www.Mfestival.com.

16

W Hey Jackie. What are you doing?

M _____ _____. I'm just _____ today. Why? What's going on?

W I was thinking about _____ _____ _____ _____. Do you want to go?

M Are the stores _____ _____ _____?

W Yeah. A lot of shops are having end-of-season sales. It's a great time to buy some _____ _____ _____ for awhile.

M That sounds great. Where should we meet?

W Why don't we meet in front of ABC Department store _____ _____ _____?

M Sounds good. Then see you there.

17

M What do you think of _____ _____ ?

W They _____ _____ . But don't you think you already have too many _____ _____ that kind of shoe?

M Yes, that's right. Okay. Let's look at your clothes.

W This sweater is so pretty. I love the _____ _____ design.

M I _____ _____ _____ .

W It's on sale for _____ dollars. What do you think? Should I _____ _____ _____ ?

M Of course, it's a great deal. Go try it on.

18

M Hey, how was your _____ _____ ?

W It was not that good because I worked over the summer at a restaurant to make _____ _____ for _____ _____ . What did you do?

M I went to summer school. I _____ from two of my classes last year so I wanted to _____ _____ _____ .

W So are you officially a _____ now?

M Yes. _____ _____ _____ , where is Stacy?

W She has _____ _____ _____ _____ completely.

M Really? Why?

W Her summer job turned into full-time work.

19

M Your bracelet _____ _____ . When did you get it?

W I got it a few days ago, but I _____ _____ it much.

M It's _____ . Is it white gold or silver?

W It's white gold.

M Where did you buy it?

W My boyfriend _____ _____ to the jewelry shop and _____ me _____ _____ _____ .

M That's so sweet. Was it for _____ _____ ?

W No, he just wanted to buy me something.

20

W Greg and Pia are best friends. Greg is really _____ _____ _____ so he wants to _____ _____ a _____ _____ at the school festival. In order to get _____ _____ about magic, he asks Pia to go to the library with him. He wants to check out some books _____ _____ _____ . However, she has a _____ _____ in an hour today. In this situation, what would Pia most likely say to Greg?

01 대화를 듣고, 여자가 원하는 머리 모양으로 가장 적절한 것을 고르시오.

①  ② ③ ④ ⑤

02 대화를 듣고, 여자가 독일어를 배우는 주된 이유를 고르시오.

① 가장 배우기 쉬운 외국어라서   ② 독일 여행을 위해서
③ 독일어가 필요한 업무 때문에   ④ 독일로 유학 가기 위해서
⑤ 독일인 남자 친구와 대화하려고

03 다음을 듣고, 무엇에 관한 내용인지 고르시오.

① 비상시 선박 탈출 방법   ② 비행 중 비상 상황 대처 요령
③ 화재 시 건물 탈출 요령   ④ 응급환자 수송 수칙
⑤ 지진 발생 시 대피 방법

04 대화를 듣고, 남자의 심경으로 가장 적절한 것을 고르시오.

① bored   ② confident   ③ irritated
④ moved   ⑤ scared

05 대화를 듣고, 여자가 매장을 방문한 목적을 고르시오.

① 가격 비교   ② 상품 구매   ③ 경품 수령
④ 매장 점검   ⑤ 불만 접수

06 대화를 듣고, 남자가 환전한 금액을 고르시오.

① 250유로　　　　　② 280유로　　　　　③ 300유로
④ 360유로　　　　　⑤ 430유로

07 대화를 듣고, 두 사람의 관계로 가장 적절한 것을 고르시오.

① 화장품 연구원 ― 화장품 체험단　　② 관광 안내원 ― 관광객
③ 해양 경찰 ― 해변 구조원　　　　　④ 점원 ― 손님
⑤ 도시가스 회사원 ― 가입자

08 대화를 듣고, 두 사람이 대화하는 장소로 가장 적절한 것을 고르시오.

① 스키장　　　　　② 운동장　　　　　③ 의상실
④ 댄스교실　　　　⑤ 아이스 링크

09 다음을 듣고, 그림의 상황에 어울리는 대화를 고르시오.

①　　　　②　　　　③　　　　④　　　　⑤

10 대화를 듣고, 여자가 룸메이트에게 화난 일이 <u>아닌</u> 것을 고르시오.

① 한밤중에 음악을 크게 듣는 것　　② 동의 없이 파티를 여는 것
③ 욕실 청소를 하지 않는 것　　　　④ 문단속을 잘 하지 않는 것
⑤ 물건을 허락 없이 사용하는 것

11 대화를 듣고, 남자가 여자에게 조언한 것으로 가장 적절한 것을 고르시오.

① 친구에게 전화하기　　　　　② 친구에게 편지쓰기
③ 친구 집 방문하기　　　　　　④ 친구 연락 기다리기
⑤ 선생님과 의논하기

12 다음을 듣고, 남자가 언급한 내용과 일치하지 <u>않는</u> 것을 고르시오.

① 전시회는 이번 달 말에 열린다.
② 개장시간은 오전 9시 30분부터 저녁 7시까지이다.
③ 사진 콘테스트, 밀랍인형 만들기 등의 행사가 있다.
④ 웹사이트에서 50% 할인 쿠폰을 받을 수 있다.
⑤ 티켓 가격은 성인은 25불, 어린이는 15불이다.

13 다음을 듣고, 광고지의 내용과 일치하지 <u>않는</u> 것을 고르시오.

> ### Mini's Garage Sale
>
> Furniture, household goods, books, clothing, and lots more
>
> Sunday 17th, November
> 8am – 4pm
>
> 1715 Elizabeth St., Fort Collins, Colorado
> 080-0700-0987

①　　　②　　　③　　　④　　　⑤

14 대화를 듣고, 여자가 대화 직후 할 일로 가장 적절한 것을 고르시오.

① 경찰서에 전화하기　　　　　② 주차장에 주차하기
③ 보험회사에 전화하기　　　　④ 자동차 서비스센터 찾아가기
⑤ 사고 차량 주인에게 전화하기

15 다음을 듣고, Seoul Korean Speech Contest에 대해 언급되지 <u>않은</u> 것을 고르시오.

① 1995년에 처음 개최되었다.　　② 3개의 분야로 나누어져 있다.
③ 대회 응시료는 무료이다.　　　④ 매년 50명 이상이 참여한다.
⑤ 1등은 전국대회에 참가할 수 있다.

[16-17] 대화를 듣고, 남자의 마지막 말에 이어질 여자의 응답으로 가장 적절한 것을 고르시오.

16
① Why did you take the History of Art?
② Oh really? Who was the instructor?
③ What tutoring program did you take?
④ I took both Biology 101 and Writing 201.
⑤ When can we register for classes for the fall semester?

17
① I'm sorry to hear that.
② I walk my dog twice a week.
③ I want to buy a beagle like yours.
④ I adapt myself to any environment.
⑤ Why was such a well−trained dog abandoned?

[18-19] 대화를 듣고, 여자의 마지막 말에 이어질 남자의 응답으로 가장 적절한 것을 고르시오.

18
① It says it will be the same as today.
② If it rains tomorrow, let's stay at home.
③ You can decide what we are going to do.
④ How about staying in and reading a book?
⑤ Yes, you should listen to tomorrow's weather forecast.

19
① It takes about 20 minutes to get to the work.
② I'm looking forward to working out with you.
③ I concentrate mostly on doing strength training.
④ As a matter of fact, I'm not interested in exercising.
⑤ I usually handle the paperwork and attend meetings.

20 다음을 듣고, 수진이 민정에게 할 말로 가장 적절한 것을 고르시오.

① There is no need for you to pick me up.
② Can you tell me where I can pick you up?
③ Sorry, but are you able to pick me up now?
④ You should have given me better directions.
⑤ I'm sorry, can you tell the way to your house?

● 다음은 **Listening Test 02**의 주요 지문입니다. 녹음을 다시 듣고, 질문에 대한 답을 완성하세요.

Q1
1 Why does the woman want to have shoulder length hair?

⤷ The reason is that _____ and
_____ with long hair.

Q2
2 Why does the woman want to learn German?

⤷ She thinks that it'll help _____ between her
German boyfriend and her.

Q3
3 When the oxygen mask drops down, what should you do?

⤷ I should _____ and then _____
_____ to tighten it.

Q11
4 What happened to Bella last weekend?

⤷ She _____ .

Q12
5 What events can you enter at the exhibition?

⤷ I can enter _____, a wax figurine contest and _____ .

Q14
6 What will the man do for the woman?

⤷ He will look for _____ in his
_____ .

Q16
7 Why couldn't she take the History of Art class last semester?

⤷ The reason is that the class was _____ by the time she _____ .

Q19
8 How often does he work out these days?

⤷ He works out _____ .

자신의 상황에 맞게 내용을 완성하고 말해 보세요.

A Have you ever made a complaint about a product you purchased? Tell your classmates about it.

Making a Complaint about a Product	
When?	(1)
Who was the complaint directed at?	(2)
What was your complaint?	(3)
What did you do?	(4)
	(5)
What was the result of your complaint?	(6)

I'd like to tell you about a time when I made a complaint. The day I made a complaint was (1)_____ and the complaint was directed at (2)_____. What I complained about was that (3)_____ _____. (4)_____ _____.

Then, (5)_____. Finally, (6)_____ _____.

B Do you agree or disagree that when we want a pet, we should adopt one from an animal shelter? Write your opinion with two reasons and give specific supporting examples.

Adopting a Pet from an Animal Shelter	
Reasons	Supporting examples
(1)	(2)
(3)	(4)

I (agree/disagree) that we should adopt a pet from an animal shelter for two main reasons. First, (1)_____.

For example, (2)_____.

Second, (3)_____.

For example, (4)_____.

In conclusion, I think that we (should/should not) get a pet from an animal shelter.

01

M Good morning. How may I help you?

W I'd like to change my _____.

M Have a seat here, please. How would you like _____ _____ _____?

W I've decided to cut my hair _____ _____ and get a perm.

M Are you sure you want to do that? Your hair is _____ and _____.

W Yes. Summer is just _____ _____ _____ and it's so hot with long hair.

M Okay. Do you want tight curls, or just a little curl _____ _____ _____?

W Make it _____, please. Also, I want it dyed _____. I hate my black hair.

M Okay. Then I'll cut your hair first.

02

M Kate, do you have any plans this Saturday?

W Yes. I have a meeting of my _____ _____ _____. Why?

M I just want to _____ _____ with you. By the way, are you studying German _____ _____ _____ _____?

W Not really.

M Then, can I ask you the _____ _____?

W Actually, my boyfriend is German.

M Oh, I didn't know that you have a boyfriend who is German. How did you _____ him?

W I met him at a _____ _____ last year. His company is in a _____ with mine. Anyway, I want to _____ _____ _____ with him in German. It'll help me _____ _____ _____ _____.

M That's a good idea. Good luck to you.

03

W Ladies and gentlemen, on behalf of the crew I ask that you please direct your attention to _____ _____ above as we review _____ _____ _____. There are six emergency exits on this aircraft. Take a minute to locate _____ _____ _____ to you. Should the cabin experience a _____ _____ _____, stay calm and listen for instructions from the cabin crew. _____ _____ will drop down from _____

_____ _____. Place the mask over your mouth and nose, like this. Pull _____ _____ to tighten it. If you are traveling with children, make sure that your own mask is on first _____ _____ your children.

04

M Mom, did you hear _____ _____?

W I didn't hear anything. What did you hear?

M I heard something stomping about _____. I can't _____ on my studying. You can't hear anything right now, but just wait and it'll _____ _____. See!

W Oh, I can hear that. Do you usually hear that sound at night?

M Yes, I think it starts _____ _____ p.m. I can hear that sound for about _____ _____ every night.

W How long have you heard that sound?

M It has been _____ _____ _____ _____.

W OK, I'll check. Maybe, the resident _____ _____ or does something at this time every night.

M Please tell her or him my _____ _____ are next week.

05

M Good afternoon. What can I do for you?

W I'd like to speak to _____ _____, please.

M May I ask you _____ _____ _____ _____?

W There's a problem with _____ _____ I made yesterday.

M What kind of problem is that?

W The milk I bought yesterday had passed _____ _____ _____.

M Have you brought _____ _____ and _____ _____?

W Here you are. Have a look at this date _____ _____ _____.

M Oh, I see. Let me check _____ _____ _____ first so that I can _____ it belongs to our market and then I'll call our _____.

W All right. Go ahead.

06

W Welcome to the European Money Exchange. How may I help you?
M I'd like to exchange _____ _____ into _____. What's the current _____ _____?
W Let me see. Today's won to euro exchange rate is _____ won _____ euro. May I see some ID, please?
M Here you are.
W How much do you want to exchange?
M I want to exchange _____ won.
W How would you like your _____?
M I'd like _____ _____ euro bills, _____ _____ euro bills and _____ _____ euro bills.
W Okay. Here you go. _____ _____, _____ _____, and _____ _____.
M Thank you.
W Have a nice trip!

07

W Good evening. What can I do for you?
M Where can I find the _____?
W It's right behind you. And the brand-name _____ _____ _____ also sell sunscreen.
M One of these here is fine. Can you _____ a good one?
W Sure. What about this one? It is much more _____ to use especially _____ _____ because it's a _____ _____.
M Oh, is it safe? I heard that when using a _____ _____, I should not _____ _____ _____.
W It is safe because there's _____ _____ in it.
M Isn't it _____?
W No. Give _____ _____ a try. You get _____ _____ if you buy _____.
M Wow! OK, I'll take them.

08

M Look at her! Isn't she so beautiful?
W Yes, she is. Now I know why she is _____ _____ _____. Seeing her performance here in the rink is _____ _____ _____ than seeing it on TV.

M You can say that again!
W She is performing like a _____. Look at her _____ _____ and how she _____ _____ _____ _____. Who else can do that?
M No one. She is the best.
W I like her _____ and colorful _____.
M You sound like you are a big fan.
W Of course. I wish I could jump and turn like her. I actually _____ _____ _____ _____ walking on the ice.
M Ha, ha. You're just a _____. Practice hard. _____ _____? You could be more famous than her.

09

① M Why did you _____ _____ our company?
   W It's because this is my _____ _____.
② M Can I have your _____ _____?
   W It's 010-0099-1100.
③ M How may I help you?
   W I'm looking _____ _____ _____ _____ to wear in an interview.
④ M _____ _____ _____ _____?
   W No, you can sit there.
⑤ M _____ _____, please?
   W This is Susie Kim.

10

M Are things going well with your new roommate?
W _____, not really.
M Why? What's the matter?
W She always listens to _____ _____ late at night, often has a party without telling me, _____ _____ the bathroom, and uses my things _____ _____ me.
M Why don't you have _____ _____ with her?
W I already did. But it _____ work _____ _____.
M _____ _____ _____. So what are you going to do?
W I will try to talk to her again tonight. I don't want to _____, but I _____ _____ _____ with her.
M I hope it will work out better this time.

11

W How was your weekend, Jason?

M I just _____ _____ _____. How about you, Bella? What did you do?

W I had a _____ weekend. I don't want to think about it.

M Why? What happened?

W Do you remember my best friend, Lisa? I _____ _____ _____ _____ with her on Saturday.

M I'm sorry to hear that. Did you _____ _____ with her?

W Not yet. I don't want to _____ _____, though. I don't think I did anything wrong.

M _____ _____ _____ _____, I would call her and _____ _____ _____ _____ to meet. You should solve the problem by talking.

W Thanks. I will do that.

12

M Good morning! The Dinosaur Exhibition finally opens _____ _____ _____ _____ this month. Thank you very much for waiting for such a long time. _____ _____ _____ 9:30 a.m. _____ 7 p.m. every day. The _____ has _____ _____ _____ special events you can enter such as a _____ _____, a wax figurine contest and a dinosaur drawing contest. A day pass can be _____ at the ticket booth. Passes are _____ dollars _____ _____ and _____ dollars _____ _____. For more information, please visit our website at www.DinoExhibition.com. You can also _____ a 15% off discount coupon there.

13

① W You can buy _____ _____ and _____ at the _____ _____.

② W The garage sale will be held on _____ _____.

③ W You can visit the place from 8 a.m. to 5 p.m.

④ W It is _____ at 1715 Elizabeth St., Fort Collins.

⑤ W The _____ _____ is 080-0700-0987.

14

M Why did you come back? I thought you _____ _____ work a few minutes ago.

W Another car hit my car in the _____ _____.

M Oh, no!

W Yes, the _____ _____ of my car is _____.

M Is there a note?

W No, there isn't. The driver _____ _____.

M Gosh! You have to call the _____ _____ _____. Do you have the number?

M I'll look for it in my _____ _____. Wait a minute. [Pause] It is 070-000-82802.

W Thank you. I'll _____ _____ _____ right now.

15

W The Seoul Korean Speech Contest was _____ _____ in 1995. The 2014 SKSC is the _____ contest. Students learning Korean at _____ and language schools present their speeches in _____ _____: beginner, intermediate, and advanced. SKSC has been the most successful Korean speech contest in Seoul since it began. SKSC attracts more than _____ _____ every year and the _____ _____ _____ are entitled to _____ _____ the National Korean Speech Contest.

16

M When does _____ for the _____ _____ begin?

W It begins on Monday, _____ _____.

M What classes are you _____ _____ _____?

W I really want to take the History of Art, but I don't know if it will be _____.

M Is the class really _____ _____?

W Yes. I tried to get in last semester, but it was _____ by the time I had registered.

M What _____ _____ are you going to take?

W I still need to take English 201, but I really _____ _____ _____.

M I took that class already. There is a lot of writing, but it's _____ _____ _____.

W Oh really? Who was the instructor?

17

W Willy, do you _____ _____ Green Park?

M Yes, how do you know?

W I _____ you the other day _____ _____ _____. You have a beagle, don't you?

M Exactly right. You seem to know the different types of dogs.

W Actually, I don't. My cousin is _____ a beagle so it's the only dog that I can _____ _____ _____. Your dog looked well-trained.

M Yes, he seems to understand _____ _____ _____ I say to him.

W How did you _____ _____? Did you use _____ _____ _____?

M Actually, I adopted him from the _____ _____ two weeks ago.

W Why was such a well-trained dog abandoned?

18

M Hi, Susan. This is Jim. What are you doing?

W Oh, hi. I have just _____ _____ a book.

M Is it _____?

W Not really. Since I have nothing to do, I'm trying to read it but it's _____.

M Then let's _____ _____ and do something.

W I'd like to, but I have to meet my uncle and aunt _____ _____ _____ for dinner. _____ _____ _____?

M All right. Let's plan something for tomorrow.

W Did you hear the _____ _____ for tomorrow?

M It says it will be the same as today.

19

W Hey, Chris! Is that you?

M Yes. How have you been?

W Not too bad. _____ _____ _____ to see you here.

M Yeah. It's been _____ _____ _____ _____ since I saw you.

W What have you been up to?

M I just _____ _____ _____.

W Really? _____ _____ do you work out?

M At least _____ _____ a week.

W What kind of _____ do you do?

M I concentrate mostly on doing strength training.

20

M Today Soojin is visiting Seoul for the first time. But it is _____ _____ for her to find her friend's house as she is _____ a _____ _____ in South Gyeongsang Province. There are so many buses and cars on the _____. People in Seoul look _____ _____ that she doesn't want to _____ _____

to ask for _____. So she _____ to call her friend, Minjung, _____ _____ _____ she can come and get her. In this situation what would Soojin most likely say to Minjung on the phone?

01 대화를 듣고, 남자가 기차역에 가기 위해 이용할 방법으로 가장 적절한 것을 고르시오.

①  ②  ③ ④ ⑤

02 대화를 듣고, 남자가 발표 순서를 바꾼 이유를 고르시오.

① 자료를 더 준비해야 해서   ② 연습 시간이 더 필요해서
③ 할머니 문병을 가야 해서   ④ 친구의 부탁으로
⑤ 감기에 심하게 걸려서

03 다음을 듣고, 무엇에 관한 내용인지 고르시오.

① 학교 축제 일정 안내   ② 동아리 가입 안내
③ 공개 오디션 안내   ④ 행사 진행요원 모집 안내
⑤ 지역 무료 콘서트 안내

04 대화를 듣고, 여자의 심경으로 가장 적절한 것을 고르시오.

① nervous   ② hopeful   ③ sorry
④ disappointed   ⑤ cheerful

05 대화를 듣고, 남자가 전화를 건 목적을 고르시오.

① 자원봉사에 참여하려고   ② 점심 도시락을 주문하려고
③ 주말 아르바이트를 구하려고   ④ 주말반 학원에 등록하려고
⑤ 주말 여행을 예약하려고

06 대화를 듣고, 남자가 선물 구입에 지불한 금액을 고르시오.

① $15 ② $25 ③ $35
④ $45 ⑤ $50

07 대화를 듣고, 두 사람의 관계로 가장 적절한 것을 고르시오.

① 자동차 정비사 — 손님 ② 슈퍼마켓 직원 — 손님
③ 교통 경찰관 — 운전자 ④ 주유소 직원 — 운전자
⑤ 카드회사 직원 — 고객

08 대화를 듣고, 두 사람이 대화하는 장소로 가장 적절한 것을 고르시오.

① museum ② furniture store ③ park
④ art gallery ⑤ flower shop

09 대화를 듣고, 여자가 구입한 좌석으로 가장 적절한 것을 고르시오.

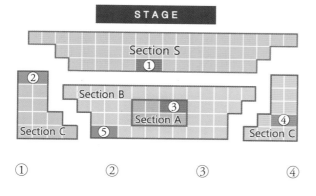

①   ②   ③   ④   ⑤

10 대화를 듣고, 남자가 해야 할 일로 여자가 언급하지 않은 것을 고르시오.

① 색깔 구분하여 세탁하기
② 식물에 물주기
③ 하루 세 번 고양이 먹이 주기
④ 식사 직후 설거지하기
⑤ 매일 바닥 쓸기

11 대화를 듣고, 여자가 남자에게 부탁한 일로 가장 적절한 것을 고르시오.

① 여행사 위치 알려주기　　　　② 여행지 추천해주기
③ 패키지여행 주의사항 알려주기　　④ 자유여행 상품 소개해주기
⑤ 여행상품 소개 이메일로 보내주기

12 대화를 듣고, 대화의 내용과 관계 깊은 속담을 고르시오.

① 소 잃고 외양간 고친다.
② 말 한마디로 천 냥 빚을 갚는다.
③ 열 번 찍어 안 넘어가는 나무 없다.
④ 낮말은 새가 듣고 밤 말은 쥐가 듣는다.
⑤ 사공이 많으면 배가 산으로 올라간다.

13 대화를 듣고, 남자가 여자를 위해 예매할 기차로 가장 적절한 것을 표에서 고르시오.

	Destination	Departure Time	Arrival Time	Class
	Train Pass Reservation			
①	Busan	06:30	10:10	Economy
②	Busan	07:10	10:45	First
③	Busan	08:00	11:35	First
④	Busan	09:15	12:47	Economy
⑤	Busan	10:20	13:42	Economy

14 대화를 듣고, 남자가 할 일로 가장 적절한 것을 고르시오.

① 바이러스 체크하기　　　　② 웹사이트 주소 확인하기
③ 인터넷 연결선 확인하기　　④ 웹사이트 다시 접속하기
⑤ 컴퓨터 재부팅하기

15 다음을 듣고, James M. Barrie에 대해서 언급되지 <u>않은</u> 것을 고르시오.

① 그는 1860년 스코틀랜드에서 태어났다.
② 그는 한때 런던에서 교사로 일했다.
③ 그는 재능 있고 성공한 작가였다.
④ 그는 1904년에 피터팬을 집필했다.
⑤ 그의 희곡에서 후크선장이 가장 재미있는 등장인물이다.

[16-17] 대화를 듣고, 여자의 마지막 말에 이어질 남자의 응답으로 가장 적절한 것을 고르시오.

16
① There won't be a next time for me.
② Why don't we go snowboarding tomorrow?
③ If you feel like that, you'd better take a long rest.
④ You should do some stretching before snowboarding.
⑤ If you practice more, you can be a professional boarder.

17
① Whenever I have a cold, I sneeze a lot.
② Well, I do have an allergic reaction to nuts.
③ I was in the hospital last May for two weeks.
④ Every fall, I am stricken with a seasonal allergy.
⑤ I often have a runny nose because of air pollution.

[18-19] 대화를 듣고, 남자의 마지막 말에 이어질 여자의 응답으로 가장 적절한 것을 고르시오.

18
① You're lucky to have a job you like to do.
② That's normal and you'll get used to it soon.
③ Do you think I should take a vacation now?
④ When will they come home from the hospital?
⑤ A working wife shouldn't do all the housework.

19
① Talking to my friends helps me a lot.
② Thanks for the massage, I appreciate it.
③ Taking a deep breath helps you stay calm.
④ Pressures at work cause me a lot of stress.
⑤ I think it's time for you to live your own life.

20 다음을 듣고, 민수가 사서에게 할 말로 가장 적절한 것을 고르시오.
① I've already checked the database.
② Can you tell me how to use the database?
③ Can I check out this book I found on that shelf?
④ Can you help me find the book I'm looking for?
⑤ You can check out this book from another library.

● 다음은 **Listening Test 03**의 주요 지문입니다. 녹음을 다시 듣고, 질문에 대한 답을 완성하세요.

Q1
1 How long will it take to Union Station if the man takes a Yellow Cab? Why?

↳ It will take _____ because it is _____.

Q3
2 For what purpose will the school musical club hold an evening of song and music?

↳ Its purpose is to _____.

Q7
3 How much money did the woman spend at the gas station? For what?

↳ She spent _____ dollars for _____ and _____ dollars for windshield _____.

Q10
4 What does the man have to do on Saturday?

↳ He has to _____ and _____ three times a day.

Q11
5 How long does the woman plan to go on a trip?

↳ She wants to go for _____.

Q13
6 According to the woman, how long does it take from Busan Station to BEXCO?

↳ It depends on _____ but it will take _____.

Q16
7 Why does his whole body ache?

↳ The reason is that he _____ for the _____.

Q17
8 What kinds of symptoms does she have related to her allergies?

↳ She _____ a lot and has a _____. Also, her throat sometimes _____ and her eyes start to _____.

자신의 상황에 맞게 내용을 완성하고 말해 보세요.

A Have you ever done any volunteer work? Fill in the table and tell your classmates about it.

My Memorable Volunteer Work	
(1) Where?	
(2) When?	
(3) What?	
(4) How did you begin it?	
(5) Why do you think it is memorable?	

I'd like to tell you about the memorable volunteer work that I did (1)_____

_____ (2)_____. My volunteer work was

(3)_____. I began this volunteer

work because (4)_____

_____. The reason why it is memorable volunteer

work is that (5)_____.

B Think about the most memorable trip you've been on. Fill in the table and tell your classmates about it.

The Most Memorable Trip	
(1) Where did you go?	
(2) When did you go?	
(3) Who did you go with?	
(4) What did you do there?	
(5) Why is it the most memorable trip?	

I'm going to talk about the most memorable trip I've been on. It was when I went

to (1)_____. I visited there (2)_____.

I went there with (3)_____. I (4)_____

_____. It is the most memorable trip

for me because (5)_____.

01

M Excuse me. Can you tell me _____ _____ _____ to Union Station?

W You can take _____ _____, over there.

M If I take the bus now during _____ _____, do you think I can _____ _____ _____ _____ _____?

W If you take the bus now, it will take _____ _____ _____ _____ _____, I guess.

M What about taking a Yellow Cab?

W There _____ _____ be a big time difference. How about taking _____ _____? You have to _____ five or six blocks to take it, but it'll be worth it.

M How long do you think it will take to the subway station _____ _____?

W It'll take about 10 _____. _____ _____ this way.

M Oh, that would be much better. Thank you.

02

W Are you done _____ _____ _____ _____ tomorrow?

M Oh, I won't be doing my presentation tomorrow.

W How come? _____ _____ _____ _____ I remember, your _____ is tomorrow.

M You're right, but I _____ _____ with Cindy last night.

W Her turn is the day after tomorrow, isn't it? Do you have a problem?

M Not me but her. I'm finished preparing mine. All I need is just to _____ _____ one _____ _____.

W Then why does she want to do it one day earlier?

M Her grandmother _____ _____ last night. So tomorrow after school, she's going to go visit her for a few days.

W I'm sorry to hear that. Anyway you're so kind to _____ _____ with her.

M That's _____ _____ _____ _____. I'm happy to help her and also to have more time to practice.

03

W Attention students. On _____ _____, our school musical club will be staging an evening of song and music in _____ of _____ _____ in the school _____. If you have a good voice, we invite you to join us in _____ _____. This is a great opportunity for you to _____ _____ _____ of many with your beautiful voice! An _____ _____ will be held on _____ _____ from 10 a.m. to 3 p.m. Kindly _____ for the audition by emailing us at musicalclub@koreahs.com. The _____ _____ is _____ _____. Hope to see you at the audition.

04

M Hi, Amy. Long time no see. How's everything going?

W Not bad. It's been a long time since I last saw you. How are you?

M I'm fine. We only have a _____ _____ _____ before _____ _____. Time flies so fast.

W It really does. How's your _____ _____ going?

M I finally got a phone call for _____ _____ _____ yesterday. I'd been waiting for it _____ _____ _____ _____.

W Wow, good for you. When are you going to have the interview?

M It's _____ _____. How about you?

W I've been searching for a job for _____ _____ _____ _____, but I haven't had _____ _____ _____ _____ yet.

M Sorry to hear that. You'll have good news soon. _____ _____.

W Anyway, _____ _____ _____ and do your best.

M I will. Thanks.

05

[Telephone rings.]

W Hello, East End Community Center. How may I help you?

M Hello, I'd like to _____ _____ _____ your _____ _____.

W What would you like to do?

M Just put me in _____ _____ _____ in which you need a hand.

W Okay. Do you have _____ _____ _____ to work?

M Yes. I will be happy if I can work _____ _____.

W Let me see. Would you be able to _____

free lunches to _____ _____ who live _____?

M Of course. I'll do that from this Saturday.

06

M Mom, Happy Birthday! This is my present for you.

W Thank you, son. Oh, this is _____ _____ I _____ _____ at the mall last month.

M Yeah, I know you didn't buy it because _____ _____ it was too _____.

W Oh, did you go shopping with me? I don't remember.

M Yes, I did. But I was looking at some other stuff and I saw you _____ _____ _____ from a _____.

W Oh, good boy. You remembered it. Son, thank you so much, but I think _____ dollars is _____ _____ for you to pay for a birthday present.

M Fortunately, they were having an end-of-season sale. I got 50% _____ and _____ _____ _____ _____, I used a _____ dollar _____ _____.

07

M What can I do for you?

W I need to _____ _____ _____ _____. Uh, can I get _____ _____ _____ _____? And can I pay by _____ _____?

M Sure. Could you please _____ _____? The tank's on the other side.

W Oops. Sorry. I'll do that.

M Thanks. [Pause] Here's your _____.

W Could you do me _____ _____ _____ and check the windshield washer fluid level?

M Okay, _____ _____ _____, please. [Pause] It's _____ _____ _____. Do you want to _____ it _____? It's 2 dollars.

W Yes, please. Here you are. Thanks.

08

W Look! These are so beautiful.

M Which do you like most?

W I can't choose only one but this white lily _____ _____ _____.

M Why don't you _____ it?

W Really? Hmmm. OK. Wow, it smells like a real lily.

M Of course it does. It just proves that here you cannot _____ _____ the real flowers and the _____ _____ by looking at them.

W You're right. Thank you for bringing me here. I

_____ so _____.

M I'm happy that you like this place so much.

W I will _____ _____ _____ which I can put in my living room.

M I'll buy it for you _____ _____ _____.

09

M Hello. May I help you?

W I'd like to buy a ticket for tonight's concert.

M Where do you want to sit? The price _____ _____ _____ the _____ of the _____.

W I see. May I see the _____ _____, then?

M Sure. Here it is.

W Thanks. I don't like seats _____ _____ _____ _____ or right _____ _____ _____ the stage. What's the _____ between sections A and B?

M It's $25.

W That's _____ _____. I'll get one seat in the _____ _____ then.

10

M Are there any special things I have to _____ _____ _____ while you _____ _____?

W Of course, honey. I was just _____ _____ _____ you some things to do while I am away.

M What are they?

W First, please don't wash _____ and white clothes _____ _____ _____ _____.

M Okay. And?

W _____ _____ _____ on Saturday, and don't forget to _____ the kitty three times a day.

M I will. I have to _____ _____ _____, don't I?

W I guess you're asking because you don't really want to do that. But there is a lot of _____ _____ these days, so you'd better _____ _____ _____ every day.

M Alright. Don't worry.

11

[Telephone rings.]

M Hello, Diamond Tours. May I help you?

W Hello, I want to _____ _____ _____ of Taiwan _____ _____.

M How many days would you like to stay?

W Five days and _____ _____.
M Would you like a full _____ _____
   or one with lots of _____ _____
   _____ _____?
W I _____ a full package tour.
M Okay. We have several tours you can choose from.
   Do you want me to _____ all of them on the
   phone?
W Well, if it is okay with you, please send me the
   _____ by email.
M Sure. _____ _____ your email address,
   please.
W It's hardworker1002@yourmail.com.

12

M Why are you _____ _____? Didn't you
   sleep well last night?
W Not really. I got up too early. I'm a _____
   _____, but I'm trying to change myself into a
   _____ _____.
M Why do you want to change?
W I saw a health program on TV a few days ago. The
   doctor said going to _____ _____ at
   night is not good for your health.
M Didn't you know that?
W People had told me before, but I didn't listen.
   I've been going to bed early and _____
   _____ _____ for three days now.
M It won't be easy to change your habit within a
   _____ _____ _____ _____ _____.
W You're right. But I will _____ _____
   _____ being tired and try hard until
   I've changed my sleeping habits. _____
   _____ _____.
M _____! Good luck.

13

M Did you _____ _____ _____
   _____ to Busan?
W _____ _____ _____. I will do it later when I
   get home.
M Do you want me to do it for you?
W Would you? Thanks. I have to _____ before
   _____ because I have a meeting at 1:00 in the
   afternoon at BEXCO.
M _____ _____ _____ does it _____
   _____ Busan Station _____ BEXCO?
W It depends on the _____ _____ but it
   will take about an hour, I guess.
M Alright. I'm sure you don't want to _____
   _____ _____, do you?
W No, I don't. And I prefer to take first class

_____ _____ _____ _____ _____.
M OK. I'll book a first class ticket for you.

14

M Lora, can you help me?
W What do you want me to do?
M Well, this _____ _____ _____.
   I don't know what I am _____ _____.
W Did you type in the _____ _____?
M Yes, I checked it _____ _____.
W _____ _____ the Internet cable? If it is
   not connected, the website won't come up.
M The _____ is fine. What should I do?
W Have you _____ _____ _____ on
   your computer?
M No. I'll do it now.

15

M James M. Barrie was a very _____ and
   _____ _____. He was _____ in
   Scotland in _____. For a time, he worked
   as a _____ in London. Then he began to
   write _____ and _____. In 1904, he
   wrote *Peter Pan*. This is his most famous and most
   _____ play. There are some very _____
   _____ in the play, but Captain Hook is by far
   the most interesting.

16

W Hey Peter. Why are you _____?
M Oh, hi Sara. I went snowboarding yesterday and my
   whole body _____.
W Was it your _____ _____?
M Yes. And I never want to go again.
W I remember the first time I went. My back was
   _____, and I couldn't sit down the next day
   as my butt _____ so much, and _____
   _____ cramped _____ I walked
   _____ _____.
M That's exactly how I feel now.
W It's only like that the first _____ _____
   _____.
M There won't be a next time for me.

17

M You've been _____ a lot lately. Are you sick or
   something?
W No. Every springtime around April, I'm _____
   _____ _____.
M I never have _____ allergies.
W Consider yourself lucky.
M What are all the _____?

W Well, I _____ _____ _____. Also, my nose becomes very _____, my throat sometimes _____, and my eyes _____ _____ _____.

M That doesn't sound good.

W No, it's not. So you don't have any allergies at all?

M Well, I do have an allergic reaction to nuts.

18

W Did your wife _____ _____ yet?

M Yes. I have a healthy son.

W Congratulations. How is your wife doing?

M She is _____, but taking a lot of _____ now.

W That's _____ _____ _____.

M I'm just glad there were _____ _____.

W If your wife and baby are both healthy, what more can you _____ _____?

M That's right. But it's been a week, and I _____ _____ that well since I have to _____ and _____ _____ of my wife and son.

W That's normal and you'll get used to it soon.

19

M What stresses you out the most?

W Probably my parents.

M How so?

W Well, when I was in school, they wanted me to get _____ _____. And now after getting a job, they want me to get a _____ _____.

M You have to _____ _____ a lot of _____ from your parents.

W Your parents are _____ _____ _____?

M Ever since I _____ home some bad grades in elementary school, they have never _____ _____.

W You're lucky.

M What do you do to _____ _____ _____ _____?

W Talking to my friends helps me a lot.

20

W Minsu is a college student. He needed to _____ _____ _____ for one of his classes. He went to the _____ _____ first to _____ _____ the book _____. It showed that the book was _____ _____. Today, he goes to the library to _____ _____ _____, but he can't find it on the _____. So he goes to the _____ _____. In this situation, what would Minsu most likely say to the librarian?

04 Listening Test

01 대화를 듣고, 락 페스티발 장소에 입장 가능한 사람을 고르시오.

① ② ③ ④ ⑤

02 대화를 듣고, 여자가 팔을 다친 이유를 고르시오.

① 차량 접촉사고로   ② 자전거를 피하려다
③ 친구와 다투다가   ④ 버스 급정거로
⑤ 빙판에 미끄러져서

03 다음을 듣고, 무엇에 관한 내용인지 고르시오.

① 전국체전 개최 공지   ② 학교운동회 안내
③ 스포츠 수업변경 안내   ④ 학교 스포츠 팀 선발 안내
⑤ 학생회 선출 투표 안내

04 대화를 듣고, 남자의 심경 변화로 가장 적절한 것을 고르시오.

① satisfied → upset   ② embarrassed → relieved
③ bored → surprised   ④ worried → nervous
⑤ excited → regretful

05 대화를 듣고, 남자가 전화한 목적을 고르시오.

① 예약 취소   ② 예약 날짜 변경   ③ 출발지 변경
④ 목적지 변경   ⑤ 특별 기내식 요청

06 대화를 듣고, 여자가 받을 거스름돈을 고르시오.

① $30　　　　　　② $35　　　　　　③ $45
④ $50　　　　　　⑤ $70

07 대화를 듣고, 두 사람의 관계로 가장 적절한 것을 고르시오.

① 손님 — 웨이터　　　　　② 손님 — 호텔 직원
③ 고객 — 음식 배달원　　　④ 운동선수 — 감독
⑤ 카페 종업원 — 사장

08 대화를 듣고, 두 사람이 대화하는 장소로 가장 적절한 것을 고르시오.

① car showroom　　　　② friend's house
③ driving school　　　　④ auto repair shop
⑤ street

09 다음을 듣고, 그림의 상황에 어울리는 대화를 고르시오.

①　　　　②　　　　③　　　　④　　　　⑤

10 대화를 듣고, 여자가 대화 직후 할 일로 가장 적절한 것을 고르시오.

① TV 시청하기　　　　　② 숙제 마무리 하기
③ 휴식 취하기　　　　　④ 방 청소하기
⑤ 중요도에 따라 할 일 정하기

11 대화를 듣고, 여자가 남자에게 부탁한 일로 가장 적절한 것을 고르시오.

① 역사 수업 함께 수강하기   ② 관련 정보 수집하기
③ 도서관에 함께 가기   ④ 발표 연습 같이하기
⑤ 도서관에서 책 대출해주기

12 대화를 듣고, 대화의 내용과 일치하지 <u>않는</u> 것을 고르시오.

① 다음 시간은 체육시간이다.
② 체육 시간에 농구 자유투 시험이 있다.
③ 남자는 농구 경기를 자주해서 시험에 자신이 있다.
④ 10개의 공을 던져서 7개를 넣어야 한다.
⑤ 여자는 남자에게 시험 전 연습할 것을 권유했다.

13 대화를 듣고, 회의를 하기로 한 날짜를 고르시오.

MAY						
SUN	MON	TUE	WED	THU	FRI	SAT
	1	2	3	4	5	6
7	8	9	① 10	11	② 12	13
14	15	③ 16	17	18	④ 19	20
21	⑤ 22	23	24	25	26	27
28	29	30				

14 대화를 듣고, 두 사람이 언급하지 <u>않은</u> 내용을 고르시오.

① 대통령 선거일   ② 남자의 생일
③ 여자의 생일   ④ 선거 가능한 법적 나이
⑤ 10대의 선거 불가 이유

15 다음을 듣고, 내용과 일치하지 <u>않은</u> 것을 고르시오.

① 벗겨지거나 찢겨진 벽지가 납중독을 일으킬 수 있다.
② 납중독은 학습 장애와 행동 장애를 일으킨다.
③ 납중독을 예방하기 위해 페인트칠한 장난감은 피해야 한다.
④ 외국에서 수입된 통조림에 의해서 납중독이 일어날 수 있다.
⑤ 자녀들에게 놀고 난 후 손을 꼭 씻어야 함을 가르쳐야 한다.

[16-17] 대화를 듣고, 여자의 마지막 말에 이어질 남자의 응답으로 가장 적절한 것을 고르시오.

16
① I'm not afraid of anything except death.
② I was rushed to the hospital last week.
③ It's because they look cute and give us honey.
④ I don't know, but it's natural to be afraid of snakes.
⑤ Since I got stung last year, I've been afraid of them.

17
① It's raining really hard right now.
② Yes, it rained cats and dogs last weekend.
③ No, it'll be warm with nothing but clear skies.
④ Not only this afternoon but the rest of the week.
⑤ I'm going climbing in Blue Mountain National Park.

[18-19] 대화를 듣고, 남자의 마지막 말에 이어질 여자의 응답으로 가장 적절한 것을 고르시오.

18
① He lives with his grandparents.
② He lives in campus housing now.
③ He is watching TV in the living room.
④ He leaves home at seven in the morning.
⑤ He works for a company manufacturing car parts.

19
① I like it very much.
② I'll pay for the tickets.
③ I will pay by Visa Card.
④ It costs more than I thought.
⑤ It costs 100,000 won per person.

20 다음을 듣고, Susie가 Sally에게 할 말로 가장 적절한 것을 고르시오.

① Why don't you study harder?
② I should have studied with you.
③ I'll keep my fingers crossed for you.
④ Let's take a lesson together once a week.
⑤ Why don't we study together in the library?

● 다음은 **Listening Test 04**의 주요 지문입니다. 녹음을 다시 듣고, 질문에 대한 답을 완성하세요.

Q2 **1** Why did the bus suddenly stop?

> ↳ The reason was that the bus tried to _____.

Q4 **2** Why didn't the man or woman hear his mobile phone ringing?

> ↳ The reason was that the man _____.

Q6 **3** What did the woman buy for her mother?

> ↳ For her mother, the woman bought _____.

Q8 **4** What's wrong with the woman's car?

> ↳ Her car is _____ while she is driving.

Q12 **5** What was the woman's advice to the man?

> ↳ She told the man to _____ and _____
> _____ during the break.

Q13 **6** Why can't they meet on Wednesday?

> ↳ They have _____ on that day, so they _____.

Q16 **7** Why isn't she afraid of horror movies?

> ↳ She knows they're _____ so there is _____ to be afraid of.

Q19 **8** What does she want to book?

> ↳ She wants to book _____ from Seoul to Daegu at
> _____ p.m. tomorrow.

자신의 상황에 맞게 내용을 완성하고 말해 보세요.

A Have you ever been hurt seriously or lightly? Tell your classmates about it.

When I Got Hurt	
(1) When did it happen?	
(2) What were you doing?	
(3) What happened?	
(4) What kind of injury did you get?	
(5) What did you learn?	

I would like to tell you about an accident in which I got hurt. It happened

(1)_____. On that day, I was (2)_____

_____. (3)_____

_____. As a result, (4)_____

_____. Due to the accident, I learned

(5)_____.

B Let's write about your favorite subject, including the details in the table below.

My Favorite School Subject	
(1) the name of the subject	
(2) when you started learning the subject	
(3) a description of the subject	
(4) the reason for liking the subject	

My favorite school subject is (1)_____, which I have learned since (2)_____

_____. It is (3)_____.

The reason I chose the subject is that (4)_____

_____

_____.

Dictation Test

01

M Jennie, are you busy _____ _____ _____?

W No, I'm not. Do you want to do something together?

M Yes, there will be an _____ _____ _____ on Friday night. Let's go enjoy it and watch the _____ _____.

W Didn't you go there _____ _____, too?

M Yes, I did. The crowd just _____ _____ _____ at the festival.

W Well, I'd love to go with you this year. I really like rock music.

M I know. That's why I'm asking you to come with me.

W What should I wear?

M Well, to _____ to the fun and _____, the organizers ask everyone to wear the same color or _____. Last year everyone wore something _____ but this year it's _____ with _____ _____.

W Oh, great. I have _____ _____ like that.

M Unfortunately, it has to be _____ _____.

02

M Cindy, I heard that you got hurt a few days ago. Are you okay?

W It wasn't that bad. But anyway I was _____ _____ _____ _____.

M Tell me what happened?

W The bus I was riding on suddenly stopped _____ _____ _____ a car _____ _____. So I fell down and _____ my arm.

M Are you okay except for the _____ _____ _____?

W Yes, I didn't hurt anything else.

M Then how long do you have to _____ _____ _____?

W I have to wear it for _____ _____.

M You were lucky _____ to have been _____ _____.

03

M Attention, students. To compete in the National Sports Day _____ _____ _____, our school will organize several sports teams. So this week we're going to have _____ _____ between classes to find our _____ _____. Each class should prepare teams for the school competition next week. The sports being played are basketball, _____, badminton and table tennis. Teachers watching these games will _____ the school team for each sport. On _____ _____ at _____ a.m. _____ _____ on the school teams will be _____.

04

W Hey, Tom. What are you doing? Are you _____ _____ something?

M Yeah, I think I _____ _____ _____.

W You mean the one you bought last week? Are you sure? I'll call your phone.

M Thanks. Can you hear it ringing?

W Yes, I can hear your ringback tone, but no one is _____ _____ _____. Can you hear any _____ or _____ around here?

M No, I can't hear anything. I can't find it anywhere. What should I do?

W I'm sure it's somewhere. Have you checked your _____ and your _____?

M Of course, that was _____ _____ _____ I did.

W Hmmm... Let me _____ _____ _____. Maybe you missed it. See! It was in the _____ _____ of your backpack.

M Wow! There it is! Huh, when did I set it _____ _____ _____? Thanks a lot.

05

[Telephone rings.]

W World Airlines. How may I help you?

M I'd like to _____ a _____ _____. Could you check _____ one is _____?

W Okay, Sir. Can I have your name and flight number please?

M My name is Greg Norman, flight WA975 leaving Incheon tomorrow.

W Actually, _____ _____ need to be requested _____ _____ two days _____ _____ _____.

M Really?

W Yes, but I'll check with the _____ _____ to see if it's possible to order one for tomorrow. _____ _____ _____ _____.

M Okay. [Pause]

W Thank you for waiting. I'm _____ _____ _____ _____. It is possible to have a vegetarian meal tomorrow.
M Thank you so much.
W No problem. Thank you for choosing World Airlines. Have a nice trip.

06

W Oh, these are beautiful!
M These _____ _____ have become very popular since a famous actress _____ _____ a TV show wearing them.
W Yeah, that's why I'm _____ _____ them. Can I have a look to see if you have a _____ _____ to the one I saw her wearing on TV.
M This is _____ _____ _____ _____ she wore. You'll like it a lot.
W Oh, it's beautiful and it really is _____ _____, too. How much is it?
M The regular price is _____ dollars, but for today only, you can get _____ _____ _____.
W I'll buy this and the silver _____ _____ _____ _____. Can you gift-wrap the silver one as it's for my mom?
M Okay. How would you like to pay for your _____?
W I'll pay _____ _____. Here's _____ dollars.
M Thank you. Here's your _____ and _____.

07

W Excuse me? There are some _____ here.
M Oh, we're sorry about that. I'll _____ them _____ right away.
W Thanks. Uh, I was _____ if you _____ _____ _____ _____.
M We have some Tabasco sauce.
W That would be great. I'll need a lot though. This food _____ _____ _____ _____ for me.
M OK, I'll be right back _____ _____ _____. [Pause] Here you are.
W Thank you very much.
M Is there anything else you need?
W Could I have _____ _____ _____ _____ _____ _____, please?
M Sure. I'll be back with it soon.

08

M Good morning, ma'am. How may I help you?
W Hello. My car is making _____ _____

_____ while I am driving. What's wrong?
M Before checking, let me ask you a few questions. Do you remember when the _____ _____?
W _____ _____ _____ _____ _____ _____, it started last week.
M Does it happen even when you _____ _____?
W I don't think so.
M _____ _____ _____ visited here before?
W No, this is my first time. One of my friends _____ this shop to me.
M Thanks. Please _____ _____ this _____ and have a seat. I will _____ _____ _____ at it.

09

① M _____ _____ is this?
  W It's 3,300 won _____ 100 grams.
② M Where do you want to _____ _____?
  W I'd like to _____ _____ the window.
③ M Please _____ me the _____.
  W Okay. Please _____ _____ _____.
④ M Excuse me. I _____ a steak but you brought me the _____ dish.
  W Oh, I'm sorry. I'll be right back with yours.
⑤ M _____ _____ _____ _____ a good Italian restaurant _____ here?
  W _____ _____ the one on 23rd Avenue?

10

M Jessica, are you still watching TV? _____ _____ _____ TV for three hours.
W Dad, I need some time to _____ _____ _____.
M I understand. But did you finish all of your homework?
W No, but it will take less than an hour to finish it. I'm _____ _____.
M Then you should finish it first. Why don't you _____ _____ _____ _____ that you have to do from 1 to 10 _____ _____?
W I think _____ _____ _____ is also important, Dad.
M You're right. But watching TV for three hours _____ _____ _____ before finishing your homework isn't right.
W Okay. I will go back to my room and finish my homework.
M Good girl!

11

M Are you busy these days?

W Yes, I'm busy preparing my _____ for my history class.

M What's your _____?

W The history of _____ _____ _____, the hanbok.

M Sounds very interesting. Where did you get all of the _____?

W I _____ _____ _____ and got some books from the library.

M Sounds like you did a lot of _____.

W I did, but I still need some more books. I could only _____ _____ three books. Can you check out some books for me?

M Sure. _____ _____ me know the titles.

W Thanks a lot.

12

M What's next?

W We have P.E. _____ _____. We have a test on _____ _____ _____ _____ in basketball.

M Are you _____? I'm not ready for it.

W But you often play basketball with your friends after school. What are you so worried about?

M But _____ _____ _____ _____ isn't easy. I practiced hard, but I'm still not really good. _____, we need to make 7 _____ _____ _____ _____ _____.

W If you are so _____, then why don't you go to the school playground and practice shooting free throws during the break?

M That's a good idea. Anyway, I will _____ _____ first in the _____ _____. I hope not many people are in the playground.

W Hurry up _____ you _____ _____ _____ time to practice before the test.

M Thanks. See you.

13

M Donna, the _____ _____ _____ _____ is on May 22, right?

W Yeah, that's correct. We need to have a meeting _____ this week _____ next week to get things ready.

M How about next Tuesday, I mean on the 16th.

W That would be fine but how about this Friday?

M _____ _____ _____ _____ _____. Then it should be _____ _____ _____ _____. Ah! We can't make it on

Wednesday. We have _____ _____ on that day, so we will finish late.

W Right. So this Friday is the best day because we don't have any _____ _____.

M Okay. Let's meet in four days and talk about it _____ _____. Please think about what we have to _____ when we meet.

W That's a good idea. It will _____ the meeting time and we will be more _____.

M See you then. Bye.

14

M Are you going to vote in the presidential election?

W When is it?

M It will be _____ _____ _____ _____ this year, on _____ 17th.

W I won't be _____ _____ _____ _____ by that time. My birthday is on December 18th.

M Oh, no. You have to wait 5 years to vote because of only one day.

W Very funny, but that's the _____. _____ _____ the _____, 19-year-olds are not _____ _____ to vote.

M I fully understand how you feel. But _____ teenagers to vote could be dangerous because teens are _____ _____.

W I _____ _____ _____ you _____. I will stop _____.

15

W As parents, we try to do _____ _____ _____ our children from dangers. But many parents don't know that their children can be _____ by _____ or _____ in their own homes. Lead poisoning causes _____ _____ and _____ _____. In order to prevent lead poisoning, we should avoid or throw away _____ _____ and _____ _____ from foreign countries. Also we should clean our homes as often as possible and teach children to _____ their hands _____ _____.

16

M What are you _____ _____?

W Nothing really. I used to be scared of a lot of things when I was young, _____ _____ _____.

M Are you afraid of _____ _____?

W No. I know they're _____ _____ so there is _____ to be afraid of.

M What about _____?

W None that I can think of. How about you?

M I get _____ _____ _____. I'm actually frightened of _____.

W Really? Why?

M Since I got stung last year, I've been afraid of them.

17

M Oh, it feels so cold this morning.

W It sure does. Early this morning my car's windshield was _____ _____ _____. I had to scrape it off before I could drive to the work.

M Who would have _____ it could be this cold in late April?

W I know. The temperature was 1 degree Celsius when I _____ _____ this morning.

M Yes, I was _____ as soon as I got out of bed.

W It is never this cold _____ _____ _____.

M Well, it's forecast to rain this afternoon. _____ _____ _____ and _____!

W How long will it rain?

M Not only this afternoon but the rest of the week.

18

M Hey, Jane. I heard you are _____ _____.

W Yeah. His name is Andy. I started dating him _____ _____ _____.

M That's so exciting. Tell me all about him. Is he good looking?

W I think he's cute but _____ _____.

M How did you meet him?

W Whenever I went to my neighborhood _____ _____, he was always there. We started talking a couple of times, and he finally _____ _____ _____.

M That's so cool. What does he _____ _____ _____ _____?

W He works for a company manufacturing car parts.

19

M Good morning, ma'am, can I help you?

W Good morning, I want to _____ _____ _____ on _____ _____ from Seoul to Daegu at _____ p.m. tomorrow. Are there seats _____ _____?

M Please wait a moment. Yes, there are _____ _____ still available.

W OK. I want to _____ _____ _____. And we want to _____ _____ the front of the plane.

M Can I have the names, please?

W Olivia Brown and Peter Smith.

M _____ _____ _____ _____ for the seats?

W I will pay by Visa card.

20

M Susie's friend, Sally, has started a _____ _____ so she's had a difficult time _____ _____ _____ her classes. _____ are coming up and she doesn't know what to do. She is _____ of _____ _____ _____. Susie tells her that the best thing for her to do is study _____ _____ _____ she can. Sally says that she won't be sleeping for the next 3 days. Susie _____ has to study for her exams. So Susie wants to _____ _____ _____ _____ to study together. In this situation, what would Susie probably say to Sally?

05 Listening Test

01 대화를 듣고, 남자가 먹은 음식이 **아닌** 것을 고르시오.

①   ②   ③   ④   ⑤

02 대화를 듣고, 캠핑장을 예약할 수 **없는** 이유를 고르시오.

① 성수기가 아니라서
② 선착순 접수라서
③ 캠핑장 보수 중이어서
④ 예약이 다 차서
⑤ 비용이 비싸서

03 다음을 듣고, 무엇에 관한 내용인지 고르시오.

① 단수 예고
② 항공기 비상 탈출 안내
③ 소방 훈련 예고
④ 정전 시 행동요령
⑤ 지진 대피 훈련 안내

04 대화를 듣고, 여자의 심경으로 가장 적절한 것을 고르시오.

① relieved
② frightened
③ worried
④ satisfied
⑤ indifferent

05 대화를 듣고, 남자가 전화한 목적을 고르시오.

① 유선 TV 수리 신청
② 전화번호 문의
③ 전자상가 개점 시간 문의
④ TV 가격 문의
⑤ 세일 기간 문의

06 대화를 듣고, 두 사람이 만나기로 한 시각으로 알맞은 것을 고르시오.

① 1:30 ② 2:00 ③ 2:30

④ 3:00 ⑤ 3:30

07 대화를 듣고, 두 사람의 관계로 가장 적절한 것을 고르시오.

① 여행 가이드 — 여행객 ② 세관원 — 여행 가이드

③ 공항 보안요원 — 승객 ④ 호텔 직원 — 손님

⑤ 항공기 조종사 — 승무원

08 대화를 듣고, 두 사람이 대화하는 장소로 가장 적절한 것을 고르시오.

① 학교 ② 조부모님 댁 ③ 식당

④ 커피숍 ⑤ 양로원

09 대화를 듣고, 여자가 가입하고자 하는 동아리를 고르시오.

①  ②  ③  ④  ⑤

10 대화를 듣고, 남자가 복권에 당첨되면 하고 싶은 일이 <u>아닌</u> 것을 고르시오.

① 부모님께 돈 드리기 ② 모교에 기부하기

③ 스포츠카 사기 ④ 제주도 별장 구입하기

⑤ 성 같은 큰집 짓기

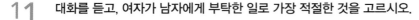

11 대화를 듣고, 여자가 남자에게 부탁한 일로 가장 적절한 것을 고르시오.

① 발표 주제 정해주기　　　　② 포인터 사용법 알려주기
③ 포인터 사주기　　　　　　④ 포인터 매뉴얼 가져다주기
⑤ 페이지 넘겨주기

12 다음을 듣고, 남자가 언급하지 <u>않은</u> 것을 고르시오.

① 방송하는 사람의 이름　　　② 방송하는 사람의 소속처
③ 물탱크 청소 일시　　　　　④ 물탱크 청소 목적
⑤ 단수 전 준비 사항

13 대화를 듣고, 표의 내용과 일치하지 <u>않는</u> 것을 고르시오.

Magazines				
	Title	Classification	Published	Stocks
①	*Muscle Mania*	Fitness	Monthly	15
②	*Golf Lovers*	Sports	Weekly	10
③	*Stars*	Entertainment	Monthly	0
④	*Gorgeous Hair*	Beauty Treatment	Yearly	1
⑤	*Street Fashion*	Fashion	Quarterly	0

14 대화를 듣고, 대화 직후 여자가 할 일로 가장 적절한 것을 고르시오.

① 재활용 바구니 구입하기　　② 재활용 마크 그리기
③ 재활용 바구니 놓아두기　　④ 재활용 쓰레기 분리하기
⑤ 재활용장에 쓰레기 버리기

15 다음을 듣고, 도서관 이용과 관련하여 언급되지 <u>않은</u> 것을 고르시오.

① 학부생들은 다섯 권까지 책을 빌릴 수 있다.
② 기한이 지난 책은 하루에 50센트씩 연체료가 부과된다.
③ 연체요금은 책 한 권당 최대 15달러이다.
④ 정기간행물과 참고도서는 3층에서 열람할 수 있다.
⑤ 토요일은 오전 9시부터 오후 8시 30분까지 운영한다.

[16-17] 대화를 듣고, 여자의 마지막 말에 이어질 남자의 응답으로 가장 적절한 것을 고르시오.

16
① I don't like that scene, either.

② I'd like to watch an action movie.

③ I was chosen to act a supporting role.

④ I'm taking the leading role in this movie.

⑤ I'm shooting a scene about driving down a highway.

17
① I cannot teach him advanced math.

② I had a lot of friends when I was a teenager.

③ I want to visit my school friends this weekend.

④ Everyone should go to school until they are 18.

⑤ He can make friends by belonging to sports teams.

[18-19] 대화를 듣고, 남자의 마지막 말에 이어질 여자의 응답으로 가장 적절한 것을 고르시오.

18
① I won't demand that I get antibiotics.

② I am healthy because I take antibiotics.

③ I'll get a stronger antibiotic that will work.

④ I'll go to the doctor and get some antibiotics.

⑤ I'll go to a different doctor closer to my house.

19
① She passed by the hospital.

② No, she didn't pass away.

③ Yes, she died in her sleep.

④ I'm sad I can't go with her.

⑤ She went to the hospital yesterday.

20
다음을 듣고, Abby가 사장에게 할 말로 가장 적절한 것을 고르시오.

① I'm due at the office at 10:00.

② Don't worry. I'll be there on time.

③ I'm reporting a car accident on 5th Avenue.

④ I'm sorry, but I'll be late because of traffic congestion.

⑤ I'm sorry, but I was pulled over by the police for speeding.

● 다음은 **Listening Test 05**의 주요 지문입니다. 녹음을 다시 듣고, 질문에 대한 답을 완성하세요.

Q1

1 Why does the woman think the man's stomach hurts?

↳ She thinks that the man's stomach hurts because he had too much

_____.

Q2

2 If you want to stay for two nights at the campsite, how much do you have to pay?

↳ I have to pay _____ for two nights.

Q6

3 How long does the man think it takes to clear customs?

↳ He thinks that it takes about _____ to clear customs.

Q8

4 When did the man use to come to the center?

↳ He used to come _____, every _____ and _____.

Q9

5 What does the woman want to major in at the university?

↳ She wants to _____.

Q11

6 What will she use the laser pointer to do?

↳ She will use it to point at _____ and to

_____.

Q15

7 How many books can graduate students check out and for how long?

↳ They can check out _____ books for _____ and the books can be

renewed up to _____.

Q18

8 What has resulted from the prescription of too many antibiotics?

↳ It has led to a _____ in _____.

● 자신의 상황에 맞게 내용을 완성하고 말해 보세요.

A What do you think of using antibiotics? Write your opinion, answering the questions in the table below.

My Opinion on Using Antibiotics	
(1) What are antibiotics?	
(2) My opinion	
(3) The reason for my opinion	

Antibiotics are (1)_____.

(However/And), I think (2)_____. The reason is

that (3)_____

_____.

Therefore, I think (2)_____ and use them in the right way.

B Please think about the ways you can recycle. Fill in the table below and tell your classmates about them.

Recycling	
Do you recycle every day?	(1)
Do you think recycling is necessary or not? Why?	(2)
What are the things that you recycle?	(3)
Please think about two items which you can make with recyclable materials.	(4) (5)

I am going to talk about recycling today. I (1) _____ every day.

I think recycling is (2)_____ because it (2)_____

and _____. I recycle (3)_____.

I will tell you two items which I can make with recyclable materials. First, I can

make (4)_____ from _____. Second, I can make

(5)_____ from _____.

01

M Mommy, I don't _____ _____ _____.

W What's the matter, sweetheart?

M I have _____ _____.

W Maybe you've _____ _____ _____ _____.

M I _____ _____ I'm going to _____.

W What did you eat for lunch?

M Not much.

W Really? What did you have today?

M Let's see. I had a _____, a can of _____ _____, _____ _____, _____, _____, and some _____ for lunch. That's all I had for today.

W _____ _____ _____ your stomach hurts! It's all that junk food.

02

M I'd like to reserve _____ _____ for next weekend.

W We don't take _____. It's _____ _____, _____ _____, _____.

M Do you _____ _____ on the weekends?

W Only _____ _____.

M What do you _____ for an _____ _____?

W _____ dollars per night.

M When do we have to _____ the campsite the next day?

W By 2 p.m.

M Can we build a fire?

W You can do that only in the _____ _____ to avoid forest fires.

M Thank you. You've been _____ _____.

03

M Attention, please! Sometime between _____ _____ and _____ _____ a fire drill will occur at Central Plaza between the hours of _____ p.m. and _____ p.m. The drill will occur on a _____ through to a _____. No other _____ _____ will be given as to what day the drill will take place on. You have to _____ the building during _____ _____ _____ _____. Please follow all safety procedures appropriately. We do apologize for the _____ this may cause you as a result. Thank you for your _____.

04

W Excuse me. Could you _____ _____ _____ _____ the book 'Introduction to Functional Grammar'?

M Okay. Let me check our computer database. Do you know _____ _____ _____ _____?

W It is _____ _____ Michael Holliday.

M Are you looking for the _____ _____?

W Yes, I am.

M Sorry, we don't have it _____ _____ at the moment. Do you want me to _____ one?

W How long will it take _____ _____ _____?

M Probably, it will take five days to a week because it comes _____ _____.

W Oh, dear! I'm _____ _____. I need it tomorrow.

05

[Telephone rings.]

W Star Cable, this is Jenny.

M I'd like to report my cable isn't _____ _____.

W What's your _____ _____ and phone number?

M 02-3769-5824.

W Mr. Brown?

M That's right.

W What seems to be the trouble?

M The low-end _____ _____ fuzzy or blurry.

W The _____ _____ we have is on _____ between _____ a.m. and _____ p.m. or between 3 p.m. and 6 p.m.

M Oh, please send your _____ between _____ and _____. Thank you.

06

W Could you _____ _____ _____ at the airport next Sunday?

M No problem. When is your _____ _____?

W I am coming in _____ 2:00 in the afternoon.

M I think that by the time you clear _____, I will be able to meet you in the arrival area around 2:30.

W Okay. But the plane _____ _____.

M Don't worry. I can _____ _____.

_____ on my smartphone using an app I have.

W I want to be able to call you on my cell phone if there is a problem.

M I'll make sure to _____ my cell phone with me and _____ _____.

W Don't wait for me for _____ _____ _____ _____ _____. If there is a problem, I can take a _____.

M You won't need to. I will be there.

07

M Hello, do you have anything _____ on you? Any _____ in your wallet, _____, _____?

W No.

M Do you have any _____ or gels?

W I have this _____ _____.

M Is it less than _____ milliliters?

W No, it is _____.

M I'm sorry, you will have to _____ _____ _____.

W Oh, alright.

M Please place your _____ and carry-on in the _____ and proceed through the _____ _____.

08

M Do you like _____ here?

W I'm very happy to help _____ _____. How about you?

M Me too. I learn a lot about life from them. They also seem to be happy _____ _____ with me.

W _____ _____ do you come here?

M I used to come _____ _____ _____, every _____ and _____ but now I come on Saturday only. How about you?

W Every weekend. _____ _____ _____ _____ coming here?

M When my grandfather _____ _____ three years ago, I missed him so much. In order to _____ _____ the _____ _____ caused by his death, I decided to come here.

W Oh, I have to go now, but let's have tea together another time.

M Okay.

09

M Did you decide which club you are _____ _____ _____?

W _____ _____. Can you help me decide? There are so many _____ _____ in my

school. So I'm still thinking about which one is best for me.

M What are you interested in?

W I'm into tennis, _____, _____, _____, and debating.

M Wow! You _____ _____ all of them. It sounds _____ to pick one.

W Hmmm... Well, I think I've just decided not to join either the tennis or photography clubs. And I'm going to _____ the English debate club from my list, too.

M Do you mean you _____ _____ the list to two?

W Actually, I have decided. Since I am planning to _____ _____ _____ at university, I will join the one that is _____ _____ it.

M That is a great choice.

10

M Please _____ _____ _____ 9.

W Why? I'm watching this _____ _____. Today is the _____ _____ so I have to see it.

M It won't take so long, please turn it on just _____ _____ _____.

W Come on. What are you going to watch?

M I'll just check the _____ _____ _____.

W What? What would you do if you _____ _____ _____?

M Well. First, I would give half of it to my parents to thank them. And I would _____ some to my _____ _____. I also would like to buy a sports car and a vacation home in Jeju Island.

W You seem to be _____ _____ _____ _____ _____, but who knows. Good luck.

M Thank you.

11

M Mina, are you _____ _____ your _____ tomorrow?

W Yes, _____ for one thing.

M What's that one thing? What is the problem?

W When I present, I am going to use a laser pointer to point at the _____ _____ or _____ and to _____ _____ _____ _____.

M So? Don't you have a pointer? I can _____ _____ _____.

W No, it's not that. I already bought one. I don't know

how to use it.

M Oh, _____ _____. Did you _____
_____ _____?

W I did, but... If you _____ _____, please
_____ _____ _____ to use it.

M Sure. Look.

12

M Ladies and gentlemen! This is Vincent Brown from
the _____ _____ _____. May
I have your _____, please? As we informed
you last week, we are going to _____ the
_____ _____ today from 9 a.m. to 1 p.m.
So the _____ _____ will be _____
_____ during that time. It is to supply clean
and safe water to you so please understand the
_____. We will _____ _____
_____ to finish _____ _____
_____ _____. Sorry for the _____.
Thank you for your _____.

13

M Let's _____ these magazines _____
_____ _____ and _____ the
_____ _____.

W Okay. If any of them are _____ _____
_____ or _____ _____
_____, we need to _____ them.

M That's right. Let's check the _____ _____
first. We have 50 _____ of *Muscle Mania* left
in stock, but we don't have any copies of *Stars*. We
need to order some.

W And we have 10 copies of the _____ magazine
Golf Lovers, so we don't need to order any more.

M We have two copies of Beauty magazine left, right?

W Beauty magazine? Are you talking about *Gorgeous
Hair*? And we only have one copy of it.

M Oh, sorry. Yes, I am. I made a mistake. I _____
_____ _____ Beauty magazine. And we
should order some more copies of the _____
magazine *Street Fashion* because there aren't any
left.

W OK. I think we are done now.

14

M What are all these _____ _____?

W They are _____ _____. Look at the
words and pictures printed on them.

M Ah! I can see the little pictures of paper, cans,
_____, and _____. Why did you buy
them? You have always _____ and taken
the _____ to the _____ _____,

haven't you?

W Yes, I have. However, I used to put all of them in the
same big box or a single plastic bag, and then I had
to separate them in the _____ _____.

M If you have these, it will be easier to recycle, won't it?

W Yes. That's _____ _____ _____.

M Where are you going to place them?

W I will put them _____ _____ the
_____ _____. I will do it now.

M Good idea.

15

W Welcome to the university library. _____
students can check out up to _____ books
for _____ _____. Graduate students
can check out _____ books for _____
_____. Books can be renewed up to
_____ _____. There is a _____
cent late fee per day for each overdue book up to a
maximum of $_____. Periodicals and
reference books _____ _____
_____ _____. The library is open
_____, 8:00 a.m. to 10:00 p.m., and
_____ _____ from 9:00 a.m. to 8:30 p.m.
The library is _____ on Sundays.

16

W Thank you for taking _____ _____
_____ from your busy schedule to answer a
few questions.

M It's my pleasure.

W Could you tell us about an _____ _____
in your life?

M Sure, I get up early at _____ in the morning.
Then I have breakfast. After breakfast, I _____
_____ _____ _____.

W Are you studying anything now?

M Yes, I'm learning _____ for the new movie
that I'm _____ _____.

W Can you tell me about the story in the movie?

M It's about a funny French family. It can make you
_____ _____ _____ at the same
time. You should watch it.

W Which scene are you _____ _____?

M I'm shooting a scene about driving down a highway.

17

M Honey, what do you think of homeschooling Tom?

W Homeschooling him?

M Yes. I think you and I are _____ _____
_____ him _____ _____.

W But do we have _____ to do that?

M We each have _____ work _____, so we can _____ our work schedules to help him.

W Okay. But why? What is good about homeschooling?

M It offers a great deal of _____ _____. He can focus on the subject matter that _____ _____ _____.

W Sounds good, but how can he _____ _____?

M He can make friends by belonging to sports teams.

18

M I heard that you went to the hospital yesterday.

W Yes I did. I had a _____ _____. I demanded that the doctor give me some _____.

M That's not right.

W What do you mean?

M If you have the flu, antibiotics _____ _____. The flu is a viral _____. The doctor shouldn't _____ something that won't help.

W But I need some _____ to get better.

M No, you don't. And haven't you heard that the prescription of too many antibiotics has led to a _____ in antibiotic-resistant infections.

W Really?

M Yes, we have no medicines to _____ _____. So what will you do next time?

W I won't demand that I get antibiotics.

19

M Sarah. You _____ _____. What's wrong?

W My grandmother just _____ _____.

M I'm so sorry to hear that. _____ did this happen?

W _____ _____ _____ _____ _____. I just came back from the funeral.

M Is there anything I can do?

W No, not really. The sad thing is that _____ _____ _____ when she _____.

M I'm sure she knew _____ _____ _____. Did she pass away in the _____?

W Yes, she died in her sleep.

20

M Today Abby is _____ to start a new job. She wants to get to work early this morning in order to make a _____ _____ on her new boss. So she _____ _____ _____ for work. However, traffic is _____ _____ for kilometers because of a car accident. Furthermore, the road traffic shows _____

_____ of _____ _____. She decides to call her boss to tell him that she is

_____ _____ _____ _____ _____.

In this situation, what would Abby probably say to her boss?

06 Listening Test

01
대화를 듣고, 챙겨갈 물품이 <u>아닌</u> 것을 고르시오.

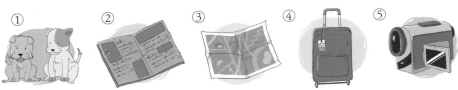

① ② ③ ④ ⑤

02
대화를 듣고, 음식점으로 차를 돌린 이유를 고르시오.

① 음식을 포장해 가려고
② 거스름돈을 덜 받아서
③ 자켓을 놓고 와서
④ 음식값이 과다 청구되어서
⑤ 지갑을 놓고 와서

03
다음을 듣고, 무엇에 관한 내용인지 고르시오.

① 야식으로 좋은 음식
② 뇌의 기능
③ 호두의 효능
④ 건강기능식품
⑤ 필수 영양소

04
대화를 듣고, 남자의 심경 변화로 가장 적절한 것을 고르시오.

① sorry → thankful
② excited → disappointed
③ bored → curious
④ frustrated → cheerful
⑤ embarrassed → jealous

05
대화를 듣고, 남자가 도서관을 방문한 목적을 고르시오.

① 학기말 시험 대비
② 발표 준비
③ 리포트 작성
④ 인터넷 사용
⑤ 배낭여행 준비

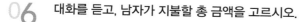

06 대화를 듣고, 남자가 지불할 총 금액을 고르시오.

① $170   ② $180   ③ $185
④ $190   ⑤ $200

07 대화를 듣고, 두 사람의 관계로 가장 적절한 것을 고르시오.

① 학원접수처 직원 — 수강생   ② 입학사정관 — 학생
③ 점원 — 고객   ④ 인사과 직원 — 면접 응시자
⑤ 변호사 — 의뢰인

08 대화를 듣고, 두 사람이 대화하는 장소로 가장 적절한 것을 고르시오.

① gas station   ② driving school
③ auto repair shop   ④ highway rest area
⑤ card company

09 다음을 듣고, 그림의 상황에 어울리는 대화를 고르시오.

①   ②   ③   ④   ⑤

10 대화를 듣고, 남자가 지난 주말에 한 일로 가장 적절한 것을 고르시오.

① 부족한 잠 보충하기   ② 여자 집 대청소 도와주기
③ 주간 계획 짜기   ④ 영화 보기
⑤ 봄맞이 대청소

11 대화를 듣고, 여자가 퇴직한 후 하고 싶어하는 것으로 가장 적절한 것을 고르시오.

① 꽃꽂이 배우기   ② 사진 찍기
③ 수필집 출간   ④ 출판사 취업
⑤ 고서 수집

12 대화를 듣고, 남자가 충고한 내용과 관계 깊은 속담을 고르시오.

① Many hands make light work.
② Look before you leap.
③ A friend in need is a friend indeed.
④ Strike while the iron is hot.
⑤ Good medicine tastes bitter.

13 대화를 듣고, 여자가 구입할 카네이션으로 가장 적절한 것을 고르시오.

Carnations on Sale			
Price	By the Piece	Bouquet Type	Basket Type
Below $10	①		
$10 – $20		②	③
$20 – $30			④
Above $30		⑤	

14 대화를 듣고, 여자가 숙제를 마친 후 두 사람이 할 일로 가장 적절한 것을 고르시오.

① 잔디 깎기   ② 시사 뉴스 시청하기
③ 소설책 읽기   ④ 날씨 확인하기
⑤ 구름 관찰하기

15 다음을 듣고, 추수감사절에 대한 내용으로 일치하지 않는 것을 고르시오.

① 추수감사절은 11월 넷째 주 목요일이다.
② 미 연방정부가 정한 첫 번째 공휴일이다.
③ 순례자들의 전통 축제에서 유래되었다.
④ 칠면조, 으깬 감자, 호박파이를 먹는다.
⑤ NFL 미식축구는 추수감사절 기간에 열린다.

[16-17] 대화를 듣고, 여자의 마지막 말에 이어질 남자의 응답으로 가장 적절한 것을 고르시오.

16
① You should call him now.
② He is taking his mind off of it.
③ Ok. I'll call you back after I've done that.
④ I'll take you out this Friday afternoon, Ok?
⑤ I'm looking forward to hearing from you.

17
① Cash. I'd like to get the discount.
② I'll go to the bank to borrow $200.
③ I don't know that motorcycle manufacturer.
④ I prefer to drive an automatic motorcycle.
⑤ Can you show me different types of motorcycles?

[18-19] 대화를 듣고, 남자의 마지막 말에 이어질 여자의 응답으로 가장 적절한 것을 고르시오.

18
① We'll ask them to pay us on time.
② We don't need to worry about it.
③ That's the reason for our meeting today.
④ We have to change the shipping company.
⑤ We're going to Canada on vacation next week.

19
① I'm really sorry to hear that.
② It's good to see you here today.
③ I'm working tomorrow afternoon.
④ Wherever it is, let's go there next time.
⑤ The old chef was worse than the new one.

20 다음을 듣고, Mrs. Wilson이 이웃에게 할 말로 가장 적절한 것을 고르시오.
① I'll stay there for two hours.
② Oh, good. I'd appreciate that.
③ I'm afraid, I can't go with you.
④ Sorry, but I can't handle four kids.
⑤ Sure. I'll take care of them at home.

● 다음은 **Listening Test 06**의 주요 지문입니다. 녹음을 다시 듣고, 질문에 대한 답을 완성하세요.

Q1

1 Where do they put their two puppies?

└→ They put their two puppies _____.

Q2

2 How often will they eat out from now on?

└→ They will eat out at least _____.

Q4

3 What does the man have to show to the woman before he can get his prize?

└→ He has to show her his _____ and _____ which the company sent to him.

Q10

4 What is the man going to do this weekend?

└→ He is going to _____ and _____.

Q12

5 Why did the man say "Congratulations!" to the woman?

└→ The reason was that the woman has been offered _____ _____ as an _____.

Q14

6 Why does the man want to check the weather?

└→ The reason is that it looks like _____.

Q15

7 When was Thanksgiving Day first celebrated and who celebrated it?

└→ Wampanoag _____ and the _____ first celebrated it in _____.

Q16

8 Why does he think that Sam must be depressed?

└→ The reason is that Sam failed the _____ for the company he really _____.

● 자신의 상황에 맞게 내용을 완성하고 말해 보세요.

A Which do you prefer doing for a vacation, going on a package tour, backpacking, or camping? Tell your classmates about it.

My Favorite Type of Vacation	
What type of vacation do you prefer?	(1)
What is the main reason?	(2)
What are other reasons?	(3)
	(4)
Which country would you like to travel in?	(5)

I prefer (1)_____. The main reason is that (2)_____

_____. There are other reasons. (3)_____

_____. Moreover, (4)_____

_____.

If I have a chance, I would like to travel (5)_____.

B Write about what you think is the most important traditional holiday in Korea after filling in the details in the table below.

The Most Important Traditional Holiday in Korea	
(1) the name of the traditional holiday	
(2) what people do on the holiday	
(3) the reason for it being the most important one	

I think that the most important Korean traditional holiday is (1)_____

_____. During the (1)_____ holidays, (2)_____

_____

_____.

I think (1)_____ is the most important traditional holiday in Korea because

(3)_____

_____.

01

M Come on. It's five o'clock. I want to be _____ _____ _____ by _____ _____.

W It's still _____ out.

M I guess we've _____ _____. Our two puppies are in the pet carrier _____ _____ _____ _____.

W Did you stop the _____ _____?

M Yes.

W I'm tired. I want to _____ _____.

M You can sleep in _____ _____. Let's double check everything. Have you got _____ _____? What about _____ _____, the camcorder and some food?

W Yes. We're _____ _____.

M Then, let's _____ _____ _____.

02

W That meal was delicious. We should _____ _____ more often.

M How about at least _____ _____ _____ _____?

W Great. Let's do that. Where's _____ _____?

M I have no idea.

W Oh, no! I _____ _____ _____ it at the restaurant.

M _____ _____ could you _____ _____ it?

W _____. I'm sorry.

M It's no _____ _____. We'll go back. Let me _____ _____. I hope it's there.

03

W Do you want to improve the functioning of your _____? Making _____ part of your diet could be a good way. The human brain needs _____ _____ like omega-3s to function properly. Walnuts have plentiful omega-3s, which make them the _____ " _____ _____." Are you tired of _____ _____ at night? Maybe a pre-bedtime snack of walnuts would help you get some shuteye. Walnuts also contain manganese, copper, iron, magnesium, and calcium — all _____ which are important for good health. Walnuts, like most nuts, can help lower cholesterol and _____

_____ _____.

04

W How may I help you?

M I came here to _____ _____ _____ _____ for the winner of the giveaway event this month.

W Oh, _____!

M Thank you. This is _____ _____ _____ I am a winner of an event. I feel like I'm _____ _____ _____ _____.

W Could you show me your ID card and the _____ we've sent?

M Here's my ID card and the _____.

W Alright. You won _____ _____ _____ in this event.

M What is the prize?

W It's a dining voucher _____ _____ dollars. Your _____ and utility _____ are _____ percent of the surface value.

M Oh, no! I can buy the voucher at a _____ of _____ percent through an Internet group purchase program.

05

W Surprise! I didn't expect to see you here. What are you reading?

M I'm reading a book on the history of Rome.

W Oh, are you taking a _____ _____ _____ this _____?

M No. You know what? I'm planning to _____ _____ _____ this summer. I believe this book will help me appreciate what I see. Anyway, _____ _____ _____ _____ _____?

W I was searching for some _____ for my _____.

M What's that about?

W It's about _____ _____. I'm writing a research paper that argues that we only use 10 percent of our brain.

M That sounds interesting. Are you going to _____ some books _____ now?

W No, the books with the articles I wanted have already been checked out.

06

M I'm looking for a suit that isn't _____ _____ _____ on a _____ _____. Can you help me find

_____ _____ _____?

W Okay. I think this _____ _____ will _____ _____ _____ you. Would you like to _____ it _____?

M Oh, that's great. How much is it?

W It's _____ dollars. Don't you need a shirt _____ _____ _____ _____?

M Yes, I need one. Could you show me _____ _____ _____ over there? It's really nice!

W You _____ _____ _____ _____ the latest fashion! That will make you look _____ _____. It's _____ dollars.

M Oh, _____ _____ _____ _____ a bit cheaper.

W Hmm… here's _____ _____. If you buy those two items, I'll give you a 10% discount _____ _____.

M Okay, then I'll buy _____ _____ _____. Thank you.

07

M Excuse me. I _____ in Science 307, but I don't know which classroom it is in.

W Well, there's a room _____ _____ on the _____ _____ outside this office.

M Yeah, I know. But Science 307 isn't _____ there. There _____ _____ some kind of _____. Could you check for me, please?

W Hmmm… ok, let me check on the computer. I'm sorry, but it says here that it was _____. You should have gotten a text message about this.

M What? I didn't get one.

W It says on the computer that an SMS was sent out to students _____ _____ _____.

M Oh, I haven't changed my cell phone number. And how can you _____ _____ _____ after offering it?

W I know it's really _____ for you, but if enough students don't _____ _____ for a course, we _____ _____ it.

08

M Hello, what can I do for you?

W Hello. Please _____ _____ _____.

M Which one? Diesel, unleaded, or super-unleaded?

W _____, please. It's _____ _____ now and I have to fill it up because I'm going to drive all day.

M Why? Are you a _____ or _____ _____ _____?

W I'm going to Busan now and _____ _____ late at night.

M That's a long drive for one day. Pretty tiring!

W It is, but I have no choice. Is it finished? Here is my card.

M [Pause] Here is the receipt. _____ _____.

09

① M I'd like to _____ in the Barista course. _____ _____ _____ _____?

W Please _____ _____ _____ first and _____ _____ _____ _____.

② M May I help you?

W I'd like to have _____ _____ _____ coffee without _____ and _____.

③ M Did you make these _____?

W Yes. Would you like to try some? _____ _____.

④ M I'd like to have hot chocolate with _____ _____ on top.

W Okay. It will be $2.50.

⑤ M Look at the _____ and choose what you'd like to have.

W I will have _____ and a diet Coke.

10

W How was your weekend? Did you have fun?

M Fun? _____ _____ _____ _____. It was very _____ and _____.

W Ha, ha. What did you do? Last Friday you said you were excited about the _____ weekend.

M Yeah, at that time I didn't know that I'd have to do _____ over the weekend.

W At least you got it done. I'm planning to do it this weekend.

M Are you? Don't _____ _____ _____ _____.

W I won't, I promise. What are you going to do this weekend then?

M I will go to see a movie and _____ _____ _____ my sleep. I need a good rest.

W That's right. I hope to see you _____ _____ _____ on Monday.

11

M Thank you for everything, Mrs. Cha. Here's a _____ _____ _____.

W What a beautiful _____ _____ it is!

M You were such a great teacher who will _____

_____ _____ _____ forever.

W Oh, thank you for saying so. I won't forget you, either.

M Let's _____ _____ _____ so we can keep this beautiful moment _____.

W Sure. Your _____ makes me thankful that I chose to be a teacher.

M What are you going to do now? Do you have a _____ _____ after you _____?

W Well, I haven't thought a lot about it. But if I have a chance, I'd like to _____ _____ _____ of essays _____ _____ my teaching experiences.

M That would be wonderful.

12

M What are you thinking about so _____, Soyoon?

W I've been _____ _____ _____ to go to the States as an _____ _____.

M Congratulations! That's what you've always wanted. Why do you have a _____ _____?

W I can't decide _____ I should _____ this offer _____ _____.

M What? What are you talking about? You should go.

W Do you really think so? Now that my dream actually has _____ _____, I am _____.

M _____ _____ _____ _____ _____, I wouldn't think about doing anything else, I'd just go. You know what? An _____ like this doesn't come very often.

W Thank you for your _____. I guess I'll have to take this chance right now.

M Good.

13

M Can I help you? Are you looking for anything _____ _____?

W I'd like to buy flowers for Parents' Day.

M I see. Do you want a _____ or a _____? Or maybe you want to buy them by the piece. We have a _____ _____.

W Well. I haven't thought about that yet. What's most _____?

M It _____ _____ the _____ _____ but people usually choose a bouquet or a basket _____ _____ by the piece.

W I see. Can you show some to me then?

M These small ones on the _____ _____ are $17 and these larger ones on the _____ _____ cost between $25 and $30.

W Oh, I like this one _____ _____

_____. It has a blue basket.

M Good choice.

14

M Lauren, are you done with your homework? It's 2 o'clock now.

W Sorry, dad. I need one more hour to be finished.

M Okay. I will wait for you. _____ _____ _____.

W Thanks. Are you done with reading your novel already?

M Yes. I will turn on the news to _____ _____ _____. It looks like _____ _____ _____ _____ soon because the sky is _____ _____ _____ _____.

W Oh, no. If it is, we can't _____ _____ as we had planned. I hope it won't rain.

M We can do it next time. Don't worry.

W I will finish my homework _____ _____ _____ _____ so we don't have to change our plan.

15

W Thanksgiving Day is the _____ _____ in November. It is a U.S. _____ _____, so schools, banks, post offices, and government offices are _____. Thanksgiving was the _____ holiday celebrated in _____. It was first celebrated in the _____ _____ _____ when the Wampanoag Indians and the Pilgrims got together for a three-day feast and festival of fun. Today, families celebrate Thanksgiving by eating _____, mashed potatoes, gravy, yams, corn, cranberry sauce, and _____ _____. Macy's Thanksgiving Day Parade and an NFL football game are _____ Thanksgiving Day _____.

16

W Hey, Bill. What are you doing?

M Nothing much. What are you up to?

W I am just _____ _____ Sam. He _____ _____ _____ lately. He _____ the final interview for the company he really wanted to work for.

M That's too bad. He must feel _____.

W Yeah. He's been _____ in his room all day for the last 3 days.

M Why don't we _____ _____ _____? We can try to take his mind off of it.

W That's a great idea. _____ _____

_____ _____ _____? I already talked to him a couple of times and it might be good for him to _____ _____ _____.

M Ok. I'll call you back after I've done that.

17

W Good morning, can I help you?

M Good morning. I want to buy a _____.

W What kind of motorcycle are you looking for?

M I want to purchase an _____ motorcycle.

W Please have a look! We have many _____ motorcycles by a variety of _____.

M How much is this one?

W It is $200.

M That's a little _____. Is there any way you can offer me a discount?

W If you pay _____ _____, you can get a _____% discount. If you use a _____ _____, you can purchase it on an _____ _____. Which way do you prefer?

M Cash. I'd like to get the discount.

18

W Thank you for coming to the meeting today, Mr. Kim.

M My pleasure, Ms Lee. Now, _____ _____ are we having around here?

W Well, unfortunately, we're having a serious problem with _____ _____ _____ _____.

M Haven't they paid yet?

W Yes, they've paid on time. The problem is they _____ _____ with the goods we've sent them.

M How can that be? We always _____ the best _____ _____.

W But they aren't happy. They say they are meeting with a _____ _____ next week.

M No way! What are we doing to _____ _____?

W That's the reason for our meeting today.

19

W I can honestly say this is the _____ _____ I'll come here.

M I have the _____ _____. I don't like this place, either.

W The service was _____ _____ and the food was _____.

M This steak is as _____ as leather and it is even quite _____.

W It _____ _____ _____ a good

restaurant. I wonder why everything has changed.

M Well, I heard that _____ _____ of this restaurant _____ and he hired a _____ _____.

W I think the new owner has reduced the quality of the ingredients in the dishes and the new chef is _____ _____ _____ cooking.

M I'm going to _____ _____ _____ the old chef is working.

W Wherever it is, let's go there next time.

20

M Mrs. Wilson takes her seven-year old son and five-year old daughter _____ _____ _____ on _____ _____. The park has quite a large playground for young children. Her children like to play on the swings, slides and teeter-tooters. They spend _____ _____ at the park. Today her neighbor _____ _____ to _____ _____ _____ to the park, too. But Mrs. Wilson _____ to take other people's children to the park. Also she doesn't want to _____ _____ _____ _____, either. In this situation, what would Mrs. Wilson probably say to her neighbor?

01 대화를 듣고, 남자와 여자가 보게 될 뮤지컬 포스터를 고르시오.

① ② ③  ④  ⑤

02 대화를 듣고, 남자가 직접 여동생의 자전거를 빌리지 <u>않는</u> 이유를 고르시오.

① 자전거를 펑크 낸 적이 있어서
② 다툰 후 화해하지 않아서
③ 빌린 돈을 갚지 않아서
④ 시험기간이라 예민해서
⑤ 자기 물건을 빌려주길 싫어해서

03 다음을 듣고, 무엇에 관한 내용인지 고르시오.

① 교복선정 투표안내
② 학교 축제 일정 안내
③ 학교 시설 안내
④ 학생회장 출마 연설
⑤ 기부금 모금 행사 안내

04 대화를 듣고, 여자의 마지막 말에 드러난 심경으로 가장 적절한 것을 고르시오.

① relieved
② indifferent
③ surprised
④ suspicious
⑤ upset

05 대화를 듣고, 남자가 문자를 보내는 목적을 고르시오.

① 약속 취소
② 구입할 물품 목록 전달
③ 날씨 안내
④ 약속 장소 변경
⑤ 과제물 문의

06 대화를 듣고, 여자가 지불할 음식의 가격을 고르시오.

① $16   ② $17   ③ $18

④ $32   ⑤ $34

07 대화를 듣고, 두 사람의 관계로 가장 적절한 것을 고르시오.

① 대학 입학처 직원 — 학생   ② 음식점 사장 — 종업원

③ 도서관 사서 — 도서 대출자   ④ 출입국 관리원 — 여행객

⑤ 채용 면접관 — 구직자

08 대화를 듣고, 두 사람이 대화하는 장소로 가장 적절한 것을 고르시오.

① 사무실   ② 전시회   ③ 교실

④ 미용실   ⑤ 음식점

09 다음을 듣고, 그림의 상황에 어울리는 대화를 고르시오.

①   ②   ③   ④   ⑤

10 대화를 듣고, 남자가 여자를 위해 할 일로 가장 적절한 것을 고르시오.

① 리포트 작성해주기   ② 리포트 기한 연장해주기

③ 리포트 제출해주기   ④ 토요일에 만나기

⑤ 리포트 검토해주기

11 대화를 듣고, 여자가 계약 연장 시 받는 혜택으로 가장 적절한 것을 고르시오.

① 무료 화상 통화
② 속도 향상 및 한 달 무료
③ 무료 점검 서비스
④ 6개월 요금 면제
⑤ 혜택 없음

12 대화를 듣고, 대화의 내용과 일치하는 것을 고르시오.

① 여자는 아들에게 사 줄 애완동물을 이미 정했다.
② 활동적인 아이에게는 같이 놀 수 있는 동물이 좋다.
③ 아이들은 우리에서 키우는 애완동물은 싫어한다.
④ 남자는 햄스터가 가장 좋다고 적극 추천해 주었다.
⑤ 여자는 이구아나나 도마뱀은 사주고 싶어하지 않는다.

13 다음을 듣고, 표의 내용과 일치하지 <u>않는</u> 것을 고르시오.

Idea Contest

① Title: Anything that makes your life easier
② Period: March. 01 – March. 31
③ Application method: Online
④ Prize giving details: 1st $2,000
　　　　　　　　　　　2nd $1,500
　　　　　　　　　　　3rd $700
⑤ Contact: 080-8080-1234 or ideacontest@contest.com

14 대화를 듣고, 여자가 이번 토요일에 할 일로 가장 적절한 것을 고르시오.

① 리포트 작성하기
② 교회 가기
③ 고아원 방문하기
④ 양로원 방문하기
⑤ 교회 친구 집 방문하기

15 다음을 듣고, 방송에서 언급하지 <u>않은</u> 것을 고르시오.

① 출발 지연 이유
② 탑승 시작 시간
③ 목적지
④ 도착 시간
⑤ 출발 탑승구

[16-17] 대화를 듣고, 여자의 마지막 말에 이어질 남자의 응답으로 가장 적절한 것을 고르시오.

16
① I'm going to the mountain this weekend.
② I want to go on a vacation with my colleagues.
③ I should have made as many friends as possible.
④ I missed the chemistry exam so I must take a make-up.
⑤ Going to parties and staying up late talking with friends.

17
① That's a little too expensive for me.
② Do you have any suites available?
③ I'm planning to visit my grandparents.
④ No, I'd like to recommend another room.
⑤ If I buy many candies, do I get a discount?

[18-19] 대화를 듣고, 남자의 마지막 말에 이어질 여자의 응답으로 가장 적절한 것을 고르시오.

18
① OK. I have made an outline of my speech.
② I have read a lot about how to write a speech.
③ Yes, you have to decide the subject matter first.
④ That's right. Look at the outline when you speak.
⑤ No, you will speak for over 20 minutes by yourself.

19
① Yes, I do mind visiting you tomorrow.
② No problem. Let's go buy some fruit first.
③ OK. His test results will come out tomorrow.
④ Then I think you should take him to the doctor's.
⑤ Not at all. Tomorrow is a good time to visit him.

20 다음을 듣고, 보미의 엄마가 그녀의 남편에게 할 말로 가장 적절한 것을 고르시오.
① Honey, I think we have a big money problem.
② Let's travel here every year as it's so much fun.
③ Keep thinking about it and you can get the answer.
④ Honey, stop worrying and start enjoying our vacation.
⑤ I think we need to go to the bank to get some money.

● 다음은 Listening Test 07의 주요 지문입니다. 녹음을 다시 듣고, 질문에 대한 답을 완성하세요.

Q1
1 How long has the Phantom of the Opera been running?

↳ It has been _____.

Q2
2 Why does the boy not have his bike?

↳ He does not have it because he _____.

Q4
3 What do you expect the woman to do after Tom comes back home safely?

↳ According to what she said, I expect her to _____.

Q10
4 What does the man recommend the woman do?

↳ She has to read her paper _____ and highlight _____

_____.

Q11
5 Why did the woman call customer service?

↳ She'd like to _____.

Q14
6 When does the woman visit the orphanage?

↳ She goes there _____.

Q16
7 Why is he not sure that he likes to work?

↳ He _____ all day and doesn't _____ to enjoy his money and car.

Q17
8 How much does she say the suite is?

↳ It's $_____, plus a _____% _____.

● 자신의 상황에 맞게 내용을 완성하고 말해 보세요.

 A Suppose you are running for president of the student council. Make a speech for the election.

A Speech for the Election	
(1) Position	
(2) Why are you running for this position?	
(3) Why should students vote for you?	
(4) What ideas do you have to improve the school?	

Good morning, students! My name is _____ and I am running

for (1)_____. I am running for this position because

(2)_____. You should

vote for me because I am (3)_____.

Some ideas I have to improve the school are (4)_____

_____. Thank you.

B Imagine your school lifts restrictions on hairstyles. What kind of hairstyle would you like to have? Draw a picture in the box. And then fill in the table below and tell your classmates about it.

My New Hairstyle	
(1) How long would your hair be?	
(2) What color would it be?	
(3) Would you have bangs? Why? Why not?	
(4) Would you prefer straight hair or wavy hair? Why?	

I'm going to talk about the hairstyle I would have if my school lifted restrictions

on hairstyles. My hair would be (1)_____. I would have (2)_____

_____. I (would / wouldn't) have bangs because (3)_____

_____. I would prefer to have (4)_____

_____ because _____.

07 Dictation Test

01

M Wow, look at these _____ _____ on the wall. Can you guess _____ _____ _____ _____?

W It looks like _____ _____ _____. I can't believe that all these musicals are now playing in the city.

M I heard that some shows have _____ _____ _____ _____.

W Oh, that might be the reason why it's so easy for people _____ _____ a _____ on Broadway when they travel to New York.

M I can see _____ _____ ones. *The Phantom of the Opera, Chicago, Jesus Christ Superstar, Les Miserables, Mamma Mia, The Lion King*, and *Wicked*.

W As we are in New York we can't _____ _____ _____. Which one would you like to see among these?

M Why don't we watch *Mamma Mia*?

W Sorry. I saw it last year. How about *The Phantom of the Opera*? It has _____ _____ for _____ _____.

M Oh, that sounds great. There must be _____ _____ _____ _____ to it

02

M Mom, I've got a problem.

W What's up?

M I have _____ _____ _____ this afternoon. All my friends are _____ _____ to the playground.

W What's your problem, then?

M You know Mike, my friend, don't you? I _____ _____ _____ _____. His bike needs to be repaired.

W Well, I don't know what I can do.

M Could you please tell Jenny to _____ _____ _____ _____? She _____ _____ _____ _____ _____ it because I _____ _____ _____ _____ the last time I used it.

W Oh, I remember that. You didn't _____ the tire. So your sister couldn't use it when she needed to.

03

M Good morning, students! My name is Michael

Woods and I am running for _____ of the _____ _____. I am running for this position because I want to be _____ _____ for all the students in this school. '_____, _____ and _____,' these are the three words that _____ _____, and three reasons why you _____ _____ for me. Some ideas I have to improve the school are more fundraisers, better food in the cafeteria, _____ in classrooms, and more electives. I want students to know they can come to me _____ _____ and I will listen to them and try to _____ _____ _____. I look forward to your votes on _____ _____. Thank you.

04

W It's 9 o'clock at night. Tom _____ _____ _____ home hours ago.

M Did you _____ Jason's house?

W Yes. I called Steve's house and Paul's house, too. I'm _____ _____.

M He _____ _____ _____ us _____ _____.

W Let's call the police.

M I heard that they _____ _____ anything _____ a person has been _____ for twenty-four hours.

W I _____ _____ _____.

M I'm sure he's _____ _____.

W If he is _____ _____, he's going _____ _____ _____.

05

M Oh, is it raining outside? You're all wet!

W It is raining _____ _____ _____. I got _____ _____ _____ _____ when I was _____ _____ _____ _____ home from the grocery store.

M According to the weather forecast this morning, it is supposed to be _____ today.

W The weather is really _____ these days. I don't think the rain will stop soon.

M Really? I am going to play soccer with my friends this afternoon.

W I think you'd better not do that. You should wait _____ _____ _____ _____.

M Yeah, you're right. I am going to _____

everyone right now.
W I hope you'll have the game tomorrow.

06

M Where's the _____? [Pause] Oh, it's here.
W Oh, let me get it this time.
M No. I'll _____ _____.
W Come on. It's _____ _____. I _____!
M Don't worry, we'll _____ _____ _____.
W All right. Let's do that this time.
M Let's see... the pasta is _____ dollars and chicken tender salad is _____ dollars. Then _____ _____ will be _____ dollars. How should we split it?
W Well, I ate the chicken tender salad so I'll pay for it. Here's the money.
M OK, I'll take it to the _____. I'll be back in a minute.

07

M What are your _____?
W Well, I have an MBA from Yale Graduate School, not to mention a _____ _____ from Harvard University.
M That's _____. Do you have any _____?
W Yes. During my college years, I _____ at a trading company.
M I see. And why do you want to _____ _____ us?
W I think your company has a _____ _____ _____ _____.
M What _____ do you want to work in?
W I'd like to work in the _____ _____.

08

M It's been a long time, Sally.
W _____ _____ _____ _____, Brian? We have the same _____ _____, so it has been quite hard to _____ _____ with you.
M Sorry for the _____. How would you like it to be done this time?
W I _____ _____ _____ showing what I would like done. Here it is.
M Oh, this is called a pin curl perm. It is the _____ _____ this spring.
W Do you think it will _____ _____ me?
M Of course. But I'll need to _____ _____ the _____ _____ first before I begin

perming your hair.
W Okay. Please don't make it too short though.
M Don't worry.

09

① M _____ _____ the Zoo, Zoo, Zoo.
  W Where can I see the _____?
② M How long will it take to _____ _____ the zoo?
  W It will take _____ _____ _____ by _____ _____.
③ M Look at the _____ over there. You _____ _____ the animals.
  W I'm sorry. I didn't see it.
④ M What do you think of this _____?
  W It looks good on you.
⑤ M I _____ what's _____ _____ you.
  W I left my lunch box _____ _____.

10

W Did you have a chance to _____ _____ _____ for me?
M Yes, I did. I just finished reading it.
W What do you think about it? Do you think it is okay?
M In my opinion, you'd better _____ the _____. It is _____ _____. It doesn't _____ _____ _____ _____ well. In other words, it is not clear enough.
W What do you _____ I do?
M Well. You have to read your paper again and _____ the sentences that are important.
W And then?
M Try to summarize and _____ what you highlighted in the conclusion. Your main point should be clearly _____.
W I will try. If it's okay with you, can you please review it again before I _____ _____ _____?
M No problem. Send it to me _____ _____.

11

[Telephone Rings.]
M Hello, Fastro Customer Service. Can I help you?
W Hello. I'd like to _____ the _____ on my Internet connection.
M May I have your name and phone number?
W This is Kate Smith. My number is 02-100-0207.
M _____. How long do you want to extend the contract for?

W For a year. Do you have any _____ _____ for customers _____ their contract?

M Well, since you've been with us for three years now, we can _____ your connection speed and give you _____ _____ _____ _____.

W Great. I will take that offer.

M A serviceman will visit your house to _____ _____ _____ next week. He will call you. Please _____ _____ _____ at that time. Thank you.

12

M Please _____ _____. How can I help you?

W I am not sure which one would be a _____ _____ _____ my son.

M Do you want to give him a pet he can _____ _____ or one which he has to _____ _____ _____ inside its cage?

W I haven't thought about that. Which type is better for a five-year-old boy?

M Well, _____ _____. If your son is _____, I _____ a puppy or a cat to play with. But if he is not _____, a _____ is a good choice.

W Any _____ _____?

M Some children like to _____ iguanas or lizards.

W Thank you for your helpful _____.

M You're welcome. I'll give you some time to think about it.

13

① **M** It is about the _____ _____.

② **M** It is a month-long _____ _____.

③ **M** You can only _____ _____.

④ **M** The difference in winnings between _____ and _____ is _____ dollars.

⑤ **M** You can ask for _____ information _____ _____ or by email.

14

M Are you done with your _____ _____ _____?

W Yes. I just finished it. How about you?

M I need some more time to finish it. I will _____ working on it over the weekend.

W That's too bad. You know what? I'm planning to do _____ _____ this weekend.

M What's that? Going _____?

W Yes. I will visit an _____ with my church friends. We go there the _____ _____ of _____ _____.

M Really? That sounds great. Can I _____ you next time?

W Why not? Why don't you go to the _____ _____ with us next weekend?

M Ok, I will. Please remind me the day before.

15

W Hello, passengers of flight 705 _____ _____ Chicago, with a stop in L.A. The _____ _____ has been _____ to 30B. Also, there will be a slight departure _____ due to the heavy snowstorm outside. The ground _____ is _____ the snow on the _____ in preparation for departure. It also looks like the flight is slightly _____, so we are offering free round-trip tickets to a few passengers willing to take a _____ _____. We should be boarding in _____ _____ _____ an hour. Thank you for your patience.

16

W Congratulations on your new job, Chris!

M Thanks, Angie. To tell you the truth, I'm _____ _____ _____ I like to work.

W Why do you say that? Last year you wanted to _____ _____ _____ university!

M I know, but that was last year. Now, it's just that I _____ _____. I work hard all day, every day.

W Oh, come on. _____ _____. You're making a _____ _____ now.

M Right. Now, I have money and a nice car. But I don't have any time to enjoy _____ of them.

W It can't be all that bad.

M No, of course it isn't. I still have my weekends.

W So tell me, what do you _____ _____ _____?

M Going to parties and staying up late talking with friends.

17

W Hello. BestStay Hotel. May I help you?

M Yes, I'd like to _____ _____ _____ for _____ on the _____ of August.

W Okay. Let me check our computer here for a moment. _____ _____, right?

M Yes, are you _____ _____ that night?

W Well, we have _____ _____ _____, complete with a kitchenette and a sauna bath. And the view of the city is great, too.

M _____ _____ is that?

W It's only $_____, plus a _____% room tax.

M That's a little too expensive for me.

18

M I have to _____ _____ _____ on international relations on Friday, and I am so _____.

W There are a lot of things you can do to make yourself _____ _____ _____ and less nervous.

M What should I do, Mary?

W First of all, you need to understand the _____ _____ _____.

M I have done a lot of research on the subject, and I believe I can answer any questions I will receive _____ _____ _____.

W Then you're ready to write your presentation. And after you write it, make a _____ _____ which you'll use to practice speaking.

M You mean I shouldn't read everything I wrote down.

W That's right. Look at the outline when you speak.

19

M My uncle was _____ yesterday.

W What seems to be _____ _____?

M He has got _____ _____. The doctor said that it was probably caused by his bad habit of _____.

W I'm sorry to hear that. So _____ _____ has he been smoking?

M I'm not really sure, but it might be about _____ years.

W Oh, that's too long. He must _____ _____ now or the cancer will _____ _____.

M I think so, too. Smoking just makes matters worse. Hopefully he can stop smoking.

W _____ _____ _____ _____ today?

M Yes, if you _____ _____.

W No problem. Let's go buy some fruit first.

20

W Bomi's family is _____ _____. They are staying in Hawaii for five days. _____ in her family is _____. She and her brother

want to go on a _____ _____ and see fish underwater. Her mother wants to _____ _____ and her father wants the family to _____ _____ in the morning and have a _____ on the beach in the evening. However, he is worried about _____ _____ _____ _____. Her mother thinks he worries too much about money and wants him _____ _____ _____ _____ _____ _____ while they are on vacation. In this situation, what would Bomi's mother probably say to her husband?

08 Listening Test

01 대화를 듣고, 여자가 구입할 TV로 가장 적절한 것을 고르시오.

① ② ③ ④ ⑤

02 대화를 듣고, 여자의 오빠가 남자에게 셔츠를 선물한 이유를 고르시오.

① 오늘이 그의 생일이어서　　　② 옷이 너무 커서
③ 도움에 대한 감사 인사로　　　④ 부탁할 일이 있어서
⑤ 자기 스타일이 아니어서

03 다음을 듣고, 무엇에 관한 내용인지 고르시오.

① 도서관 개관 시간　　　② 층별 도서 안내
③ 도서관 사서 모집　　　④ 도서 대출 방법
⑤ 도서관 벌금 안내

04 대화를 듣고, 남자의 심경으로 가장 적절한 것을 고르시오.

① cheerful　　　② anxious　　　③ relaxed
④ lonely　　　⑤ confident

05 대화를 듣고, 남자가 여자를 방문한 목적을 고르시오.

① 임대료를 납부하려고　　　② 배송 온 택배를 가지러
③ 입주자 주소를 확인하려고　　　④ 층간 소음 신고를 위해
⑤ 자동차 키를 맡기려고

06 대화를 듣고, 남자가 지불할 총 금액을 고르시오.

① $114　　　　　　② $120　　　　　　③ $144
④ $152　　　　　　⑤ $160

07 대화를 듣고, 두 사람의 관계로 가장 적절한 것을 고르시오.

① 경찰관 — 운전자　　　　　② 여행가이드 — 관광객
③ 호텔 직원 — 손님　　　　　④ 출입국 관리원 — 이민자
⑤ 지역 주민 — 이방인

08 대화를 듣고, 두 사람이 대화하는 장소로 가장 적절한 것을 고르시오.

① 레코드 가게　　　　② 마라톤 접수처　　　　③ 한강
④ 운동장　　　　　　⑤ 마술 쇼

09 다음을 듣고, 그림의 상황에 어울리는 대화를 고르시오.

①　　　　②　　　　③　　　　④　　　　⑤

10 대화를 듣고, 두 사람의 대화에서 언급되지 않은 것을 고르시오.

① 영어 말하기 대회 개최 요일　　② 영어 말하기 대회 점심 메뉴
③ 영어 말하기 대회 제공 음료　　④ 영어 말하기 대회 개최 장소
⑤ 대회 전날 점검해야 할 물품

11 대화를 듣고, 남자가 여자에게 제안한 일로 가장 적절한 것을 고르시오.

① 차량 인도하기   ② 응급차 부르기   ③ TV 시청하기

④ 보트 타기   ⑤ 낚시하기

12 대화를 듣고, 대화의 내용과 일치하지 <u>않는</u> 것을 고르시오.

① 그들의 아들은 수석으로 졸업할 것이다.

② 여자는 아들의 담임선생님한테서 전화를 받았다.

③ 남자는 고등학교를 수석으로 졸업했다.

④ 그들의 딸은 춤추고 노래하는 것을 좋아한다.

⑤ 남자는 딸이 재능을 살릴 수 있게 도와 줄 것이다.

13 다음을 듣고, 청첩장의 내용과 일치하지 <u>않는</u> 것을 고르시오.

WEDDING INVITATION
Donna & Vincent

Request the Honor of Your Presence
as They Exchange Their Marriage Vows
on September 13, 2015
At Noon

The Grand Building
123 Elizabeth Street, Brooklyn, New York
Lunch and Merriment to Follow

①   ②   ③   ④   ⑤

14 대화를 듣고, 대화 직후 여자가 할 일로 가장 적절한 것을 고르시오.

① 문화센터 방문하기   ② 문화센터 프로그램 알아보기

③ 신청서 작성하고 수강료 내기   ④ 중국어 말하기 능력 테스트 하기

⑤ 수강료 환불 받기

15 다음을 듣고, 고래에 대해서 언급되지 <u>않은</u> 것을 고르시오.

① 세상에서 가장 큰 동물이다.

② 공기를 분수공을 통해서 폐로 불어넣는다.

③ 바다에서의 삶에 적응한 유일한 포유류이다.

④ 항상 무리를 지어 이동한다.

⑤ 몇몇 종들은 사냥 때문에 멸종위기에 처해있다.

[16-17] 대화를 듣고, 여자의 마지막 말에 이어질 남자의 응답으로 가장 적절한 것을 고르시오.

16
① Mine is on October 10th.
② Thank you for encouraging me.
③ I wish you good luck tomorrow.
④ I failed to get my poom belt again.
⑤ You had your taekwondo test today.

17
① I'm sorry but I can't go there.
② Let's wait and see how it works.
③ Sure, I can stay here for a long time.
④ Yes, it's pretty painful during the night.
⑤ The pain has been constant for three days.

[18-19] 대화를 듣고, 남자의 마지막 말에 이어질 여자의 응답으로 가장 적절한 것을 고르시오.

18
① He must be really fond of you.
② Of course, he can do that for me.
③ Many people have failed, so he will too.
④ With that attitude, I'm sure he'll succeed.
⑤ He shouldn't quit school to work full time.

19
① I'm sorry to hear that.
② How poor he is to be all alone.
③ You deserve it to get this award.
④ I bet you're very proud of your son.
⑤ You enjoyed talking with him, didn't you?

20 다음을 듣고, Maria가 그녀의 엄마에게 할 말로 가장 적절한 것을 고르시오.
① Mom, I'm hungry. When can I eat lunch?
② Mom, look at the gift for you in the garden.
③ Mom, I can water the plants instead of you.
④ Mom, I want to live in a house with a garden.
⑤ Mom, thank you for giving me this special gift.

● 다음은 Listening Test 08의 주요 지문입니다. 녹음을 다시 듣고, 질문에 대한 답을 완성하세요.

Q1
1 Why does the man want a 40 or 42-inch rather than a 50-inch screen TV?

┗→ The reason is that a 50-inch screen is _____.

Q2
2 Why did the woman's brother buy the shirt?

┗→ He bought the shirt _____ as it was _____.

Q4
3 What did the man plan to do before watching the musical?

┗→ He planned to have _____ in a _____ with the woman.

Q8
4 What is the training schedule for the first day?

┗→ She will _____ and do some _____.

Q12
5 What is their daughter interested in?

┗→ She is interested in _____.

Q14
6 What kinds of courses does the culture center offer?

┗→ The center offers various courses in _____.

Q15
7 How do whales breathe?

┗→ They breathe in air _____ and it goes into their _____.

Q18
8 What does his brother plan to do after graduation?

┗→ He plans to _____ first, and then he will _____ for his
_____.

● 자신의 상황에 맞게 내용을 완성하고 말해 보세요.

A Have you ever bought something on impulse? Tell your classmates about it.

What I Bought Impulsively

(1) A useful item	
(2) When and why did you get it?	
(3) A useless item	
(4) When and why did you get it?	
(5) Why was it useless?	
(6) So what did you do with it?	

I'd like to contrast two items I bought on impulse. First of all, one of the useful items I bought on impulse was (1)_____. I bought it (2)_____ _____. I'm still happy about buying it. On the contrary, one useless item I have bought on impulse was (3)_____. I bought it (4)_____. It was useless for me because (5)_____. So (6)_____ _____.

B Think about the most memorable award you have ever received. Fill in the table below and tell your classmates about it.

The Most Memorable Award

(1) What was the title of the award?	
(2) When did you receive it?	
(3) Why did you get the award?	
(4) How did you feel when you received it?	
(5) Why is it the most memorable award to you?	

I'm going to talk about the most memorable award I have ever received. The award is (1)"_____." I received it when (2)_____ _____. The award is presented to any student who (3)_____ _____. I was (4)_____ when I received it. It is my most memorable award because (5)_____ _____.

01

M I'm looking for a television to _____ in my living room. Can you recommend one?

W The _____ and 50-inch _____ are the most popular sizes for the living room. How about a 50-inch Smart TV?

M I've heard a lot about Smart TVs, but I don't know anything about them. Could you tell me _____ _____?

W Okay. A Smart TV is a _____ _____ _____. It includes various functions such as a _____ television system, a set-top box, _____ _____ _____ _____ and game consoles _____ _____.

M Oh, fantastic. Well, I have some Blu-Ray movies. Can I play them with it?

W Of course. It also _____ as a Blu-Ray player.

M Sound perfect. But I think a 50-inch screen is _____ _____ _____ for my _____ _____ _____. Do you have a _____ or _____-inch _____?

W We have _____.

M Okay, then I'll take a _____-inch one.

02

W Hey, Chris! This is my brother's _____ for you.

M What's this _____ for? My birthday is _____ _____ _____ _____.

W He knows that. Just open it.

M Wow, this shirt is _____ _____ that I really like. By the way, could you tell me why he is giving this to me?

W This morning, my brother said it isn't _____ _____. He bought it yesterday _____ _____ as it was 50% _____. Unfortunately, it's _____.

M I'm sorry to hear that.

W He said you are _____ _____ _____ to wear this style.

M It's my good luck I guess. How do I look?

W Oh, he was right! It _____ really _____ _____ you. You look very _____.

M Yeah, I'm _____ _____ _____ _____ with you. Say thanks to him.

03

M Please return _____ by their _____ _____ as someone else is waiting for them.

If items are not returned by their _____ _____, other users, who have _____ or placed holds on these items, are _____. To _____ this, the library levies _____. If you have _____ _____ on your record, you will not be allowed _____ _____ until these are _____. Students in their _____ _____ will not be able _____ _____ _____ until _____ _____ to the library have been _____. Remember that you need never pay a _____ _____ if you return your loans _____ _____!

04

M Hi, Cindy. It's me, Tom. I'm here _____ _____ _____ the theater. Where are you now?

W Hi, Tom. I'm terribly sorry. I'm still _____ _____ _____ _____. I left the office early, but I've been _____ _____ _____ for over _____ _____ _____.

M When do you expect to be here?

W I'm not sure. I _____ _____ _____ this route. It's completely _____ _____.

M Oh, according to the _____ _____, there is a bad _____ on the road near the concert hall.

W I thought as much.

M I _____ a table for a light dinner in a restaurant near the concert hall where we're going to watch the musical, I'll have to _____ it.

W Sorry, I can't help it. The traffic is terrible. Anyway I'll do my best to get there _____ _____ _____ _____.

M I hope we won't _____ _____ _____ due to the traffic jam.

05

M Good morning. Could you do me a favor?

W What can I do for you?

M I have to _____ this package to one of your _____. Unfortunately, there's _____ _____ _____ on it.

W Have you tried to _____ _____ _____?

M Of course, I did. But she didn't _____ _____ her cell phone. There's _____

_____ to my _____ _____ as well.

W Alright, let me check the name on the box, and then I'll check _____ _____ _____.

M Okay, have a look at this. Her name is Martha Jones.

W Oh, she lives in _____ _____. Just _____ the box here and _____ _____ _____ her package is here.

M Thank you so much.

06

W May I help you?

M Yes, I'd like to reserve _____ _____ _____ tonight's Mozart concert.

W What section would you like? We have seats in the _____ _____ and seats in the _____ _____ available.

M How much is each section?

W A ticket in the _____ _____ is _____ dollars, and a ticket in the _____ _____ is _____ dollars.

M Do _____ and _____ get a discount?

W Yes, they do. Students and seniors receive a 10% _____ with proper ID.

M I'd like 1 seat for a _____, 2 seats for _____, and 1 seat for a _____ in the _____ _____.

W How would you like to pay, sir?

M With this debit card, please.

07

M Excuse me, how do I get to Hoyts' Theater?

W I'll _____ _____ _____ _____. I'm going there myself _____ _____ _____ _____ _____.

M I'm rather _____ for time. Do you know a _____?

W Sure. _____ _____.

M You really know _____ _____ well. Have you lived here long?

W Yes. I've lived here all my life.

M By the way, _____ _____ _____?

W It's _____ _____. Can you see _____ _____ over there?

M Yes, I can. You are very _____ to strangers. Without you, I would have _____ _____ and _____ _____ for hours. Thank you very much.

08

M How do you feel today?

W Not bad. What's the _____ _____ for today?

M Since this is your first day, you will _____ _____. First, you'll do some running to warm up.

W Good. I like running. I can run _____ _____ without _____.

M That's good. What's your _____ time to run 10 kilometers?

W About an hour and a half.

M In a month from now, you will be able to do it in _____ _____ _____.

W But the Hangang Marathon is three weeks from now. I'm going to run the 10km course and I want to be faster by then.

M Don't _____ magic. Just try to _____ _____ _____ this time and try again next year.

09

① M Where can I _____ a formal suit or tuxedo for my _____?

   W Here is the _____ number of a shop downtown.

② M Do you know to whom the _____ is to _____?

   W No. Do you?

③ M I'm very happy that you are _____.

   W Thank you. I _____ it all to you.

④ M Let's go to the _____ now _____ we will be late.

   W Okay.

⑤ M Thank you for your _____ and _____.

   W You deserve it.

10

M How is the _____ for the English Speech Contest going?

W You mean the one for first year students _____ _____, don't you?

M Yes. I'd like to double check all the _____.

W Here is a list of everything that I have _____. What do you think about the _____ _____?

M Are sandwiches and fruit going to be _____?

W I think so. And we will _____ coffee, fresh fruit juice and mineral water for drinks.

M Good. What about the tables and chairs? Do we have enough of them?

W We will prepare 10% _____ _____ the _____ _____ of people.

M And please check the microphone and the speakers at least _____ _____ _____.

W I will, sir. Don't worry. Everything will go fine without any _____.

11

W Why are you _____ the car over?

M Can't you hear the _____ _____? We have to pull over to the _____ _____ _____ _____.

W Oh, sorry. Now I can hear it.

M My goodness. Look at the cars! They are not _____ _____ _____ _____.

W Oh, no! I can't _____ my _____. I saw it on TV the other day. Many people don't _____ _____ _____ the way when they see the _____ _____.

M _____ _____ they are! What would they think it were them who needed help?

W I know. What should we do? We can't just sit and do nothing here.

M How about helping to _____ _____ so the ambulance can _____ _____?

W Great idea.

12

W Honey! I'm so _____ _____ our son, Jimmy. Don't be so _____, but listen to this!

M What is it? Please stop _____ _____ _____ _____ and tell me.

W I got a call from his _____ _____ this morning and she said Jimmy is going to _____ the top of his class.

M Oh, really? I graduated the top of my class when I was in grade 8, too.

W _____ _____ _____, _____ _____ _____.

M Ha, ha. Right. I hope Sally will be like him, but I think she is more interested in _____ and _____ than studying.

W But she is really good at them. I think having _____ and _____ for doing something is _____, too. Studying isn't everything.

M That's a reasonable explanation. Let's try to encourage her to develop her _____ _____.

13

① M It is a _____ _____ _____ for the marriage of Donna and Vincent.

② M The wedding will be _____ _____ _____, _____.

③ M The _____ will be at 12 o'clock.

④ M The venue _____ _____ _____ Elizabeth Street, Brooklyn.

⑤ M You can _____ _____ after the ceremony.

14

M Welcome to Seoul Culture Center. May I help you?

W I'd like to see a list of the various courses for _____ _____. Do you have a timetable of the courses?

M Here it is. You'd better decide which types of courses you _____ _____ _____. We offer _____ and _____ courses in art, music, _____ _____ and sports.

W I see. The Chinese conversation class sounds interesting to me.

M What do you think about your Chinese-speaking _____? Are you a beginner, intermediate, or advanced speaker?

W I'm definitely a beginner. What should I do in order to _____ _____ _____ _____?

M Please fill out this _____ _____ and make a _____ at the _____ _____.

W Okay. Thank you for your kind _____.

15

W Whales are large, magnificent, intelligent, aquatic mammals. They _____ _____ _____ through a blowhole and then it goes into their _____. They are the only _____ that live their entire lives in the water, and the only mammals that have _____ _____ _____ in the _____. They are the biggest animals in the world, even bigger than any of the _____ were. Many whales _____ over _____ _____ every year, sometimes in groups, from cold water feeding grounds to warm water breeding grounds. Some whale species are _____ because of _____ that still exists in countries such as _____.

16

W Bill, where are you going?

M I'm going to my taekwondo school to take _____ _____.

W I didn't know you took taekwondo lessons. _____ _____ do you have now?

M I have a poom belt which is a _____ _____ _____ belt.

W Wow, you _____ _____ _____.

_____ taekwondo. I started to learn it two months ago, too.

M You did? Great. It is really helpful in _____ your _____ and _____. Practice it every day to be healthy.

W Okay, I will. I have a _____ _____ _____ tomorrow.

M Don't be _____ and you can _____.

W Thanks. What about your next belt test?

M Mine is on October 10th.

17

W Hello. I'm Doctor Smith. What's the _____ with you today?

M I have some _____ right here, in my back and shoulders.

W How much does it _____?

M It's pretty bad. Both my back and shoulders really hurt.

W How would you _____ the pain _____ _____ _____?

M I can't say. I don't have a lot of _____ with pain. It's really hard to say.

W Well, _____ would be _____ and a _____ means somewhere in the middle, a _____ kind of pain.

M I'd say an _____ out of ten.

W Okay. That's _____ _____. Does it stay for a long time or does it come and go?

M The pain has been constant for three days.

18

M My brother's _____ _____ will be held tomorrow. He will finally have finished his four years of studies.

W That's great. Congratulate him for me.

M Ok, I will. I think he'll be very _____.

W What does he plan to do _____ _____?

M He plans to _____ _____ _____ _____, and then he will go back to school for his _____ _____.

W You mean he will _____ his job to go back to school full time?

M No, he needs to work to _____ _____. He will work full-time and go to school part-time at night.

W It will be _____ to hold a _____ _____ while going to school, won't it?

M It won't be easy, but he says many people _____ _____ _____. So he can, too.

W With that attitude, I'm sure he'll succeed.

19

M How are you feeling these days?

W I have been waiting for _____ _____ of _____ _____ _____. So I'm anxious and nervous.

M When is the result going to _____ _____?

W In a week. I have so much time on my hands and I have _____ _____ _____.

M Good luck to you. How about reading books? That's always a good way _____ _____ _____.

W That's true. How about you? How are you these days?

M I'm pretty good these days. My kid just _____ _____.

W That's great to hear. He _____ _____ _____ now. It's been a year since I saw your son.

M Yeah. He has _____ _____ _____ this year. And he's reading storybooks all _____ _____ _____ these days.

W I bet you're very proud of your son.

20

M Today is Arbor Day. Maria and her daddy are _____ _____ _____ in their garden. Her mom is preparing lunch and _____ _____ what they are doing. Her daddy tells her trees are _____ for the _____ as they create oxygen and _____ a home for birds and other small animals. Maria decides to _____ a tree for her mom in the _____ _____ the garden. After planting it, she wants to show it to her mom. In this situation, what would Maria probably say to her mom?

01 대화를 듣고, 여자가 구입할 컴퓨터로 가장 적절한 것을 고르시오.

① ② ③ ④ ⑤

02 대화를 듣고, 여자의 열대어가 죽은 이유를 고르시오.

① 산소발생기가 없어서 　　　② 먹이가 부족해서

③ 물 온도가 너무 낮아서 　　　④ 스트레스를 받아서

⑤ 수질이 나빠져서

03 다음을 듣고, 무엇에 관한 내용인지 고르시오.

① 학생증 발급 방법 　　　② 온라인 티켓 수령 방법

③ 콘서트 홍보 전략 　　　④ 학생 할인 티켓

⑤ 오페라 하우스 소개

04 대화를 듣고, 남자의 심경으로 가장 적절한 것을 고르시오.

① pleased 　　　② excited 　　　③ worried

④ annoyed 　　　⑤ embarrassed

05 대화를 듣고, 여자가 커뮤니티 센터에 전화한 목적을 고르시오.

① 유료강습 일정문의 　　　② 상연 중인 공연 문의

③ 센터 위치 문의 　　　④ 대관 문의

⑤ 시설 이용료 문의

06 대화를 듣고, 여자가 지불할 총 금액을 고르시오.

① $144   ② $264   ③ $270
④ $432   ⑤ $480

07 대화를 듣고, 두 사람의 관계로 가장 적절한 것을 고르시오.

① 여행가이드 — 관광객   ② 철도 역무원 — 승객
③ 버스 매표소 직원 — 승객   ④ 지하철 역무원 — 무임탑승객
⑤ 버스 운전기사 — 학생

08 대화를 듣고, 두 사람이 대화하는 장소로 가장 적절한 것을 고르시오.

① 병원   ② 바닷가   ③ 신발가게
④ 운동장   ⑤ 공연장

09 다음을 듣고, 그림의 상황에 어울리는 대화를 고르시오.

①   ②   ③   ④   ⑤

10 대화를 듣고, 남자가 여자를 위해 할 수 있는 일이 <u>아닌</u> 것을 고르시오.

① 팜플렛 제작 도와주기   ② 쇼핑몰에 같이 가기
③ 미용실에 들르기   ④ 선전 구호 만들기
⑤ 팜플렛용 사진 찍어주기

11 대화를 듣고, 여자가 남자에게 부탁한 일로 가장 적절한 것을 고르시오.

① 사회학 과제 설명해주기   ② 과제 발표 함께 하기

③ 발표 연습 후 조언해주기   ④ 발표 순서 정해주기

⑤ 방과 후에 만나기

12 대화를 듣고, 두 사람이 이야기하는 내용과 일치하는 것을 고르시오.

① 여자는 저녁으로 야채 수프를 만들고 있다.

② 남자는 야채 먹는 것을 좋아한다.

③ 여자는 입맛이 까다롭다.

④ 남자는 패스트푸드를 좋아한다.

⑤ 남자는 식습관을 고치기로 약속했다.

13 다음을 듣고, 포스터의 내용과 일치하지 <u>않는</u> 것을 고르시오.

LOST

① **Pet Dog:**
② Male/ Cocker spaniel / ③ White with light brown hair on ears
④ **Last Seen:**
Running on the grass in April Park
⑤ **If You Have Any Information:**
Please call the number below
010-100-8282

REWARD!!

14 대화를 듣고, 여자가 이번 주말에 할 일로 가장 적절한 것을 고르시오.

① 아파트 둘러보기   ② 아파트 계약하기

③ 이삿짐 센터 알아보기   ④ 이사하기

⑤ 남자의 이사 도와주기

15 다음을 듣고, 고대 이집트인에 대해서 언급되지 <u>않은</u> 것을 고르시오.

① 파라오를 신이라고 믿었다.   ② 오직 왕만이 미라가 될 수 있었다.

③ 사후 세계가 있다고 믿었다.   ④ 파라오의 몸을 보존하기 위해서 애썼다.

⑤ 영혼이 알아보도록 몸을 미라로 만들었다.

[16-17] 대화를 듣고, 여자의 마지막 말에 이어질 남자의 응답으로 가장 적절한 것을 고르시오.

16
① Sure. It's on you, right?
② Yes, I'll visit that hotel tomorrow.
③ Don't worry, I'll be there on time.
④ Why aren't you working tonight?
⑤ No, I don't want to hang out with him.

17
① You're right. These foods are safe to eat.
② You are thinking about safety a lot these days.
③ Then I should grow a bigger and better tomato.
④ Well, I'll never eat genetically modified foods.
⑤ I dislike eating tomatoes since they aren't tasty.

[18-19] 대화를 듣고, 남자의 마지막 말에 이어질 여자의 응답으로 가장 적절한 것을 고르시오.

18
① That sounds like a lot of fun.
② I like chocolate bars so much.
③ Well, I really hope it works today.
④ There are no snacks in the machine.
⑤ Kick the ball a lot harder next time.

19
① Let's take this cute black puppy.
② My best friend is raising a kitten.
③ We can bring dogs and cats in here.
④ That's right. You can take any animal.
⑤ We can buy some fish in a small bowl.

20 다음을 듣고, 치과의사가 Jamie에게 할 말로 가장 적절한 것을 고르시오.
① You have two cavities to be filled right now.
② You may feel some pain when I am drilling.
③ Why did you pull out this tooth on the right?
④ Why has it been three years since you last visited?
⑤ As the cavity's so big, I want to pull this tooth out.

● 다음은 Listening Test 09의 주요 지문입니다. 녹음을 다시 듣고, 질문에 대한 답을 완성하세요.

Q1
1 What is the benefit of an all-in-one desktop computer?

↳ You can _____ because it has _____ together.

Q2
2 According to the woman, when do the tropical fish get stressed?

↳ They get stressed when they have to _____.

Q3
3 What do students have to do when they book a ticket online?

↳ They have to _____ into the _____.

Q8
4 Before taking their present vacation, why hadn't they been on a trip for a long time?

↳ The reason is that they were so _____ working and _____ _____.

Q10
5 Write three places where they are going to go.

↳ They are going to go to _____, _____ and _____.

Q12
6 What does the boy prefer to eat?

↳ He prefers to eat _____ like _____.

Q15
7 Why did the ancient Egyptians make mummies?

↳ They made mummies for the pharaoh's _____ to _____ his _____.

Q17
8 Based on her saying, list three reasons why genetic modification is used.

↳ To grow _____, to have more _____, and to be _____ to _____ and _____.

● 자신의 상황에 맞게 내용을 완성하고 말해 보세요.

A How do you prepare for exams? Have you ever crammed to prepare for an exam? Tell your classmates about it.

How to Prepare for Exams

(1) What is the first thing you do?	
(2) What subject do you spend more time on?	
(3) What subject did you cram for the night before the test?	
(4) What was the result of your cramming?	
(5) What will you do to prepare for your next exam?	

I'd like to tell you about how I prepare for exams. The first thing I do is (1)_____

_____. I try to spend more time on (2)_____

_____. For my most recent exams, I crammed all

night for the (3)_____ test. As a result, I (4)_____

_____. For my next exam, I will (5)_____

_____.

B What do you think of genetically modified foods? Write your opinion, including the details in the table below.

Genetically Modified Crops

(1) What are genetically modified crops?	
(2) My opinion of eating them	
(3) The reason for my opinion	

Genetically modified crops are (1)_____

_____. In my opinion, I think (2)_____.

The reason I think this is that (3) _____

_____.

Therefore, I think we can say they (are/aren't) safe and (2)_____

_____.

01

W Hi. I saw the sign 'Display Models on Sale.' Among them, are there any computers?

M Yes, there are some. Which type do you want, a _____ or a _____?

W Could you show me _____ _____ _____?

M Okay. How about this all-in-one desktop computer? It is a really popular model because it has _____ _____ and _____ together, so you can _____ _____. The discounted price is _____ dollars.

W Wow, it looks very _____ and _____. It's quite attractive. Could you recommend a laptop?

M Okay. The most popular one is this ultra book.

W _____ _____ it is! And it's _____ _____. How much is it?

M It's _____ dollars.

W Oh, that's too much for me. I'll take the _____ one.

02

M How are the _____ _____ you bought last month doing?

W Of the ones I bought there are only _____ _____, but they are doing great, I guess.

M How come there are only 2 left? As I remember, you bought _____ _____ fish and _____ _____ fish. Isn't it correct?

W You're right. Unfortunately, _____ _____ _____ I bought them, 1 male fish died. Then the next day 5 female fish died as they _____ _____ _____ the fish tank onto the floor.

M It's _____. Do you know why they did that?

W They _____ _____ _____ the fish tank when they _____ _____. Especially when they have to _____ _____ a new tank, I've heard that it happens a lot.

M Oh, I see. Then, are you going to buy more fish and put them into the fish tank?

W No. I _____ _____ that. You know what? My female goofy fish _____ _____ to _____ baby fish last week.

M Wow! _____!

03

W Do you want _____ _____ _____ _____ to great shows? Well, it's possible if you're a full-time student. Guard that _____ _____ like _____, because it's _____ _____ _____ in it. You can buy a student ticket for most shows at the Opera House for _____ _____ _____ $20. If you are a full time student, you have to _____ 'STUDENT' into the _____ _____ _____ when you book a ticket online. These online tickets can be picked up from the box office _____ _____ _____ to the performance. That's when you'll need to show your _____ student ID. If you cannot book online, you can buy student tickets on the day of a show for as little as _____ dollars.

04

W Wow! Finally, the _____ _____ are _____.

M I guess you did very well.

W No! Believe it or not, I _____ _____ this time. I am just happy because my _____ _____ are _____. How about you?

M I think I _____ _____ _____ _____.

W I can't believe it. You told me you studied hard for the test.

M Yeah. I wanted to do well so I _____ the _____ _____ before taking the math exam.

W You were _____ _____ _____ _____ on your test, weren't you? I had the same experience once before.

M I _____ _____ _____ _____ to my mom. I _____ _____ _____ _____ what I had learned that day at the end of each day. What should I tell her?

W Just tell her _____ _____. If you try to hide it, you won't be able to _____ it for very long.

05

[Telephone rings.]

M Townsville Community Center. How can I help you?

W I want to _____ a workshop. Can I _____ one of your seminar rooms?

M It _____ on _____ _____. For example, all the Saturdays in July have already been _____. What day are you thinking of?

W Oh, I was thinking of Saturday _____ _____ _____. Then, is Sunday _____ _____ _____ available?

M I'm afraid that day has already been reserved as well.

W Can you tell me the _____ _____?

M Sunday July the _____ is still available.

W That sounds great! Then, could you please _____ a seminar room on that day _____ _____ _____ of Jane Smith?

M Okay. We have _____ such as projectors, screens and _____ _____ which can be used for a small _____. Are you going to need to use some of these?

W Oh, I think I'll need a _____ and _____.

06

W Hi, I'd like to _____ _____ the Pilates beginner class.

M Okay. We have two classes for beginners: a _____ _____ and an _____ _____.

W How much is _____ _____ _____ for each?

M For the _____ one, it costs 100 dollars, and the _____ one is _____ dollars.

W What's the difference between the two classes?

M There is a difference in the number times it meets per week. The _____ class meets _____ a week, but the _____ class meets five times a week.

W Then I'll take the _____ _____.

M I got it. If you pay _____ _____ _____ at one time, you can get a 10% discount off the total price.

W Okay, I'll pay _____ _____ card for three months now. Could you make it _____ _____ _____ _____? It's interest-free, so it's easier for me.

07

M I'd like a ticket for Blacktown, please.

W There are _____ _____ _____ buses to Blacktown today. We run four nonstop buses per day, but the last bus left _____ _____ _____.

M What should I do then?

W You can get a bus to Burwood and _____ _____ onto a bus for Blacktown.

M That's fine. Then give me _____ _____ _____ to Burwood, please.

W Okay. The next Burwood bus _____ _____ ten minutes, but since you need to _____ you are better off waiting for _____ _____ minutes for the _____ bus.

M Oh, thanks for the information. I'll get that one. How much is the ticket?

W It's _____ dollars.

M Okay, here you are.

08

M I _____ so _____. What about you? Do you feel the same as me?

W Yeah, I do. My work has been _____ _____ _____ so much these days, but all the _____ _____ are gone now.

M I feel _____. When was the last time we _____ _____ on the sand together?

W _____ 5 years ago. Before coming here, we hadn't gone on a trip since I got _____ with Laura.

M I'm so sorry.

W Don't say so. We were just _____ _____ and _____ our children. We are here now anyway.

M Look at Laura and Ralph. They are enjoying making a _____.

W They are _____ their hands at us. Let's go to them.

09

① M How would you like to _____ _____ _____? _____ _____ or _____?

W By plane, please.

② M How much _____ _____ _____?

W It _____ 13kg. Can you help me move it?

③ M _____ _____ _____ _____?

W It is not _____ _____ to ask a woman her _____.

④ M How can I get to the _____ _____?

W Sorry, I'm a _____ here.

⑤ M How much is this?

W It's $25. It's on sale.

10

M Amy! I heard that you are going to _____ in the school _____ _____. Is it right?

W I haven't decided yet, but I'm _____

_____ about doing it.

M _____ _____. Just go for it. You are the _____ _____ for the position. I will help you _____ _____ _____ I can.

W You give me the _____ to be a _____.

M Let's go to a photo shop and get some pictures taken for a poster and _____. I will help you make both of them. Let's think about a _____.

W Thank you.

M Before you take the picture, let's go to a dress shop and buy a nice dress. And then let's go to a beauty salon to get your hair and _____ done for the photo.

W I don't know how to _____ you for all this.

M _____ _____ _____ _____? I'm sure you will be elected president of the _____ _____.

11

M Were you looking for me?

W Yes. I really _____ _____ _____. Do you have some free time _____ _____ _____ _____?

M What do you want me to do for you?

W I will give a _____ in my _____ class the day after tomorrow, so I want to practice presenting in front of you.

M Okay. So do you want me to give you _____ _____ on _____ _____ _____ your presentation right now?

W YES! Can you?

M No problem. I _____ _____ you _____ your presentation as often as you can.

W Thank you so much. When can I _____ you?

M See you _____ _____ school.

12

M Mom. What's that _____? What are you making?

W I'm making _____ _____ for lunch.

M Vegetable soup? Oh, mom! You know how much I _____ _____ _____ _____ _____. Why are you making that? I'm not going to eat it.

W Tim, listen! Vegetables are good for your health. You have to eat a _____ _____. Don't be so _____.

M But they are _____ _____ _____ _____. I _____ _____ eat pizza or hamburgers.

W You'd better _____ your _____ _____. Stop eating fast food from now on and try to eat proper meals.

M Mom, please…

W _____ _____! I want you to _____ _____ and be _____ _____ any _____.

13

M I lost my pet dog. It is _____ and the _____ of the dog is Cocker Spaniel. Its hair is _____ _____, but its ears are _____ _____ light brown hair. I saw him for the last time in April Park _____ _____ a _____ _____. If you have seen him around your neighborhood or have any _____, please _____ me at 010-100-8282. There is a small _____ of $50 for information that results in finding him. Please don't just _____ _____. I _____ _____ _____ _____ from you.

14

M _____ _____ _____ _____ this apartment?

W I like it. I like its _____, _____ and the _____. And especially, the price is _____.

M Why don't you _____ _____ _____ now then?

W I will. When can I _____ _____?

M When do you want to? Anytime is fine because _____ is living here now.

W Then I will _____ into this place this coming weekend.

M You will be _____ _____ throughout the week. If you need a recommendation for a moving company just let me know.

W Okay, I will. Thank you.

15

W The ancient Egyptians believed in many gods. They also believed that their kings, called pharaohs, were _____. They believed that there was a life _____ _____ and the pharaoh could take care of them even after he had _____. Because of this, they wanted the pharaoh to have a good afterlife. One way to give the pharaoh a good afterlife was _____ _____. Egyptians believed it was important for the pharaoh's _____ to _____ _____ _____. This is the reason the Egyptians made _____.

16

W Hey, Max. I just got hired to work _____ _____ _____ at the buffet restaurant in the Rideau Hotel.

M Congratulations. That's great!

W I'm so happy. To work there has always been _____ _____ and it has finally _____ _____ _____.

M When do you start?

W I start _____ _____.

M You're going to have to put in a lot of hours you know.

W I know. I'm a _____ _____, but just the _____ of working there makes _____ _____ _____.

M I bet you'll do a good job.

W Thanks. I'm going to _____ _____. Can you join me?

M Sure. It's on you, right?

17

M What's that?

W It's a bigger and better tomato. It's been genetically _____.

M You're not going to eat that, are you?

W Yes. I'm making a salad. Want one?

M No way. I don't want to eat it. Who knows what kind of _____ _____ it has?

W It's perfectly _____. It's been modified to grow _____, have _____ _____, and be resistant to _____ and pests.

M And it may contain _____ _____ as part of its genetic makeup that they didn't tell you about.

W Farmers use _____ _____ with animals and crops to bring us bigger and better food. This tomato is _____ _____.

M It is different because scientist _____ its genes.

W Oh, it's still safe to eat!

M Well, I'll never eat genetically modified foods.

18

W Finally, it's break time. I'm going to the _____ _____. Do you _____ _____, John?

M No, thanks, Sara.

W Don't you like snacks or chocolate bars?

M I like them, but I don't _____ them from these _____ _____.

W Why not?

M Last week, that machine _____ my coins. _____ _____ _____; no snack, no money back.

W That's _____. So, what did you do?

M I _____ the machine a few times, but _____ _____.

W Well, I really hope it works today.

19

M Mom, can we take one of these puppies?

W I would love to _____ a puppy, but we _____ _____ _____. We live in an apartment. A dog in an apartment is not a good idea.

M But my friend who _____ _____ _____ _____ has a dog.

W Yes, I know many people raise dogs in their apartments, but I think it's _____ good for _____ _____ _____ the dog.

M If we _____ _____ _____ _____, can we have a dog?

W Yes, of course. Someday you can have a dog, if we ever live in a house.

M Do we have a plan to live in a house?

W Not really. But it _____ _____ _____.

M Then is there _____ _____ we can take home today?

W We can buy some fish in a small bowl.

20

M Jamie is at the _____ _____ today since he has a _____ on the right side of his mouth. He bought _____ _____ at the drugstore, but the _____ _____ _____. As his last dental check-up was three years ago, he is _____ that he may have a serious problem. An x-ray technician took x-rays of his teeth. Fortunately, he has only _____ _____. The dentist is _____ one of the cavities and filling it. However, he will have to _____ _____ the other tooth which is _____ _____ _____. In this situation, what would the dentist probably say to Jamie?

01 대화를 듣고, 여자가 찾고 있는 가방으로 가장 적절한 것을 고르시오.

① ② ③ ④ ⑤

02 대화를 듣고, Mike가 도망간 이유를 고르시오.

① 야구 연습을 하려고
② 숙제 하기 싫어서
③ 심부름하기 귀찮아서
④ 불량배가 따라와서
⑤ 이웃집 유리창을 깨서

03 다음을 듣고, 무엇에 관한 내용인지 고르시오.

① 산행 시 유의 사항
② 입산 시간 안내
③ 야생 동물 보호
④ 새 등산로 개장
⑤ 등산로 폐쇄

04 대화를 듣고, 남자의 심경을 가장 잘 나타낸 것을 고르시오.

① surprised
② excited
③ nervous
④ indifferent
⑤ jealous

05 대화를 듣고, 여자가 여행사를 방문한 목적을 고르시오.

① 크루즈 여행 예약
② 패키지 여행 예약
③ 항공권 구입
④ 예약 취소
⑤ 예약 재확인

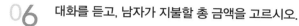

06 대화를 듣고, 남자가 지불할 총 금액을 고르시오.

① $240

② $300

③ $330

④ $390

⑤ $480

07 대화를 듣고, 두 사람의 관계로 가장 적절한 것을 고르시오.

① 택시 기사 — 승객

② 여행가이드 — 관광객

③ 은행 직원 — 고객

④ 관광버스기사 — 여행객

⑤ 택배 기사 — 고객

08 대화를 듣고, 두 사람이 대화하는 장소로 가장 적절한 것을 고르시오.

① 도서관

② 컴퓨터 AS센터

③ 창고

④ 고객 서비스센터

⑤ 서점

09 대화를 듣고, 여자가 구입할 이불로 가장 적절한 것을 고르시오.

10 대화를 듣고, 남자가 오늘 아침에 한 일로 가장 적절한 것을 고르시오.

① 공항에 사촌 마중 나가기

② 조조 영화보기

③ 회사에 정시 출근하기

④ 프랑스 출장 준비하기

⑤ 인터뷰 준비하기

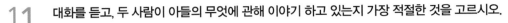
11 대화를 듣고, 두 사람이 아들의 무엇에 관해 이야기 하고 있는지 가장 적절한 것을 고르시오.

① 식습관   ② 장래 희망   ③ 교우 관계
④ 공부 태도   ⑤ 취미 생활

12 대화를 듣고, 대화의 내용과 일치하는 속담으로 가장 적절한 것을 고르시오.

① Well begun is half done.
② All that glitters is not gold.
③ A rolling stone gathers no moss.
④ A bad workman always blames his tools.
⑤ When a leopard dies, it leaves its skin; a man, his reputation.

13 대화를 듣고, 남자가 구입할 USB로 가장 적절한 것을 고르시오.

Model	Capacity	Price	Cable
① Mega 3.0	32GB	$55	O
② Mega 2.0	16GB	$35	X
③ Mega 1.0	8GB	$20	O
④ Vega 2.0	16GB	$30	O
⑤ Vega 1.0	8GB	$20	X

14 대화를 듣고, 여자가 전화 통화 후에 할 일로 가장 적절한 것을 고르시오.

① 케이크 사러 가기   ② 파티 음식 준비하기   ③ 집 꾸미기
④ 설거지 하기   ⑤ 집안 치우기

15 다음을 듣고, 마야인에 관련하여 언급되지 않은 것을 고르시오.

① 멕시코와 중앙아메리카에 살았다.
② 신세계에서 가장 위대한 문명을 세웠다.
③ 사람을 제물로 바치는 의식이 있었다.
④ 땅의 신을 가장 위대한 신으로 숭배했다.
⑤ 천문학과 점성술을 중요하게 여겼다.

[16-17] 대화를 듣고, 여자의 마지막 말에 이어질 남자의 응답으로 가장 적절한 것을 고르시오.

16
① Walking is good for your health.
② Is there any risk of heart damage?
③ I could never get used to it either.
④ But you can save someone's life.
⑤ I'm sorry to hear of your health troubles.

17
① I don't think he needs to pay you a fine.
② No, it's not overdue so there is no fine.
③ Yes, when that happens, he has to pay me $1.
④ My parents never had to clean up after me.
⑤ No, I don't want to live with a messy person.

[18-19] 대화를 듣고, 남자의 마지막 말에 이어질 여자의 응답으로 가장 적절한 것을 고르시오.

18
① It's not a bad day to go for a ride.
② Be careful, and keep your eyes open.
③ I got a bargain when I bought this bike.
④ Go faster! The road is so flat and straight.
⑤ I'm learning so I can't stay balanced on my bike.

19
① I'm glad we can finally both agree.
② I'm sorry, but it sounds boring to me.
③ I want to walk in the park every day, too.
④ Our neighbor is a real interesting character.
⑤ I wish we could get along with our neighbors.

20
다음을 듣고, Ms. Adams가 그녀의 고객에게 할 말로 가장 적절한 것을 고르시오.

① I'm really sorry I'm late.
② What time should we make it?
③ It's already been sold to another family.
④ I wish we could live in a new apartment.
⑤ Come quickly, or someone else might take it.

● 다음은 **Listening Test 10**의 주요 지문입니다. 녹음을 다시 듣고, 질문에 대한 답을 완성하세요.

Q1

1 Where is this conversation taking place?

↳ It is taking place at the _____ for subway line _____.

Q2

2 What does Mike's mom want Mike to do?

↳ She wants Mike to tell Mr. Johnson he _____ and he will

_____.

Q5

3 How can she have her own room if she goes on a package tour?

↳ She can have her own room for _____.

Q10

4 Where did the man go this morning and why did he go there?

↳ He went to _____ to pick up _____.

Q13

5 Why does the man need a new USB?

↳ He needs one to _____ for his _____.

Q14

6 What did the woman ask the man to buy and why?

↳ She asked the man to _____ because the one she has

_____.

Q15

7 What were the features of Mayan civilization?

↳ They were the worship of _____ , the existence of _____,

the importance of _____ and _____, rituals of _____,

and the building of elaborate _____.

Q16

8 What is the sticker on his driver's license?

↳ It indicates that he has _____ for the _____.

● 자신의 상황에 맞게 내용을 완성하고 말해 보세요.

 A   Please try to recall a moment when you broke a promise. Fill in the table and tell your classmates about it.

I Broke a Promise When...	
(1) When did you break a promise?	
(2) Who did you make it to?	
(3) What was it about?	
(4) What was the person's reaction when you broke it?	
(5) How did you resolve it and what was the result?	

I'm going to talk about a moment when I broke a promise. It was (1)_____

_____. I made the promise to (2)_____. It was about

(3)_____ but I didn't keep

it. (He/ She) (4)_____

_____. I (5)_____

_____. (Fortunately/ Unfortunately), (5)_____

_____.

B   Do you want to live in a big city or in the country? Fill in the table below and write your opinion.

In a Big City or in the Country?	
The place	
The 1st reason	
The 2nd reason	
My conclusion	

When people talk about where they prefer to live, different people have

different points of view. From my personal perspective, I prefer to live in (a big

city / the country). First, _____

_____.

Second, _____.

In sum, I want to live in _____ because _____.

01

W Excuse me. I'm looking for a bag I accidently left on subway line 5 last night. Could you check if anyone has _____ _____ _____?

M I will check. [Pause] We have 3 bags that were _____ _____ to the Lost and Found last night. Can you _____ your bag for me?

W It is a _____ _____ tote bag with a shoulder strap. It is a woven bag.

M Is there _____ _____ about it?

W Well, the bag is woven _____ _____ of dark brown leather and camel brown leather. So its color is _____ _____.

M Can you describe the contents of your bag?

W There is a wallet made of the _____ _____ as the bag inside it. I hope it wasn't _____.

M I think this is yours. Check it and if it is yours, _____ _____ _____, please.

W Oh, I'm sure it's mine. I really _____ your help.

02

W What's up, Mike? You look _____.

M Well, Tom and I were shagging flies and he hit a ball over the _____ and _____ a window in Mr. Johnson's house.

W Then what happened?

M We both _____ _____.

W What a surprise!

M I feel bad about _____ _____, but…

W I want you to _____ _____ to Mr. Johnson's house and tell him you broke the window and you'll _____ _____ it.

M Mom, I didn't _____ it, Tom did.

W That's not the point. You were there, so you both are _____. Don't shy away from _____ _____.

03

M Attention, visitors! McKinley Mountain Maintenance Department has scheduled a _____ of the South Eastern _____ from _____ _____ to _____ _____. This trail will be _____ closed due to the _____ of _____ _____ _____ _____ in large numbers which pose a _____ _____ to visitors.

Efforts are underway to _____ _____ _____ and to _____ _____ in this area. The trail will _____ after the work has been _____. For further information, please contact Robert Donovan at 360-856-5700. Thank you for your patience.

04

W If you take Judy to the _____ _____ at _____ o'clock and keep her busy until _____, her friends will all have _____ at our house by _____. Do you think _____ _____ is enough for you two to _____ _____?

M It will be alright. When she comes back, she'll be _____ _____.

W I want her best friend Wendy to _____ _____ _____ _____.

M I'm sure she won't _____ _____ _____.

W _____ _____ _____ will be coming?

M We've invited _____.

W I hope there'll be a good _____.

M Aren't you _____ _____ _____ Judy's going to be?

W I am Just make sure you _____ her _____ _____ until 12:30.

M Don't worry. Trust me.

W Oh, here comes Judy. _____ _____ _____.

05

M How can I help you?

W I'm here to _____ _____ _____ _____ to Bangkok.

M Are you traveling with anyone?

W No, I'm going to travel _____. Do I have to _____ _____ _____ with someone else if I get a _____ _____? I don't want to.

M Don't worry about it. You can have your _____ _____ for a small extra payment.

W Okay, I'll do that. Then, could you check flights? I would like to _____ _____ _____.

M I'm afraid that no tickets are available for _____. _____ _____ you can leave is _____ _____. Is that okay with you?

W It should be fine.

M Here are your tickets and _____ _____.
As soon as you arrive at the airport, find our
_____ _____ at _____
_____ _____.

06

W Welcome to Mount Cook Ski Resort! How can I help
you?

M Hi, I would like to buy two day _____
_____ _____.

W The regular price for a day pass is _____
dollars. And with that pass you can enjoy skiing
and snowboarding from _____ a.m. to
_____ p.m.

M Oh, can't I ski _____ _____?

W No, with a day pass you can't To do that, you should
buy a _____ _____ It's 60 dollars.

M Do you have _____ passes for periods of
several days? I'm going to stay at this resort for
_____ _____.

W Yes, we have them. It is _____ dollars for a
full-day pass for three days.

M Okay. I'll have _____ _____ passes for
three days. And my friend and I have to _____
_____ and skiing gear for the three days.

W Renting clothing is 10 dollars _____
_____ per day and skiing gear is 20 dollars per
person per day.

07

M _____ _____, ma'am?

W The Canadian Embassy. It's behind City Hall. You
can _____ _____ _____ there if
there is too much traffic around City Hall.

M All right, ma'am.

W Could you _____ _____ _____?
I'm _____ _____ _____. I have to
_____ _____ _____ to renew my
passport before they close at 5 pm.

M I'll do my best.

W Is it possible to _____ _____? This lane
is _____ _____!

M Oh, you really are a _____ _____.

W Excuse me, but what did you say?

M No, nothing.

08

M Excuse me. This is my _____ _____
coming here. Can I ask you _____
_____ _____?

W Of course. What can I do to help?

M I don't know the best way to find a book I want.

W First, _____ _____ the book you
want on the computer over there. It will show you
where you can find it and whether it is _____
_____ or _____ _____
_____.

M What should I do if it is out of stock?

W Then you can go to the _____ _____
_____ and get a copy _____ for you.

M If I want to order a book, do you know if I have to
put some money down first?

W I'm sorry. I'm _____ _____ about that.

M I see. Thank you very much for helping me.

09

M Is there _____ _____ _____ you'd
like to buy, ma'am?

W I'm looking for a comforter for my daughter.

M There are _____ _____ _____
designs for kids. What kind of design do you
_____ _____ _____?

W Which one is _____ with kids these days? Can
you _____ one of them to me, please?

M This way, please. Take a look at these _____,
_____, and _____ _____
_____.

W Oh, the last one sounds great to me.

M Which one do you prefer: Mickey Mouse, Cinderella
riding in a _____ _____ or Snow White
and the Seven Dwarfs?

W _____ _____ _____, please.

10

W Why didn't you _____ my phone call this
morning?

M I'm sorry, I was very busy so I _____
_____ _____ to call you back.

W What were you doing?

M I had to go to the _____ _____
_____ _____ my cousin from
_____. My uncle called me _____
_____ and asked me to do it. So I _____
_____ _____ work.

W Oh, that's too bad. You said your _____ is
very _____ about getting to work _____
_____.

M I explained my _____ to him and he
understood.

W Good. So where is your cousin now? In your house?

M Yes. He is probably _____ _____ his
_____ _____ tomorrow.

11

W Honey, do you know what our son Jack is doing now?

M Isn't he doing his homework in his room?

W No! He read _____ _____ right after finishing _____ _____, and now he is playing computer games.

M How about _____ _____ _____? It's Sunday today. He needs some time to _____ _____ _____.

W What? Are you serious? But he has to do his homework for tomorrow.

M Honey, listen. I don't want to _____ my son to study hard. As you know, _____ _____ is not everything.

W You're right. Let's leave him for a while and _____ him to act responsibly in the future. However, if he _____ _____ _____ this way, I'll have to talk to him.

M Alright. That's a good idea.

12

M Grandma, is it that important to _____ _____ _____ you make with someone?

W _____ _____ it is! It is one of the best ways to build a _____ _____. Moreover, building _____ is very important in your life.

M But you know it is hard to keep every promise you make. Haven't you ever _____ _____ _____?

W I surely have.

M Then do you have a _____ _____ among people?

W Ha, ha. Of course not. Whenever I broke a promise because of some _____ _____, I _____ _____ and _____ _____ to the person.

M Ok, I'll try to do that, too.

W There is a saying "A man _____ but his name _____." So keeping a promise and having a good _____ are very important.

13

W Are you still looking for a new USB, Ken?

M Yes, but I can't decide which one would be best for me. I have to _____ the _____, the _____ of a _____, and the _____.

W Let's _____ _____ _____ each of them _____ _____ _____. How large do you need it to be?

M Actually, I just realized that it doesn't really matter because it will only be for my in-class _____. I will _____ just a few files on it.

W What about the price? What's your _____? It is usually the most important _____.

M Less than 25 dollars. _____ _____, _____ _____, though.

W There are two choices left. And they are the same price and capacity. The difference is only the _____ of a cable.

M I don't need to think about it. I will pick the one with the cable.

14

[Telephone rings.]

W Hello, Ted. Are you _____ _____ _____?

M Hi, Jenny. Yes, I'm still _____ _____ _____. Why?

W Please don't forget to _____ _____ the wine shop and get _____ _____ ice wine.

M I already bought it _____ the lunchtime. Don't worry about it.

W Good. I was about to go to the _____ to buy a cake, but the wine just _____ _____ _____ _____.

M Is there anything else you want me to get?

W Please get a new wine opener. The one in the house has a _____ _____ so it is quite hard to open _____.

M Alright. You have had a hard job _____ all the food and _____ the house. I will do the dishes and _____ _____ after the party.

W Thank you. I'm going to buy a chocolate cake. Is it _____?

M Sure. It's really delicious.

W Okay. I'll go get it now

15

W The Mayan people of Mexico and Central America had the greatest civilization in the New World. These _____ Mesoamerican people developed one of the _____ _____ cultures before the _____ of the _____. Their _____ was characterized by the _____ of _____ _____, especially the gods of sun, rain and corn. Other features were the existence of a priestly class, the _____ of _____ and astrology, rituals of _____ _____, and the building of elaborate pyramidal temples.

16

W What is this _____ on your driver's license?

M It indicates that I've signed up for the _____ _____ program.

W You mean you're going to donate your organs?

M Yes. If anything _____ _____ _____ _____, I want my organs to go to other people who need them.

W So you want somebody else to have your heart and liver?

M That's right. Also, my eyes, kidneys, or anything else that can be given to someone else. _____ _____ _____ to donate your organs?

W Me? No way. I'll never agree to doctors _____ _____ my body after I die.

M But you won't need those organs when you're dead.

W That might be true, but I _____ _____ somebody else walking around with my heart.

M But you can save someone's life.

17

W It is _____ _____ how you and Henry can be roommates. You're very tidy and he's not.

M It's not always easy, but we're _____ _____ _____.

W Isn't he really _____ all the time? Whenever I see him, his clothes are not clean and his hair is _____.

M His room is just as you would _____ it _____ _____.

W How can you live with him then?

M He keeps the _____ _____ in _____ _____. However, I often have to _____ _____ the living room, and sometimes have to pick up and _____ _____ _____ _____.

W That's very _____ of you.

M And he has just agreed to pay a _____ sometimes.

W Pay a _____? You mean when he's really messy.

M Yes, when that happens, he has to pay me $1.

18

W I'm really glad to ride a bike again. It's _____ _____ since I rode a bicycle last.

M This is the only way to travel. You get to really see the _____ and enjoy the _____ _____.

W Hey, watch out! You _____ rode into that huge pothole. Watch out or you might fall off your bike.

M Thanks for the warning.

W Not at all. This asphalt needs to be repaired.

M Oh, slow down! There's a _____ _____ _____.

W I didn't see that coming. I almost _____ _____ on that slippery section of path. Sorry, I nearly swerved into you. Are you okay?

M Yes, I'm fine. I thought this would be an easy ride since it's _____ all the way. I didn't _____ for these _____ _____ _____.

W Be careful, and keep your eyes open.

19

W I want to live _____ _____ _____. We can _____ to most amenities.

M Downtown is always _____ and _____. And the crime rate is really high as well.

W If we live downtown, we won't have to worry about the _____ _____ and the _____. We can walk to work and take public transportation.

M I want to _____ _____ somewhere for a while, not move every couple of years.

W Is that why you want to live in the suburbs? I think the suburbs have _____ _____.

M That's not true.

W Downtown has a dynamic and interesting character.

M I want to live in a _____ _____. I want to garden in the backyard and take a walk in the local park.

W I'm sorry, but it sounds boring to me.

20

M Ms. Adams is a _____ _____ _____. Now, she is waiting for her clients to show them a _____ _____ whose price is quite _____ for the area. It is a _____ _____ apartment with _____ _____ nearby and a nice view. Another real estate agent has _____ _____ that is interested in it, so Ms. Adams needs to _____ _____ if her clients want it. However, her clients _____ _____ _____ at the appointed time. She tries to call them several times and finally _____ _____ _____ _____. In this situation, what would Ms. Adams probably say to her clients?

01 대화를 듣고, 남자가 취해야 할 자세로 가장 적절한 것을 고르시오.

①   ②  ③   ④   ⑤

02 대화를 듣고, 여자가 남자에게 줄 책을 주문한 이유를 고르시오.

① 생일 선물로 주려고　　　　　② 발표 자료로 쓰기 위해
③ 커피를 엎질러서　　　　　　④ 깨진 컵을 대신할 선물로
⑤ 책을 잃어버려서

03 다음을 듣고, 무엇에 관한 내용인지 고르시오.

① 해외여행의 효용　　　　　　② 여행자 보험의 역할
③ 해외여행 취소 시 유의점　　④ 의료보험의 필요성
⑤ 해외여행 시 건강 관리 요령

04 대화를 듣고, 남자의 심경으로 가장 적절한 것을 고르시오.

① lonely　　　　　② jealous　　　　　③ concerned
④ satisfied　　　　⑤ cheerful

05 대화를 듣고, 남자가 전화한 목적을 고르시오.

① 구급차를 부르려고　　　　　② 화재 신고하려고
③ 응급처치 방법을 물어보려고　④ 교통사고 보험처리를 위해
⑤ 환자의 가족을 찾기 위해

06 대화를 듣고, 남자가 지난 주 저축한 용돈이 얼마인지 고르시오.

① \$0　　　　　　② 50 cents　　　　　　③ \$1.70

④ \$2.50　　　　　⑤ \$5.50

07 대화를 듣고, 두 사람의 관계로 가장 적절한 것을 고르시오.

① 철도 매표원 — 승객　　　　　② 승객 — 승객

③ 카페점원 — 손님　　　　　　④ 버스기사 — 경찰

⑤ 구청 공무원 — 역무원

08 대화를 듣고, 두 사람이 대화하는 장소로 가장 적절한 것을 고르시오.

① 공항　　　　　　② 주민 센터　　　　　　③ 선물가게

④ 사진관　　　　　⑤ 안경원

09 다음을 듣고, 그림의 상황에 어울리는 대화를 고르시오.

①　　　　②　　　　③　　　　④　　　　⑤

10 다음을 듣고, 여자가 독도에 대해 언급하지 않은 것을 고르시오.

① the geography　　　　　　② the climate and ecology

③ the population　　　　　　④ the natural resources

⑤ the territorial dispute

11 대화를 듣고, 남자가 여자에게 부탁한 일로 가장 적절한 것을 고르시오.

① 말하기 대회에 참가하기   ② 성적 수정해 주기
③ 면담 대상자 되어주기   ④ 선생님 만나러 함께 가기
⑤ 과제를 대신 제출해주기

12 대화를 듣고, 대화의 내용과 일치하는 것을 고르시오.

① 두 사람은 오늘 처음 만났다.
② 여자는 매일 같은 일상을 보내고 있다.
③ 남자는 소개팅 상대를 무척 마음에 들어 한다.
④ 남자는 여자에게 데이트 신청을 했다.
⑤ 여자는 소개팅을 한 남자의 연락을 기다린다.

13 대화를 듣고, 두 사람이 말 타기 시내투어를 이용할 시간으로 가장 적절한 것을 고르시오.

Horseback City Tour

Departure from Gwanghwamun	Arrival at Gwanghwamun
① 8:00 a.m.	9:00 a.m.
② 9:30 a.m.	10:30 a.m.
③ 11:00 a.m.	12:00 p.m.
Lunch Break	
④ 2:00 p.m.	3:00 p.m.
⑤ 3:30 p.m.	4:30 p.m.

14 대화를 듣고, 남자가 대화 직후 할 일로 가장 적절한 것을 고르시오.

① 잠시 휴식을 취한다.   ② 여자 친구에게 사과하러 간다.
③ 인터뷰를 준비한다.   ④ 여자친구의 전화를 기다린다.
⑤ 도서관에 간다.

15 다음을 듣고, 북극곰에 관한 내용으로 일치하지 <u>않는</u> 것을 고르시오.

① 하얀 털은 주로 먹이에 몰래 다가가기 위한 위장용이다.
② 주로 물개를 먹는다.
③ 방수가 되는 보호털을 가지고 있다.
④ 햇빛을 흡수하는 검은색 피부를 가지고 있다.
⑤ 다 자란 암컷은 무게가 약 650킬로그램 나간다.

[16-17] 대화를 듣고, 여자의 마지막 말에 이어질 남자의 응답으로 가장 적절한 것을 고르시오.

16
① That's all right.
② I agree with you.
③ That's a good idea.
④ I hope you're right.
⑤ Don't you think so?

17
① To tell you the truth, I am not rich.
② I declare I didn't do anything wrong.
③ No, I don't want to tell you anything.
④ We all have valid passports for this trip.
⑤ Here's the receipt for some duty-free items we bought.

[18-19] 대화를 듣고, 남자의 마지막 말에 이어질 여자의 응답으로 가장 적절한 것을 고르시오.

18
① You need a better job with a higher salary.
② We don't have enough money to pay our bills.
③ You need a good credit rating to borrow money.
④ I have never made an overdue payment in my life.
⑤ Not paying bills on time can make your credit bad.

19
① Don't worry and things will be better.
② They seemed pretty well-behaved to me.
③ I'm happy to have a good time with you.
④ Yes, I know you were not a polite teenager.
⑤ That's right. They are just learning to walk.

20 다음을 듣고, 의사가 Jack에게 할 말로 가장 적절한 것을 고르시오.

① You need to eat more fruits and vegetables.
② Don't skip any meals. Eat three meals a day.
③ As you're busy, you have to eat a lot of fast food.
④ Fried chicken is really delicious when you're hungry.
⑤ Getting regular exercise is the only thing you need to do.

다음은 **Listening Test 11**의 주요 지문입니다. 녹음을 다시 듣고, 질문에 대한 답을 완성하세요.

Q1

1 What do you have to do to keep your balance when you do the stretching exercise the woman suggests?

└➤ In order to keep my balance, I have to _____.

Q2

2 What did the woman do to take responsibility after damaging a borrowed book?

└➤ She has ordered _____ from an _____.

Q6

3 How much money does the man spend on subway tickets for five days?

└➤ He spends _____ on subway tickets for five days.

Q10

4 How's the weather in Dokdo?

└➤ It is mostly _____. There are only about _____ throughout the year.

Q12

5 What does she say about the man who she met on a blind date?

└➤ She says that he is _____, _____, and _____.

Q14

6 Why didn't the man sleep a wink last night?

└➤ The reason was that he had _____ over the phone.

Q15

7 What is the role of the polar bear's black skin?

└➤ The role of it is to _____ of the sun.

Q18

8 What does she think is the reason he has been turned down for a credit card?

└➤ She thinks the reason is that his _____ is bad because he didn't _____.

● 자신의 상황에 맞게 내용을 완성하고 말해 보세요.

A What do you think of using credit cards? Write your opinion, filling in the table below.

Using Credit Cards	
(1) The advantage(s)	
(2) The disadvantage(s)	
(3) Your suggestion	

Credit cards (1)_____.

On the other hand, they (2)_____

_____. And (2)_____

_____. Therefore, it is strongly recommended that (3)_____

_____.

B Describe your ideal man or woman based on the questions below. Fill in the table and tell your classmates about him/her.

My Ideal Man / Woman	
(1) Name and job	
(2) Appearance	
(3) Personality	
(4) Ability	
(5) Why the person is your ideal type	

I am going to talk about my ideal (man/ woman). (His/ Her) name is (1)_____

_____. (He/ She) is (1)_____. (He/ She) (2)_____

_____. People say that (he/ she)

(3)_____. (He/ She) is good at (4)_____

_____. (He/ She) is my ideal

(man/ woman) because (5)_____.

In addition, (5)_____.

11 Dictation Test

01

M I feel like my legs are _____ because I have been _____ for a long time.

W How about doing some _____ _____? In my experience, they are easy but _____.

M That's a good idea. Can you recommend something?

W Okay. I'll _____ _____ _____ one of my favorites. First, plant your feet flat on the ground, about shoulder-width _____. Your feet should be slightly outward, not _____ _____.

M Is it okay?

W Right. Then, look straight ahead and _____ _____ _____ as if you were going to _____ _____ in a chair, keeping your heels _____ _____ _____.

M It is getting difficult.

W Good, so far. Don't allow your knees to go _____ _____ _____. In a controlled manner, slowly _____ _____ down and back so that your upper legs are nearly _____ with the floor.

M Oh, it's really hard to _____ _____ _____.

W In that case, _____ your arms for balance.

02

W Tom, I'm sorry, but I'm afraid I have some bad news for you.

M What's it? Haven't you finished making the PowerPoint for _____ _____?

W That's not it. Fortunately, I finished it _____ _____. Do you remember that you _____ me your science _____ last week?

M Of course I remember. Did you _____ it?

W No, that's not it. By mistake last night, I _____ _____ coffee mug _____ and _____ _____ on your book.

M Oh, no! You _____ _____ _____ more _____.

W I should have. I was too sleepy. I'm terribly sorry.

M Do you think it will be _____ _____ _____ _____ it?

W I guess so. I have ordered a _____ from an Internet bookstore, but it won't arrive _____ _____ _____ _____ of this week.

M That's Ok. I don't need it until then.

03

M When planning your next holiday, make sure you do your _____ and that you have a _____ _____ in case things _____ _____. Take out appropriate _____ _____ which should cover you for such things as _____, lost luggage, and _____ _____ _____. Check your _____ _____ _____ as it may also depend on where you travel. Travel insurance should cover _____ _____ incurred during _____ _____; however, your national health plan always covers medical expenses incurred when travelling in this country. And always _____ _____ _____ for appropriate health advice before _____ _____.

04

W I got a letter from Grandma today. Well, it's not exactly a letter, but it doesn't _____.

M What do you mean? What did you get?

W She sent me a _____ _____.

M Good for you.

W And she sent me a _____ _____ for _____ _____.

M Wow! Let me see it, you _____ _____. I wish I had fifty dollars. I need a new backpack.

W Well, you'll have to wait. I'm going to buy some _____ for myself.

M Can I see the gift card?

W Why? It's not _____!

M I know. Hmm... My middle school _____ is _____. I'm sure I'll get some money then.

W I'm going to have so much fun shopping today.

M Hey, I don't want to hear that.

05

[Telephone rings.]

W Hello, _____ services!

M We need an _____ quick!

W What's the _____ _____?

M 45 Barton Street.

W What's the telephone number you're calling from?

M 02-9823–5698.

W What's the problem? Tell me exactly _____ _____.

M A man was drinking _____ _____ _____ in an armchair and he

suddenly _____ .
W How old is he?
M He looks like he is in his _____ .
W Is he _____ ?
M No.
W Is he _____ ?
M Yes.
W I am sending the _____ to help you now,

_____ _____ _____

and I'll tell you _____ _____

_____ _____ _____ .

06

W I _____ _____ my weekly allowance

_____ _____ _____ .

M How can you _____ _____ your
allowance so fast?
W I don't know. I think I didn't spend much, but all my
money _____ _____ .
M I think you you'd better _____ _____

_____ your spending. Do you know how I

_____ my weekly allowance?
W No, tell me. I'm listening.
M My allowance is _____ dollars _____

_____ . When I receive my allowance, the first
thing I do is to put 5 dollars into my _____

_____ .
W Wow! I always thought that my 20 dollars a week
allowance _____ _____ .
M Next thing I do is to put _____ dollars into a

_____ _____ in my wallet. That's for the

_____ _____ going to and from school
for 5 days.
W Then what about _____ _____ of your
allowance?
M I can use it to do my own thing. For example, last
week, I bought a _____ for studying. That was
1 dollar. And I spend 2 dollars 50 cents on a movie
ticket. Then, I put the _____ _____ in
my piggy bank.

07

M Is this the _____ _____ _____

_____ ?
W No, it's _____ _____ .
M Oh, I see. Wow, it's really _____ . Is it always
like this?
W Only during _____ _____ .
M _____ _____ _____ I thought
that _____ _____ was finished at
around _____ in the morning. By the way, do
you know _____ _____ the trains run?

W _____ _____ _____ , I believe.
They run _____ _____ during

_____ _____ _____ .
M That's good to know. Well, I guess I'd better buy my
ticket now and go down to the platform. Bye.
W Yes, take care.

08

M Please sit down on the chair over there and

_____ _____ . Is this for a _____ ?
W Yes. Do I have to _____ _____ the

_____ and _____ ?
M They are small. You don't need to. However
your _____ are _____

_____ . Please put a hairpin in your hair so
that your eyes are _____ .
W Okay. What about the _____ _____ ?
Are they fine, too?
M I'm afraid they aren't. Big horn-rimmed glasses are

_____ .
W The _____ is quite _____ . Anyway, I'm
ready.
M Three! Two! One! Oh, wait! Don't show your

_____ . Just make a _____ _____ .
W Alright.
M That's _____ . Please come back _____

_____ _____ . I will _____ them.

09

① M May I help you?
  W I am _____ _____ this sweater in a
  medium.
② M Can I _____ _____ _____ on
  this sweater?
  W Sure. Do you _____ _____

  _____ with you?
③ M Why don't you _____ _____

  _____ ?
  W Okay. Where is the _____ _____ ?
④ M Do you have this in a medium?
  W I'll check if we have it _____ _____

  _____ _____ .
⑤ M Where can I buy a sweater nearby here?
  W There's one clothing shop _____

  _____ _____ this street.

10

W Dokdo is in the _____ of the East Sea. Dokdo

_____ 91 small
including two main islets called Seodo (Western
Island) and Dongdo (Eastern Island). The weather is

_____ _____ and cloudy. There are only about 45 clear days throughout the year. About 126 bird _____ have been found to _____ the islets. The islets lie in rich fishing _____ which may also _____ large _____, about 600 million tons of _____ _____. It has great _____ to become a main source of clean energy in the future. The island chain is _____ by both South Korea and Japan. However, Dokdo is Korean _____ without a shadow of a _____.

11

W Sunuk, what did you get in English conversation class?

M I got a C. Mrs. Francisco gave me a _____ _____ _____ I expected.

W _____ _____ to your score? Didn't you say you made a _____ _____ last week?

M Yeah, I did. She even told me to _____ _____ _____ the _____ _____ in _____.

W Why did she give you a low grade then?

M I actually went to her and asked her. She said I missed _____ _____. If I submit it by tomorrow, she will change my grade.

W Good! What is the assignment?

M I need to _____ a friend and _____ _____ _____ about the interview. So if you don't mind, I want you to be the _____.

W No problem. Let's start now.

12

M Long time no see. How have you been?

W I've been doing well. How about you?

M My _____ _____ is just _____ the same thing _____. I heard you went on a _____ _____ yesterday. How was it?

W People are talking about it already? Who told you?

M Come on. It's not important. Tell me about it.

W _____ _____ _____, considering his _____, he is my _____ _____. He is tall, _____, and _____.

M Sounds like you really like him. Did he ask you out again?

W [Sighing] No. I'm waiting for his call.

M I hope your _____ with him develops.

13

M Look at the horses. It is _____ to see horses _____ _____ _____ of downtown.

W You're right. Why don't we _____ _____

_____ _____? We can _____ _____ _____ riding horses on such a fine day.

M Let's go to the _____ _____ and check the _____.

W It takes an hour and visits several _____ _____ around here. What time is it, now?

M It's exactly 9:00. There's one tour in thirty minutes, but it's _____ _____.

W What about the next one? _____ _____ _____ for us?

M _____, yes. Let's go on it and _____ _____ after that.

W Hooray! I'm so excited.

14

W Why do you have _____ _____ _____ _____, Carter?

M I had a _____ _____ my girlfriend last night over the phone, so I couldn't _____ _____.

W Really? Why?

M She got mad at me because she sent me 5 _____ _____, but I didn't _____ _____ any of them.

W Why not? What were you doing?

M I was in the _____ so my cell phone was _____ _____ _____. I didn't know about them. Then I saw the messages as I was going to bed.

W Did you _____ that to her?

M Yes, but her _____ didn't _____ _____.

W Don't worry. She just needs some time. If you are so _____, go to her and say sorry. _____ _____ is the best way.

M Okay, I will. Thanks for the _____.

15

W The polar bear is one of the most _____ animals in the world. It has a beautiful _____ _____ of _____ which is partly for _____ but also it allows it to _____ _____ on its _____. Their typical prey are _____. The polar bear's coat also has special hairs that are water _____ and a dense underfur for _____. But under their fur, polar bears have _____ _____ to soak up the warming rays of the sun. A full grown adult _____ polar bear will weigh approximately 650kg while a _____ will weigh about _____ _____ _____. The polar bear can only be found in the Northern Hemisphere.

16

W Were you excited today? It was your first day of work.

M Yes. I was. Last night I was really _____ _____ to going to work for the first time.

W What was more _____, starting university or starting work?

M It's difficult to choose one over the other. How about you?

W For me, I think starting school was more exciting.

M Does that mean work _____ _____ _____ now?

W It's different for everyone, but because I knew school was going to be so much fun, I really got _____ about it.

M But work is a _____ _____ of our lives. I'm looking forward to _____ _____ I have fun at my job.

W That's a _____ _____ to have. I think you won't have any problems at your work.

M I hope you're right.

17

W Your passports, please. What is your final _____?

M We're going to Los Angeles.

W _____ _____ is your stay?

M We'll be there _____ _____ _____.

W What is the _____ _____ _____ _____?

M I'm going there _____ _____ and my family is _____ me _____ _____.

W Whom are you traveling with?

M I'm with my wife and children.

W Are you bringing in _____ _____ _____? Any plants, fruits and vegetables, meats, or animals?

M No. I am not bringing _____ _____.

W Do you have anything _____ _____?

M Here's the receipt for some duty-free items we bought.

18

M This is the _____ _____ I've been _____ _____ for a credit card in a month. I don't know what I'm doing wrong.

W Have you checked your _____ _____ recently? Maybe your credit is bad.

M I have a _____ job with a _____ _____, which they can easily check, and I don't have any _____, so what could be the problem?

W Have you had a credit card _____?

M Yes.

W Did you always make your payments on time?

M Well, no. I _____ _____ to pay the _____.

W Then that may be _____ _____.

M What do you mean by that?

W Not paying bills on time can make your credit bad.

19

M I'm surprised at the _____ _____ _____ on this tour.

W Oh, really? I hadn't noticed.

M Well, we'll be spending the next _____ _____ with these people so I think I should _____ _____ _____ some of them.

W That's nice.

M Did you see that thirty-something couple with _____ _____? I'm really _____ they're on this tour.

W _____ _____ _____. They will spend all their time taking care of their kids.

M And how about that group of _____? Some of them look like they're in their _____.

W Yes, I see them. They may be old, but they seem _____ _____.

M But what really _____ _____ is those middle-aged couples travelling with their _____ children. They are at an age when they can act out and _____.

W They seemed pretty well-behaved to me.

20

M Jack is a _____ man _____ _____. Every morning on his way to work, he drops by a donut shop and purchases a _____ _____ and a cup of coffee. He likes this morning routine because it is _____ and _____. He doesn't have to cook breakfast or wash the dishes. Today Jack goes to the doctor for a _____ _____. His doctor tells him that his cholesterol _____ is so high that he has to _____ _____. He is also told that he has to _____ _____ foods that are _____ _____ _____. So he asks his doctor _____ _____ _____ _____ he should eat. In this situation, what would his doctor probably say to him?

01 대화를 듣고, 두 사람이 점심으로 먹을 음식으로 가장 적절한 것을 고르시오.

① ②  ③ ④ ⑤

02 대화를 듣고, DVD 대여를 연장할 수 <u>없는</u> 이유를 고르시오.

① 찾는 사람이 많아서   ② 보유 DVD가 적어서
③ 대출 기간을 지키지 않아서   ④ 도서관 휴무일이어서
⑤ 단체 상영 예정이어서

03 다음을 듣고, 무엇에 관한 내용인지 고르시오.

① TV 광고의 효과   ② TV 시청 등급 안내
③ TV의 유해성   ④ TV 프로그램 소개
⑤ TV 자막 방송 안내

04 대화를 듣고, 여자의 마지막 말에 나타난 심경으로 가장 적절한 것을 고르시오.

① moved   ② anxious   ③ disappointed
④ scared   ⑤ excited

05 대화를 듣고, 남자가 전단지를 만드는 목적을 고르시오.

① 잃어버린 개를 찾기 위해   ② 키우던 개를 분양하려고
③ 애견 카페 홍보를 위해   ④ 애견 모임 행사 안내를 위해
⑤ 애견 돌봄 서비스 홍보를 위해

06 대화를 듣고, 두 사람이 만나기로 한 시각을 고르시오.

① 오전 7시 　　　② 오전 7시 30분 　　　③ 오전 8시
④ 오전 9시 　　　⑤ 오전 9시 30분

07 대화를 듣고, 두 사람의 관계로 가장 적절한 것을 고르시오.

① safety guide — tour guide 　　② immigrant official — police
③ pilot — flight attendant 　　④ travel agent — traveler
⑤ airline clerk — passenger

08 대화를 듣고, 두 사람이 대화하는 장소로 가장 적절한 것을 고르시오.

① bank 　　　　　　　② management office
③ department store 　　④ driving school
⑤ immigration office

09 다음을 듣고, 그림의 상황에 어울리는 대화를 고르시오.

① 　　　　② 　　　　③ 　　　　④ 　　　　⑤

10 대화를 듣고, 두 사람이 대화 직후 할 일로 가장 적절한 것을 고르시오.

① Jenny의 성적표 확인하기 　　② Jenny의 소지품 검사하기
③ Jenny를 불러 이야기 하기 　　④ Jenny의 선생님과 상담하기
⑤ Jenny의 친구에게 전화하기

11 대화를 듣고, 여자가 남자에게 부탁한 일로 가장 적절한 것을 고르시오.

① 어린이 날 선물 추천해 주기 ② 어린이 날 선물 함께 사러 가기
③ 장난감 가게 위치 알려주기 ④ 인형 옷 만드는 법 알려주기
⑤ 인형의 집 사주기

12 대화를 듣고, 대화의 내용과 관계 깊은 속담을 고르시오.

① Well begun is half done.
② Blood is thicker than water.
③ Where there's a will, there's a way.
④ Like father, like son.
⑤ Many hands make light work.

13 다음을 듣고, 표의 내용과 일치하지 <u>않는</u> 것을 고르시오.

> ## Open Campus Tour
>
> ① When? on Sunday April 17th from 10 a.m. to 5 p.m.
> ② Where? at Hana College
> ③ What? Senior students will guide you and answer your questions about the school
> ④ To whom? Only high school seniors who have already been accepted to Hana College
> ⑤ How? Fill out the application form and submit it online
> Visit the website at www.hanacollege.com

14 대화를 듣고, 여자가 할 일로 가장 적절한 것을 고르시오.

① 좌석 번호 확인하기 ② 남자에게 모자 벗으라고 말하기
③ 남자와 자리 바꿔 앉기 ④ 남자에게 몸을 숙여 달라고 말하기
⑤ 친절한 말투로 말하기

15 다음을 듣고, 노벨상과 관련하여 언급되지 <u>않은</u> 것을 고르시오.

① Alfred Nobel의 이름을 따서 지어졌다.
② 1901년 처음 시상되었다.
③ 처음에는 다섯 개 분야로 나눠 시상했다.
④ 1996년에 노벨경제학상이 추가되었다.
⑤ 각각의 상은 매년 최대 3명까지 수여될 수 있다.

[16-17] 대화를 듣고, 여자의 마지막 말에 이어질 남자의 응답으로 가장 적절한 것을 고르시오.

16
① My hobby is playing the cello.

② He must be feeling on top of the world.

③ My father is interested in playing golf.

④ Great. I'm glad he's taken up an instrument.

⑤ Maybe he needs time to find out what interests him.

17
① Yes, how much does it cost?

② No thanks. I don't want to read a book.

③ Sure, I'll tell other people to come here.

④ If the price is reasonable, I will take it.

⑤ Sorry, I don't have enough money to buy it.

[18-19] 대화를 듣고, 남자의 마지막 말에 이어질 여자의 응답으로 가장 적절한 것을 고르시오.

18
① Okay, let's take a taxi.

② I'll text you the address.

③ You can dress casually.

④ My house is near the A−Mart.

⑤ It's an hour to get to the ski resort.

19
① That would be fun.

② Yes, everything is set.

③ Yes, I completely cleaned it up.

④ No, it'not as messy as it looks.

⑤ No, thank you. I can do it by myself.

20 다음을 듣고, Samantha가 여동생에게 할 말로 가장 적절한 것을 고르시오.

① Thanks for telling me. I forgive you.

② Thanks for letting me wear your jeans.

③ Can you take these to the dry cleaner's for me?

④ Do you know where I can buy new jeans?

⑤ Did you wear these jeans without asking me?

● 다음은 Listening Test 12의 주요 지문입니다. 녹음을 다시 듣고, 질문에 대한 답을 완성하세요.

Q1
1 Why didn't the woman order a steak when she went to the Four Seasons Restaurant the first time?

↳ Her sister, who _____, wouldn't let her _____.

Q2
2 What are two limitations for borrowing DVDs?

↳ You can borrow only _____ at a time, and you must return them _____ as they don't allow DVD loans _____.

Q5
3 What is the man going to do during the vacation?

↳ He is going to take care of _____ when they _____.

Q8
4 What advantage does he get by having an account with the bank?

↳ He can get _____ than the going rate.

Q11
5 Why did the man mention Tim's Toy Store on Guil Street?

↳ The reason is that the store is _____ so she can get items _____ _____.

Q13
6 When is the campus tour?

↳ It is on Sunday, _____.

Q15
7 When were the Nobel Prizes first awarded?

↳ They were first awarded in _____, _____ after Alfred Noble's _____.

Q17
8 When is the next shuttle scheduled to leave and how long does it take to get to the airport?

↳ It leaves in _____ and it takes about _____ to get to the airport.

● 자신의 상황에 맞게 내용을 완성하고 말해 보세요.

A Which do you prefer, watching sports on TV or in person? Tell your classmates about your preference.

Watching Sporting Events

(1) Which do you prefer, watching sports on TV or in person?	
(2) Why? (two reasons)	
(3) What was the most memorable sporting event you have ever watched?	
(4) Why can't you forget it?	

I prefer watching sports (1)(on TV / in person). The first reason is that (2)_____

_____. The second reason

is that (2)_____

_____. The most memorable sporting event I have ever watched (on TV /

in person) is (3)_____

_____. I can't forget it because (4)_____

_____.

B Do you think it is necessary to have a hobby? Write your opinion, filling in the table below.

Having a Hobby

(1) What is a hobby?	
(2) My opinion	
(3) The 1st reason for my opinion	
(4) The 2nd reason for my opinion	

A hobby is (1)_____. And I think (2)_____

_____. The reason for my opinion is (3)_____

_____. In addition,

(4)_____

_____. Therefore, I think (2)_____

_____.

01

M Have you been to the Four Seasons Restaurant before?

W Yes, I went there with my sister about _____ _____ _____.

M What did you have?

W I was going to have a steak, but my sister is a _____ and she wouldn't let me have a steak. I had a _____ _____ and my sister had tomato _____. They were both really delicious.

M What is the specialty of the restaurant? Is it pizza?

W No, it's marinated barbequed pork ribs with _____ _____.

M Sound delicious. Do they grill the ribs _____ _____ to get a real barbequed _____?

W Yes, they do. I saw them doing that _____ the restaurant in a huge barbeque pit. The next time I go, I will try it.

M How about trying it today for lunch? It's _____.

W Great. I'd love to go there for lunch.

02

M Hi. Are you ready to _____ _____?

W Yes, please. Here's my _____ _____ and the books and DVDs I want to _____ _____.

M Ok. You can return these books in _____ _____, but you have to return these DVDs in _____ _____. And you are only allowed to borrow two DVDs at a time. So which two DVDs do you want?

W Why can't I borrow all of them?

M There's _____ _____ a _____ for our DVDs. So we _____ the number of _____ to two and we don't allow DVD loans to be _____.

W Then it means _____ I have watched them _____ _____, I have to return them _____ _____ _____, right?

M _____ _____ _____ _____.

W I see. I'll take these two.

03

M _____ _____ _____ _____ _____ of TV Parental Guidelines? TV programs fall into one of _____ _____ _____: TV-Y, TV-Y7, TV-G, TV-PG, TV-14 or TV-MA.

Then, content descriptors of D, L, S, V, and FV are added to the ratings. Each alphabetic letter _____ _____ _____ if a show contains suggestive dialogue, coarse language, sexual content, violence, or fantasy violence. For example, a program rated TV-Y7-FV is designed to be _____ _____ children of all ages. The program is _____ _____ _____ _____ frighten younger children, but is generally more _____ as it has some fantasy violence.

04

M Did you watch Yuna Kim's _____ _____ on TV last night? It was so wonderful.

W Oh, I went to the ice rink to see it _____ _____ with my family.

M I feel terrible about missing the _____ _____ to see her perform live. Last week when I tried to buy tickets _____, they were _____ _____.

W I was just lucky. My mom and dad are _____ _____ _____ hers, so they booked tickets quickly after they went on sale a month ago.

M I should have done that. I always leave things until the last minute.

W I think she _____ _____ _____ _____ as the queen of figure skating with last night's performance. My whole family cried when she gave her _____ _____ saying that she was happy but also sad _____ _____ _____ _____.

M Maybe we will never see perfect jumps like the ones we saw last night again.

05

W Hey, Tom. What are you making?

M I'm making _____ to advertise my new small business. I will _____ _____ _____ people's dogs when they go on holidays.

W I guess that is your part-time job during this vacation.

M Yes. It's a perfect idea, _____ _____? I know about dogs _____ _____ _____ and I love dogs.

W I _____ _____ _____ _____ _____. Oh, I heard that my aunt has to _____ _____ a business trip next week. I'll call and ask her about using _____ _____. [Pause]

M What did she say?

W She said she would like to use your service.

M Thanks a lot. As she is my _____ _____, I'll take care of her dog one day _____ _____ _____.

W Great. She will be happy about that.

06

W I can't wait! Gold Coast Water Park will be open tomorrow! And we're both going. I guess another hot summer is just _____ _____.

M When it's hot, nothing can _____ a water park.

W I was lucky to only spend $50 on two tickets because of their _____ _____ for _____ _____. You know I got more than 50% off.

M You did a good job! I can't wait to enjoy all the _____ _____ there.

W What time shall we meet tomorrow?

M Did you _____ _____ the opening times on the website?

W Yes. _____ _____ are from 9:30 a.m. to 9:30 p.m. on weekdays and from 9 a.m. to 11 p.m. on weekends and holidays. It will take about _____ _____ to get there by car. Let's meet at 8:00 am.

M 8:00? I think it'll take longer to drive there than an hour. Why don't we meet _____ _____ _____ because we have to _____ _____ _____ _____?

W Oh, I didn't think of it. I'll see you then.

07

M Oh, you're traveling with an _____ today.

W Yes, my daughter Mia. She's _____ _____.

M Okay. I'll need to see your daughter's _____ _____ to prove that she is _____ _____ _____ of age.

W Here you are. Say, would we be able to get _____ _____ _____ _____? I may have to _____ _____ with her if she gets fussy.

M Sure. I'll put you near the _____ too.

W Thanks. Can I take _____ _____ to the gate?

M Yes, we'll check it in as over-sized _____ after you board. Are you just checking these two bags today?

W Yes, I'll take my knapsack as my carry-on.

M Okay. Here is your _____ _____.

Be at the gate one hour prior to the _____ _____. You will be able to _____ because you are traveling with an _____.

08

W Can I help you?

M I would like to _____ Korean won into Japanese _____. What's the _____ _____ for today?

W It is 10.50 won per 1 yen. How much would you like to exchange?

M I'd like to exchange 300,000 won. Here are the _____.

W Do you _____ _____ _____ with us?

M Why? Is there a _____?

W Yes. I can give you a slightly better exchange rate _____ the _____ _____.

M Really? How nice. I do have an account here. Do you need the number?

W Yes, and please show me either your _____ card or driver's _____.

09

① **M** I like your _____ _____. How much is it?

  W It is $_____.

② **M** I'm so sorry. My hand just _____.

  W Oh, no! I _____ _____ _____ the file that I was working on.

③ **M** Would you like to drink _____ _____ _____ _____?

  W I'd love to. Thank you.

④ **M** Do you know how to _____ _____ all your files?

  W I don't know how. Can you teach me?

⑤ **M** What's up? You _____ _____ _____.

  W My computer _____ _____. What should I do?

10

M Honey. It is very _____ _____ _____ Jenny's report card.

W Why? Are there any serious problems?

M Look at this _____ that shows her _____ from the beginning of the year. They have been decreasing _____ _____ _____.

W Really? What do you think is the _____ _____? She always studies in her room, doesn't she?

M In my _____, she doesn't focus on her studies.

정답 및 해석 p.103

We never _____ up on her. We don't know whether she is really studying or not.

W Do you mean she is telling us a _____ and doing _____ _____?

M I'm not sure, but there is a _____.

W Why don't we just call Jenny and ask her _____? I don't want to _____ our _____ daughter.

M That's good. Let's ask her if anything is _____. She might have a problem that we don't know about.

11

M Have you _____ what you're going to buy Rose for Children's Day?

W No. Have you?

M I have _____ _____ _____ a Barbie doll.

W Wow! She will love it. Can you _____ a good _____ for me to get her?

M Well. How about buying some _____ or a house for the _____ I bought?

W That sounds great. Thanks for the _____.

M One more thing, the Tim's Toy Store on Guil Street is having a sale. You can get _____ _____ _____ at the _____ _____ _____ there.

W Sounds wonderful. I will go there _____ _____.

12

M Rebecca, what are you doing?

W I'm _____ these _____ cards into _____.

M Will you send them by mail or deliver them _____ _____?

W _____ _____ _____. If they live _____, I'll give them in person. And if they live _____ _____, I'll send them by mail.

M I see. Do you want me to _____ _____ the people's names on the each envelope?

W Oh, thank you. But please write in _____ _____ at the _____.

M No problem.

W _____ _____ your help, I can finish _____ _____ _____ _____ I thought. Thanks.

13

M _____, prospective students! Hana College is _____ a _____ _____ on Sunday, _____ 17th from 10 a.m. to 5 p.m.. _____ students are _____ to guide you and answer

your _____ about our school. Anyone who is _____ _____ _____ to our school is _____ to go on the tour. You can _____ _____ the _____ _____ and _____ it online. A free lunch will be _____ during the tour! _____ _____ _____, please visit our website at www.hanacollege.com.

14

W Please show me the tickets. What are our _____ _____?

M They are J55 and J56 You sit in J55, I'll _____ _____ J56.

W Okay. Uh-oh. I can't see the _____ well. The man _____ _____ _____ in front of me is _____ _____ _____ _____. He is tall and he is sitting very straight.

M Then let's _____ places. You sit in mine, I'll sit in yours.

W Great idea. That's very kind of you. But it might be a little _____ for you, too. I don't want to cause you too much trouble.

M It's okay. I will ask him to _____ _____ his cap.

W Ask him _____, or he might be _____.

M Don't worry. I will.

15

W The Nobel Prizes were _____ _____ Alfred Nobel, the Swedish chemist and _____ of dynamite. The prizes were first awarded in _____, five years after Alfred Nobel's _____. They were awarded in _____ _____: chemistry, physics, physiology or medicine, literature, and peace. And the _____ _____, _____, was added in _____. The prizes can only be awarded to _____, except the Peace Prize. Each award can be given to a maximum of three people per year. Each prize constitutes a gold medal, a _____, and a sum of money. If there are _____ winners for one subject, the award money is _____ _____ among the winners.

16

M Who were you talking to on the phone?

W My mother. We were talking about my dad's _____.

M Your father retired a couple of _____ _____. That was a good thing, right?

W Well, it's _____ that he doesn't have to

_____ _____, but he hasn't found a useful way to spend his time yet.

M Why doesn't he take up a _____? That would give him something interesting to _____ his time.

W My mother has tried to interest him in various things, but _____ _____ _____.

M How about encouraging him to take up golf or bowling?

W He wouldn't be interested in those hobbies. I think he needs something _____ _____ like playing a musical instrument.

M Maybe he needs time to find out what interests him.

17

W Did you enjoy your stay with us?

M Yes, very much. However, I have a _____ that leaves in about _____ _____, so what is the _____ _____ to get to the airport?

W We do have a _____ _____ _____ service.

M That sounds great, but will it get me to the airport _____ _____?

W Yes, it should. The next shuttle leaves _____ _____ _____, and it takes approximately 25 minutes to get to the airport.

M Fantastic. I'll just wait in the _____ _____. Will you please let me know when it is _____?

W Of course, sir. If you like, you can _____ _____ _____ with the porter and he can _____ your bags onto the _____ for you when it arrives.

M That would be great, thank you.

W Would you like to sign the _____ _____ while you wait?

M Sure, I'll tell other people to come here.

18

W Any plans for this weekend?

M I'm thinking of _____ _____.

W But you won't have fun because the ski resorts haven't _____ _____ _____ _____.

M Maybe you're right. Do you know what the _____ is _____ _____ _____ _____ on Saturday?

W The report says that it will be windy and dry with _____ _____ _____ _____ _____.

M Okay. Then I'd better not go skiing this weekend. How about you? Do you have any plans?

W Saturday is my sister's birthday, and we are

_____ _____ _____ _____ _____. Can you come?

M _____, I can come to her party. Will it be at your house?

W No. My aunt has a larger house with a big _____ room where everyone can play. So we're having the party there.

M Oh, good! _____ _____ _____?

W I'll text you the address.

19

M Have you decided where to go for _____ _____?

W We've decided on Guam.

M I've _____ _____ _____. It's a fantastic place.

W What did you do there?

M There is an _____ _____ of leisure activities in Guam. I went scuba diving and snorkeling.

W That's good. I'm _____ _____ _____ our honeymoon.

M How long are you planning to stay there?

W We decided on _____ _____. We are leaving on _____ and returning on _____.

M That should be _____ _____. Do you have all your travel plans _____ _____?

W Yes, everything is set.

20

W Samantha has a favorite pair of white jeans that she wears only on _____ _____. Yesterday her younger sister wore them _____ getting her _____. Her sister went to a movie theater with her boyfriend and he accidentally _____ Coke on the white jeans. Her sister _____ _____ _____ _____ in the drawer without saying anything to Samantha. Today, Samantha is _____ to her friend's housewarming party and she _____ that she wants to _____ those white jeans with a blouse. Putting them on, she sees the _____. She knows the jeans were clean when she put them in the _____ a few days ago. In this situation, what would Samantha probably say to her sister?

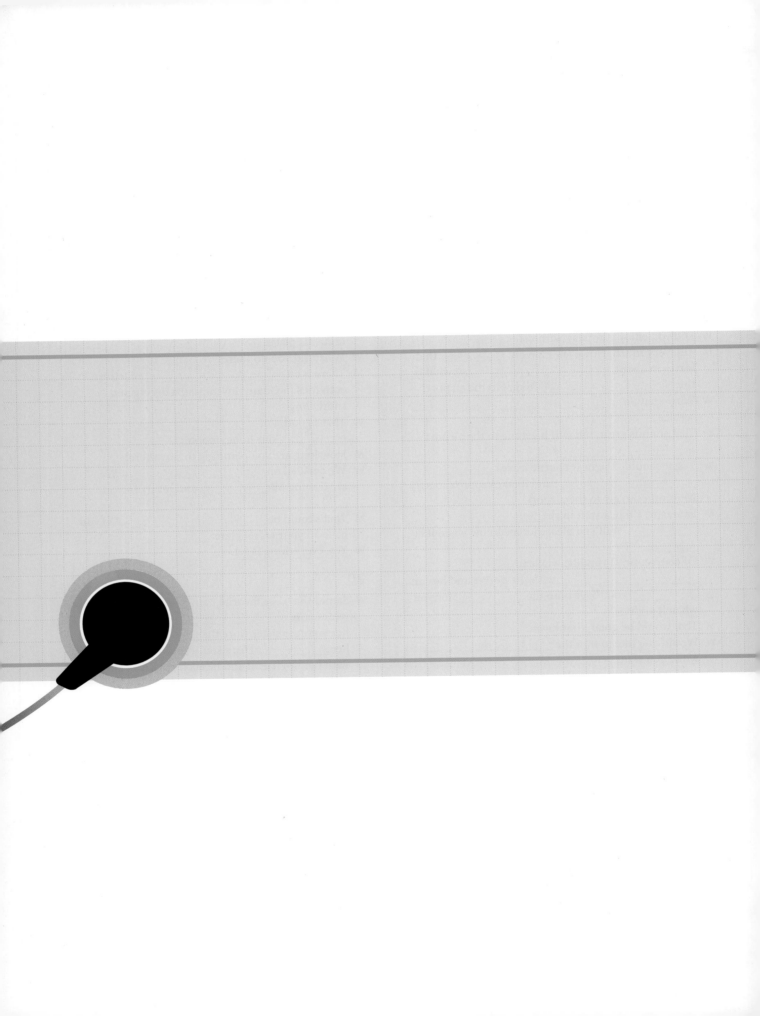

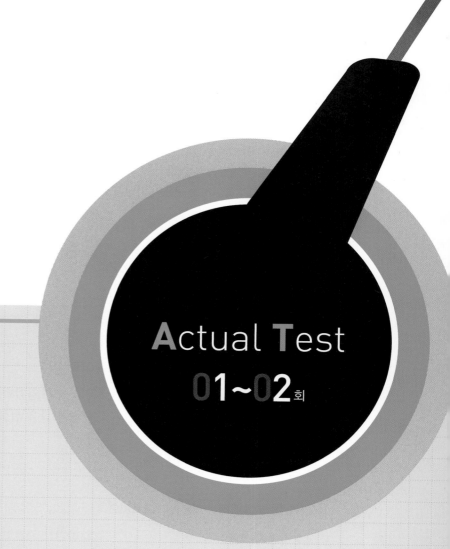

Actual Test
01~02회

01 대화를 듣고, 여자가 좋아하는 운동이 <u>아닌</u> 것을 고르시오.

①   ②   ③  ④   ⑤

02 대화를 듣고, 남자가 선물을 바꿔야 하는 이유를 고르시오.

① 아빠가 책을 싫어해서　　　　② 아빠가 읽었던 책이어서
③ 아빠가 CD를 좋아해서　　　　④ 형과 같은 선물을 사서
⑤ 형이 다른 선물을 추천해줘서

03 다음을 듣고, 무엇에 대한 내용인지 고르시오.

① 신형자동차 모델 소개　　　　② 라디오 프로그램 소개
③ 자동차 리콜 안내　　　　　　④ 자동차 회사 입사 안내
⑤ 자동차 딜러 소개

04 대화를 듣고, 남자의 심경으로 가장 적절한 것을 고르시오.

① bored　　　　　② curious　　　　　③ disappointed
④ pleased　　　　 ⑤ jealous

05 대화를 듣고, 여자가 Brandon에게 연락하는 목적을 고르시오.

① 안부를 묻기 위해서
② 사촌의 전화번호를 알기 위해서
③ 주말 일정을 묻기 위해서
④ 일자리 정보를 얻기 위해서
⑤ 조언을 듣기 위해서

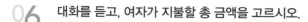

06 대화를 듣고, 여자가 지불할 총 금액을 고르시오.

① $68   ② $72   ③ $80

④ $90   ⑤ $100

07 대화를 듣고, 두 사람의 관계로 가장 적절한 것을 고르시오.

① librarian — student   ② doctor — patient

③ writer — reader   ④ customer — clerk

⑤ employer — employee

08 대화를 듣고, 두 사람이 대화하는 장소로 가장 적절한 것을 고르시오.

① a concert hall   ② an art museum   ③ a zoo

④ a laboratory   ⑤ a subway station

09 다음을 듣고, 그림의 상황에 어울리는 대화를 고르시오.

①   ②   ③   ④   ⑤

10 다음을 듣고, 여자가 언급하지 <u>않은</u> 것을 고르시오.

① 불국사의 창건 연대

② 불국사와 석굴암의 관계

③ 다보탑과 석가탑

④ 불국사의 UNESCO 세계유산 등재

⑤ 전쟁으로 인한 불국사의 파괴

11 대화를 듣고, 여자가 남자에게 제안한 것으로 가장 적절한 것을 고르시오.

① 책을 정기적으로 읽어라.　　② 읽고 싶은 책은 구입해야 한다.

③ 어려운 책은 읽지 마라.　　④ 자신의 책을 빌려 주겠다.

⑤ 도서관에서 책을 빌려 읽어라.

12 대화를 듣고, 대화의 내용과 일치하지 <u>않는</u> 것을 고르시오.

① 아들은 어제 플루트 연습을 했다.

② 오늘 저녁에 대회가 있을 예정이다.

③ 아들은 대회 우승을 자신하고 있다.

④ 엄마는 아들에게 더 연습하라고 충고한다.

⑤ 아들은 레슨 후 더 연습할 예정이다.

13 다음을 듣고, 안내문의 내용과 일치하지 <u>않는</u> 것을 고르시오.

> ## Construction Notice
>
> **What:** Removal and Relocation of Existing Underground Utilities
> **When:** Saturday, October 4, 2014 through Sunday, November 2, 2014
> **Work Hours:** 9 am to 7 pm Monday through Friday
> 　　　　　　　　7 am to 6 pm Saturday through Sunday
> **Where:** Construction on Sadang Station in the Lane 4
> **Work Description:** removing and relocating existing underground utilities at Sadang Station
> **Major work activities:** asphalt removing, soil excavation, relocating new utilities and restoring asphalt
> **Further Information:** Seoul Subway Public Works Department (070-1234-5678)

①　　　　②　　　　③　　　　④　　　　⑤

14 대화를 듣고, 대화 직후 여자가 할 일로 가장 적절한 것을 고르시오.

① 시계를 확인한다　　　　② 지하철 티켓을 구입한다

③ 콘서트 티켓을 구입한다　　④ 핸드폰을 구입한다

⑤ 핸드폰으로 인터넷 검색을 한다

15 다음을 듣고, 온라인 쇼핑에 대해서 언급되지 <u>않은</u> 것을 고르시오.

① 이용 수단　　　② 결재 방법　　　③ 이용 가능 시간

④ 이용 가능 장소　　⑤ 선호 연령대

[16-17] 대화를 듣고, 여자의 마지막 말에 이어질 남자의 응답으로 가장 적절한 것을 고르시오.

16
① No problem. I won't miss her at all.
② That's right. Don't forget to call me.
③ You're right. Bill will call you next time.
④ OK. I know I must not answer your phone.
⑤ OK, even if I'm busy, I'll return your call.

17
① If so, I'm wondering when she can visit me today.
② Then, I'm wondering if she can visit me at 3 p.m.
③ I'm wondering where I should meet her at 3 p.m.
④ I'm wondering how you know I'm from Pennsylvania.
⑤ If she's going to be late, I'm wondering how late she'll be.

[18-19] 대화를 듣고, 남자의 마지막 말에 이어질 여자의 응답으로 가장 적절한 것을 고르시오.

18
① Watching TV is a good way to relax after school.
② Bill spent six hours reading books this afternoon.
③ Six hours of homework every night is too much.
④ Spending six hours on TV is too long for a teenager.
⑤ You have to spend many hours reading magazines.

19
① Mr. Brilliant is an interesting movie.
② Let's recommend a good movie for Richard.
③ No. That is the only movie I've watched recently.
④ Sorry, I don't know the movie review website.
⑤ Never download and watch a movie on the Internet.

20 다음을 듣고, Henry의 엄마가 Henry에게 할 말로 가장 적절한 것을 고르시오.
① Why don't you practice soccer longer?
② Let's go out and get new soccer shoes.
③ Why don't you tell the secret to your father?
④ Why don't you ask your friends to lend them to you?
⑤ I'm really disappointed that you didn't play in the game.

01

W I have to _____ _____ _____ for our school newspaper.

M Oh, really? When do you have to finish it by?

W That's not the problem. I don't know _____ _____ _____ _____ _____.

M _____ _____ writing about sports?

W Good idea. I think many students like to _____ _____ about sports.

M What sports do you like?

W I like all _____ _____ _____ _____.

M So you like baseball, volleyball, basketball, and soccer, don't you?

W That's right. I love _____, too. How about you?

M I don't like ball sports. I like swimming.

02

W Mike, why are you so busy?

M I have to _____ a big party this evening.

W Is today your father's birthday?

M Yeah. All the things are _____, but…

W But what? You _____ a book for your father _____ _____ _____ _____, didn't you?

M Yeah. I did it. But I found out that my brother _____ _____ _____ the same thing.

W I'm sorry to hear that. You _____ _____ _____ _____ earlier with him.

M Yes, I should have.

W Did you _____ _____ _____ for your father yet?

M Not yet. I have to take the book back to the bookstore, but I don't know what I should buy _____.

W What about a music CD?

M That's a good idea. Thanks a lot.

03

M Hello, _____! This is Ben Simon from the Chipan Motor Corporation. First of all, we _____ _____ _____ you that our new model the NPE1 has some problems. We are issuing a _____ _____ for this model. If your car is this model, you can _____ it to any Chipan Motor's service center and the recalled part will be _____. Of course, this _____

_____ is bothersome for you. But you have to do it so that you can _____ _____. For further information, you can _____ _____ your car dealer or any of Chipan Motor's service centers.

04

[Telephone rings.]

M Hello?

W Hello, it's me, Jenny. I have something to tell you.

M What is it?

W I can't _____ _____ this Friday night. I'm sorry, but I won't be there.

M Why? Is there a problem?

W I really want to come to the party for your parents' 30th wedding _____, but I forgot I had a _____ _____.

M Oh my goodness! I already told my parents that you _____ _____ _____.

W I'm so sorry. Can you tell them that I couldn't be with them _____ _____ a _____ _____?

M I don't believe it. Do you really want me to _____ _____ _____ to them?

W Sorry again!

05

M Hi, Betty!

W Hi, Brian. How was your weekend?

M I _____ _____ _____ _____ with _____ _____. Do you know my cousins, Brandon and James?

W Of course. How are they?

M They're fine. Brandon _____ a _____ for this _____.

W Really? I _____ _____ _____ _____. I really want to get a scholarship so I don't have to work part time.

M If you talk to him, he will give you _____ _____ about all the scholarship that students can _____ _____.

W Great. Can you tell me his phone number or his email address?

M Sure. His phone number is 010-6789-1234, and his _____ _____ is Brandon@email.ac.kr.

W Thanks a lot. I can't wait to hear his _____ about how to get a scholarship.

06

W Good morning. I'd like to get train tickets to Irvine, please.

M Good morning. When would you like to go?

W I'd like tickets for the _____ of _____, which is _____ _____.

M There are three trains _____ on that day. They are at _____ in the morning and _____ and _____ in the afternoon.

W I need four tickets, two _____ _____ and two _____ _____. How much are the tickets?

M It _____ _____ the train. The 10:15 is $20, and both the 3:00 and 4:30 are $30. And children can get a 10% discount.

W Why do the different trains have different _____?

M The former is a _____ _____; the latter is an _____ _____. The express is more expensive.

W Both my husband and I have train membership cards. Can we get a discount?

M Sure, we give our members a 10% _____ on weekdays.

W Okay, I want four tickets for the _____ _____.

07

W Good afternoon.

M Good afternoon. How can I help you?

W I am looking for a book for a birthday _____.

M _____ _____ _____ _____ _____ do you want?

W Can you _____ some books for _____ _____ _____?

M Sure. This book, which was _____ by Sir. Arthur, is a bestseller in the young adult genre.

W Unfortunately, the person who I will give the present to read that book last week.

M Oh, really? Well, what about this other one by _____ _____ _____ _____?

W Are you _____ at the book _____ After Twilight?

M Yes. That's right. This is the first book written by Sir Arthur.

08

W Excuse me? I have something to ask you.

M Okay. You can ask me _____ you want to know.

W I don't mean to be _____, but do you

_____ _____ I ask you the name of this painting?

M Oh! I don't mind at all This painting is called Number 5.

W Could you tell me who painted it?

M Sure Jackson Pollack _____ this painting _____ _____.

W I think this painting is _____. How did he paint this?

M I know he _____ a _____ _____ called the drip painting technique.

W Really? It sounds difficult, but the _____ is very interesting.

M Don't worry about it. Many _____ in here think it is difficult to understand.

09

① W What are you _____ _____?
  M I am _____ _____ _____.
② W Are you reading a book now?
  M I am _____ _____ go out to buy _____.
③ W Why are you _____ a _____ _____?
  M I am _____ a _____ _____ _____.
④ W What are you doing _____ _____ _____?
  M I am _____ this paper.
⑤ W What are you _____ _____?
  M I am making a paper boat _____ _____ to music.

10

W Bulguksa is a very _____ _____, which is _____ _____ Gyeongju, South Korea. The temple has several of Korea's _____ _____. Inside the temple, Dabotap is located on the right side and Seokgatap is _____ _____ _____ _____. Both of them are known as wonderful _____ _____. In 1995, Bulguksa was included in the list of UNESCO World Heritage Sites. Bulguksa _____ _____ in 751 under King Gyeongdeok, the 35th ruler of the kingdom of Silla, but over the years it was _____ because of _____ and _____. _____ work beginning in the 1960s has brought Bulguksa to its current form.

11

M Hi, Mina. What did you do last weekend?

W I read the book Freakonomics _____

_____ _____.

M *Freakonomics*? What is the book about?

W It's a non-fiction book which blends _____ _____ with _____.

M Can you tell me about it more specifically?

W It _____ economic _____ to a variety of _____ in very _____ _____.

M Is it interesting to read?

W Yes. In fact, I _____ _____ think _____ was a very difficult subject, but I don't any more thanks to this book.

M Really? I want to read the book right now. Can you _____ _____ _____ _____ _____?

W Sorry, I can't. I'll read it again today. You can _____ it from our school library.

12

W Michael, do you remember your flute lesson this evening?

M I _____ _____ about the lesson. Thanks, mom!

W Did you finish your homework yesterday?

M Yes, mom. I also _____ _____ _____ yesterday, so you _____ _____ _____ _____ about it.

W Do you think you will win the _____?

M Of course, mom. I'm the best _____ in my school.

W Michael, don't speak so _____.

M OK. I know there will be many other good _____ in the contest.

W You're right. You had better practice much more if you want to be the winner.

M I really _____ your advice. After taking the lesson, I will practice for more than an hour.

13

① W It is a _____ _____ put up by the Seoul Subway Public Works Department.

② W The construction will _____ _____ _____ _____.

③ W The construction activities will include the _____ and restoration of the asphalt.

④ W The construction activities will end in early _____.

⑤ W _____ wants to get more _____ can _____ the Seoul Subway Public Works Department by phone.

14

W Jeff, do you have a problem these days?

M I _____ I do. I feel everything's not okay these days.

W I'm sorry to hear that. What is it that's _____ you?

M My problem is that I don't know _____ _____ _____ _____.

W Have you tried to _____ _____ _____? What about going to a concert?

M A concert? It sounds great. Is there a good concert coming up?

W Yes, a K-pop Star Concert _____ _____ _____ this Friday night.

M Really? What time does it start?

W Sorry. I don't remember when the concert _____ _____.

M I don't have my cell phone with me. So can you _____ _____ _____ _____ for me?

15

M Online shopping is very popular today. It is a form of _____ _____, and it is called e-shopping. Consumers can _____ _____ goods or services from many sellers on the Internet. Now, through cell phones, consumers can easily shop online by using shopping apps. _____ _____ generally use their _____ _____, electronic transfers and _____ _____ to pay for their purchases. In addition, online stores are _____ _____ 24 hours a day, so many consumers can _____ online shopping _____ _____ _____.

16

W Hi, Brad.

M Hi, Vicky.

W How did you know to come here? Who told you to come here?

M Yesterday Bill told me to come here.

W Really? I _____ _____ _____ all day long yesterday. I was very _____ yesterday because you didn't _____ _____ _____.

M Sorry, I _____ _____ _____ _____ because I was really busy helping my mom.

W By the way, did Bill tell you _____ _____ _____?

M No, I _____ Bill while shopping with my mom at the mall. _____ _____, Vicky.

W Okay. It is _____ that we met each other here. But I don't want the same thing to ever happen again.

M OK, even if I'm busy, I'll return your call.

17

[Telephone rings.]
W Hello, this is HCM. How may I help you?
M Yes, this is Andrew Rice from Pennsylvania. I'd like to talk to Ms. Parker.
W I'm sorry. She can't talk to you because she is _____ _____ _____ now.
M Can I _____ _____ _____ _____?
W Sure. Could you _____ _____ _____ _____ because I have to get a pen _____ _____ _____?
M Okay. When you're ready, let me know. [Pause]
W Thank you. I'm ready.
M I want to check _____ she can visit my office at _____ p.m. today.
W Sorry, she isn't _____ to visit your office at that time because she already has _____ _____.
M If so, I'm wondering when she can visit me today.

18

M Thank you for coming.
W _____ _____ _____. What seems to be wrong with Bill?
M Well, we are worried about Bill's failure _____ _____.
W Please continue explaining Bill's situation to me.
M He _____ _____ any books since he became _____ _____ watching TV.
W Well, you know spending a lot of time watching TV can make people _____ _____ _____ to _____.
M We have just found out that he usually watches TV all afternoon after school.
W How many hours does he watch TV every day?
M Every day he _____ _____ _____ _____ watching TV.
W Spending six hours on TV is too long for a teenager.

19

M Hi, Betty! Richard and I are _____ _____ _____ _____ the movie theater.
W Really? Can I join you?
M Sure. The movie we are going to see is Mr. Brilliant.
W What? Mr. Brilliant? I saw it yesterday.
M Really? How is the movie? _____ _____ _____?
W Not at all. It is really _____. I was so _____ _____ _____ _____

on the movie.
M Really? I don't believe it. The _____ of the movie are really _____, aren't they?
W I read all the reviews, too, and then I decided to watch the movie. But it was terrible.
M Can you _____ _____ interesting movie?
W No. That is the only movie I've watched recently.

20

M The annual _____ _____ will be held at Henry's school next Friday. He _____ _____ _____ _____ the soccer competition for 2 years. But he may not _____ _____ this year's competition because he can't find his soccer shoes. Although he looked everywhere for them, he couldn't find them. He tried to _____ _____ _____ from a few of his friends, but they don't have any _____ _____. All his classmates and homeroom teacher _____ him to play and be _____ of the soccer team, and it is certain that they will be _____ if he can't. In this situation, what would Henry's mom probably say to Henry?

Actual Test

01 대화를 듣고, 남자가 찾고 있는 집으로 가장 적절한 것을 고르시오.

① ② ③ ④ ⑤

02 대화를 듣고, 남자가 과제를 늦게 제출한 이유를 고르시오.

① 과제를 잃어버려서   ② 마감 기한을 몰라서
③ 컴퓨터 사용이 서툴러서   ④ 컴퓨터 수리가 오래 걸려서
⑤ 컴퓨터가 바이러스에 감염되어서

03 다음을 듣고, 무엇에 관한 내용인지 고르시오.

① 구내 식당 수리 공고   ② 신임 교장 인사
③ 변경된 교칙 공고   ④ 구내 식당 판매 물품 변경
⑤ 신축 구내 식당 이용 안내

04 대화를 듣고, 여자의 심정으로 가장 적절한 것을 고르시오.

① pleased   ② satisfied   ③ worried
④ jealous   ⑤ angry

05 대화를 듣고, 남자가 여자에게 전화를 건 목적을 고르시오.

① 과제를 설명해 주려고   ② 여자가 좋아하는 것을 물어보려고
③ 과제 내용을 물어보려고   ④ 과제의 마감 기한을 알려주려고
⑤ 과제를 함께 하자고 제안하려고

06 대화를 듣고, 여자가 받을 거스름돈으로 가장 적절한 것을 고르시오.

① \$5 ② \$5.50 ③ \$10
④ \$13.50 ⑤ \$15

07 대화를 듣고, 두 사람의 관계로 가장 적절한 것을 고르시오.

① patient — doctor ② student — teacher
③ sales person — customer ④ employee — boss
⑤ interviewer — interviewee

08 대화를 듣고, 두 사람이 대화하는 장소로 가장 적절한 것을 고르시오.

① hair salon ② playground ③ living room
④ animal clinic ⑤ school

09 다음을 듣고, 그림의 상황에 어울리는 대화를 고르시오.

① ② ③ ④ ⑤

10 대화를 듣고, 남자가 대화 직후 할 일로 가장 적절한 것을 고르시오.

① 회원권 문의 ② 회원권 갱신
③ 예약 취소 ④ 회원가입 신청서 작성
⑤ 예약금 환불

11 대화를 듣고, 남자가 여자에게 부탁한 일로 가장 적절한 것을 고르시오.

① 뮤지컬 함께 보러 가기　　　　② 세종문화회관 위치 설명해주기
③ 뮤지컬 예매 취소하기　　　　④ 뮤지컬 예매 시간 변경하기
⑤ 과제 마무리 도와주기

12 대화를 듣고, 여자에 대한 내용으로 일치하는 것을 고르시오.

① 여자는 테니스 대회에서 우승했다.
② 여자는 작년 챔피언에게 패배했다.
③ 사람들은 여자의 우승을 확신했다.
④ 여자는 집중력을 높이기 위해 실전 경기를 관람한다.
⑤ 여자는 음악 감상과 낮잠 자기를 제일 좋아한다.

13 대화를 듣고, 메모의 내용과 일치하지 <u>않는</u> 것을 고르시오.

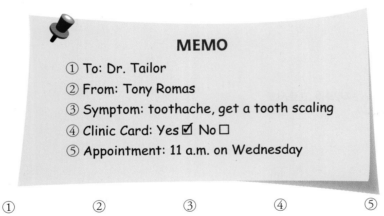

MEMO
① To: Dr. Tailor
② From: Tony Romas
③ Symptom: toothache, get a tooth scaling
④ Clinic Card: Yes ☑ No ☐
⑤ Appointment: 11 a.m. on Wednesday

①　　　　②　　　　③　　　　④　　　　⑤

14 대화를 듣고, 남자가 대화 직후 할 일로 가장 적절한 것을 고르시오.

① 자물쇠 수리공 부르기　　　　② 새 핸드폰 구입하기
③ 경비 아저씨에게 가기　　　　④ 아파트 관리사무소에 가기
⑤ 쓰레기 분리수거 하기

15 다음을 듣고, 여자가 언급하지 <u>않은</u> 것을 고르시오.

① 강연 주체　　　　② 강연 요일　　　　③ 강연료
④ 강사　　　　　　⑤ 강연 장소

[16-17] 대화를 듣고, 남자의 마지막 말에 이어질 여자의 응답으로 가장 적절한 것을 고르시오.

16
① My mom is a good driver, too.
② Could you drive me to school?
③ I went to bed at 2 a.m. last night.
④ I usually get up at 6:30 in the morning.
⑤ Please give me a wakeup call at 6 o'clock.

17
① Where did you buy the air conditioner?
② Okay, I will. Please wait for me for a while.
③ Oh, really? I'll check the batteries right away.
④ When is the air conditioner being delivered?
⑤ Don't worry. The batteries have some power left.

[18-19] 대화를 듣고, 남자의 마지막 말에 이어질 여자의 응답으로 가장 적절한 것을 고르시오.

18
① Try to look on the bright side all the time.
② May I have your student ID number, please?
③ Didn't you know the deadline was three days ago?
④ Thank you very much. I was really worried about it.
⑤ What are the qualifications to apply for the scholarship?

19
① Okay. Here you are.
② When is the sale over?
③ Really? I thought they are on sale.
④ Sorry for the inconvenience. I'll recharge it.
⑤ What kind of credit card would you like to issue?

20 다음을 듣고, Teresa가 영어 선생님에게 할 말로 가장 적절한 것을 고르시오.

① I wonder if you can be the first presenter.
② Cheer up! I'm sure you will do better next time.
③ Do you know where the nurse's room is?
④ Just let me know when you can give your presentation.
⑤ I'm feeling sick, so can I give my presentation next class?

01

W How may I help you?

M I'm looking for a new house to _____ _____. Could you show me some houses that are _____?

W What kind of house do you _____ _____ _____?

M I want a two-story house with a _____ _____.

W I see. Do you prefer a house _____ _____ _____ or _____ _____?

M The _____.

W Anything else?

M It would be good if it _____ _____ _____ rather than _____ or _____.

W I'll show you some houses that have what you want. Let's go.

02

W What's up? You look stressed.

M I am really stressed. My school _____ is really late.

W Why? You never _____ _____ late papers.

M _____ _____ _____ _____, I was working on it for a week and had almost finished it, but…

W But what? What happened?

M My computer was _____ _____ _____ _____ a few days ago and I lost all my files.

W Oh, no! Were you able _____ _____ _____ _____ from the computer?

M Fortunately, yes. But I couldn't _____ the _____ _____ because I hadn't _____ _____ my computer.

W Does it mean you had to write the paper all over again?

M Yes. I've _____ _____ _____ _____ days to do it. I'm almost done.

W I'm very sorry to hear you've had so much trouble.

03

M Good morning, students. I'm Paula Hilton, the _____ _____. I will tell you about our school's _____ plan. As we _____ before, we are planning to renovate the school cafeteria. It will _____ _____ _____ starting next Monday. We will keep serving lunch, but as half the cafeteria is being renovated, there are _____ _____. The lunch times for every class will now be changed. Your homeroom teacher will tell you your new lunch time. Sorry for the _____ and thank you for understanding. I'm sure the cafeteria will serve you better after the _____. Thank you.

04

W Excuse me. _____ _____ _____ _____ do I have to wait? I _____ about 20 _____ _____.

M Sorry, ma'am. I will go to the kitchen and _____ _____ _____. I will be right back.

W Thank you.

M [Pause] It's coming up _____ _____! Please wait a few more seconds.

W Okay. I'm so hungry. [Pause]

M Here's your _____, ma'am.

W What's this? This is not _____ _____ _____ _____. I ordered seafood cream spaghetti, not tomato meatball spaghetti.

M Oh, I'm _____ sorry. I'll be right back with your order.

W _____ _____ _____. I'd like to _____ my order. I'm leaving!

05

[Cell phone rings.]

W Hi, Taemin. What's up?

M I'd like to ask you about the English _____. I _____ _____ the memo. What do I have to _____ _____?

W You need to write about some of your _____ _____ such as your favorite _____, _____, or _____.

M How long does it have to be?

W The teacher said _____ _____. You have to include an _____, a _____, and a _____, too.

M I see. When is the _____ _____, then?

W It is this _____. You'd better start to write it now.

M Thank you very much.

06

W Excuse me. I'm _____ _____ notebooks. How much are they?

M It _____. _____ _____ _____ notebooks do you want?

W Well. I have no idea. It is for my 10-year-old boy. Could you please _____ some to me?

M Sure. Come here. These are good ones for children that age. _____ ones are $1 and ones with _____ _____ _____ on them are $1.50 each.

W I see. I will take 5 of each. Could you please _____ them?

M Sure. But there is an _____ _____ _____ $2. Do you still want it done?

W Yes, please. Here is $20.

M Thank you. Here is your _____.

07

W Dr. Flahive. Can I talk to you _____ _____ _____?

M Yes. _____ _____ _____.

W My brother in Seattle is in the hospital now, but there is no one to _____ _____ _____ him.

M Really? That's too bad. Do you need to _____ some _____ _____?

W I'm sorry, but yes. Can I take a _____ _____?

M Of course. We're not busy this week and I'm planning to _____ the _____ _____ who I _____ yesterday.

W Thank you so much.

M But tell Mrs. White to take care of your work _____ you're gone.

W Yes, I will. I hope she'll be understanding, too.

08

M Wow! She has beautiful _____ _____ and ears.

W She sure does. Thanks for saying so.

M _____ _____ _____ her?

W She used to be _____ and liked to play with me, but these days she just _____ _____ _____ or _____ her house.

M What about her _____? Does she _____ _____?

W Not really. She doesn't even take care of her little puppies.

M Hmm… Let's _____ _____ _____.

_____ and see the _____.

W When will the result _____ _____?

M It usually takes 3 days. Please come again on _____.

09

① **W** What do you want _____ _____ _____?

  M I want some _____.

② **W** Oh, no. What are you doing?

  M I'm sorry, mom. I'll start _____ _____.

③ **W** Aren't you _____? Have a snack first.

  M No thanks, mom. I have to _____ _____ _____.

④ **W** What are you doing, sweetie?

  M I'm playing a _____ _____. It's so much fun.

⑤ **W** _____ _____ to go to school?

  M Almost. Please wait _____ _____ _____.

10

W Hello, sir. _____ _____ Oak Inn. How may I help you?

M Do you _____ _____ _____ _____ for tonight?

W Did you _____ _____ _____ _____?

M No. I didn't.

W Let me _____ first. Please wait _____ _____ _____. [Pause] A _____ _____ is _____. Is it okay for you?

M Yes, I'm by myself. How much is it?

W Do you have an A-1Suites _____ card? If you have it, you can get a _____.

M No. This is my _____ _____ here.

W I see. If you'd like one, please _____ this _____. You can _____ _____ _____ within a few minutes.

M Okay. I will.

11

M Did you buy the tickets for the _____?

W Yes, I did. We are going to see Les Miserables. It is playing at the Sejong Center for the Performing Arts.

M Really? What time is it?

W It is at 1 p.m. _____, _____.

M Hmm… To tell you the truth, I had a _____

_____ finishing my _____. I couldn't
sleep _____ all week.

W Do you mean you want me to _____
_____ _____?

M No, no. It's not that. I just want to go in the
evening not the afternoon. I want to _____
_____ really late and _____ _____
_____ my sleep.

W I see. I will check _____ we can go in the
evening or not. I'll let you know.

M Thank you very much.

12

M Terra! _____ _____ winning the Tennis
Championship! How do you feel now?

W Thank you very much. I feel great! Fantastic!

M People didn't _____ that you would
_____ last year's champion, Vera Chang. Were
there any _____ _____ or _____
_____ _____?

W Well, I didn't think in a _____ _____
and just tried to _____ _____ the ball
until the end of the match.

M You focused really well throughout the match. How
do you learn to _____ so well?

W Well, I usually _____ _____ some
rock music and play it very _____ while
practicing. That way, I can _____ _____
_____ the noise of a real _____.

M That's _____! What are you going to do now?

W I just want to go home and take a nap.

13

[Telephone rings.]

W Hello. This is Dr. Tailor's _____ _____.
How may I help you?

M Hello. This is Tony Romas. I'd like to _____
_____ _____ with Dr. Tailor.

W _____ _____ _____ our clinic
before?

M Yes. I have a clinic card.

W Good. Can you describe your problem?

M I have a _____. It's not too painful, but I want
it checked out. And I'd like to get my teeth scaled
after the doctor's _____.

W No problem. Can you come in at 11 tomorrow
morning? I mean _____.

M I'm afraid I can't. I have an important meeting. Is it
_____ to make it the _____
_____?

W That's fine. See you then.

14

W Hey, Dennis. What are you doing here?

M Oh, Gillian. I _____ _____ my cell
phone in here, but it's _____.

W You mean in this _____ _____? Oh, no.
How did that happen?

M I was _____ _____ when the phone
rang so I took the call. After the call I put it into this
recycling bin _____ _____.

W I'm sorry to hear that. You'd better go to the
_____ _____ _____. They might
have a key for this bin.

M I did. But the office isn't open now. The office hours
are over.

W Did you ask the _____ _____, then? He
might have one.

M That's a good idea. I'll go and ask him. Thank you
very much.

15

W Listen well, everyone. Before I _____ the
_____, I will make an _____. Our
school's _____ _____ will offer a special
_____ _____ every Wednesday for 5
weeks _____ _____ _____ _____. This
Wednesday, June 4, HeavTec's CEO Rose Martin will
give a lecture on _____ _____ in room
101. You will be given a _____ with a pen in
the _____ _____ on that day. I'm sure it
will help you think in a _____ _____.
Please _____ and _____ us for a
wonderful time. Hope to see all of you there.

16

M Good morning, Apple. Why have you come to
school so early today?

W Hi, Jack. Didn't you know that I always come to
school _____ _____ _____ every
day? You are very early today.

M Every day? Are you _____?

W Of course I am.

M Why?

W I come early because my mom _____ me
_____ _____ on her way to work.

M What do you do before the class starts, then?

W _____ _____. I sometimes _____
or _____ the lessons or listen to music.

M Wow! You're a really good student. What time do
you usually _____ _____?

W I usually get up at 6:30 in the morning.

17

[Telephone rings.]

M Hello, this is Gold Star Electronics _____ _____. How may I help you?

W Hello. I had an _____ _____ _____ this morning. It was working quite well right after your _____ had installed it.

M And?

W But when I turned it on with a _____ _____ just a while ago, nothing happened. It is not working.

M I see. We're very sorry for the _____. Let me ask you a few _____ before sending someone.

W Okay. Go ahead.

M Did you check the _____ of the remote control?

W Of course I did. They are both new.

M Good. Could you please check the _____ _____ whether it is on? It is _____ _____ _____ the air conditioner.

W Okay, I will. Please wait for me for a while.

18

M May I help you?

W Yes, please. I have a question about this _____ _____.

M What is it?

W I actually _____ my application three days ago. However, I just _____ _____ that I _____ _____ _____ on the application form.

M Oh, no. Do you mean you put down the _____ _____?

W Unfortunately, yes. If _____, I'd like to change the student ID number. Can I?

M Let me _____. May I have your name, please?

W I'm Eva Rosa.

M Oh! Yours isn't in the _____ of being _____ yet. Just _____ _____ the _____ information on this form.

W Thank you very much. I was really worried about it.

19

M It is $57.50 _____ _____. Are you going to _____ _____ _____ or by _____ _____?

W By credit card.

M Do you have a store _____ card, too? You can get points for your purchase.

W Yes, here it is.

M Please sign on the _____. [Pause] Here is your _____. Thank you.

W Wait! Wait! I was _____ the wrong price for the three cans of soda. The sodas should be $2 not $6. They're on sale.

M Oh, really? Let me see it.

W Look! It says $6. It is not the _____ _____.

M Oh, I am so sorry for that. I'll _____ this and _____ it. Can I have your credit card again?

W Okay. Here you are.

20

M Teresa is going to _____ _____ _____ tomorrow in English class. She has been _____ and _____ for over a week. She even practiced _____ _____ _____ a mirror and _____ it one day. Today is the day of the presentation. She has breakfast and goes to school. However, she _____ has a _____ and breaks out in a _____ _____ right before the English class starts. She is sick and knows it is impossible for her to give her presentation. So she _____ _____ go to the _____ _____. In this situation, what would Teresa most likely say to her English teacher?

Vocabulary **R**eview

01	bicycle rack	자전거 보관대
	frame	골격
	saddle	안장
02	feature phone	피처폰 (저성능 휴대전화)
	handle	취급하다, 다루다
	branch retail store	직영대리점
03	exclusive	독점적인, 전용의
	limited offer	한정판매
	personalized	개인 맞춤형의
04	gorgeous	아주 멋진
	shouldn't have p.p.	~하지 말았어야 했는데(했다)
	come out of	~에서 나오다
05	raw fish	생선회
	family reunion	가족모임
06	catch the movie	영화를 보다
	admission price	입장료
	hectic	빡빡한, 정신없이 바쁜
07	attachment	첨부
	should have p.p.	~했어야 했는데(하지 않았다)
	forward	(편지 등을) 전송하다
08	push a cart	카트를 밀다
	a loaf of bread	빵 한 덩어리
	ingredient	재료
09	take a picture	사진을 찍다
	annual event	연례행사
	develop a picture	사진을 현상하다
10	convenience	편리, 편의
	a variety of	다양한
	be located on	~에 위치하다
11	participate in	~에 참가하다

12	obviously	확실히, 분명히
	give a hand	도움을 주다
	competition	경쟁, 경연
	negative	부정적인
	calm down	진정하다
13	application form	지원서
	tuition	수업, 수업료
	can't afford to-V	~할 여유가 없다
14	somewhere around here	여기 근처 어딘가에
	a little while ago	방금
	customer service center	고객 서비스 센터
15	direct bus	직행 버스
	journey	여정, 여행
	miss out on	~을 놓치다
16	head for	~로 향하다
	end-of-season sale	시즌 마감 세일
	for awhile	잠시 동안, 한동안
17	try on	~을 (시험 삼아) 입어보다
	bargain	거래
18	withdraw from	~에서 철수하다
	make up	만회하다, 보충하다
	drop out of	~에서 중도하차하다
	full-time work	정규직
19	bracelet	팔찌
	jewelry shop	보석가게
	pick out	고르다
20	be interested in	~에 흥미[관심]가 있다
	trick	묘기

02 Vocabulary Review

01	shoulder length	어깨 길이
	wavy	웨이브가 있는, 물결모양의
	dye	염색하다
02	reduce	줄이다
	cultural gap	문화적 차이
	on behalf of	~을 대신[대표]하여
03	emergency procedure	비상시 절차
	cabin	객실, 선실
	pressure loss	압력 손실
	stay calm	침착함을 유지하다
04	stomp	발을 세게 구르다
	resident	거주자
05	expiration date	유통기한
	bar code	(상품의) 바코드
	verify	확인하다, 입증하다
06	money exchange	환전소
	current	현재의
	exchange rate	환율
07	sunscreen	자외선 차단제
	convenient	편리한
	sticky	끈적이는
08	the world's best	세계 최고의
	facial expression	얼굴 표정
	splendid	화려한
09	apply for	~에 지원하다
	formal dress	정장
	Is this seat taken?	자리 있어요?
10	honestly	솔직히
	complain	불평하다
	stand	참다

11	have a big fight with	~와 크게 싸우다
	make peace	화해하다
	set up a time	시간을 정하다
12	exhibition	전시회
	wax figurine	밀랍인형
	day pass	일일 이용권
13	household goods	가사용품
	garage sale	창고 세일
	contact number	연락처
14	car insurance company	자동차 보험 회사
	address book	주소록
	make a call	전화하다
15	category	부류, 유형
	attract	끌다, 모으다
	participant	참가자
16	registration	등록
	available	이용 가능한
	instructor	강사
17	raise	키우다, 기르다
	tell A from B	A와 B를 구별하다
	adopt	입양하다
18	abandon	버리다
	boring	지루한
	weather forecast	일기 예보
19	a couple of	둘의
	work out	운동하다
	concentrate on	~에 집중하다
	do strength training	근력 운동하다
20	for the first time	처음으로
	pick up	(차에) 태우러 가다

03 Vocabulary Review

01	rush hour	혼잡 시간대
	worth	～할 가치가 있는
	on foot	걸어서
02	as far as	～하는 한
	turn	차례, 순서
	fall down	쓰러지다
03	stage	무대에 올리다
	auditorium	강당
	in celebration of	～을 축하하여
04	graduation	졸업
	nervous	긴장한
05	take part in	참여하다
	urgent	급한
	senior citizen	노인
06	from a distance	멀리서
	on top of that	게다가
	gift certificate	상품권
07	buck	(미국·호주의) 달러
	turn around	돌리다, 돌려 세우다
	washer fluid	워셔액, 세정액
08	look real	진짜처럼 보이다
	distinguish between A and B	A와 B를 구별하다
	artificial flower	조화
09	vary	다르다
	seating plan	좌석배치도
	right in front of	바로 앞의
10	keep in mind	명심하다, 유념하다
	be away	부재중이다
11	five days and four nights	4박 5일
	package tour	패키지여행

	detail	세부사항
12	exhausted	지친
	a night owl	올빼미 족
	put up with	참다, 견디다
13	book a ticket	표를 예매하다
	traffic condition	교통상황
14	rather than	～보다는
	correct	정확한, 옳은
	connection	연결 상태
15	check for virus	바이러스를 체크하다
	for a time	한동안
	remarkable	주목할 만한
16	by far	단연, 훨씬
	limp	절뚝거리다
	ache	아프다
	cramp	경련이 나다, 쥐가 나다
17	lately	최근에
	stricken with	～에 시달리는
	itch	간지럽다
	reaction	반응
18	give birth	아기를 낳다
	complication	합병증
	get used to	～에 익숙해지다
19	deal with	～을 다루다, 처리하다
	pressure	압박감
	expect	기대하다
20	search for	～을 찾다
	circulation desk	대출대
	librarian	사서

04 Vocabulary Review

01	overnight	밤샘
	organizer	주최자, 조직자
	pattern	무늬
02	injured	부상을 당한
	avoid	피하다
	fracture	골절상을 입다
03	athlete	운동선수
	select	선택하다
	announce	알리다, 발표하다
04	ringback tone	통화연결음
	vibration	진동
	silent mode	무음 모드
05	request	요청하다
	vegetarian meal	채식 식사
	catering department	(항공) 기내식 담당 부서
06	appear on TV show	TV쇼에 출연하다
	taste	취향
	gift-wrap	선물 포장하다
07	crumb	부스러기
	wipe up	닦다
	refill on one's coke	콜라 한 잔 더, 콜라 리필
08	make a funny noise	이상한 소리를 내다
	fill out	작성하다
	take a look	점검하다
09	per	～ 마다, ～ 당
	be seated	앉다
	by the window	창가에
10	rest one's mind	머리를 식히다
	number	번호를 매기다
	in a row	연속적으로

11	traditional	전통적인
	research	조사, 연구
	check out	(도서관에서 책을) 대출하다
12	next period	다음 시간[교시]
	shoot a free throw	자유투를 던지다
	concerned	걱정하는
13	field trip	현장 체험 학습
	shorten	단축하다
	constructive	건설적인
14	vote	투표하다
	mature	성숙한
	influenced	영향을 받는
15	be poisoned	중독되다
	permanent	영구적인
	lead	납
16	canned goods	통조림 제품
	fake	가짜의, 거짓된
	be frightened	겁을 먹다
17	get stung	(벌에) 쏘이다
	frost	서리
	scrape	긁어내다
18	Celsius	섭씨
	ask ~ out	～에게 데이트 신청하다
	manufacture	생산하다
19	parts	부품
	flight	항공편
	front	앞, 정면
20	keep up with	～을 따라잡다
	fail in the exam	시험에 낙제하다

05 Vocabulary Review

01	stomachache	복통
	catch the flu	독감에 걸리다
	vomit	토하다
02	first come first served	선착순
	fill up	가득차다
	designated	지정된
03	fire drill	소방훈련
	evacuate	떠나다, 대피하다
	apologize	사과하다
04	second edition	2판
	overseas	해외
	in trouble	난처한, 곤경에 빠진
05	area code	지역번호
	first opening	가장 빠른 시간
	technician	기술자
06	customs	세관
	delay	지연되다
	track	추적하다
07	carry-on	휴대용 짐
	proceed	진행하다
	metal detector	금속탐지기
08	elderly	연장자, 노인
	pass away	죽다, 사망하다
	enormous	매우 큰
09	choir	합창단
	broadcasting	방송
	debate	토론(하다)
10	final episode	마지막 회
	win the lottery	복권에 당첨되다
	donate	기부하다

11	stress	강조하다
	lend	빌려주다
	manual	사용 설명서
12	water supply	수도 공급
	cut off	중단하다
	cooperation	협조
13	organize	정리하다, 조직하다
	arrange	조정하다
	quarterly	분기별
14	recycling bin	재활용 쓰레기통
	separate	분리하다
	recycling area	재활용장
15	undergraduate	학부의
	graduate student	대학원생
	renew	갱신하다, 재개하다
	overdue	기한이 지난
	periodical	정기간행물
16	average	평범한, 보통의
	shoot	촬영하다
17	flexible	탄력적인, 유동적인
	a great deal of	많은
18	antibiotics	항생제
	viral infection	바이러스성 감염
	prescribe	처방하다
19	look terrible	기분이 안 좋아 보이다
	funeral	장례식
	make a good impression	좋은 인상을 주다
20	be backed up	차가 정체 되다
	furthermore	더욱이, 게다가

01	delivery	배달
	camper	캠핑카
	hit the road	길을 나서다
02	eat out	외식하다
	must have p.p.	~임에 틀림없다
	big deal	큰 거래, 중대 사건
03	function	기능, 기능하다
	plentiful	풍부한
	nutrient	영양소
04	giveaway event	경품행사
	dining voucher	외식상품권
	tax and utility charge	제세공과금
	surface value	액면가
05	semester	학기
	appreciate	이해하다
	article	기사, 글
06	look good on	~에 잘 어울리다
	have an eye for	~을 보는 안목이 있다
07	enroll	등록하다
	room assignment sheet	방배정표
	bulletin board	게시판
08	Please fill it up.	(주유소에서) 가득 채워주세요.
	empty	텅 빈
	unleaded	(휘발유가) 무연의
09	form	양식, 형식
	pay the tuition fee	수강료를 납부하다
	Help yourself.	(음식을) 마음껏 드세요
10	approach	다가오다
	spring-cleaning	봄맞이 대청소
	remain in one's mind	~의 기억에 남다

11	gratitude	감사
	based on	~을 바탕으로 한
	exchange student	교환학생
12	have a long face	우울한 표정을 짓다
	opportunity	기회
	in particular	특히
13	piece	(꽃의) 한 송이, 조각
	wide selection	폭넓은 선택
	Take your time.	천천히 해.
14	be covered with	~로 뒤덮이다
	mow the lawn	잔디를 깎다
	federal	연방정부의
15	pilgrim	순례자
	mashed	으깬
	concerned	걱정하는
16	lately	최근에
	take one's mind off	(걱정거리를) 잊게 하다
	automatic	자동의
17	on an installment basis	할부로
	prefer	더 좋아하다
	unfortunately	불행히도
18	client	고객
	manufacturer	제조업자
	smelly	(역겨운)냄새가 나는
19	leather	가죽
	ingredient	재료
20	swing	그네
	handle	다루다

01	performance	공연
	familiar	친숙한, 익숙한
	phantom	유령
02	borrow	빌리다
	repair	수리하다
	flat tire	펑크 난 타이어
03	run for	~에 출마하다
	student council	학생회
	dedicated	헌신적인
04	by now	지금쯤은
	missing	실종된
	punished	벌받는, 혼나는
05	rain cats and dogs	비가 억수같이 쏟아지다
	be[get] caught in the rain	비를 만나다
	unpredictable	예측 불가능한
06	tender	(고기 등이) 부드러운, 연한
	insist	주장하다
	split	쪼개다, 나누다
07	qualification	자격요건
	not to mention	~은 말할 것도 없고
	intern at	~에서 인턴으로 근무하다
08	inconvenience	불편
	in style	유행하는
	look good on	~에 잘 어울리다
09	damaged	손상된
	get to	~에 도착하다
	feed	먹이를 주다
10	conclusion	결론
	summarize	요약하다
	restate	고쳐 말하다

11	extend	연장하다
	contract	계약
	confirmed	확인된
12	It depends.	경우에 따라 다르다
	exotic	이국적인
	lizard	도마뱀
13	life saving	인명 구조
	winnings	상금
	further information	기타문의
14	senior center	양로원
	orphanage	고아원
	remind	생각나게 하다
15	bound for	~행의
	departure gate	출발 탑승구
	heavy snowstorm	폭설
	runway	활주로
	board	탑승하다
16	to tell the truth	사실을 말하자면
	get out of	~에서 벗어나다
	make a good salary	돈을 잘 벌다
17	complete with	~이 완비된
	kitchenette	작은 부엌
18	give a presentation	발표하다
	thoroughly	완전히, 철저히
	do research on	~을 연구하다
19	be hospitalized	입원하다
	lung	폐
	mind	꺼려하다
20	be on vacation	휴가중이다
	submarine	잠수함

	hybrid	혼성체, 혼합물
01	device	장치
	Blu-Ray	광디스크 저장 매체
	on impulse	충동적으로
02	nonrefundable	환불되지 않는
	on the same page	같은 생각을 하고 있는
	discourage	막다, 말리다
03	levy fines	벌금을 부과하다
	loan	대출
	stuck in traffic	교통이 막힌[정체된]
04	be backed up	밀려있다, 꽉 막히다
	traffic report	교통 방송 안내
	resident	거주자
	receiver	수신자, 받는 사람
05	unit	(공동주택내의) 한 가구
	reply to	~에 답변하다, 대응하다
06	general section	일반구역
	senior	연장자, 노인
	pressed	압박을 받는
07	shortcut	지름길
	hospitable	환대하는, 친절한
	training schedule	훈련 일정
08	exercise lightly	가볍게 운동하다
	do one's best	최선을 다하다
	graduation ceremony	졸업식
09	auditorium	강당
	praise	칭찬, 찬양
	organize	조직하다
10	arrangement	배열, 준비
	without any incidents	별일 없이

	pull over	차를 갓길에 세우다
11	emergency	응급 상황
	selfish	이기적인
12	passion	열정
	talent	재능
	venue	개최지
13	presence	참석
	vow	서약
	timetable	시간표
14	proficiency	능숙, 숙달
	reception desk	접수처
	magnificient	웅장한
	blowhole	분수공
15	adapt to	~에 적응하다
	endangered	멸종위기에 처한
	be good at	~을 잘하다
16	succeed	성공하다
	rate	등급을 매기다
	unbearable	참을 수 없는
17	moderate	중간의, 적당한
	severe	심한
	master's degree	석사 학위
18	support	부양하다, 지탱하다
	attitude	태도, 자세
	anxious	걱정하는
19	kindergarten	유치원
	Arbor Day	식목일
20	environment	환경
	oxygen	산소

09 Vocabulary Review

01	display	진열, 전시
	all-in-one	둘(이상)을 하나로 만든, 일체형의
	former	이전의, 앞서의
02	tropical fish	열대어
	incredible	믿을 수 없는
	give birth to	~을 출산하다, 낳다
03	guard	지키다, 보호하다
	worth its weight	아주 유용한, 대단히 귀중한
	promotion code	판촉용 부호
	valid	유효한, 정당한
04	flunk a test	시험에 떨어지다, 낙제하다
	cram	벼락치기로 공부하다
	concentrate on	~에 집중하다
05	workshop	강습
	surcharge	추가 요금
06	regular	정규의
	intensive course	집중 코스
	in monthly installments	할부로
	interest-free	무이자의
07	direct	직행의
	transfer	갈아타다
08	negative	부정적인
	peaceful	평화로운
	pregnant	임신한
09	send the parcel	소포를 보내다
	weigh	무게가 나가다
	stranger	낯선 사람
10	run in the election	선거에 출마하다
	hesitate	망설이다
	candidate	후보

	sociology	사회학
11	the day after tomorrow	내일 모레
	rehearse	예행연습을 하다
	balanced diet	균형 잡힌 식단
12	picky	까다로운
	correct	바로 잡다
	breed	(개의)품종
13	reward	보상, 사례
	walk by	지나치다
	reasonable	타당한
14	view	전망
	pack	짐을 싸다
	ancient	고대의
15	afterlife	사후 세계
	mummy	미라
16	hire	고용하다
	flutter	두근거리다
	genetically modified	유전자가 조작된
17	gene	유전자
	mutation	돌연변이
	selective breeding	선발번식
	break time	휴식 시간
18	vending machine	자동판매기
	swallow	삼키다
19	puppy	강아지
	someday	언젠가
	have a toothache	치통이 있다
20	check-up	검진
	pull out	뽑다

10 Vocabulary Review

01	turn in	~을 돌려주다, 반납하다	
	woven	엮은, 짠	
	contents	내용물	
02	shagging flies	배팅연습, 연습 야구	
	take off	도망가다	
	responsibility	책임	
03	closure	폐쇄	
	safety hazard	안전 위협 요소	
	pose	(위험, 문제를) 제기하다	
	underway	진행중인	
04	keep one's mouth shut	입을 닫다, 함구하다	
	give away	~을 폭로하다, 누설하다	
	a good turnout	(모임에) 많이 나타남	
	button one's lip	함구하다, 비밀을 지키다	
05	depart	출발하다	
	travel itinerary	여행일정	
06	gear	장비	
	per person per day	하루에 인당	
07	step on it	속도를 내다	
	go nowhere	아무 성과[진전]를 못보다	
	backseat driver	뒷좌석 운전자	
08	ask for a hand	도움을 요청하다	
	look up	검색하다	
	out of stock	재고가 없는	
09	have in mind	염두에 두다	
	striped	줄무늬의	
	floral	꽃무늬의	
10	at dawn	새벽에	
	strict	엄격한	
	on time	정각에	

11	refresh one's mind	정신을 맑게 하다	
	force	강요하다	
	trust	믿다	
12	a good reputation	호평	
	unavoidable	피치 못할	
	apologize	사과하다	
13	capacity	용량	
	inclusion	포함	
	budget	예산	
14	stop by	들르다	
	come to one's mind	떠오르다, 생각나다	
	dull	무딘	
15	civilization	문명	
	sophisticated	세련된	
	worship	숭배	
	astrology	점성술, 점성학	
16	sacrifice	희생, 제물	
	organ	장기, 기관	
	donation	기부	
17	tolerant	아량이 넓은	
	untidy	단정하지 않은	
	common area	공용 지역	
18	passable	공용 지역	
	pothole	움푹 패인 곳	
	swerve	방향을 바꾸다	
19	bustling	혼잡한	
	commute time	통근 시간	
	real estate agent	부동산 중개인	
20	appointed	약속된, 지정된	
	get hold of	~와 연락하다	

11 Vocabulary Review

	numb	감각이 없는
01	shoulder-width	어깨 넓이로
	parallel with	~과 평행한
	encyclopedia	백과사전
02	knock something over	~을 넘어뜨리다
	stained	얼룩진
	replacement	대체물
	safety net	안전망, 안전장치
03	insurance	보험
	medical expense	의료비
	incur	비용을 발생시키다
	matter	중요하다
04	lucky duck	행운아
	gift card	졸업
	collapse	무너지다, 쓰러지다
05	conscious	의식이 있는
	paramedics	긴급 의료진
	use up	다 써버리다
06	separate section	별도구역, 특별한 공간
	leftover	남은 것
07	what a shame	부끄러워라
	stay still	가만히 있다
08	bangs	앞머리
	banned	금지된
	get a refund	환불 받다
09	try on	입어보다
	fitting room	탈의실
	consist of	~로 구성되다
10	islet	섬
	species	품종

	speech contest	말하기 대회
11	mark	점수
	interviewee	인터뷰 받는 사람
	blind date	소개팅
12	appearance	외모
	well-built	체격이 좋은
	tourist spot	관광명소
13	sold out	매진된
	room	(빈)공간, 자리
	have a long face	시무룩해 보이다
14	have a quarrel with	~와 말다툼을 하다
	sleep a wink	한숨 자다
	unique	독특한, 유일한
	sneak up	~에게 몰래 다가가다
15	water repellent	방수의
	soak up	흡수하다
	hemisphere	반구
16	portion	부분
	attitude	태도
17	accompany	~와 동행하다
	restricted	제한된
	be turned down	거절당하다
18	credit	신용
	debt	빚
	pay the bills	청구서를 지불하다
	variety	각양각색, 다양성
19	rebel	반항하다
	well-behaved	예의 바른
20	regular	정기적인, 규칙적인
	level	수치

12 Vocabulary Review

01	marinated	양념에 재운
	flavor	맛, 풍미
	treat	대접, 한턱
02	demand	요구, 수요
	loan	대여
	renew	갱신하다
03	Parental Guidelines	보호자 지침서
	rating	순위, 등급
	fall into	~로 나뉘다
	suggestive dialogue	외설적인 대화
	coarse language	거친 말투
04	retirement performance	은퇴 공연
	in person	직접, 몸소
	remark	말
05	leaflet	전단지, 광고지, 안내지
	better than anyone	누구보다도 더 나은
06	around the corner	아주 가까운
	factor in	고려하다
07	infant	유아
	lavatory	화장실
	stroller	유모차
08	exchange A into B	A를 B로 바꾸다
	have an account	계좌가 있다
	benefit	혜택
09	slip	미끄러지다
	lose a file	파일을 잃다
	crash	(컴퓨터가) 기능을 멈추다
10	report card	성적표
	evaluation	평가
	doubt	의심하다

11	present	선물
	information	정보
12	insert into	~에 집어넣다
	envelope	봉투
	at the bottom	아래쪽에
13	attention	주목
	senior students	2학년 학생들
	submit	제출하다
14	block one's view	시야를 막다
	uncomfortable	불편한
	annoyed	짜증내는, 화내는
15	be named after	~의 이름을 따서 짓다
	chemist	화학자
	physiology	생리학
	economics	경제학
16	be split	나눠지다
	occupy one's time	~의 시간을 쏟다
	challenging	도전적인
17	approximately	대략, 약
	load	짐을 싣다
	guestbook	방명록
18	with little chance of snow	눈이 올 확률이 없는
	throw a party	파티를 열다
	basement	지하실
19	have been there	거기 가본 적이 있다
	in order	정리된
20	occasion	행사
	permission	허락
	spill	쏟다

13 Vocabulary Review

01	all kinds of	모든 종류의 ~
	ball sports	구기 종목
	volleyball	배구
02	discuss	의논하다
	instead	대신
03	motor corporation	자동차 회사
	regret to-V	~하게 되어 유감이다
	recall notification	리콜 공지
	bothersome	성가신
04	previous	이전의
	appointment	약속
	tell a lie	거짓말하다
05	receive	받다
	scholarship	장학금
	envy	부러워하다
06	available	이용 가능한
	adult	어른
	regular train	정기열차
	get a discount	할인을 받다
07	author	저자
	point out	~을 가리키다
08	rude	무례한
	creative method	창의적인 방법
09	be about to-V	막 ~하려고 하다
	scissors	가위
10	national treasure	국보
	invasion	침략
	restoration	복원
11	theory	이론
	blend A with B	A를 B와 섞다

	specifically	구체적으로
	thanks to	~ 덕택으로
12	boastfully	자랑하며, 허풍 떨면서
	competitor	경쟁자
13	construction	건설
	last	지속하다
	removal	제거
14	relieve one's stress	스트레스를 해소하다
	be held	개최되다
15	consumer	소비자
	purchase	구입하다, 구매
	electronic transfer	온라인 이체
	access	접속하다
16	keep –ing	계속해서 ~하다
	forget to-V	~할 것을 잊다
17	conference	설명회, 회의
	leave a message	메시지를 남기다
18	failure	실패
	be wrong with	~에 문제가 있다
	concentrate	집중하다
	be addicted to -ing	~에 중독되다
19	on the way to	~로 가는 길에
	review	비평, 논평
	fantastic	환상적인
20	annual	연례의
	captain	주장

14 Vocabulary Review

	have in mind	염두에 두다
01	two-story	2층의
	latter	후자
	believe it or not	믿거나 말거나
02	be infected with a virus	바이러스에 감염되다
	recover	회복하다
	principal	교장
03	renovation	수리
	seat	좌석
	order	주문하다
04	Never mind.	신경 쓰지 마세요. 괜찮아요
	cancel one's order	~의 주문을 취소하다
	assignment	과제
05	delete	지우다, 삭제하다
	conclusion	결론
	solid	단색의
06	additional charge	추가 요금
	change	거스름돈
07	take days off	며칠 쉬다, 휴가를 내다
	understanding	이해심 있는
	couch	소파
08	stay in	~에 머무르다
	appetite	식욕
	take a blood test	혈액 검사를 하다
09	sweetie	사랑하는 사람을 부를 때 쓰는 호칭
	Are you ready to-V?	~할 준비가 되었니?
	make a reservation	예약하다
10	single room	1인실
	membership card	회원권
	tough	힘든, 거친

11	cancel	취소하다
	catch up on	~을 따라잡다
	champion	우승자
12	strategy	전술, 전략
	negative	부정적인
	awesome	멋진
	dental clinic	치과
13	describe	기술하다
	toothache	치통
14	accidently	잘못해서, 사고로
	separate trash	쓰레기를 분류하다
	dismiss the class	수업을 해산하다. 마치다
15	student union	학생회
	in a row	연속으로
16	preview	예습
	review	복습
	technician	기술자
17	install	설치하다
	inconvenience	불편
	scholarship application	장학금 신청
18	process	과정
	evaluate	심사하다
	in total	총, 합
19	receipt	영수증
	recharge	재결제하다
	record	녹화하다
20	cold sweat	식은 땀
	staff room	교무실

MEMO

MEMO

MEMO

MEMO

MEMO

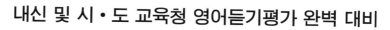

내신 및 시·도 교육청 영어듣기평가 완벽 대비

Listening
올리고
Level 4

중학영어듣기 모의고사

정답 및 해석

01 ③	02 ③	03 ①	04 ④	05 ③
06 ⑤	07 ②	08 ③	09 ①	10 ③
11 ③	12 ④	13 ②	14 ⑤	15 ④
16 ③	17 ④	18 ②	19 ③	20 ④

01

M How may I help you?

W I'd like to report that my daughter's <u>bicycle</u> <u>was</u> <u>stolen</u>.

M When and where did you last see it?

W I haven't seen the bicycle since I <u>locked</u> it to the bicycle <u>rack</u> in my apartment complex at around 5 p.m. yesterday.

M Do you know the <u>brand</u> <u>name</u> and <u>model</u> <u>number</u> of it?

W Unfortunately, I don't remember them.

M Can you <u>describe</u> the bike for me?

W It has <u>a</u> <u>pink</u> <u>frame</u> with a violet basket in front of the handlebars. The <u>saddle</u> and <u>tires</u> are <u>white</u>.

M Any other special <u>features</u>?

W Oh, I almost forgot. It has <u>training</u> <u>wheels</u> because my daughter is young.

남 어떻게 도와드릴까요?

여 제 딸아이의 자전거가 도난당한 것을 신고하고 싶습니다.

남 언제 어디서 마지막으로 그것을 봤나요?

여 어제 오후 5시경 저희 아파트 단지에 있는 자전거 보관대에 그것을 묶어둔 이후로 자전거를 보지 못했습니다.

남 브랜드명과 모델넘버를 아시나요?

여 불행하게도 그것을 기억하고 있지 않습니다.

남 저에게 자전거에 대해 설명해 주시겠습니까?

여 그것은 분홍색 주골격에 핸들 앞에 보라색 바구니가 달려있습니다. 안장과 바퀴는 흰색입니다.

남 다른 특별한 특징들은요?

여 오, 깜빡 할 뻔했네요. 딸이 어려서 보조바퀴가 달려 있습니다.

•• **stolen** 도난당한 **bicycle rack** 자전거 보관대 **apartment complex** 아파트 단지 **frame** 골격 **saddle** 안장

02

M Can I help you?

W Yes, please. I'd like to buy a <u>cell</u> <u>phone</u>.

M I think you'll like this one. It's <u>the</u> <u>latest</u> and most <u>popular</u> smartphone.

W Does this have many <u>games</u> on it?

M Of course. And you have access to more games online. You can <u>surf</u> <u>the</u> <u>Internet</u> at anytime and from anywhere.

W Oh, that's not good. I don't want to let my son <u>use</u> <u>the</u> <u>Internet</u>. Don't you have any <u>feature</u> <u>phones</u>?

M No, I'm afraid not. We only <u>handle</u> smartphones.

W Is there any place that I can buy one?

M You'd better go to a <u>branch</u> <u>retail</u> <u>store</u>. I'll give you the <u>address</u> and phone number of one.

W Thank you very much.

남 도와 드릴까요?

여 네, 부탁드립니다. 휴대전화를 사고 싶습니다.

남 이것이 마음에 드실 겁니다. 최신형에 가장 인기 있는 스마트폰입니다.

여 게임이 많이 들어있나요?

남 물론입니다. 그리고 인터넷으로 더 많은 게임에 접근할 수도 있습니다. 언제 어디에서든 인터넷 서핑도 가능합니다.

여 오, 그건 안 좋네요. 제 아들이 인터넷을 이용하도록 내버려 두고 싶지 않네요. 저성능 휴대전화는 없나요?

남 네, 없습니다. 저희는 스마트폰만 취급합니다.

여 그걸 살 만한 곳 있을까요?

남 직영대리점에 가보시는 게 좋을 것 같습니다. 한 곳의 주소와 전화번호를 드리겠습니다.

여 정말 감사합니다.

•• **feature phone** 피처폰 (저성능 휴대전화) **handle** 취급하다, 다루다 **branch retail store** 직영대리점

03

M Are you a <u>huge</u> <u>fan</u> of movies? The Cinema Theater Insider is our <u>exclusive</u> membership-based <u>movie</u> <u>club</u> which is for behind the scenes access to the <u>latest</u> <u>events</u>, special offers and <u>entertainment</u> <u>news</u> at the Cinema Theater. As a Cinema Theater Insider you will receive exclusive invitations to member-only movie events, access to <u>limited</u> <u>offers</u> for <u>10 tickets</u> to the 'Members' Movie of The Week' for <u>30</u> dollars, and a free personalized <u>weekly</u> newsletter. Join now. It's free.

남 열렬한 영화팬이신가요? Cinema Theater Insider는 저희 영화관 회원들만을 위한 영화 클럽으로 최신 이벤트, 특가 행사, Cinema Theater 연예뉴스에 비공식적으로 접근할 수 있습니다. Cinema Theater Insider로서 여러분은 회원전용 영화 행사 초대장을 받게 될 것이며, '금주의 회원 영화' 티켓 10매를 30달러에 한정 판매하는 것과 무료 개인 맞춤형 주간 뉴스레터를 받으실 수 있습니다. 지금 가입하세요. 무료입니다.

•• **exclusive** 독점적인, 전용의 **behind the scenes** 무대 뒤에서, 막후에서 **limited offer** 한정판매 **personalized** 개인 맞춤형의

04

M Wow! Is this the bag you wanted to buy <u>for so long</u>?

W Yes, I finally <u>bought it</u> yesterday.

M It looks <u>gorgeous</u>. You <u>must</u> <u>be</u> <u>happy</u> to have it.

W I was. But unfortunately, I'm not happy about it now.

M Why? Is there any problem with it?

W I found it for a <u>cheaper</u> <u>price</u> at another store.

M Oh, then why don't you <u>get</u> <u>a</u> <u>refund</u>?

W The clerk said I can't.

M Why not?

W That's because I don't have the <u>receipt</u>. I <u>shouldn't</u> <u>have</u> <u>thrown</u> it <u>away</u> right after I came out of the shop.

남 와! 이게 네가 그렇게 오랫동안 사고 싶어 했던 바로 그 가방이니?
여 응. 나 드디어 어제 샀어.
남 그거 아주 멋진데. 그걸 갖게 되어 틀림없이 기쁘겠구나.
여 그랬지. 그런데 불행하게도 지금은 기쁘지 않아.
남 왜? 무슨 문제 있니?
여 다른 가게에서 저렴한 가격에 그것을 발견했어.
남 오, 그럼 환불하지 그래?
여 판매원이 안 된다고 했어.
남 왜 안 돼?
여 그건 내가 영수증이 없기 때문이야. 가게를 나오자마자 그걸 버리는 게 아니었는데.

① 질투하는 ② 안심되는 ③ 만족스러운
④ 후회스러운 ⑤ 당황스러운

•• **gorgeous** 아주 멋진 **get a refund** 환불받다 **clerk** 점원 **receipt** 영수증 **shouldn't have p.p.** ～하지 말았어야 했는데(했다) **come out of** ～에서 나오다

05

M What did you do last weekend?

W I did <u>nothing but</u> watch DVDs at home. What about you?

M I went to Busan with my family.

W Did you <u>see</u> <u>the</u> <u>sea</u> and have <u>some</u> <u>raw</u> <u>fish</u> at the Jagalchi Market?

M No, we didn't have <u>enough</u> <u>time</u>.

W Then what did you do there?

M We had <u>a</u> <u>family</u> <u>reunion</u> near the Centum City Department Store, which is <u>the largest</u> in Asia.

W Did you go shopping at the department store?

M No, but we enjoyed <u>foot</u> <u>spa</u> there.

W Wow! That sounds cool. Enjoying <u>foot</u> <u>spa</u> at the <u>department</u> <u>store</u>!

남 지난 주말에 뭐했니?
여 집에서 DVD만 봤어. 너는?
남 나는 우리 가족과 부산에 갔었어.
여 바다도 보고 자갈치 시장에서 회도 먹었니?
남 아니, 시간이 충분하지 않았어.
여 그럼 거기서 뭐했니?
남 아시아에서 가장 큰 백화점인 Centum City 백화점 근처에서 가족모임을 했어.
여 그 백화점에서 쇼핑 했니?
남 아니, 하지만 거기서 족욕은 즐겼어.
여 와! 멋진데. 백화점에서 족욕을 즐기다니!

•• **raw fish** 생선회 **family reunion** 가족모임 **foot spa** 족욕

06

W Did you see <u>the</u> <u>latest</u> *Mission Impossible* movie <u>yet</u>?

M Not yet. I heard that it's much more exciting than <u>previous</u> <u>movies</u> in the series.

W　Let's catch the movie tomorrow. What about watching it in the early morning? Then the admission price is reduced.

M　I'd love to, but I'm going to be super busy tomorrow.

W　Well, what are you supposed to do tomorrow?

M　I should go to the library to take an hour-long storytelling lesson beginning at 10 a.m. Thirty minutes after that, I have an appointment with the dentist.

W　And after that?

M　After lunch, I have to go to the nursing home near my house and help clean there. Then, I'll tell some stories to the elderly.

W　Wow, you have a pretty hectic schedule tomorrow. Just let me know when you are free.

··

여　너 최신 〈Mission Impossible〉 영화 봤니?

남　아직 못 봤어. 이전 시리즈의 작품들보다 훨씬 흥미진진하다고 들었는데.

여　내일 그 영화 보자. 이른 아침에 보는 거 어때? 그럼 입장료가 줄어들잖아.

남　나도 그러고 싶은데, 내일은 굉장히 바쁠 것 같아.

여　그럼, 내일 뭘 하기로 되어있는데?

남　오전 10시에 시작하는 1시간짜리 스토리텔링 수업을 받으러 도서관에 가야 해. 수업 끝나고 30분 후, 치과 예약이 있어.

여　그리고 그 다음엔?

남　점심식사 후에, 집 근처 양로원에 가서 거기 청소하는 거 도와야 해. 그런 다음, 어르신들께 이야기를 들려드릴 거야.

여　와, 너 내일 정말 빡빡한 일정이구나. 그냥 네가 시간 있을 때 알려줘.

●●
catch the movie 영화를 보다　**admission price** 입장료　**reduce** 줄이다　**hectic** 빡빡한, 정신없이 바쁜

07

M　I haven't got your essay yet. Did you email me it as an attachment?

W　Yes, of course. I sent it to you the day before yesterday.

M　Is that so? Unfortunately, I couldn't find yours even in the spam mailbox.

W　The address I sent it to was admin@cyjedu.com.

M　Oh, I see. That's why I couldn't get yours.

W　Is it wrong?

M　You should have sent it to admin@cyjedu.net, not with the extension ".com"

W　Oh, I didn't know.

M　Could you just send your essay to me by this evening and then forward to me the initial e-mail you sent to admin@cyjedu.com?

W　Okay, I'll do that.

··

남　네 에세이를 아직 받지 못했구나. 그것을 첨부해서 내게 이메일 보냈니?

여　네, 물론이죠. 그걸 엊그제 보냈어요.

남　그랬니? 불행하게도, 스팸메일함에서도 네 것을 찾을 수 없었단다.

여　제 에세이를 보낸 주소가 admin@cyjedu.com 이었어요.

남　오, 알겠구나. 그것 때문에 내가 네 메일을 받지 못했구나.

여　잘못됐나요?

남　확장자명 ".com" 이 아니라 admin@cyjedu.net으로 보냈어야 한단다.

여　그걸 몰랐네요.

남　오늘 저녁까지 네 에세이를 나에게 보낸 다음 admin@cyjedu.com으로 보낸 처음 이메일을 나에게 전송할수 있겠니?

여　네, 그럴게요.

●●
attachment 첨부　**spam mailbox** 스팸 메일함　**should have p.p.** ~했어야 했는데　**extension** 확장자명　**forward** (편지 등을) 전송하다

08

M　Do you have a 100-won coin? I think we need to push a cart.

W　Here it is.

M　Thank you. What do we have to get?

W　Let me check the list. We need to buy a loaf of bread, milk, butter, and eggs.

M　And I ate all of strawberry jam this morning. Let's get another jar.

W　Okay. How about getting the ingredients for dinner? You said you'd like to have chicken soup, didn't you?

M　You're right. Which section would you like to go to first? What do you want to get first?

W　Well, the items that do not need to be put in the

refrigerator.

M That's a great idea.

W Let's go and get everything.

남 100원짜리 동전 있어? 우리 카트를 밀어야 할 것 같아.

여 여기 있어.

남 고마워. 우리 무얼 사야 하지?

여 목록을 확인해 볼게. 빵 한 덩어리랑, 우유, 버터, 그리고 계란을 사야 해.

남 그리고 내가 오늘 아침에 딸기잼을 다 먹었어. 한 병 사자.

여 알았어. 저녁 재료들을 사는 건 어때? 닭고기 수프 먹고 싶다고 했었잖아, 아니야?

남 맞아. 어느 구역 먼저 갈까? 어떤 것부터 먼저 구입하고 싶어?

여 음. 냉장고에 넣을 필요가 없는 것부터 사자.

남 좋은 생각이야.

여 가서 전부 사자.

① 철물점   ② 공원   ③ 식료품점
④ 빵집   ⑤ 식당

●●
push a cart 카트를 밀다 **a loaf of bread** 빵 한 덩어리 **ingredient** 재료 **section** 구역 **refrigerator** 냉장고

09

W What a nice picture! When did you take it?

M It was on New Year's Day. My family takes a family picture every year on that day. It's an annual event.

W Really? Sounds interesting! So do you always carry it in your wallet?

M Yes. But we also develop a large sized picture and hang it on the wall in the house.

W On the wall? Wow! Where did you hang this year's picture?

M Well, my dad wanted to place it over the dining table in the kitchen. And my mom wanted to hang it over her and dad's bed on the second floor.

W Well, where was it finally hung?

M You know what? I put it in the living room on the first floor. I wanted everyone to see it easily.

W That sounds good.

여 정말 멋진 사진이다! 언제 찍은 거야?

남 새해에. 우리 가족은 매년 그날에 가족 사진을 찍어. 연례 행사야.

여 정말? 흥미로운데! 그래서 항상 지갑에 가지고 다니는 거야?

남 응. 하지만 큰 크기의 사진도 현상해서 집의 벽에 걸어 둬.

여 벽에? 우와! 올해 사진은 어디에 걸었어?

남 어. 아빠는 주방의 식탁 위에 두기를 원하셨어. 그런데 엄마는 2층에 있는 엄마, 아빠 침대 위쪽에 걸고 싶어 하셨지.

여 그럼 최종적으로 어디에 걸렸어?

남 그거 알아? 내가 1층에 있는 거실에 걸었어. 모두가 쉽게 볼 수 있었으면 해서.

여 좋네.

●●
take a picture 사진을 찍다 **annual event** 연례행사 **develop a picture** 사진을 현상하다 **dining table** 식탁 **over** ~위쪽에

10

M Jaeil's Fitness Center, which opened on August 28, 2011, is the biggest and has the latest equipment in the city. It is open from 6am till 11pm on weekdays, and from 7am to 9pm on weekends for your convenience. We offer a variety of free programs like yoga, Pilates, and aerobics. It is located on 5th Avenue. If you have any questions, please contact us at 02-702-9896. Please come and enjoy yourself!

남 2011년 8월 28일에 개장한 Jaeil 휘트니스 센터는 이 도시에서 가장 크고 최신 장비를 갖추고 있습니다. 센터는 여러분의 편의를 위해 주중에는 오전 6시부터 밤 11시까지, 주말에는 오전 7시부터 밤 9시까지 개장합니다. 저희는 요가, 필라테스, 그리고 에어로빅 같은 다양한 무료 프로그램을 제공합니다. 5번가에 위치해 있습니다. 문의사항이 있으시면 02-702-9896으로 연락주세요. 오셔서 좋은 시간 가지시길 바랍니다.

●●
fitness center 휘트니스 센터 **on weekdays** 주중에 **on weekends** 주말에 **convenience** 편리, 편의 **a variety of** 다양한 **be located on** ~에 위치하다 **contact** 연락하다

11

W Hello, Taeyoon. Why are you so busy these days?

M Hello, Mrs. Han. I am going to participate in the Korea Mathematics Olympiad at the end of the month.

W Wow. Are you almost ready?

M Not really. I am trying to solve sample questions

from previous Olympiads, but they aren't easy at all.

W Obviously. How many questions were you able to solve?

M I guess 50% of them. Can you give me a hand to answer the rest of them?

W Hmm… I'll check my schedule and let you know in an hour.

M I'm really grateful for your help.

W Well, I'm not sure if I have any time yet. So don't say that yet.

··

여 안녕, 태윤. 너 요즘 왜 그렇게 바쁘니?

남 안녕하세요, 한 선생님. 제가 이번 달 말에 한국 수학 올림피아드에 참가해서요.

여 우와! 거의 다 준비 됐니?

남 꼭 그렇진 않아요. 이전 올림피아드 문제를 풀어보려고 노력은 하는데 쉽지가 않네요.

여 당연하지. 얼마나 많이 풀 수 있었니?

남 50%쯤이요. 나머지 문제들을 풀 수 있게 도와주시겠어요?

여 음… 내 일정 확인해보고 한 시간 내에 알려줄게.

남 도와주셔서 정말 감사합니다.

여 아직 시간이 날지 확실하지 않아. 그러니 아직 그런 말은 마.

··

these days 요즘에 **participate in** ~에 참가하다 **previous** 이전의
obviously 확실히, 분명히 **give a hand** 도움을 주다 **rest** 나머지

12

W What's the matter? You don't look fine.

M I'm so worried about tomorrow's piano competition.

W Don't worry about that. You've been practicing so hard.

M I really hope I've practiced enough. But… could you give me some tips to relax?

W Sure! Get enough sleep tonight. Never think in a negative way, and you should trust yourself.

M I will try to do those things.

W Then, tomorrow, on the day of the competition, listen to classical music. It will help you calm down.

M Thank you very much for your advice. I'm sure it

will help me.

W I will keep my fingers crossed for you!

··

여 무슨 일이니? 안 좋아 보여.

남 내일 피아노 경연대회가 너무 걱정되어서.

여 걱정하지 마. 열심히 연습했잖아.

남 충분히 연습을 했기를 바래. 그런데… 진정할 수 있는 요령 좀 알려줄래?

여 물론! 오늘 밤에 충분히 자. 절대 부정적인 생각은 하지 말고 너 자신을 믿어야 해.

남 그렇게 하도록 노력할게.

여 그런 다음 내일, 경연 당일에 클래식 음악을 들어. 마음을 진정시키는 데 도움이 될 거야.

남 충고 고마워. 그게 도움이 될 거라 확신해.

여 행운을 빌게!

··

competition 경쟁, 경연 **relax** 휴식을 취하다 **negative** 부정적인
trust 믿다 **calm down** 진정하다 **Keep my fingers crossed for
you!** 행운을 빌게!

13

M Are you done with submitting your university application form?

W Yes, I finally have applied to a university. It was hard to pick one.

M How did you choose the university that you applied to?

W Well, first, the cost of the yearly tuition. I can't afford to pay more than $4,500 a year, so I excluded those which are more expensive.

M What about your major? You were interested in education, weren't you?

W Yes, I was. But recently, I have become more interested in psychology, so I chose it.

M I didn't know about that. Is there anything else that is important?

W I think it would be good to choose one with a dormitory, but the availability of a scholarship is more important.

M Wow! What good thinking! I'm sure you will be accepted. Good luck!

··

대학	전공	연간 학비(달러)	기숙사	장학금
①	심리학	4,900	○	○
②	심리학	4,400	X	○
③	심리학	4,200	○	X
④	교육학	5,400	X	○
⑤	교육학	4,200	○	X

남 대학 지원서 제출 다 했니?

여 응. 마침내 한 대학에 지원했어. 하나를 고르기 힘들었어.

남 네가 지원한 대학은 어떻게 선택했어?

여 음. 첫째로, 연간 학비. 나는 한 해에 4,500달러 이상을 낼 여유가 없어서 더 비싼 곳들은 제외시켰어.

남 전공은? 교육학에 관심 있었잖아, 아닌가?

여 응, 맞아. 그런데 최근에 심리학에 관심이 더 있어서 그것으로 선택했어.

남 그것에 대해서는 몰랐네. 그밖에 중요한 것이 있어?

여 기숙사가 있는 곳을 택하는 게 좋겠지만 장학금을 받을 수 있는지가 더 중요하다고 생각해.

남 우와! 훌륭한 생각인걸! 넌 분명 합격할거야. 행운을 빌어!

•• **submit** 제출하다 **application form** 지원서 **tuition** 수업, 수업료 **can't afford to-V** ~할 여유가 없다 **exclude** 제외시키다 **education** 교육학 **psychology** 심리학 **dormitory** 기숙사 **scholarship** 장학금

14

M What's wrong, Dahee? You look worried.

W Oh, Hanul. I left my cell phone somewhere around here.

M How did that happen? Wasn't it in your hand?

W Right. I was holding it a little while ago, but…

M I remember. I saw you holding it. Did you look in your pockets and bag?

W Of course I did. I didn't find it. What should I do?

M Why don't you call your cell phone? Someone might answer it.

W I already did that, too. No one answered it.

M Then, let's go to the customer service center. They might have it.

W Okay.

남 다희야, 무슨 일이니? 걱정이 있어 보이네.

여 오, 하늘아. 나 여기 어딘가에 핸드폰을 떨어뜨린 것 같아.

남 어떻게 된 일이지? 네 손에 있지 않았어?

여 맞아. 방금 전에 손에 들고 있었는데…

남 기억 나. 네가 들고 있는 거 봤어. 주머니나 가방 속 찾아봤어?

여 물론 했지. 없어. 어떻게 해야 하지?

남 네 핸드폰에 전화해 보는 게 어때? 누군가가 전화를 받을 수 있잖아.

여 그것도 벌써 해봤어. 아무도 전화를 안 받아.

남 그러면 고객 서비스 센터에 가자. 가지고 있을 지도 몰라.

여 알았어.

•• **drop** 떨어뜨리다 **somewhere around here** 여기 근처 어딘가에 **a little while ago** 방금 **No one** 아무도 ~않다 **customer service center** 고객 서비스 센터

15

M The Boryeong Mud Festival in Korea is held on Daecheon Beach every year in July. Direct buses do run from Seoul and it takes about 3 hours to get to Daecheon Beach. If you are coming from one of the big cities in the southeast, be prepared for an even longer journey, more than 4 hours. However, the festival is free and it's awesome! Arrive early in the day or you will miss out on some of the day's fun activities. If you need more information, please visit our website www.Mfestival.com.

남 한국의 보령 진흙 축제가 매해 7월에 대천해수욕장에서 개최됩니다. 직행버스가 서울에서 운행되고 대천해수욕장까지 3시간 걸립니다. 만약 남동쪽의 대도시들 중 한 곳에서 오신다면, 4시간 이상의 더 긴 여정을 대비하셔야 합니다. 하지만, 축제는 무료이고 멋집니다! 낮에 일찍 도착하지 않으면 그 날의 재미있는 활동들 중 일부를 놓치게 될 것입니다. 정보가 더 필요하시다면, 저희 웹사이트 www.Mfestival.com을 방문해 주시기 바랍니다.

•• **be held** 개최되다 **direct bus** 직행 버스 **journey** 여정, 여행 **miss out on** ~을 놓치다

16

W Hey Jackie. What are you doing?

M Nothing much. I'm just relaxing today. Why? What's going on?

W I was thinking about heading to the mall. Do you want to go?

M Are the stores having any sales?

W Yeah. A lot of shops are having end-of-season sales. It's a great time to buy some clothes you've wanted for awhile.

M That sounds great. Where should we meet?

W Why don't we meet in front of ABC Department Store in 30 minutes?

M Sounds good. Then see you there.

여 안녕, Jackie. 뭐 하는 중이야?

남 별거 없어. 오늘은 쉬고 있는 중이야. 왜? 무슨 일 있어?

여 나는 쇼핑몰에 가면 어떨까 하는데. 같이 갈래?

남 상점들이 세일중이야?

여 응. 많은 상점들이 시즌 마감 세일중이야. 네가 한동안 원했던 몇몇 옷들을 사기에 아주 좋은 때야.

남 좋네. 어디서 만날까?

여 30분 후에 ABC백화점 앞에서 만나는 거 어때?

남 좋아. 그러면 거기서 보자.

① 만나서 반가워.
② 좋아. 내일 만나자.
④ 안 돼. 오늘은 쉬어야 해.
⑤ 좋은 생각이야. 한 시간 후에 데리러 갈게.

•• **head for** ~로 향하다 **end-of-season sale** 시즌 마감 세일 **for awhile** 잠시 동안, 한동안

17

M What do you think of these shoes?

W They look comfortable. But don't you think you already have too many pairs of that kind of shoe?

M Yes, that's right. Okay. Let's look at your clothes.

W This sweater is so pretty. I love the low neck design.

M I bet it's expensive.

W It's on sale for 20 dollars. What do you think? Should I try it on?

M Of course, it's a great deal. Go try it on.

남 이 신발 어때?

여 편안해 보여. 하지만 너는 그런 종류의 신발을 이미 너무 많이 가지고 있다고 생각하지 않니?

남 그래, 맞아. 좋아, 네 옷 좀 보자.

여 이 스웨터 너무 예쁜 거 같아. 목 부분이 깊게 파인 디자인이 마음에 들어.

남 분명 비쌀 거야.

여 세일해서 20달러야. 어때? 한 번 입어 볼까?

남 물론이지. 진짜 괜찮은 가격이네. 가서 한번 입어 봐.

① 물론이죠. 이것은 어떠세요?
② 진짜 싸네요. 살게요.
③ 몇 개 더 입어봤으면 좋겠어요.
⑤ 맞아요. 하지만, 그것은 입을 만한 가치가 있어요.

•• **try on** ~을 (시험 삼아) 입어보다 **bargain** 거래

18

M Hey, how was your summer vacation?

W It was not that good because I worked over the summer at a restaurant to make enough money for my tuition. What did you do?

M I went to summer school. I withdrew from two of my classes last year so I wanted to make them up.

W So are you officially a junior now?

M Yes. By the way, where is Stacy?

W She has dropped out of school completely.

M Really? Why?

W Her summer job turned into full-time work.

남 안녕, 여름방학 어떻게 보냈어?

여 수업료를 벌기 위해서 여름 동안 음식점에서 일했기 때문에 그렇게 좋지 않았어. 넌 뭘 했니?

남 여름학기 수업을 들었어. 작년에 수강신청을 취소한 과목이 두 개 있어서 그 과목들을 보충하고 싶었거든.

여 그래서 너 이제 정식으로 3학년이 된 거야?

남 응. 그런데 Stacy는 어디에 있어?

여 그녀는 완전히 학교를 중퇴했어.

남 정말? 왜?

여 그녀의 여름 직장이 정규직으로 바뀌었거든.

① 그녀는 가능한 한 열심히 공부하기를 원했어.
③ 나는 그녀에게 학업에 집중하라고 충고했어.
④ 그녀도 수업료를 벌려고 일했어.
⑤ 그녀가 정부로부터 장학금을 받았기 때문이야.

•• **withdraw from** ~에서 철수하다 **make up** 만회하다, 보충하다 **drop out of** ~에서 중도하차하다 **turn into** ~로 바뀌다 **full-time work** 정규직

19

M Your bracelet <u>looks</u> <u>awesome</u>. When did you get it?

W I got it a few days ago, but I <u>haven't</u> <u>worn</u> it much.

M It's <u>gorgeous</u>. Is it white gold or silver?

W It's white gold.

M Where did you buy it?

W My boyfriend <u>took</u> <u>me</u> to the jewelry shop and <u>let</u> me <u>pick</u> <u>it</u> <u>out</u>.

M That's so sweet. Was it for <u>anything</u> <u>special</u>?

W <u>No, he just wanted to buy me something.</u>

남 네 팔찌 멋지다. 언제 샀니?

여 며칠 전에. 하지만 자주 차지는 않았어.

남 아주 아름다워. 백금이니 아니면 은이니?

여 백금이야.

남 어디서 구입했니?

여 내 남자친구가 나를 보석가게로 데려가서 그것을 고르게 했어.

남 너무 멋지다. 특별한 뭔가를 위한 것이었어?

여 <u>아니, 그는 나에게 그냥 뭔가를 사주고 싶었대.</u>

① 그는 그 팔찌에 100달러를 지불했어.

② 그래, 나는 그에게 말끔한 넥타이를 사줬어.

④ 그들의 일주년 결혼기념일이 12월 23일이야.

⑤ 우리는 약혼을 축하하기 위해서 제주도에 갔어.

●● bracelet 팔찌 **jewelry shop** 보석가게 **pick out** 고르다

20

W Greg and Pia are best friends. Greg is really <u>interested</u> <u>in</u> <u>magic</u> so he wants to <u>put</u> <u>on</u> a <u>magic</u> <u>show</u> at the school festival. In order to get <u>more</u> <u>information</u> about magic, he asks Pia to go to the library with him. He wants to check out some books <u>on</u> <u>magic</u> <u>tricks</u>. However, she has a <u>dentist</u> <u>appointment</u> in an hour today. In this situation, what would Pia most likely say to Greg?

여 Greg과 Pia는 가장 친한 친구 사이이다. Greg는 정말 마술에 관심이 있어서 학교 축제에서 마술 쇼를 보여주기를 원한다. 마술에 관한 정보를 더 얻기 위해서, 그는 Pia에게 함께 도서관에 가자고 부탁한다. 그는 마술묘기에 관한 책을 대출하고 싶어 한다. 하지만, 그녀는 오늘 한 시간 후에 치과 진료 약속이 있다. 이런 상황에서, Pia는 Greg에게

뭐라 말할 것 같은가?

① 나와 함께 도서관에 갈래?

② 어떤 종류의 책을 빌리고 싶어?

③ 한 시간 후에 도서관 앞에서 만나자.

④ 미안하지만 나는 지금 치과에 가야해.

⑤ 생각해보자. 그래. 같이 진찰 받으러 가자.

●● be interested in ~에 흥미[관심]가 있다 **put on** (연극 등을)공연하다 **trick** 묘기 **have a dentist appointment** 치과 진료 약속이 있다

Further **S**tudy 정답   p. 14

1 I think this conversation is taking place <u>at a police station</u>.

2 She does not want to <u>let her son use the Internet</u>.

3 The reason is that she found it for <u>a cheaper price</u> at <u>another store</u>.

4 The reason is that he needs it <u>to get a cart</u>.

5 He is planning to <u>participate in the Korea Mathematics Olympiad</u> at the end of the month.

6 It was the cost of the <u>yearly tuition</u>.

7 It is held on <u>Daecheon Beach</u> in Korea every year <u>in July</u>.

8 He <u>withdrew</u> from <u>two</u> of his classes last year so he wanted to <u>make them up</u>.

On **Y**our **O**wn 모범답안   p. 15

A

My Lost Possession	
(1) What did you lose?	my bicycle
(2) When and where did you last see it?	when I locked it to the bicycle rack in my apartment complex at around 5 p.m. yesterday
(3) Can you describe it for me?	It has a pink main frame with a violet basket in front of the handlebars. The saddle and tires are white.
(4) What did you do after you saw it was gone?	I reported it to the policeman.

I'd like to tell you about (1)my lost bicycle. The last time I saw it was (2)when I locked it to the bicycle rack in my apartment complex at around 5 p.m. yesterday. The features of it are as follows. (3)It has a pink frame with a violet basket in front of the handlebars. The saddle and tires are white. After I noticed it had been stolen, (4)I reported it to the policeman.

내가 잃어버린 물건	
(1) 무엇을 잃어버렸는가?	내 자전거
(2) 언제, 어디에서 그것을 마지막으로 보았나?	어제 오후 5시경 아파트 단지에 있는 자전거 보관대에 잠금장치를 해 두었을 때
(3) 그것에 대해 설명할 수 있는가?	그것은 분홍색 주골격에 핸들 앞에 보라색 바구니가 달려있다. 안장과 바퀴는 흰색이다.
(4) 없어진 것을 알아차린 후 무엇을 했나?	그것을 경찰관에게 신고했다.

제 잃어버린 자전거에 대해 말씀 드리고 싶습니다. 제가 마지막으로 그것을 본 것은 어제 오후 5시경 아파트 단지에 있는 자전거 보관대에 묶었을 때였습니다. 그것의 특징은 다음과 같습니다. 그것은 분홍색 주골격에 핸들 앞에 보라색 바구니가 달려있습니다. 안장과 바퀴는 흰색입니다. 도둑맞은 것을 알아차린 후 저는 그것을 경찰관에게 신고했습니다.

B

Getting a Low Grade	
(1) What kind of test was it?	a midterm exam
(2) Which subject did he/she get a low grade in?	English
(3) What were the main reasons he/she got a low grade?	crammed and didn't finish memorizing the main texts in the textbook
(4) What did you tell him/her?	Cheer up! You can do better on the final. I'll give you a hand.
(5) If you were in his/her shoes, what would you do?	I would review and preview every day before going to bed.

I'm going to talk about my best friend who is depressed about getting a low grade on a test. The test was (1)a midterm exam. She got a low grade in (2)English. According to her, the main reasons she got a low score were she (3)crammed and didn't finish memorizing the main texts of the textbook. So I told

her to (4)cheer up because she can do better on the final. And I also told (4)her if she needs my help I will give her a hand. If I were in her shoes, (5)I would try to review and preview every day before going to bed.

낮은 점수를 받고서	
(1) 어떤 종류의 시험이었습니까?	중간 고사
(2) 어떤 과목에서 그가/그녀가 낮은 점수를 받았습니까?	영어
(3) 그/그녀가 낮은 점수를 받게 된 주요 원인은 무엇입니까?	벼락치기/ 교과서 본문 암기를 마치지 못함
(4) 그/그녀에게 무엇이라고 이야기 했습니까?	힘내! 기말에선 더 잘 할 수 있을 거야. 내가 도와줄게.
(5) 당신이 같은 상황에 놓여있다면, 어떻게 하겠습니까?	매일 자기 전에 복습과 예습을 하겠다

저는 시험에서 낮은 점수를 받아 우울해 하고 있는 저의 가장 친한 친구에 대해 이야기를 할 것입니다. 그 시험은 중간고사였습니다. 그녀는 영어에서 낮은 점수를 받았습니다. 그녀에 따르면, 그녀가 낮은 점수를 받은 주된 이유들은 그녀는 벼락치기를 했고 교과서의 주요 문장들 외우기를 끝내지 않아서 입니다. 그래서 저는 그녀에게 기말고사 때 더 잘할 수 있으니 힘을 내라고 말했습니다. 그리고 저는 또한 그녀에게 만일 제 도움이 필요하면 그녀를 도와주겠다고 말했습니다. 만일 제가 같은 상황에 처했다면, 저는 매일 잠자리에 들기 전 예습과 복습을 하도록 노력할 것입니다.

01 ④	02 ⑤	03 ②	04 ③	05 ⑤
06 ②	07 ④	08 ⑤	09 ①	10 ④
11 ①	12 ④	13 ③	14 ③	15 ③
16 ②	17 ⑤	18 ①	19 ③	20 ③

01

M Good morning. How may I help you?

W I'd like to change my hairstyle.

M Have a seat here, please. How would you like your hair done?

W I've decided to cut my hair shoulder length and get a perm.

M Are you sure you want to do that? Your hair is long and pretty.

W Yes. Summer is just around the corner and it's so hot with long hair.

M Okay. Do you want tight curls, or just a little curl at the ends?

W Make it wavy, please. Also, I want it dyed light brown. I hate my black hair.

M Okay. Then I'll cut your hair first.

남 안녕하세요. 어떻게 도와드릴까요?

여 머리 모양을 바꾸고 싶습니다.

남 여기 앉으세요. 머리를 어떻게 해드릴까요?

여 머리를 어깨 길이로 자르고 파마를 했으면 해요.

남 정말 그렇게 하시고 싶으세요? 머리가 길고 예쁜데.

여 네. 여름이 이제 성큼 다가왔고 긴 머리로는 너무 더워요.

남 좋습니다. 꼬불꼬불한 파마를 원하세요, 아니면 끝에 살짝 말리는 것을 원하세요?

여 굵은 파마 부탁 드려요. 또한, 밝은 갈색으로 염색하고 싶네요. 제 검은 머리카락이 싫거든요.

남 알겠습니다. 그럼 커트 먼저 하겠습니다.

●●
shoulder length 어깨 길이 **curl** 둥글게 말리는 머리카락 **wavy** 웨이브가 있는, 물결모양의 **dye** 염색하다

02

M Kate, do you have any plans this Saturday?

W Yes. I have a meeting of my German study club. Why?

M I just want to go shopping with you. By the way, are you studying German to travel to Germany?

W Not really.

M Then, can I ask you the main reason?

W Actually, my boyfriend is German.

M Oh, I didn't know that you have a boyfriend who is German. How did you meet him?

W I met him at a business meeting last year. His company is in a partnership with mine. Anyway, I want to have a conversation with him in German. It'll help me reduce the cultural gap.

M That's a good idea. Good luck to you.

남 Kate, 이번 토요일에 계획 있니?

여 응. 독일어 스터디 동아리 모임이 있어. 왜?

남 그냥 너랑 쇼핑 가고 싶어서. 그건 그렇고, 독일 여행하려고 독일어 배우는 거니?

여 그렇진 않아.

남 그럼 주된 이유를 물어도 될까?

여 사실, 내 남자 친구가 독일인이야.

남 오, 네게 독일인 남자친구가 있는 줄 몰랐어. 어떻게 그를 만났니?

여 작년 회사 업무회의에서 그를 만났어. 그의 회사가 우리 회사와 협력 관계에 있거든. 어쨌든, 난 그와 독일어로 대화하고 싶어. 그러면 내가 문화적인 차이를 줄이는 데 도움이 될 거야.

남 좋은 생각이다. 행운을 빌어.

●●
German 독일어, 독일인 **Germany** 독일 **business meeting** 업무회의 **partnership** 협력관계, 동업관계 **reduce** 줄이다 **cultural gap** 문화적 차이

03

W Ladies and gentlemen, on behalf of the crew I ask that you please direct your attention to the monitors above as we review the emergency procedures. There are six emergency exits on this aircraft. Take a minute to locate the exit closest to you. Should the cabin experience a sudden pressure loss, stay calm and listen for instructions from the cabin crew. Oxygen masks will drop down from above your seat. Place the mask over your mouth and nose, like this. Pull the strap to tighten it. If you are traveling with children, make sure that your own mask is on first before helping your children.

··

여 신사 숙녀 여러분, 승무원을 대표하여 부탁 말씀 드립니다. 비상시 절차를 확인 중이오니 위쪽에 설치된 모니터에 주목해 주세요. 이 비행기에는 6개의 비상탈출구가 있습니다. 여러분 자리에서 가장 가까운 비상탈출구의 위치를 잠깐 찾아보세요. 만약 객실에 급격한 기압 손실이 발생할 때엔, 침착하게 객실승무원의 지시를 들으세요. 산소마스크가 좌석 위에서 떨어질 것입니다. 이렇게 입과 코 위로 마스크를 놓으세요. 줄을 꽉 잡아 당겨서 단단히 조여주세요. 어린이와 함께 여행 중이시면, 어린이를 돕기 전에 먼저 여러분의 마스크를 우선적으로 착용할 수 있도록 하세요.

••
on behalf of ~을 대신[대표]하여 **crew** 승무원 **emergency procedure** 비상시 절차 **locate** 위치를 찾다 **cabin** 객실, 선실 **pressure loss** 압력 손실 **stay calm** 침착함을 유지하다 **oxygen mask** 산소마스크 **strap** 줄

04

M Mom, did you hear that sound?

W I didn't hear anything. What did you hear?

M I heard something stomping about overhead. I can't concentrate on my studying. You can't hear anything right now, but just wait and it'll start again. See!

W Oh, I can hear that. Do you usually hear that sound at night?

M Yes, I think it starts around 11 p.m. I can hear that sound for about 30 minutes every night.

W How long have you heard that sound?

M It has been more than three weeks.

W OK, I'll check. Maybe, the resident upstairs exercises or does something at this time every night.

M Please tell her or him my final exams are next week.

··

남 엄마, 저 소리 들었어요?

여 아무 것도 못 들었는데. 무슨 소릴 들은 거니?

남 제 머리 위에서 뭔가 쿵쿵거리는 소리를 들었어요. 공부에 집중할 수가 없어요. 지금은 들을 수 없지만 기다려 보면 다시 시작할 거에요.

보세요!

여 오, 들리는 구나. 보통 밤에 저 소리가 들리니?

남 네. 제 생각엔 밤 11시경부터 시작되는 것 같아요. 매일 밤 30분 정도 저 소리를 들을 수 있어요.

여 저 소리를 들은 것은 얼마나 되었니?

남 삼 주는 더 되었어요.

여 그래, 내가 확인하마. 아마도 위층에 사는 사람이 매일밤 이 시간에 운동이나 뭔가를 하는 것 같구나.

남 그분께 제 기말고사가 다음 주라고 말씀 전해주세요.

① 지루한   ② 자신만만한   ③ 짜증이 난
④ 감동한   ⑤ 겁먹은

••
stomp 발을 세게 구르다 **overhead** 머리 위에서 **concentrate** 집중하다 **resident** 거주자

05

M Good afternoon. What can I do for you?

W I'd like to speak to your manager, please.

M May I ask you what it is about?

W There's a problem with the purchase I made yesterday.

M What kind of problem is that?

W The milk I bought yesterday had passed the expiration date.

M Have you brought the receipt and the product?

W Here you are. Have a look at this date on the bottle.

M Oh, I see. Let me check the bar code first so that I can verify it belongs to our market and then I'll call our manager.

W All right. Go ahead.

··

남 안녕하세요. 무엇을 도와드릴까요?

여 매니저와 얘기하고 싶어요.

남 무엇 때문에 그러시는지 여쭤봐도 될까요?

여 제가 어제 구입한 물건에 문제가 있어서요.

남 무슨 문제인지요?

여 제가 어제 산 우유가 유통기한이 지난 것이었어요.

남 영수증과 제품을 가져오셨습니까?

여 여기 있습니다. 여기 병 위에 날짜를 보세요.

남 아, 알겠습니다. 저희 마트의 상품이 맞는지 확인을 위해 우선 상품의 바코드를 확인하고 매니저를 부르겠습니다.

여 알겠습니다. 어서 하세요.

expiration date 유통기한 **bar code** (상품의) 바코드 **verify** 확인하다, 입증하다

06

W Welcome to the European Money Exchange. How may I help you?

M I'd like to exchange Korean won into euro. What's the current exchange rate?

W Let me see. Today's won to euro exchange rate is 2,000 won per euro. May I see some ID, please?

M Here you are.

W How much do you want to exchange?

M I want to exchange 560,000 won.

W How would you like your bills?

M I'd like 2 fifty euro bills, 8 twenty euro bills and 4 five euro bills.

W Okay. Here you go. 2 fifties, 8 twenties, and 4 fives.

M Thank you.

W Have a nice trip!

여 European 환전소입니다. 어떻게 도와드릴까요?

남 한국돈 원을 유로로 바꾸고 싶습니다. 현재 환율이 어떻게 되나요?

여 어디 볼까요. 오늘의 원유로 환율은 1유로 당 2,000원 입니다. 신분증 볼 수 있을까요?

남 여기 있습니다.

여 얼마를 바꾸고 싶으세요?

남 560,000 원을 바꾸고 싶습니다.

여 지폐를 어떻게 드릴까요?

남 50유로 지폐 2장, 20유로 지폐 8장, 5유로 지폐 4장 주세요.

여 네. 여기 있습니다. 50유로 2장, 20유로 8장, 5유로 4장입니다.

남 감사합니다.

여 즐거운 여행 되세요!

money exchange 환전소 **exchange** 맞바꾸다 **current** 현재의
exchange rate 환율 **bill** 지폐

07

W Good evening. What can I do for you?

M Where can I find the sunscreen?

W It's right behind you. And the brand-name cosmetics shops upstairs also sell sunscreen.

M One of these here is fine. Can you recommend a good one?

W Sure. What about this one? It is much more convenient to use especially at the beach because it's a spray type.

M Oh, is it safe? I heard that when using a spray product, I should not spray my face.

W It is safe because there's no gas in it.

M Isn't it sticky?

W No. Give this tester a try. You get one free if you buy two.

M Wow! OK, I'll take them.

여 안녕하세요. 무엇을 도와드릴까요?

남 네, 어디에서 자외선 차단제를 찾을 수 있을까요?

여 바로 뒤에 있습니다. 그리고 위층 유명 브랜드 화장품 상점에서도 자외선 차단제를 팝니다.

남 여기 이것들 중 하나가 좋네요. 괜찮은 거 하나 추천해 주시겠어요?

여 네. 이거 어떠세요? 스프레이 타입이라 특히 해변에서 훨씬 편리하실 거예요.

남 오, 그거 안전한가요? 스프레이 제품을 쓸 때, 얼굴에 뿌려서는 안 된다고 들어서.

여 이것은 가스가 들어있지 않기 때문에 안전합니다.

남 끈적이지는 않나요?

여 네. 이 테스터를 한번 써 보세요. 두 개를 구입하시면 하나를 무료로 드립니다.

남 와! 좋아요. 그걸로 할게요.

sunscreen 자외선 차단제 **cosmetics** 화장품 **recommend** 추천하다
convenient 편리한 **spray** 스프레이, 분무 **sticky** 끈적이는 **tester**
테스터, 시험사용

08

M Look at her! Isn't she so beautiful?

W Yes, she is. Now I know why she is the world's best. Seeing her performance here in the rink is much more exciting than seeing it on TV.

M You can say that again!

W She is performing like a swan. Look at her facial expression and how she dances to the music. Who else can do that?

M No one. She is the best.

W I like her splendid and colorful costume.

M You sound like you are a big fan.

W Of course. I wish I could jump and turn like her. I actually have a hard time walking on the ice.

M Ha, ha. You're just a beginner. Practice hard. Who knows? You could be more famous than her.

남 그녀를 봐! 정말 아름답지 않니?

여 맞아. 그녀가 왜 세계 최고인지 이제야 알겠어. 이곳 링크에서 직접 공연을 보는 것이 TV에서 보는 것보다 훨씬 흥미로워.

남 말할 필요 없이 사실이야.

여 백조처럼 공연하네. 얼굴 표정과 음악에 맞추어 춤추는 모습을 봐. 누가 저렇게 할 수 있을까?

남 아무도 못하지. 그녀는 최고야.

여 나는 그녀의 화려하고 색채가 다양한 의상이 좋아.

남 넌 열렬한 팬인 것 같아.

여 물론이야. 나는 그녀처럼 점프하고 회전할 수 있으면 좋겠어. 나는 사실 얼음 위에서 걷기도 힘들어.

남 하하. 너는 초보자잖아. 열심히 연습해. 누가 알아? 네가 그녀보다 더 유명해질지.

the world's best 세계 최고의 **swan** 백조 **facial expression** 얼굴 표정 **dance to music** 음악에 맞추어 춤을 추다 **splendid** 화려한

09

① M Why did you apply for our company?

W It's because this is my dream company.

② M Can I have your teacher's phone number?

W It's 010-0099-1100.

③ M How may I help you?

W I'm looking for a formal dress to wear in an interview.

④ M Is this seat taken?

W No, you can sit there.

⑤ M Who's speaking, please?

W This is Susie Kim.

---

① 남 왜 저희 회사에 지원하셨습니까?

여 저의 꿈의 회사이기 때문입니다.

② 남 당신 선생님의 전화번호를 알 수 있을까요?

여 010-0099-1100입니다.

③ 남 무엇을 도와드릴까요?

여 인터뷰에서 입을 정장을 찾고 있습니다.

④ 남 자리 있나요?

여 아니요, 앉으셔도 돼요.

⑤ 남 전화를 거신 분은 누구세요?

여 저는 Susie Kim입니다.

apply for ~에 지원하다 **dream company** 꿈의 직장 **formal dress** 정장 **Is this seat taken?** 자리 있어요?

10

M Are things going well with your new roommate?

W Honestly, not really.

M Why? What's the matter?

W She always listens to loud music late at night, often has a party without telling me, never cleans the bathroom, and uses my things without asking me.

M Why don't you have a serious talk with her?

W I already did. But it didn't work at all.

M That's too bad. So what are you going to do?

W I will try to talk to her again tonight. I don't want to complain, but I can't stand living with her.

M I hope it will work out better this time.

남 새 룸메이트와 잘 지내고 있니?

여 솔직히 말하자면, 아니.

남 왜? 뭐가 문제야?

여 그녀는 밤 늦게 음악을 크게 틀고, 나에게 말도 없이 파티를 열고, 화장실 청소는 전혀 하지 않고, 나에게 묻지도 않고 내 물건을 사용해.

남 그녀와 심각하게 이야기 해보지 그래?

여 벌써 했지. 하지만 소용없어.

남 안됐구나. 그래서 어떻게 할 거야?

여 오늘 밤에 다시 이야기 해 보려고. 불평은 하기 싫은데 그녀와 함께 사는 것을 견딜 수가 없네.

남 이번에는 잘 되길 바랄게.

go well with ~와 잘 지내다 **honestly** 솔직히 **not at all** 전혀 ~가 아니다 **complain** 불평하다 **stand** 참다

11

W How was your weekend, Jason?

M I just stayed at home. How about you, Bella? What did you do?

W I had a <u>terrible</u> weekend. I don't want to think about it.

M Why? What happened?

W Do you remember my best friend, Lisa? I <u>had a big fight</u> with her on Saturday.

M I'm sorry to hear that. Did you <u>make peace</u> with her?

W Not yet. I don't want to <u>say sorry</u>, though. I don't think I did anything wrong.

M <u>If I were you</u>, I would call her and <u>set up a time</u> to meet. You should solve the problem by talking.

W Thanks. I will do that.

여 Jason, 주말 어땠어?

남 그냥 집에 있었어. Bella, 너는? 뭐했어?

여 끔찍한 주말을 보냈어. 생각도 하고 싶지 않아.

남 왜? 무슨 일이 있었는데?

여 내 가장 친한 친구 Lisa 기억나? 토요일에 그녀와 크게 싸웠어.

남 안됐구나. 화해는 했어?

여 아직. 하지만 미안하다고 하기 싫어. 내가 잘못했다고 생각하지 않아.

남 만일 내가 너라면, 그녀에게 전화해서 만날 약속을 잡을 거야. 대화로 문제를 풀어야 해.

여 고마워. 그렇게 해 볼게.

•• **terrible** 끔찍한 **have a big fight with** ~와 크게 싸우다 **make peace** 화해하다 **If I were you** 만일 내가 너라면 **set up a time** 시간을 정하다

12

M Good morning! The Dinosaur Exhibition finally opens <u>at the end of</u> this month. Thank you very much for waiting for such a long time. It's <u>open from</u> 9:30 a.m. <u>to</u> 7 p.m. every day. The <u>exhibition</u> has <u>a variety of</u> special events you can enter such as a <u>photo contest</u>, a wax figurine contest and a dinosaur drawing contest. A day pass can be <u>purchased</u> at the ticket booth. Passes are <u>25</u> dollars <u>for adults</u> and <u>15</u> dollars <u>for children</u>. For more information, please visit our website at www. DinoExhibition.com. You can also <u>download</u> a 15% off discount coupon there.

남 좋은 아침입니다! 공룡 전시회가 마침내 이번 달 말에 열립니다. 그렇게 오랜 시간 동안 기다려 주셔서 정말 감사합니다. 매일 아침 9시30분부터 저녁 7시까지 개장합니다. 전시회에는 사진 선발대회, 밀랍인형 경연, 그리고 공룡 그리기 대회와 같은 여러분이 참여할 수 있는 다양한 특별한 행사들이 있습니다. 일일 이용권은 매표소에서 구입할 수 있습니다. 성인은 25달러이며 어린이는 15달러입니다. 더 많은 정보를 위해 저희 웹사이트 www.DinoExhibition.com을 방문해 주세요. 그 곳에서 15% 할인 쿠폰도 다운로드 받으실 수 있습니다.

•• **exhibition** 전시회 **a variety of** 다양한 **wax figurine** 밀랍인형 **day pass** 일일 이용권 **purchase** 구입하다

13

① W You can buy <u>household goods</u> and <u>clothing</u> at the <u>garage sale</u>.

② W The garage sale will be held on <u>November 17th</u>.

③ W You can visit the place from 8 a.m. to 5 p.m.

④ W It is <u>located</u> at 1715 Elizabeth St., Fort Collins.

⑤ W The <u>contact number</u> is 080-0700-0987.

> **Mini의 창고 세일**
> 가구, 가사용품, 책, 옷, 그리고 더 많은 물품들
> 11월 17일, 일요일
> 오전 8시 – 오후 4시
> 1715 Elizabeth St., Fort Collins, Colorado
> 080-0700-0987

① 여 당신은 창고 세일에서 가사용품과 의류를 구입할 수 있습니다.

② 여 창고세일은 11월 17일에 열립니다.

③ 여 오전 8시부터 오후 5시까지 방문할 수 있습니다.

④ 여 위치는 Fort Collins, Elizabeth길, 1715번지입니다.

⑤ 여 연락처는 080-0700-0987입니다.

•• **household goods** 가사용품 **garage sale** 창고 세일 **be held** 열리다, 개최되다 **contact number** 연락처

14

M Why did you come back? I thought you <u>left for</u> work a few minutes ago.

W Another car hit my car in the <u>parking lot</u>.

M Oh, no!

W Yes, the <u>left side</u> of my car is <u>damaged</u>.

M Is there a note?

W No, there isn't. The driver drove off.

M Gosh! You have to call the car insurance company.

W Do you have the number?

M I'll look for it in my address book. Wait a minute. [Pause] It is 070-000-8282.

W Thank you. I'll make the call right now.

남 왜 돌아왔어? 몇 분 전에 출근했다고 생각했는데?

여 주차장에서 다른 차가 내 차를 들이받았어.

남 오, 저런!

여 그래, 내 차 왼쪽이 망가졌어.

남 쪽지가 있어?

여 아니, 없어. 운전자가 가버렸어.

남 이런! 자동차 보험 회사에 전화해야겠다.

여 전화번호 있어?

남 주소록을 찾아볼게. 잠시 기다려. 070-000-8282야.

여 고마워. 바로 전화할게.

●●
damage 손해를 입히다 **car insurance company** 자동차 보험 회사
address book 주소록 **make a call** 전화하다

15

W The Seoul Korean Speech Contest was first held in 1995. The 2014 SKSC is the 20th contest. Students learning Korean at universities and language schools present their speeches in three categories: beginner, intermediate, and advanced. SKSC has been the most successful Korean speech contest in Seoul since it began. SKSC attracts more than 50 participants every year and the first prize winners are entitled to participate in the National Korean Speech Contest.

여 Seoul Korean Speech Contest는 1995년에 처음 개최되었습니다. 2014년의 SKSC는 20번째 대회입니다. 대학교와 어학원에서 한국어를 공부하는 학생들은 말하기를 세 개의 분야, 즉 초급, 중급, 고급으로 나누어 발표합니다. SKSC는 시작한 이래로 서울에서 가장 성공적인 대회가 되어 왔습니다. SKSC는 매년 50명 이상의 참가자들이 참여하고 1등 수상자는 National Korean Speech Contest에 참여할 자격을 부여 받습니다.

●●
category 부류, 유형 **attract** 끌다, 모으다 **participant** 참가자

16

M When does registration for the summer session begin?

W It begins on Monday, February 17.

M What classes are you planning to take?

W I really want to take the History of Art, but I don't know if it will be available.

M Is the class really that popular?

W Yes. I tried to get in last semester, but it was full by the time I had registered.

M What other classes are you going to take?

W I still need to take English 201, but I really don't like writing.

M I took that class already. There is a lot of writing, but it's not that bad.

W Oh really? Who was the instructor?

남 여름 학기 등록은 언제 시작하니?

여 2월 17일 월요일에 시작해.

남 어떤 수업을 수강할 계획이니?

여 미술사를 정말 수강하고 싶지만 수강할 수 있을지 모르겠어.

남 그 강의가 그렇게 인기가 많니?

여 응. 지난 학기에 등록하려고 노력했는데 내가 등록하려고 할 때 이미 정원이 찼더라구.

남 다른 수업들은 뭘 들을 거야?

여 영어 201을 수강해야 하는데, 작문은 정말 싫어.

남 나는 이미 그 수업을 들었어. 작문이 많기는 하지만 그렇게 나쁘지는 않아.

여 정말? 강사가 누구였어?

① 왜 미술사를 수강했니?
③ 어떤 강습 프로그램을 수강했니?
④ 나는 생물학 101과 작문 201 둘다 수강했어.
⑤ 가을 학기 등록은 언제 할 수 있니?

●●
registration 등록 **available** 이용 가능한 **instructor** 강사

17

W Willy, do you live near Green Park?

M Yes, how do you know?

W I saw you the other day walking your dog. You have a beagle, don't you?

M Exactly right. You seem to know the different types of dogs.

W Actually, I don't. My cousin is raising a beagle so it's the only dog that I can tell from the others. Your dog looked well-trained.

M Yes, he seems to understand almost every word I say to him.

W How did you train him? Did you use any special method?

M Actually, I adopted him from the animal shelter two weeks ago.

W Why was such a well-trained dog abandoned?

. . . .

여 Willy. 너 Green Park 근처에 사니?

남 응. 어떻게 알았어?

여 며칠 전에 네가 개를 산책시키는 걸 봤어. 비글종이지, 그렇지 않니?

남 맞아. 너 개의 다른 종에 대해서 아는 것 같구나.

여 실은 그렇지 않아. 내 사촌이 비글을 길러서 그것은 내가 구별할 수 있는 유일한 종이야. 너의 개는 훈련이 잘 된 것 같더라.

남 응. 그는 내가 말하는 거의 모든 말을 이해하는 것 같아.

여 어떻게 훈련시켰니. 특별한 방법을 사용했니?

남 사실, 이 주 전에 그를 동물보호소에서 입양했어.

여 그렇게 잘 훈련된 개가 왜 버려졌을까?

① 유감이야.

② 나는 한 주에 두번 개를 산책시킨다.

③ 너의 개처럼 비글을 사고 싶어.

④ 나는 어떤 환경에도 잘 적응한다.

●●
the other day 일전에. 며칠 전에 **raise** 키우다. 기르다 **tell A from B** A와 B를 구별하다 **adopt** 입양하다 **animal shelter** 동물 보호소
abandon 버리다

18

M Hi, Susan. This is Jim. What are you doing?

W Oh, hi. I have just been reading a book.

M Is it interesting?

W Not really. Since I have nothing to do, I'm trying to read it but it's boring.

M Then let's get together and do something.

W I'd like to, but I have to meet my uncle and aunt in an hour for dinner. How about tomorrow?

M All right. Let's plan something for tomorrow.

W Did you hear the weather forecast for tomorrow?

M It says it will be the same as today.

. . . .

남 안녕, Susan. 나 Jim이야. 뭐하고 있는 중이니?

여 오, 안녕. 그냥 책 읽고 있었어.

남 재미있니?

여 별로. 할 일이 없어서 책을 읽고 있긴 한데 지루해.

남 그럼 만나서 뭔가 하자.

여 그러고 싶지만, 한 시간 후에 저녁을 먹기 위해서 삼촌과 숙모를 만나야 해. 내일은 어때?

남 괜찮아. 내일 뭘 할지 계획을 세우자.

여 내일 일기예보 들었니?

남 오늘과 같을 거라고 하더라.

② 내일 비가 온다면, 집에 있자.

③ 우리가 무엇을 할지 네가 정할 수 있어.

④ 안에 있으면서 책 읽는 거 어때?

⑤ 그래, 너는 내일 일기 예보를 들어야 해.

●●
boring 지루한   **weather forecast** 일기 예보

19

W Hey, Chris! Is that you?

M Yes. How have you been?

W Not too bad. What a surprise to see you here.

M Yeah. It's been a couple of months since I saw you.

W What have you been up to?

M I just started working out.

W Really? How often do you work out?

M At least three times a week.

W What kind of workout do you do?

M I concentrate mostly on doing strength training.

. . . .

여 안녕, Chris! 너니?

남 응. 어떻게 지냈니?

여 뭐. 괜찮아. 여기서 너를 보다니 너무 놀랍다.

남 응. 두 달 만에 보는 거네.

여 어떻게 지냈어?

남 나는 막 운동을 시작했어.

여 정말? 얼마나 자주 운동해?

남 최소한 일 주일에 세 번은 해.

여 어떤 종류의 운동을 하니?

남 나는 주로 근력운동에 집중해.

① 직장에 도착하는 데 대략 20분이 걸려.
② 너와 함께 운동하는 걸 기대하고 있어.
④ 사실, 나는 운동에 흥미가 없어.
⑤ 나는 대개 서류작업을 하고 회의에 참석해.

•• **Not too bad.** (안부인사에 대답할 때) 뭐, 괜찮아. **a couple of** 둘의
work out 운동하다 **concentrate on** ~에 집중하다 **do strength
training** 근력 운동하다

20

M Today Soojin is visiting Seoul for the first time. But
it is <u>not</u> <u>easy</u> for her to find her friend's house as
she is <u>from</u> a <u>small</u> <u>town</u> in South Gyeongsang
Province. There are so many buses and cars on
the <u>street</u>. People in Seoul look <u>so</u> <u>busy</u> that she
doesn't want to <u>bother</u> <u>them</u> to ask for <u>directions</u>.
So she <u>decides</u> to call her friend, Minjung, <u>to</u> <u>ask</u>
<u>if</u> she can come and get her. In this situation what
would Soojin most likely say to Minjung on the
phone?

남 오늘 수진은 처음으로 서울을 방문한다. 그러나 그녀는 경상남도의
작은 마을 출신이라 그녀의 친구 집을 찾기가 쉽지 않다. 거리에는
버스와 자동차가 너무 많다. 서울 사람들은 너무 바쁘게 보여서 그녀는
길을 묻기 위해 그들을 귀찮게 하고 싶지 않다. 그래서 그녀는 친구,
민정에게 그녀를 데리러 와달라고 전화를 하기로 결심한다. 이런
상황에서, 수진은 민정에게 전화로 뭐라고 말을 할 것 같은가?

① 너는 나를 데리러 올 필요 없어.
② 내가 어디로 너를 데리러 가야 하는지 말해줄래?
③ 미안하지만 지금 나 데리러 와줄 수 있어?
④ 너는 나에게 방향을 좀 더 정확하게 말해줬어야 해.
⑤ 미안한데 너의 집으로 가는 길을 좀 알려 줄 수 있니?

•• **for the first time** 처음으로 **bother** 귀찮게 하다 **pick up** (차에)
태우러 가다

1 The reason is that <u>summer is just around the
corner</u> and <u>it's so hot</u> with long hair.
2 She thinks that it'll help <u>her reduce the cultural gap</u>
between her German boyfriend and her.
3 I should <u>place the mask over my mouth and nose</u>
and then <u>pull the strap</u> to tighten it.
4 She <u>had a big fight with her best friend, Lisa.</u>
5 I can enter <u>a photo contest</u>, a wax figurine contest
and <u>a dinosaur drawing contest.</u>
6 He will look for <u>the car insurance company's phone
number</u> in his <u>address book.</u>
7 The reason is that the class was <u>full</u> by the time
she <u>registered.</u>
8 He works out <u>at least three times a week.</u>

A

Making a Complaint about a Product	
When?	(1) last Sunday
Who was the complaint directed at?	(2) at K Mart
What was your complaint?	(3) The milk I bought the day before had already passed the expiration date.
What did you do?	(4) I went to see the manager of customer service with the receipt and the product. (5) I asked for a refund.
What was the result of your complaint?	(6) They had to take the product off the shelves and check its expiration date.

I'd like to tell you about a time when I made a
complaint. The day I made the complaint was (1)<u>last
Sunday</u> and the complaint was directed at (2)<u>K Mart.</u>
What I complained about was that (3)<u>the milk I bought
the day before had already passed the expiration date.</u>
(4)<u>I went to see the manager of customer service</u>

with the receipt and the product. Then, (5)I asked for a refund. Finally, (6)they had to take the product off the shelves and check its expiration date.

제품에 대한 불만 제기하기	
언제?	(1) 지난 일요일
누구를 향한 항의였나?	(2) K 마트
항의 내용은 무엇이었나?	(3) 전날 구입했던 우유가 이미 유통기한이 지났었다는 것
무엇을 했나?	(4) 영수증과 물건을 가지고 고객센터 매니저를 만나러 갔다.
	(5) 환불을 요청했다.
항의의 결과는 무엇인가?	(6) 그 상품을 선반 위에서 회수하여 유통기한을 확인해야만 했다.

제가 항의를 제기했던 때에 관해 말씀 드리고 싶습니다. 제가 항의를 제기했던 날은 지난 일요일이었고 K마트를 향한 항의였습니다. 제가 항의했던 것은 전날 구입했던 우유가 이미 유통기한이 지났었다는 것입니다. 저는 영수증과 물건을 가지고 고객센터 매니저를 만나러 갔습니다. 그 다음, 환불을 요청했습니다. 마침내 그들은 그 상품을 선반 위에서 회수하고 유통기한을 확인해야만 했습니다.

B

Adopting a Pet from an Animal Shelter	
Reason	Supporting example
(1) We can feel proud to rescue an abandoned animal.	(2) If the animals aren't adopted right away, they can be put to sleep.
(3) We can save the money to get cute animals.	(4) Pets from animal shelters only cost a little while pets at a pet store can cost more than 100,000 won.

I agree that we should adopt a pet from an animal shelter for two main reasons. First, (1)we can feel proud to rescue an abandoned animal. For example, (2)if the animals aren't adopted right away, they can be put to sleep. Second, (3)we can save money by getting a cute animal from an animal shelter. For example, (4)pets from animal shelters only cost a little while pets at a pet store can cost more than 100,000 won. In conclusion, I think that we should get a pet from an animal shelter.

동물보호소에서 애완동물을 입양하는 것	
이유	뒷받침하는 예
(1) 버려진 동물을 구조하여 자부심을 느낄 수 있음	(2) 그 동물들이 즉시 입양되지 않는다면, 그들은 안락사 당할 수 있음
(3) 귀여운 동물을 얻으면서 돈을 절약할 수 있음	(4) 동물보호소의 애완동물은 비용이 적게 들지만 애완동물 가게에서는 가격이 십만 원 이상임

나는 두 가지 이유로 동물보호소로부터 애완동물을 입양해야 한다는 것에 동의한다. 첫 번째로, 버려진 동물을 구조하는 것에 대해서 우리는 뿌듯함을 느낄 수 있다. 예를 들어, 그 동물들이 즉시 입양되지 않는다면, 그들은 안락사 당할 수 있다. 두 번째로 우리는 귀여운 동물을 보호소에서 얻음으로써 돈을 절약할 수 있다. 예를 들어, 동물보호소의 애완동물은 비용이 적게 들지만 애완동물 가게에서는 가격이 십만 원 이상이다. 결론적으로, 나는 동물보호소로부터 애완동물을 얻어야 한다고 생각한다.

03 Listening Test 정답   p. 30

01 ②	02 ④	03 ③	04 ④	05 ①
06 ③	07 ④	08 ⑤	09 ⑤	10 ④
11 ⑤	12 ③	13 ③	14 ①	15 ②
16 ①	17 ②	18 ②	19 ①	20 ④

01

M Excuse me. Can you tell me how to get to Union Station?

W You can take bus 384, over there.

M If I take the bus now during rush hour, do you think I can catch my train in an hour?

W If you take the bus now, it will take more than an hour, I guess.

M What about taking a Yellow Cab?

W There might not be a big time difference. How about taking the subway? You have to walk five or six blocks to take it, but it'll be worth it.

M How long do you think it will take to the subway station on foot?

W It'll take about 10 minutes. Go straight this way.

M Oh, that would be much better. Thank you.

....

남 실례합니다. Union역까지 어떻게 갈지 알려주시겠어요?

여 저기에서 384번 버스를 타세요.

남 이 혼잡 시간에 버스를 타면 제가 1시간 내에 기차를 탈 수 있을까요?

여 지금 버스를 탄다면, 적어도 1시간 이상은 걸릴 거예요.

남 택시를 타는 것은 어때요?

여 이 시간대엔 시간 차이가 별로 없을 거예요. 지하철 타는 건 어때요? 그걸 타려면 대여섯 블록은 걸어야 하지만 해볼 만한 가치가 있죠.

남 지하철 역까지는 걸어서 얼마나 걸릴까요?

여 약 10분 정도 걸릴 거예요. 이쪽으로 쭉 가세요.

남 오, 그게 훨씬 낫겠어요. 감사합니다.

●●
rush hour 혼잡 시간대, 러시아워 **Yellow Cab** 택시 **worth** ~할 가치가 있는 **on foot** 걸어서

02

W Are you done preparing for your presentation tomorrow?

M Oh, I won't be doing my presentation tomorrow.

W How come? As far as I remember, your turn is tomorrow.

M You're right, but I traded places with Cindy last night.

W Her turn is the day after tomorrow, isn't it? Do you have a problem?

M Not me but her. I'm finished preparing mine. All I need is just to practice it one last time.

W Then why does she want to do it one day earlier?

M Her grandmother fell down last night. So tomorrow after school, she's going to go visit her for a few days.

W I'm sorry to hear that. Anyway you're so kind to change turns with her.

M That's what friends are for. I'm happy to help her and also to have more time to practice.

....

여 내일 발표 준비는 다 했니?

남 오, 난 내일 발표하지 않을 거야.

여 어째서? 내가 기억하기로는, 네 순서는 내일인데.

남 네 말이 맞는데, 어젯밤에 Cindy와 순서를 바꿨어.

여 그녀의 순서는 내일 모레인데, 그렇지? 너한테 무슨 문제 있니?

남 난 아니고 그녀에게. 난 준비 다 했어. 내게 필요한 건 최종연습 한번 하는 거야.

여 그럼 그녀는 왜 하루 일찍 하고 싶은 거야?

남 어제 밤 그녀의 할머니가 쓰러지셨대. 그래서 그녀는 내일 방과 후부터 며칠 동안 할머니를 방문할 거야.

여 유감이다. 어쨌든 그녀와 순서를 바꿔주다니 너 참 친절하다.

남 친구 좋다는 게 뭐겠니. 그녀를 돕게 되어서 그리고 연습할 시간을 더 갖게 되어서 기뻐.

●●
as far as ~하는 한 **turn** 차례, 순서 **fall down** 쓰러지다

03

W Attention students. On May 8, our school musical club will be staging an evening of song and music in celebration of Parents' Day in the school auditorium. If you have a good voice, we invite you to join us in the concert. This is a great opportunity for you to touch the hearts of many with your beautiful voice! An open audition will be held on March 17 from 10 a.m. to 3 p.m. Kindly register for the audition by emailing us at musicalclub@koreahs.com. The closing date is January 14. Hope to see you at the audition.

....

여 학생 여러분 주목해주세요. 5월 8일 저희 학교 뮤지컬 동아리가 학교 강당에서 어버이날을 축하하는 노래와 음악의 밤을 무대에 올릴 것입니다. 만약 여러분이 좋은 목소리를 가졌다면, 저희는 그 콘서트에 여러분을 초대합니다. 이것은 당신의 아름다운 목소리로 많은 사람들의 가슴을 감동시킬 절호의 기회입니다! 공개오디션은 3월 17일 오전 10시에서 오후 3시 사이에 열릴 것입니다. musicalclub@koreahs.com 으로 이메일을 보내 오디션에 등록해 주세요. 마감일은 1월 14일입니다. 오디션에서 뵙기를 바랍니다.

●●
stage 무대에 올리다 **auditorium** 강당 **in celebration of** ~을 축하하여 **opportunity** 기회 **register** 등록하다

04

M Hi, Amy. Long time no see. How's everything going?

W Not bad. It's been a long time since I last saw you. How are you?

M I'm fine. We only have a <u>few</u> <u>months</u> <u>left</u> before <u>our</u> <u>graduation</u>. Time flies so fast.

W It really does. How's your <u>job</u> <u>search</u> going?

M I finally got a phone call for <u>a</u> <u>job</u> <u>interview</u> yesterday. I'd been waiting for it <u>for</u> <u>three</u> <u>months</u>.

W Wow, good for you. When are you going to have the interview?

M It's <u>next</u> <u>Monday</u>. How about you?

W I've been searching for a job for <u>the</u> <u>past</u> <u>two</u> <u>months</u>, but I haven't had <u>any</u> <u>job</u> <u>interviews</u> yet.

M Sorry to hear that. You'll have good news soon. <u>Cheer</u> <u>up</u>.

W Anyway, <u>don't</u> <u>be</u> <u>nervous</u> and do your best.

M I will. Thanks.

....

남 안녕, Amy. 오랜만이야. 어떻게 지내?

여 그저 그래. 너 본지 오랜만이다. 넌 어때?

남 잘 지내. 우리 졸업이 몇 달 안 남았네. 시간 참 빠르다.

여 정말 그래. 네 구직 활동은 어떻게 되어가니?

남 어제 마침내 인터뷰를 위한 전화를 받았어. 그 전화 3개월 동안 기다려왔었지.

여 와, 잘 됐다. 인터뷰는 언제 할 예정이니?

남 다음 주 월요일이야. 넌 어때?

여 지난 두 달간 일을 구해봤는데 아직 인터뷰를 하지 못했어.

남 그렇다니 유감이다. 곧 좋은 소식 있을 거야. 기운 내.

여 어쨌든. 긴장하지 말고 최선을 다 해.

남 그럴게. 고마워.

① 긴장한   ② 희망찬   ③ 미안한
④ 실망스러운   ⑤ 유쾌한

•• **graduation** 졸업   **nervous** 긴장한   **do one's best** 최선을 다하다

05

[Telephone rings.]

W Hello, East End Community Center. How may I help you?

M Hello, I'd like to <u>take</u> <u>part</u> <u>in</u> your <u>volunteer</u> <u>program</u>.

W What would you like to do?

M Just put me in <u>any</u> <u>urgent</u> <u>place</u> in which you need a hand.

W Okay. Do you have <u>any</u> <u>preferred</u> <u>day</u> to work?

M Yes. I will be happy if I can work <u>on</u> <u>weekends</u>.

W Let me see. Would you be able to <u>deliver</u> free lunches to <u>senior</u> <u>citizens</u> who live <u>alone</u>?

M Of course. I'll do that from this Saturday.

....

[전화벨이 울린다.]

여 안녕하세요. East End 주민 센터입니다. 무엇을 도와 드릴까요?

남 안녕하세요. 자원봉사 프로그램에 참여하고 싶습니다.

여 어떤 일을 하고 싶으신가요?

남 그냥 제 손길이 필요한 급한 분야 아무데나 저를 합류시켜 주세요.

여 알겠습니다. 특별히 선호하는 요일이 있으신가요?

남 네. 주말마다 일할 수 있다면 좋겠습니다.

여 어디 볼까요. 독거 노인들께 무료 점심 배달이 가능하실까요?

남 물론이지요. 이번 토요일부터 하겠습니다.

•• **take part in** 참여하다   **volunteer program** 자원봉사 프로그램
urgent 급한   **deliver** 배달하다   **senior citizen** 노인

06

M Mom, Happy Birthday! This is my present for you.

W Thank you, son. Oh, this is <u>the</u> <u>sweater</u> I <u>tried</u> <u>on</u> at the mall last month.

M Yeah, I know you didn't buy it because <u>you</u> <u>thought</u> it was too <u>expensive</u>.

W Oh, did you go shopping with me? I don't remember.

M Yes, I did. But I was looking at some other stuff and I saw you <u>trying</u> <u>it</u> <u>on</u> from a <u>distance</u>.

W Oh, good boy. You remembered it. Son, thank you so much, but I think <u>100</u> dollars is <u>too</u> <u>much</u> for you to pay for a birthday present.

M Fortunately, they were having an end-of-season sale. I got 50% <u>off</u> and <u>on</u> <u>top</u> <u>of</u> <u>that</u>, I used a <u>15</u> dollar <u>gift</u> <u>certificate</u>.

....

남 엄마, 생신 축하 드려요! 이건 제 선물이에요.

여 고마워, 아들. 오, 이건 내가 지난 달 쇼핑몰에서 입어봤던 스웨터인데.

남 네, 비싸다고 생각하셔서 사지 않으셨던 거 알아요.

여 어, 나랑 쇼핑 갔었니? 난 기억이 안 나는데.

남 갔었어요. 하지만 전 다른 물건을 보고 있다가 멀리서 엄마가 그걸 입어보는 걸 봤어요.

여 오, 착한 녀석. 그걸 기억했구나. 아들, 정말 고맙지만, 내 생각에 100달러는 네가 생일 선물로 쓰기엔 너무 많은 돈 같구나.

남 운 좋게도, 계절 마감 할인행사 중이었어요. 50% 할인을 받고 거기에 더해 15달러 상품권을 사용했어요.

try on 입어보다 **from a distance** 멀리서 **on top of that** 게다가 **gift certificate** 상품권

07

M What can I do for you?

W I need to get some gas. Uh, can I get fifty bucks worth? And can I pay by credit card?

M Sure. Could you please turn around? The tank's on the other side.

W Oops. Sorry. I'll do that.

M Thanks. [Pause] Here's your receipt.

W Could you do me a big favor and check the windshield washer fluid level?

M Okay, pop the hood, please. [Pause] It's a little low. Do you want to fill it up? It's 2 dollars.

W Yes, please. Here you are. Thanks.

남 무엇을 도와드릴까요?

여 기름이 필요해요. 어, 50 달러어치 넣을 수 있을까요? 신용카드로 결제할 수 있나요?

남 물론이죠. 차를 좀 돌려 세워 주시겠어요? 탱크가 다른 편에 있네요.

여 이런. 죄송합니다. 돌릴게요.

남 감사합니다. 여기 영수증이요.

여 부탁 하나 드리려고 하는데 워셔액 수위 좀 확인해 봐 주실 수 있을까요?

남 네, 덮개를 열어주세요. 약간 낮네요. 채우시겠어요? 2달러입니다.

여 네, 넣어주세요. 여기 2달러 있습니다. 감사합니다.

buck (미국·호주의) 달러 **turn around** 돌리다. 돌려 세우다 **washer fluid** 워셔액, 세정액 **pop** 뻥하고 튀다. 열다 **hood** (자동차) 덮개, 후드 **fill up** 채워 넣다

08

W Look! These are so beautiful.

M Which do you like most?

W I can't choose only one but this white lily looks so real.

M Why don't you smell it?

W Really? Hmmm. OK. Wow, it smells like a real lily.

M Of course it does. It just proves that here you cannot distinguish between the real flowers and the artificial flowers by looking at them.

W You're right. Thank you for bringing me here. I feel so refreshed.

M I'm happy that you like this place so much.

W I will buy a bouquet which I can put in my living room.

M I'll buy it for you as a present.

여 봐! 이것들은 정말 아름다워.

남 어떤 것이 가장 좋아?

여 단 하나만 고를 수는 없지만 이 흰색 백합이 정말 진짜 같아.

남 냄새를 맡아보는 건 어때?

여 정말? 음. 좋아. 와, 진짜 백합 향기 같은 게 나.

남 물론 그렇지. 그게 바로 이곳에선 보는 것만으로는 생화와 조화를 구분할 수가 없다는 증거야.

여 네 말이 맞아. 여기 데려와 줘서 고마워. 기분이 정말 상쾌해.

남 이곳을 이렇게나 좋아한다니 나도 기뻐.

여 거실에 놓을 꽃다발을 사야겠어.

남 선물로 내가 사줄게.

① 박물관　　　② 가구점　　　③ 공원
④ 미술관　　　⑤ 꽃가게

look real 진짜처럼 보이다 **distinguish between A and B** A와 B를 구별하다 **artificial flower** 조화 **refreshed** 상쾌한 **bouquet** 부케, 꽃다발

09

M Hello. May I help you?

W I'd like to buy a ticket for tonight's concert.

M Where do you want to sit? The price varies depending on the location of the seat.

W I see. May I see the seating plan, then?

M Sure. Here it is.

W Thanks. I don't like seats either on the side or right in front of the stage. What's the price difference between sections A and B?

M It's $25.

W That's quite big. I'll get one seat in the cheaper

남 안녕하세요? 무엇을 도와드릴까요?

여 오늘 밤 콘서트 티켓을 구매하고 싶습니다.

남 어떤 자리에 앉고 싶으세요? 좌석의 위치에 따라 가격이 다릅니다.

여 그렇군요. 좌석배치도를 볼 수 있을까요?

남 물론이죠. 여기 있습니다.

여 고맙습니다. 저는 가장자리 좌석이나 무대 바로 앞의 좌석은 싫습니다. A구역과 B구역의 가격 차이는 어떻게 되나요?

남 25달러입니다.

여 꽤 크네요. 그렇다면 더 저렴한 구역 좌석으로 하겠습니다.

●●
vary 다르다 **depending on** ~에 따라서 **location** 위치 **seat** 좌석 **seating plan** 좌석배치도 **right in front of** 바로 앞의 **difference** 차이 **quite** 꽤

10

M Are there any special things I have to <u>keep in mind</u> while you <u>are away</u>?

W Of course, honey. I was just <u>about to tell</u> you some things to do while I am away.

M What are they?

W First, please don't wash <u>colored</u> and white clothes <u>at the same time</u>.

M Okay. And?

W <u>Water the plants</u> on Saturday, and don't forget to <u>feed</u> the kitty three times a day.

M I will. I have to <u>wipe the floor</u>, don't I?

W I guess you're asking because you don't really want to do that. But there is a lot of <u>fine dust</u> these days, so you'd better <u>wipe the floor</u> every day.

M Alright. Don't worry.

남 안 계실 동안 제가 알고 있어야 할 특별한 것들이 있나요?

여 물론이지. 지금 막 내가 없는 동안 해야 할 것들을 너에게 말하려고 했었어.

남 무엇인데요?

여 먼저, 색깔 있는 옷과 흰 옷을 동시에 빨지 말아라.

남 네. 그리고요?

여 토요일에 식물에 물을 주고 하루에 세 번 새끼 고양이 밥 주는 걸 잊어선 안 돼.

남 그럴게요. 바닥도 닦아야 하죠, 그렇죠?

여 그건 정말 하고 싶지 않아서 물어보는 거구나. 그렇지만 요즘 미세 먼지가 많으니 매일 바닥을 쓰는 것이 더 나을 것 같아.

남 알겠어요. 걱정하지 마세요.

●●
keep in mind 명심하다, 유념하다 **be away** 부재중이다 **at the same time** 동시에 **water the plants** 식물에 물을 주다 **feed** 먹이를 주다 **fine dust** 미세 먼지 **wipe the floor** 바닥을 쓸다

11

[Telephone rings.]

M Hello, Diamond Tours. May I help you?

W Hello, I want to <u>take a tour</u> of Taiwan <u>next month</u>.

M How many days would you like to stay?

W Five days and <u>four nights</u>.

M Would you like a full <u>package tour</u> or one with lots of <u>options and free time</u>?

W I <u>prefer</u> a full package tour.

M Okay. We have several tours you can choose from. Do you want me to <u>explain</u> all of them on the phone?

W Well, if it is okay with you, please send me the <u>details</u> by email.

M Sure. <u>Give me</u> your email address, please.

W It's hardworker1002@yourmail.com..

[전화벨이 울린다.]

남 여보세요. Diamond 투어입니다. 무엇을 도와 드릴까요?

여 여보세요. 저는 다음 달에 Taiwan 여행을 하고 싶습니다.

남 며칠 동안이나 머무르고 싶으세요?

여 4박 5일이요.

남 전일정 패키지여행을 원하세요, 아니면 선택과 자유시간이 많은 여행을 원하세요?

여 전일정 패키지여행을 더 선호합니다.

남 알겠습니다. 선택하실 수 있는 몇 가지 여행이 있습니다. 전화상으로 그것들을 모두 설명 드릴까요?

여 음. 괜찮으시다면, 이메일로 세부사항들을 보내주세요.

남 물론입니다. 이메일 주소를 알려주세요.

여 hardworker1002@yourmail.com입니다.

●●
five days and four nights 4박 5일 **package tour** 패키지여행 **option** 선택, 선택권 **on the phone** 전화상으로 **detail** 세부 사항

12

M Why are you <u>so exhausted</u>? Didn't you sleep well

last night?

W Not really. I got up too early. I'm a <u>night owl</u>, but I'm trying to change myself into a <u>morning person</u>.

M Why do you want to change?

W I saw a health program on TV a few days ago. The doctor said going to <u>sleep late</u> at night is not good for your health.

M Didn't you know that?

W People had told me before, but I didn't listen. I've been going to bed early and <u>getting up early</u> for three days now.

M It won't be easy to change your habit within a <u>short period of time</u>.

W You're right. But I will <u>put up with</u> being tired and try hard until I've changed my sleeping habits. <u>Wish me luck</u>.

M <u>Absolutely</u>! Good luck.

··

남 왜 그렇게 지쳤어? 어젯밤에 잠을 잘 못 잤니?

여 별로 못 잤어. 너무 일찍 일어났어. 나는 올빼미 족이지만 아침 형 인간으로 바꿔보려고 노력 중이야.

남 왜 바꾸고 싶어?

여 며칠 전에 TV에서 건강 프로그램을 봤어. 의사가 밤늦게 잠을 자는 것은 건강에 좋지 않다고 해서.

남 그걸 몰랐어?

여 이전에 사람들이 나에게 말했지만 듣지 않았지. 지금 3일째 일찍 자고 일찍 일어나고 있어.

남 짧은 시간 안에 습관을 바꾼다는 것은 쉽지 않을 거야.

여 네 말이 맞아. 그렇지만 피곤한 걸 참고 내 수면 습관을 바꿀 때까지 노력할 거야. 행운을 빌어줘.

남 당연하지! 행운을 빌어.

•••
exhausted 지친 **a night owl** 올빼미 족 **a morning person** 아침 형 인간 **put up with** 참다, 견디다 **absolutely** 당연히

13

M Did you <u>book a train ticket</u> to Busan?

W <u>Not yet</u>. I will do it later when I get home.

M Do you want me to do it for you?

W Would you? Thanks. I have to <u>arrive</u> before <u>noon</u> because I have a meeting at 1:00 in the afternoon at BEXCO.

M <u>How long</u> does it <u>take from</u> Busan Station <u>to</u> BEXCO?

W It depends on the <u>traffic conditions</u>, but it will take about an hour, I guess.

M Alright. I'm sure you don't want to <u>arrive too early</u>, do you?

W No, I don't. And I prefer to take first class <u>rather than economy class</u>.

M OK. I'll book a first class ticket for you.

··

열차 승차권 예약				
	목적지	출발시간	도착시간	좌석 등급
①	부산	06:30	10:10	일반실
②	부산	07:10	10:45	특실
③	부산	08:00	11:35	특실
④	부산	09:15	12:47	일반실
⑤	부산	10:20	13:42	일반실

남 부산으로 가는 기차표 예매했니?

여 아니 아직. 집에 가면 하려고.

남 너 대신 해줄까?

여 그럴 수 있어? 고마워. BEXCO에서 오후 1시에 회의가 있어서 12시 전에 도착해야 해.

남 부산역에서 BEXCO까지 얼마나 걸려?

여 교통상황에 따라 다르지만 아마 한 시간 정도 걸릴 것 같아.

남 알았어. 너무 일찍 도착하는 건 원하지 않지, 그렇지?

여 응. 그리고 나는 일반실 보다 특실을 더 선호해.

남 좋아. 너를 위해 특실을 예약할 게.

••
book a ticket 표를 예매하다 **take** (시간이) 걸리다 **depend on** ~에 달려있다 **traffic condition** 교통상황 **first class** 특실 **rather than** ~보다는 **economy class** 일반실

14

M Lora, can you help me?

W What do you want me to do?

M Well, this <u>website won't open</u>. I don't know what I am <u>doing wrong</u>.

W Did you type in the <u>correct address</u>?

M Yes, I checked it <u>several times</u>.

W <u>What about</u> the Internet cable? If it is not connected, the website won't come up.

M　The connection is fine. What should I do?

W　Have you checked for viruses on your computer?

M　No. I'll do it now.

남　Lora, 나 좀 도와줄래?

여　내가 무엇을 해주길 바래?

남　이 웹사이트가 열리지 않아. 무엇을 잘못했는지 모르겠어.

여　주소를 정확하게 타이핑했어?

남　응. 여러 번 확인했어.

여　인터넷 연결선은? 연결이 잘 안 되어있으면, 웹사이트는 열리지 않아.

남　연결 상태는 좋아. 어떻게 해야 하지?

여　컴퓨터의 바이러스는 체크한 적 있어?

남　아니. 지금 할게.

●●
correct 정확한, 옳은　**connection** 연결 상태　**check for virus**
바이러스를 체크하다

15

M　James M. Barrie was a very talented and
successful writer. He was born in Scotland in 1860.
For a time, he worked as a reporter in London.
Then he began to write plays and novels. In 1904,
he wrote *Peter Pan*. This is his most famous and
most popular play. There are some very remarkable
characters in the play, but Captain Hook is by far
the most interesting.

남　James M. Barrie는 매우 재능 있고 성공한 작가였습니다. 그는
1860년에 스코틀랜드에서 태어났습니다. 그는 한동안 런던에서
기자로 일했습니다. 그런 다음 그는 연극과 소설을 쓰기 시작했습니다.
1904년에, 그는 〈피터팬〉을 썼습니다. 이것은 그의 가장 유명하고
인기 있는 희곡입니다. 그 희곡에는 몇몇 매우 주목할 만한
등장인물들이 있지만 후크선장이 단연 가장 흥미롭죠.

●●
talented 재능 있는　**for a time** 한동안　**remarkable** 주목할 만한　**by
far** (최상급 수식) 단연

16

W　Hey Peter. Why are you limping?

M　Oh, hi Sara. I went snowboarding yesterday and
my whole body aches.

W　Was it your first time?

M　Yes. And I never want to go again.

W　I remember the first time I went. My back was
sore, and I couldn't sit down the next day as my
butt hurt so much, and my legs cramped whenever
I walked too fast.

M　That's exactly how I feel now.

W　It's only like that the first couple of times.

M　There won't be a next time for me.

여　안녕, Peter. 왜 다리를 절고 있니?

남　오, 안녕 Sara. 어제 스노우보드 타러 가서 온 몸이 쑤시고 아파.

여　처음 가는 거였어?

남　응. 그리고 다시는 가고 싶지 않아.

여　나도 처음 갔을 때가 기억나. 등이 아팠고 다음 날 엉덩이가 아파서
앉을 수도 없었고, 빨리 걸을 때마다 다리에 쥐가 났어.

남　정확하게 내가 지금 느끼는 증상들이야.

여　처음 몇 번만 그래.

남　나에게 다음 번은 없을 거야.

② 내일 스노우보드 타러 가는 거 어때?

③ 그렇게 느낀다면, 너는 충분한 휴식을 취해야 해.

④ 스노우보드 타기 전에 준비운동을 해야 해.

⑤ 연습을 더 한다면, 너는 전문 선수가 될 수 있을 거야.

●●
limp 절뚝거리다　**ache** 아프다　**sore** 아픈　**butt** 엉덩이　**cramp** 경련이
나다, 쥐가 나다

17

M　You've been sneezing a lot lately. Are you sick or
something?

W　No. Every springtime around April, I'm stricken
with allergies.

M　I never have seasonal allergies.

W　Consider yourself lucky.

M　What are all the symptoms?

W　Well, I sneeze a lot. Also, my nose becomes very
runny, my throat sometimes itches, and my eyes
start to water.

M　That doesn't sound good.

W　No, it's not. So you don't have any allergies at all?

M　Well, I do have an allergic reaction to nuts.

남 너 최근에 재채기를 많이 하는 거 같아. 너 어디 아픈 거니?
여 아니. 매년 4월 즈음 봄철에, 나는 알러지에 시달려.
남 나는 계절에 따른 알러지는 없어.
여 행운이라고 생각해.
남 증상은 어때?
여 음. 재채기가 많이 나. 또한, 콧물이 계속 흐르고, 목이 가끔 간지럽고, 눈물이 나기 시작해.
남 안 좋구나.
여 응, 안 좋아. 너는 어떤 종류의 알러지도 없니?
남 글쎄. 나는 견과류에 대해 알러지 반응이 있어.

① 나는 감기에 걸릴 때마다 재채기가 많이 나.
③ 나는 지난 5월에 두 주 동안 입원했어.
④ 매년 가을마다. 나도 계절 알러지로 고생해.
⑤ 나는 종종 대기오염 때문에 콧물이 흘러.

lately 최근에   **stricken with** ~에 시달리는   **seasonal** 계절에 따른
itch 간지럽다   **reaction** 반응

18

W Did your wife give birth yet?
M Yes. I have a healthy son.
W Congratulations. How is your wife doing?
M She is tired, but taking a lot of rest now.
W That's good to hear.
M I'm just glad there were no complications.
W If your wife and baby are both healthy, what more can you ask for?
M That's right. But it's been a week, and I haven't slept that well since I have to work and take care of my wife and son.
W That's normal and you'll get used to it soon.

여 당신 부인은 벌써 아기 낳으셨어요?
남 네. 건강한 아들을 갖게 되었어요.
여 축하합니다. 부인은 어떠세요?
남 피곤해 하긴 하지만 지금 휴식을 많이 취하고 있어요.
여 잘 됐네요.
남 합병증이 없어서 기뻐요.
여 아내분과 아기 모두 건강하다면, 더 바랄게 뭐가 있겠어요?
남 맞아요. 하지만 일주일이 되었는데 일도 하고 아내와 아들도 돌봐야 해서, 저는 제대로 잠을 못 자고 있어요.
여 그건 정상적인 것이고 곧 익숙해지실 거예요.

① 당신이 좋아하는 일을 가진 것은 행운이예요.
③ 당신은 내가 지금 휴가를 가야한다고 생각하나요?
④ 그들이 언제 병원에서 집으로 오나요?
⑤ 일하는 아내는 그 모든 집안일을 해선 안돼요.

give birth 아기를 낳다   **complication** 합병증   **normal** 정상적인   **get used to** ~에 익숙해지다

19

M What stresses you out the most?
W Probably my parents.
M How so?
W Well, when I was in school, they wanted me to get good grades. And now after getting a job, they want me to get a better job.
M You have to deal with a lot of pressure from your parents.
W Your parents are not like that?
M Ever since I brought home some bad grades in elementary school, they have never expected much.
W You're lucky.
M What do you do to deal with the stress?
W Talking to my friends helps me a lot.

남 무엇이 너를 가장 스트레스 받게 하니?
여 아마도 내 부모님.
남 어떻게 그래?
여 음, 학교 다닐 때는 내가 좋은 성적 받길 원하셨고, 지금 직장을 구한 후에는, 더 좋은 직업을 가지길 원하셔.
남 너는 부모님이 주시는 많은 압박감을 견뎌야 하구나.
여 너희 부모님은 안 그러셔?
남 내가 초등학교 때 나쁜 성적을 받은 이후로는 많이 기대를 안 하셔.
여 넌 운이 좋구나.
남 넌 스트레스를 해소하기 위해 무엇을 하니?
여 친구들에게 이야기 하는 것이 많은 도움이 돼.

② 그 메시지에 대해 고맙게 생각 해.
③ 심호흡하기는 네가 진정하는 데 도움을 줘.
④ 직장에서의 압박이 많은 스트레스를 줘.
⑤ 네 자신의 삶을 살 때라고 생각해.

deal with ~을 다루다. 처리하다   **pressure** 압박감   **expect** 기대하다

20

W Minsu is a college student. He needed to <u>find</u> <u>a book</u> for one of his classes. He went to the <u>library</u> <u>website</u> first to <u>search for</u> the book <u>online</u>. It showed that the book was <u>still available</u>. Today, he goes to the library to <u>check</u> <u>it</u> <u>out</u>, but he can't find it on the <u>shelves</u>. So he goes to the <u>circulation desk</u>. In this situation, what would Minsu most likely say to the librarian?

여 민수는 대학생이다. 그는 강의에 필요한 책 한 권을 찾아야 했다. 그는 온라인으로 책을 찾기 위해서 먼저 도서관 웹사이트에 들어갔다. 그 책은 열람 가능하다고 나왔다. 오늘, 그는 그것을 대출하기 위해서 도서관에 갔지만 서가에서 책을 찾을 수 없다. 그래서 그는 대출대로 간다. 이런 상황에서 민수는 사서에게 뭐라고 할 것 같은가?

① 저는 이미 데이터베이스를 확인해 봤어요.
② 데이터베이스를 사용하는 방법을 저에게 말씀해주시겠어요?
③ 저 서가에서 찾은 책을 빌릴 수 있을까요?
④ 제가 찾고 있는 책을 찾는 것을 도와주시겠어요?
⑤ 당신은 다른 도서관에서 이 책을 대출하실 수 있습니다.

•• **search for** ~을 찾다 **circulation desk** 대출대 **librarian** 사서

Further Study 정답   p. 34

1 It will take <u>more than an hour</u> because it is <u>rush hour</u>.
2 Its purpose is to <u>celebrate Parents' Day</u>.
3 She spent <u>50</u> dollars for <u>gas</u> and <u>2</u> dollars for windshield <u>washer fluid</u>.
4 He has to <u>water the plants</u> and <u>feed the kitty</u> three times a day.
5 She wants to go for <u>five days and four nights</u>.
6 It depends on <u>the traffic conditions</u>, but it will take <u>about an hour</u>.
7 The reason is that he <u>went snowboarding yesterday</u> for the <u>first time</u>.
8 She <u>sneezes</u> a lot and has a <u>runny nose</u>. Also, her throat sometimes <u>itches</u> and her eyes start to <u>water</u>.

On Your Own 모범답안   p. 35

A

My Memorable Volunteer Work	
(1) Where?	in my neighborhood
(2) When?	during the last winter vacation
(3) What?	to deliver free lunches to senior citizens who live alone
(4) How did you begin it?	Minsu, my friend, asked me to deliver the lunches for him after he hurt his leg playing soccer.
(5) Why do you think it is memorable?	The senior citizens who got the delivered lunches thanked me a lot.

I'd like to tell you about the memorable volunteer work that I did (1)<u>in my neighborhood</u> (2)<u>during the last winter vacation</u>. My volunteer work was (3)<u>to deliver free lunches to senior citizens who live alone</u>. I began this volunteer work because (4)<u>Minsu, my friend, asked me to deliver the lunches for him after he hurt his leg playing soccer</u>. The reason why it is memorable volunteer work is that (5)<u>the senior citizens who got the delivered lunches thanked me a lot</u>.

기억에 남는 봉사활동	
(1) 어디서?	우리 동네에서
(2) 언제?	작년 겨울방학 동안
(3) 무엇을?	독거노인들에게 무료 점심을 배달하는 것
(4) 어떻게 그 일을 시작하게 되었는가?	내 친구, 민수가 축구를 하다가 다리를 다친 후 자신을 대신해 점심을 배달해 달라고 부탁했다.
(5) 왜 그 일이 기억에 남는가?	배달된 점심을 받은 노인들이 내게 무척 고마워 하셨다.

우리 동네에서 작년 겨울방학 동안 제가 했던 기억에 남는 봉사활동에 대해 말씀 드리겠습니다. 제 봉사활동은 독거노인들에게 무료 점심식사를 배달하는 것이었습니다. 제가 이 일을 시작하게 된 것은 제 친구, 민수가 축구를 하다가 다리를 다친 후 자기를 대신해 점심을 배달해 달라고 부탁했기 때문입니다. 그것이 왜 제게 기억에 남는 봉사활동이냐 하면, 배달된 점심을 받은 노인들이 제게 무척 고마워 하셨기 때문입니다.

B

The Most Memorable Trip	
(1) Where did you go?	Hong Kong
(2) When did you go?	two years ago
(3) Who did you go with?	with my family
(4) What did you do there?	went to a night market and Disneyland
(5) Why is it the most memorable trip?	It is the first trip everyone in my family went on together.

I'm going to talk about the most memorable trip I've been on. It was when I went to (1)Hong Kong. I visited there (2)two years ago. I went there with (3)my family. I (4)went to a night market and Disneyland. It is the most memorable trip for me because (5)it is the first trip everyone in my family went on together.

가장 기억에 남는 여행	
(1) 어디에 갔는가?	홍콩
(2) 언제 갔는가?	이년 전
(3) 누구와 함께 갔는가?	가족과 함께
(4) 거기서 무엇을 했는가?	야시장과 디즈니랜드에 갔음
(5) 그것이 당신에게 왜 가장 기억에 남는 여행인가?	우리 가족 모두가 함께 간 첫 여행이어서

저는 제게 가장 기억에 남는 여행에 대해서 이야기 하겠습니다. 그것은 제가 홍콩에 갔을 때 입니다. 저는 그곳에 2년 전에 방문 했습니다. 저는 가족과 함께 갔습니다. 저는 그 곳에서 야시장과 디즈니랜드에 갔었습니다. 그 여행이 제게 가장 기억에 남는 이유는 가족 모두가 함께 한 첫 여행이었기 때문입니다.

01 ⑤	02 ④	03 ④	04 ②	05 ⑤
06 ①	07 ①	08 ④	09 ④	10 ②
11 ⑤	12 ③	13 ②	14 ②	15 ①
16 ⑤	17 ④	18 ⑤	19 ③	20 ⑤

01

M Jennie, are you busy this Friday night?

W No, I'm not. Do you want to do something together?

M Yes, there will be an overnight rock festival on Friday night. Let's go enjoy it and watch the sun rise.

W Didn't you go there last year, too?

M Yes, I did. The crowd just went mad with excitement at the festival.

W Well, I'd love to go with you this year. I really like rock music.

M I know. That's why I'm asking you to come with me.

W What should I wear?

M Well, to add to the fun and excitement, the organizers ask everyone to wear the same color or pattern. Last year everyone wore something red, but this year it's blue with white dots.

W Oh, great. I have a skirt like that.

M Unfortunately, it has to be a top.

남 Jennie, 이번 금요일 밤에 바쁘니?

여 아니. 뭐 함께 하고 싶은 것 있니?

남 응. 금요일 밤에 밤샘 락 페스티발이 있어. 가서 즐기고 일출을 보자.

여 너 작년에도 가지 않았니?

남 응. 그랬지. 관객들이 축제에서 신이 나서 열광의 도가니였어.

여 올해 너랑 가고 싶어. 난 록음악을 정말 좋아하거든.

남 알아. 그래서 너에게 나랑 함께 가자고 하는 거야.

여 무슨 옷을 입어야 하니?

남 재미와 흥미를 더하려고 주최측에서 모두에게 같은 색이나 무늬를 입게 해. 작년엔 모두 빨간 옷을 입었지만 올핸 하얀 땡땡이가 있는 파랑이야.

여 오, 잘됐다. 나 그걸로 치마가 있어.

남 불행하게도, 상의여야만 해.

••
overnight 밤샘   **excitement** 흥분, 신남   **organizer** 주최자, 조직자
pattern 무늬

02

M Cindy, I heard that you got hurt a few days ago. Are you okay?

W It wasn't that bad. But anyway I was <u>injured</u> <u>on</u> <u>a</u> <u>bus</u>.

M Tell me what happened?

W The bus I was riding on suddenly stopped <u>to</u> <u>avoid</u> <u>hitting</u> a car <u>cutting</u> <u>in</u>. So I fell down and <u>fractured</u> my arm.

M Are you okay except for the <u>cast</u> <u>on</u> <u>your</u> <u>arm</u>?

W Yes, I didn't hurt anything else.

M Then how long do you have to <u>wear</u> <u>this</u> <u>cast</u>?

W I have to wear it for <u>two</u> <u>weeks</u>.

M You were lucky <u>not</u> to have been <u>hurt</u> <u>seriously</u>.

남 Cindy, 며칠 전에 너 다쳤다고 들었어. 괜찮아?
여 그렇게 심하진 않았어. 하지만 아무튼 버스에서 부상을 당하긴 했어.
남 무슨 일이 일어났었는지 말해봐.
여 내가 타고 있던 버스가 끼어드는 차를 피하려다 갑자기 멈춰 섰어. 그래서 넘어졌고 팔이 골절되었어.
남 팔에 한 이 깁스를 제외하고는 다 괜찮은 거야?
여 응. 다른 데는 다치지 않았어.
남 그럼 이 깁스는 얼마 동안 해야 하니?
여 2주 동안 하고 있어야 해.
남 심각하게 다치지 않아 다행이야.

••
injured 부상을 당한   **suddenly** 갑자기   **avoid** 피하다   **cut in**
끼어들다   **fracture** 골절상을 입다   **except for** ~을 제외하고   **cast** 깁스
seriously 심각하게

03

M Attention, students. To compete in the National Sports Day <u>competition</u> <u>next</u> <u>month</u>, our school will organize several sports teams. So this week we're going to have <u>some</u> <u>matches</u> between classes to find our <u>best</u> <u>athletes</u>. Each class should prepare teams for the school competition next week.

The sports being played are basketball, <u>volleyball</u>, badminton and table tennis. Teachers watching these games will <u>select</u> the school team for each sport. On <u>May</u> <u>25</u> at <u>9</u> a.m. <u>the</u> <u>players</u> on the school teams will be <u>announced</u>.

남 주목해 주세요, 학생 여러분. 다음 달 있을 전국 스포츠의 날 대회에서 경쟁하기 위해, 우리 학교는 스포츠 팀 몇 개를 조직하려고 합니다. 그래서 이번 주에 우수 선수들을 선발하기 위해 반 대항 경기를 몇 번 가질 예정입니다. 각 학급은 다음 주에 있을 학교 선발전을 위해 자체 팀을 준비해야 합니다. 하게 될 운동 경기는 농구, 배구, 배드민턴, 탁구입니다. 이 경기를 지켜보는 선생님들이 각 스포츠의 학교 대표팀을 선발할 것입니다. 5월 25일 오전 9시에 학교대표팀 선수들이 공고될 것입니다.

••
compete 경주하다, 겨루다   **match** 경기, 경주   **athlete** 운동선수
select 선택하다   **announce** 알리다, 발표하다

04

W Hey, Tom. What are you doing? Are you <u>looking</u> <u>for</u> something?

M Yeah, I think I <u>lost</u> <u>my</u> <u>smartphone</u>.

W You mean the one you bought last week? Are you sure? I'll call your phone.

M Thanks. Can you hear it ringing?

W Yes, I can hear your ringback tone, but no one is <u>picking</u> <u>it</u> <u>up</u>. Can you hear any <u>sound</u> or <u>vibration</u> around here?

M No, I can't hear anything. I can't find it anywhere. What should I do?

W I'm sure it's somewhere. Have you checked your <u>bag</u> and your <u>pockets</u>?

M Of course, that was <u>the</u> <u>first</u> <u>thing</u> I did.

W Hmmm... Let me <u>check</u> <u>your</u> <u>backpack</u>. Maybe you missed it. See! It was in the <u>inside</u> <u>pocket</u> of your backpack.

M Wow! There it is! Huh, when did I set it <u>in</u> <u>silent</u> <u>mode</u>? Thanks a lot.

여 이봐, Tom. 뭐 하니? 너 뭘 찾고 있는 거니?
남 응, 나 스마트폰을 잃어버린 것 같아.
여 지난 주에 네가 샀던 그 거 말이니? 확실해? 네 전화로 내가

전화해볼게.

남 고마워. 연결음이 들리니?

여 응. 연결음이 들려. 하지만 아무도 안 받네. 이 주위에서 무슨 소리나 진동 소리 안나니?

남 아니, 아무것도 안 들려. 아무데서도 못 찾겠어. 어떻게 하지?

여 분명 어딘가에 있을 거야. 네 가방이랑 주머니 확인해 봤니?

남 물론이지. 그게 내가 가장 먼저 한 거야.

여 음… 내가 네 가방을 확인해볼게. 네가 놓쳤을 수도 있어. 봐! 배낭 안주머니에 있었네.

남 와! 거기 있네! 어. 언제 내가 무음 모드로 설정했지? 정말 고마워.

① 만족한 → 화가 난
② 당황한 → 안심한
③ 지루한 → 깜짝 놀란
④ 걱정하는 → 긴장한
⑤ 신난 → 유감스런

ringback tone 통화 연결음 **vibration** 진동 **silent mode** 정숙 모드. 무음 모드

05

[Telephone rings.]

W World Airlines. How may I help you?

M I'd like to request a vegetarian meal. Could you check if one is available?

W Okay, Sir. Can I have your name and flight number please?

M My name is Greg Norman, flight WA975 leaving Incheon tomorrow.

W Actually, vegetarian meals need to be requested at least two days before your departure.

M Really?

W Yes, but I'll check with the catering department to see if it's possible to order one for tomorrow. Hang on a second.

M Okay. [Pause]

W Thank you for waiting. I'm back with good news. It is possible to have a vegetarian meal tomorrow.

M Thank you so much.

W No problem. Thank you for choosing World Airlines. Have a nice trip.

[전화벨이 울린다.]

여 세계 항공입니다. 어떻게 도와 드릴까요?

남 채식 식사를 요청 드리고 싶습니다. 가능한지 확인 좀 부탁 드려도 될까요?

여 네, 손님. 성함과 편명을 말씀해 주시겠습니까?

남 제 이름은 Greg Norman 이고 내일 인천을 떠나는 WA975편입니다.

여 사실은, 채식 식사는 출발 최소 이틀 전에 요청하셔야 합니다.

남 정말요?

여 네, 하지만 내일 하나를 주문하는 것이 가능한지 기내식 담당 부서에 확인해 보겠습니다. 끊지 말고 기다려 주세요.

남 네.

여 기다려 주셔서 감사합니다. 좋은 소식 갖고 돌아왔습니다. 내일 채식 식사가 가능하십니다.

남 정말 감사합니다.

여 천만에요. 세계 항공을 선택해주셔서 감사합니다. 즐거운 여행 되세요.

request 요청하다 **vegetarian meal** 채식 식사 **catering department** (항공) 기내식 담당 부서. (호텔) 연회 담당 부서

06

W Oh, these are beautiful!

M These stone bracelets have become very popular since a famous actress appeared on a TV show wearing them.

W Yeah, that's why I'm interested in them. Can I have a look to see if you have a similar style to the one I saw her wearing on TV.

M This is exactly the same design she wore. You'll like it a lot.

W Oh, it's beautiful and it really is my taste, too. How much is it?

M The regular price is 50 dollars, but for today only, you can get 30 percent off.

W I'll buy this and the silver one with black stones. Can you gift-wrap the silver one as it's for my mom?

M Okay. How would you like to pay for your purchase?

W I'll pay by cash. Here's 100 dollars.

M Thank you. Here's your change and receipt.

여 오, 이것들 예쁜데요!

남 이 원석 팔찌는 한 유명 여배우가 TV쇼에 하고 나온 이후 인기가 있어요.

여 네, 그것이 바로 제가 그것들에 관심이 있는 이유이죠. 그녀가 TV에 하고 나온 걸 본 그것과 비슷한 스타일이 있다면 한 번 볼 수 있을까요?

남 이것이 바로 그녀가 착용했던 것과 정확히 같은 디자인입니다. 아주 맘에 드실 거예요.

여 오, 아름답고 제 취향에 딱 이네요. 얼마예요?

남 정상 가격은 50달러이지만, 오늘 딱 하루 30% 할인 받으시게 됩니다.

여 이것과 검은 돌로 만든 은제품을 살게요. 은제품은 엄마를 위한 거니까 선물 포장 해주시겠어요?

남 네. 구매하신 것은 어떻게 결제하시겠습니까?

여 현찰로 지불할게요. 100달러 여기 있습니다.

남 감사합니다. 여기 잔돈과 영수증 있습니다.

stone bracelet 원석 팔찌   **appear on TV show** TV쇼에 출연하다   **taste** 취향   **gift-wrap** 선물 포장하다   **purchase** 구매   **pay by cash** 현찰로 지불하다

07

W Excuse me? There are some crumbs here.

M Oh, we're sorry about that. I'll wipe them up right away.

W Thanks. Uh, I was wondering if you had any hot sauce.

M We have some Tabasco sauce.

W That would be great. I'll need a lot though. This food isn't spicy enough for me.

M OK, I'll be right back with a bottle. [Pause] Here you are.

W Thank you very much.

M Is there anything else you need?

W Could I have a refill on my coke, please?

M Sure. I'll be back with it soon.

여 실례합니다. 여기 부스러기가 좀 있네요.

남 오, 죄송합니다. 지금 당장 그것들을 말끔히 닦겠습니다.

여 감사합니다. 어, 매운 소스가 있으신지 궁금하네요.

남 타바스코 소스가 있습니다.

여 그거 좋겠네요. 근데 제가 좀 많이 필요할 것 같아요. 이 음식이 제겐 그다지 맵지 않네요.

남 네, 병째 가지고 오겠습니다. 여기 있습니다.

여 정말 감사합니다.

남 다른 필요하신 건 없으세요?

여 콜라 한 잔 더 부탁 드려도 될까요?

남 물론이죠. 곧 준비해 드리겠습니다.

crumb 부스러기   **wipe up** 닦다   **spicy** 매운   **refill on one's coke** 콜라 한 잔 더, 콜라 리필

08

M Good morning, ma'am. How may I help you?

W Hello. My car is making a funny noise while I am driving. What's wrong?

M Before checking, let me ask you a few questions. Do you remember when the noise started?

W As far as I remember, it started last week.

M Does it happen even when you drive slowly?

W I don't think so.

M Have you ever visited here before?

W No, this is my first time. One of my friends recommended this shop to me.

M Thanks. Please fill out this form and have a seat. I will take a look at it.

남 좋은 아침입니다. 부인. 무엇을 도와드릴까요?

여 안녕하세요. 운전할 때 차에서 이상한 소리가 나서요. 무엇이 문제인가요?

남 검사를 하기 전에 몇 가지 여쭈어 보겠습니다. 언제부터 소리가 났는지 기억하세요?

여 제 기억으로는 지난 주에 시작했어요.

남 천천히 운전 하실 때도 나타나나요?

여 그런 것 같지 않습니다.

남 이곳에 이전에 방문하신 적 있으세요?

여 아니요. 이번이 처음입니다. 제 친구들 중 한 명이 이 가게를 추천해 주었어요.

남 감사합니다. 이 양식 작성해 주시고 앉아 계세요. 제가 점검해 보겠습니다.

① 자동차 전시장   ② 친구네 집   ③ 자동차 운전 학원
④ 카센터   ⑤ 거리

make a funny noise 이상한 소리를 내다   **as far as** ~하는 한에서   **recommend** 추천하다   **fill out** 작성하다   **take a look** 점검하다

09

① M How much is this?

W It's 3,300 won per 100 grams.

② M Where do you want to be seated?

W I'd like to sit by the window.

③ M Please bring me the check.

W Okay. Please wait a moment.

④ M Excuse me. I ordered a steak but you brought me the wrong dish.

W Oh, I'm sorry. I'll be right back with yours.

⑤ M Could you recommend a good Italian restaurant around here?

W How about the one on 23rd Avenue?

---

① 남 이것은 얼마인가요?

여 100그램당 3,300원입니다.

② 남 어디에 앉기를 원하세요?

여 창가에 앉고 싶습니다.

③ 남 계산서를 가져다 주세요.

여 네. 잠시만 기다려 주세요.

④ 남 실례합니다. 제가 스테이크를 주문했는데 잘못된 음식을 가져다 주셨어요.

여 오, 죄송합니다. 손님 것으로 바로 가져다 드릴게요.

⑤ 남 이 근처에 있는 좋은 Italian 식당 추천해 주시겠어요?

여 23번가에 있는 것 어떠세요?

•• **per** ~ 마다, ~ 당 **be seated** 앉다 **by the window** 창가에 **check** 계산서 **order** 주문하다 **wrong** 잘못된

10

M Jessica, are you still watching TV? You've been watching TV for three hours.

W Dad, I need some time to rest my mind.

M I understand. But did you finish all of your homework?

W No, but it will take less than an hour to finish it. I'm almost done.

M Then you should finish it first. Why don't you number the things that you have to do from 1 to 10 according to importance?

W I think taking a rest is also important, Dad.

M You're right. But watching TV for three hours in a row before finishing your homework isn't right.

W Okay. I will go back to my room and finish my homework.

M Good girl!

남 Jessica, 너 아직도 TV 보니? 벌써 3시간째 보고있는 거야.

여 아빠, 머리를 식힐 시간이 필요해요.

남 이해해. 하지만 너 숙제는 다 했어?

여 아니오. 그렇지만 한 시간 내에 끝낼 수 있어요. 거의 다 했어요.

남 그러면 숙제 먼저 끝내거라. 네가 해야 할 일을 중요도에 따라 1부터 10까지 순서를 매기는 것이 어떠니?

여 쉬는 것 또한 중요하다고 생각해요, 아빠.

남 네 말이 맞아. 그렇지만 숙제도 하지 않고 3시간 연속으로 TV를 보는 것은 옳지 않아.

여 알았어요. 방에 가서 숙제 끝낼게요.

남 착하구나!

•• **rest one's mind** 머리를 식히다 **number** 번호를 매기다 **according to importance** 중요도에 따라서 **in a row** 연속적으로

11

M Are you busy these days?

W Yes, I'm busy preparing my presentation for my history class.

M What's your topic?

W The history of traditional Korean clothing, the hanbok.

M Sounds very interesting. Where did you get all of the information?

W I searched the web and got some books from the library.

M Sounds like you did a lot of research.

W I did, but I still need some more books. I could only check out three books. Can you check out some books for me?

M Sure. Just let me know the titles.

W Thanks a lot.

남 너 요즘 바쁘니?

여 응. 역사 수업 발표 준비를 하느라 바빠.

남 주제가 뭐야?

여 한국 전통의상인 한복의 역사에 대한 것이야.

남 흥미롭게 들리는 걸. 모든 정보는 어디에서 얻니?

여 웹사이트도 찾아보고 몇몇 책은 도서관에서 찾았어.

남 조사를 많이 한 것 같구나.

여 그랬지. 하지만 아직 책이 좀 더 필요해. 나는 세 권만 대출할 수 있었어. 내 대신 책 좀 대출받아 줄 수 있겠니?

남 물론이지. 제목 알려줘.
여 정말 고마워.

•• **these days** 요즘 **presentation** 발표 **traditional Korean clothing** 한국 전통의상 **research** 조사, 연구 **check out** (도서관에서 책을) 대출하다

12

M What's next?

W We have P.E. next period. We have a test on shooting a free throw in basketball.

M Are you serious? I'm not ready for it.

W But you often play basketball with your friends after school. What are you so worried about?

M But shooting a free throw isn't easy. I practiced hard, but I'm still not really good. Moreover, we need to make 7 out of 10 shots.

W If you are so concerned, then why don't you go to the school playground and practice shooting free throws during the break?

M That's a good idea. Anyway, I will get changed first in the locker room. I hope not many people are in the playground.

W Hurry up or you won't have time to practice before the test.

M Thanks. See you.

남 다음 시간은 뭐야?
여 다음 시간은 체육이야. 농구 자유투 던지기 시험이 있어.
남 정말이야? 나 준비 안되었는데.
여 그렇지만 너는 방과 후에 친구들과 농구 경기를 자주 하잖아. 뭐가 그렇게 걱정이니?
남 하지만 자유투를 던지는 것은 쉽지 않아. 열심히 연습했지만 아직 잘 못해. 게다가 우리는 10개 던져서 7개를 넣어야 해.
여 만일 그렇게 신경 쓰이면, 쉬는 시간에 운동장에 가서 자유투를 연습하지 그러니?
남 좋은 생각이야. 어쨌든, 먼저 탈의실에서 옷을 갈아입어야겠어. 운동장에 사람이 많지 않았으면 좋겠어.
여 서둘러 그렇지 않으면 시험 보기 전에 연습할 시간이 없을 거야.
남 고마워. 이따 봐.

•• **next period** 다음 시간[교시] **shoot a free throw** 자유투를 던지다 **moreover** 게다가 **concerned** 걱정하는 **get changed** (옷을)

갈아입다 **locker room** 탈의실 **or** 그렇지 않으면

13

M Donna, the spring field trip is on May 22, right?

W Yeah, that's correct. We need to have a meeting either this week or next week to get things ready.

M How about next Tuesday, I mean on the 16th.

W That would be fine but how about this Friday? The sooner the better.

M Then it should be the day after tomorrow. Ah! We can't make it on Wednesday. We have extra-curricular activities on that day, so we will finish late.

W Right. So this Friday is the best day because we don't have any extra-curricular activities.

M Okay. Let's meet in four days and talk about it in detail. Please think about what we have to discuss when we meet.

W That's a good idea. It will shorten the meeting time and we will be more constructive.

M See you then. Bye.

남 Donna, 봄 현장 체험 학습이 5월 22일이지, 그렇지?
여 응, 맞아. 우리 이번 주나 다음 주에 준비를 위한 회의가 필요할 것 같아.
남 다음 주 화요일 어때? 내 말은 16일에.
여 괜찮을 것 같긴 한데 이번 금요일은 어때? 빠를수록 더 좋잖아.
남 그러면 내일 모레여야 하는데. 아! 수요일에는 안 되지. 그 날에는 과외활동들이 있어 늦게 끝나.
여 맞아. 그래서 이번 금요일이 가장 좋아. 방과 후 수업도 없잖아.
남 좋아. 오늘부터 4일 후에 만나서 자세한 이야기 나누자. 만나서 논의할 것에 대해 생각해 둬.
여 좋은 생각이야. 그러면 회의시간이 단축되고 더 건설적일 거야.
남 그럼 그 때보자. 안녕.

•• **field trip** 현장 체험 학습 **either A or B** A 혹은 B **the 비교급 the 비교급** 더 ~할 수록 더 ~하다 **extra-curricular activity** 과외 활동 **discuss** 논의하다 **shorten** 단축하다 **constructive** 건설적인

14

M Are you going to vote in the presidential election?

W When is it?

M It will be at the end of this year, on December 17th.

W I won't be of age to vote by that time. My birthday is on December 18th.

M Oh, no. You have to wait 5 years to vote because of only one day.

W Very funny, but that's the reality. According to the law, 19-year-olds are not mature enough to vote.

M I fully understand how you feel. But allowing teenagers to vote could be dangerous because teens are easily influenced.

W I couldn't agree with you more. I will stop complaining.

남 대통령 선거에 투표할 꺼야?

여 언제인데?

남 올해 연말 12월 17일이야.

여 나는 그 때가 되면 투표할 나이가 되지 않아. 내 생일이 12월 18일 이거든.

남 오, 이런. 단 하루 때문에 5년을 기다려야 하는 구나.

여 정말 웃기지만 현실이야. 법에 의하면 19세는 투표를 하기에 충분히 성숙하지 않다는 거야.

남 네가 어떻게 느낄 지 충분히 이해해. 하지만 10대들은 쉽게 영향을 받아서 투표를 허락하기에는 위험할 수 있어.

여 네 말에 동감해. 그만 투정해야겠다.

vote 투표하다 **presidential election** 대통령 선거 **reality** 현실 **according to** ~에 따르면 **mature** 성숙한 **fully** 충분히 **influenced** 영향을 받는 **I couldn't agree with you more.** 내 말에 동의해 **complain** 불평하다

15

W As parents, we try to do everything to protect our children from dangers. But many parents don't know that their children can be poisoned by peeling or chipping paint in their own homes. Lead poisoning causes permanent learning and behavioral problems. In order to prevent lead poisoning, we should avoid or throw away painted toys and canned goods from foreign countries. Also we should clean our homes as often as possible and teach children to wash their hands after playing.

여 부모로서 우리는 자녀들을 위험에서 보호하기 위해서 모든 것을 하려고 합니다. 그러나 많은 부모님들은 가정에서 벗겨지거나 떨어져 나간 페인트로 인해 자녀들이 중독될 수 있다는 것을 모릅니다. 납중독은 영구적으로 학습과 행동 문제를 일으킵니다. 납중독을 예방하기 위해서, 우리는 페인트칠된 장난감과 외국으로부터 수입된 통조림제품 사용을 피하거나 버려야 합니다. 또한, 우리 가정을 가능한 한 자주 청소를 하고 아이들에게 놀고 난 후에는 손을 씻어야 한다는 것을 가르쳐야 합니다.

be poisoned 중독되다 **lead** 납 **permanent** 영구적인 **behavioral** 행동의 **avoid** 피하다 **canned goods** 통조림 제품

16

M What are you afraid of?

W Nothing really. I used to be scared of a lot of things when I was young, but not anymore.

M Are you afraid of horror movies?

W No. I know they're all fake so there is nothing to be afraid of.

M What about animals?

W None that I can think of. How about you?

M I get scared pretty easily. I'm actually frightened of bees.

W Really? Why?

M Since I got stung last year, I've been afraid of them.

남 당신은 무엇을 무서워하세요?

여 실은 별로 없어요. 어렸을 적에는 많을 것들에 두려움을 느꼈었는데 지금은 아니에요.

남 공포영화 무서워하세요?

여 아뇨. 전부 가짜라는 것을 알기 때문에 무서울 것이 없어요.

남 동물은 어때요?

여 생각나는 게 없어요. 당신은 어떤가요?

남 저는 매우 쉽게 겁먹고는 한답니다. 저는 사실 벌을 아주 무서워해요.

여 정말이요? 왜요?

남 작년에 벌에 쏘인 이후로, 벌이 무서워요.

① 나는 죽음 외엔 어떤 것도 무섭지 않아요.

② 나는 지난 주에 병원으로 실려갔어요.

③ 그들은 귀여워 보이고 우리에게 꿀을 주기 때문이에요

④ 잘 모르겠지만, 뱀을 두려워하는 것은 자연스러워요.

17

M Oh, it feels so cold this morning.

W It sure does. Early this morning my car's windshield was <u>covered</u> <u>with</u> <u>frost</u>. I had to scrape it off before I could drive to the work.

M Who would have <u>thought</u> it could be this cold in late April?

W I know. The temperature was 1 degree Celsius when I <u>woke</u> <u>up</u> this morning.

M Yes, I was <u>freezing</u> as soon as I got out of bed.

W It is never this cold <u>even</u> <u>in</u> <u>March</u>.

M Well, it's forecast to rain this afternoon. <u>It'll</u> <u>be</u> <u>cold</u> and <u>wet</u>!

W How long will it rain?

M <u>Not only this afternoon but the rest of the week.</u>

남 아, 오늘 아침 너무 추워요.

여 정말 그래요. 오늘 이른 아침에 제 차의 앞 유리가 서리로 덮여있었어요. 출근하기 전에 그것을 긁어내야만 했지요.

남 4월 말에 이런 추위를 누가 생각이나 했겠어요?

여 맞아요. 오늘 아침 잠에서 깼을 때 섭씨 1도였어요.

남 네. 침대에서 나오자마자 얼어버리는 줄 알았어요.

여 3월에도 이렇게 춥진 않아요.

남 어, 일기예보에는 오늘 오후에 비가 온다네요. 추운데다 습도까지 높다니!

여 비가 얼마나 오래 올까요?

남 <u>오늘 오후뿐만 아니라 이번 주 내내요.</u>

① 지금 비가 세차게 내리고 있어요.
② 네, 지난 주말에 비가 억수같이 왔어요.
③ 아니요, 맑은 하늘에 따뜻한 날씨가 될 거예요.
⑤ 저는 블루마운틴 국립공원으로 등산 갈 거예요.

18

M Hey, Jane. I heard you are <u>seeing</u> <u>someone</u>.

W Yeah. His name is Andy. I started dating him <u>a</u> <u>week</u> <u>ago</u>.

M That's so exciting. Tell me all about him. Is he good looking?

W I think he's cute but <u>not</u> <u>gorgeous</u>.

M How did you meet him?

W Whenever I went to my neighborhood <u>coffee</u> <u>shop</u>, he was always there. We started talking a couple of times, and he finally <u>asked</u> <u>me</u> <u>out</u>.

M That's so cool. What does he <u>do</u> <u>for</u> <u>a</u> <u>living</u>?

W <u>He works for a company manufacturing car parts.</u>

남 안녕, Jane. 네가 누군가와 만나고 있다는 이야길 들었어.

여 맞아. 그의 이름은 Andy야. 나는 일 주일 전에 그와 데이트를 시작했어.

남 정말 흥미롭다. 그에 관해서 전부 이야기 해줘. 그는 잘 생겼니?

여 그는 귀엽긴 하지만 아주 멋지진 않아.

남 그를 어떻게 만났니?

여 내가 우리 동네 커피숍에 갈 때 마다 그가 거기에 있었어. 우리는 몇 번 이야기를 나눴고, 마침내 그가 나에게 데이트 신청을 했어.

남 정말 멋지다. 그는 무슨 일을 하니?

여 <u>그는 자동차 부품을 생산하는 회사에 다녀.</u>

① 그는 그의 조부모님과 같이 산다.
② 그는 지금 교내 기숙사에 산다.
③ 그는 거실에서 TV를 보는 중이다.
④ 그는 아침 7시에 집에서 나온다.

19

M Good morning, ma'am, can I help you?

W Good morning, I want to <u>book</u> <u>a</u> <u>seat</u> on <u>the</u> <u>flight</u> from Seoul to Daegu at <u>9:30</u> p.m. tomorrow. Are there seats <u>still</u> <u>available</u>?

M Please wait a moment. Yes, there are <u>some</u> <u>seats</u> still available.

W OK. I want to <u>book</u> <u>2</u> <u>tickets</u>. And we want to <u>sit</u> <u>near</u> the front of the plane.

M Can I have the names, please?

W Olivia Brown and Peter Smith.

M <u>How</u> <u>will</u> <u>you</u> <u>pay</u> for the seats?

W I will pay by Visa card.

남 안녕하세요, 부인. 도와드릴까요?

여 안녕하세요, 내일 오후 9시 30분에 서울에서 대구로 가는 비행기편 예약하고 싶어요. 아직 자리가 있나요?

남 잠시만 기다려 주세요. 네, 아직 자리가 있네요.

여 좋아요. 두 사람 자리를 예약하고 싶어요. 비행기 앞쪽 좌석에 앉고 싶고요.

남 이름 말씀해 주시겠어요?

여 Olivia Brown과 Peter Smith입니다.

남 어떻게 지불하시겠어요?

여 <u>비자카드로 지불할게요.</u>

① 저는 그것이 아주 마음에 들어요.
② 표 값은 제가 낼게요.
④ 생각했던 것보다 값이 비싼데요.
⑤ 한 사람당 10만원입니다.

•• **flight** 항공편, 비행편 **available** 이용 가능한 **front** 앞, 정면

20

M Susie's friend, Sally, has started a <u>part-time</u> job so she's had a difficult time <u>keeping</u> <u>up</u> <u>with</u> her classes. <u>Exams</u> are coming up and she doesn't know what to do. She is <u>afraid</u> of <u>failing</u> <u>her</u> <u>exams</u>. Susie tells her that the best thing for her to do is study <u>as</u> <u>much</u> <u>as</u> she can. Sally says that she won't be sleeping for the next 3 days. Susie <u>also</u> has to study for her exams. So Susie wants to <u>ask</u> <u>if</u> <u>she</u> <u>wants</u> to study together. In this situation, what would Susie probably say to Sally?

......

남 Susie의 친구, Sally는 아르바이트를 시작해서 수업을 따라가는 것을 힘들어한다. 시험이 다가오고 있는데 그녀는 무엇을 해야 하는지 모르고 있다. 그녀는 시험에 낙제할까봐 두려워한다. Susie는 그녀에게 그녀가 할 수 있는 최선의 일은 최대한 많이 공부를 하는 것이라고 말해준다. Sally는 앞으로 3일동안 잠을 자지 않을 거라고 이야기한다. Susie 또한 시험 공부를 해야 한다. 그래서 Susie는 그녀에게 함께 공부하자고 물어보고 싶다. 이런 상황에서, Susie는 Sally에게 뭐라고 이야기 할 것 같은가?

① 공부를 더 열심히 하는 게 어때?
② 너와 함께 공부했어야 했는데.
③ 행운을 빌게.
④ 일주일에 한 번씩 같이 수업 듣자.
⑤ 도서관에서 함께 공부할까?

•• **keep up with** ~을 따라잡다 **fail in the exam** 시험에 낙제하다

Further **S**tudy 정답   p. 44

1 The reason was that the bus tried to <u>avoid hitting a car cutting in</u>.

2 The reason was that the man <u>set the mobile phone in silent mode</u>.

3 For her mother, the woman bought <u>a silver bracelet with black stones</u>.

4 Her car is <u>making a funny noise</u> while she is driving.

5 She told the man to <u>go to the playground</u> and <u>practice shooting free throws</u> during the break.

6 They have <u>extra-curricular activities</u> on that day, so they <u>finish late</u>.

7 She knows they're <u>all fake</u> so there is <u>nothing</u> to be afraid of.

8 She wants to book <u>a seat on the flight</u> from Seoul to Daegu at <u>9:30</u> p.m. tomorrow.

On **Y**our **O**wn 모범답안   p. 45

A

When I Got Hurt	
(1) When did it happen?	one Saturday morning last May
(2) What were you doing?	standing in front of the bus door to get off at the library
(3) What happened?	Suddenly the bus stopped to avoid hitting a car cutting in.
(4) What kind of injury did you get?	I fell down and fractured my right arm.
(5) What did you learn?	how important it is to be healthy, and how important it is to obey traffic rules

I would like to tell you about an accident in which I got hurt. It happened (1)<u>one Saturday morning last May</u>.

On that day, I was (2)standing in front of the bus door to get off at the library. (3)Suddenly the bus stopped to avoid hitting a car cutting in. As a result, (4)I fell down and fractured my right arm. Due to the accident, I learned (5)how important it is to be healthy, and how important it is to obey traffic rules.

다쳤을 때	
(1) 언제 발생했나?	지난 오월 어느 토요일 아침에
(2) 무엇을 하고 있었나?	도서관에서 내리기 위해 버스 문 앞에 서있었다
(3) 무슨 일이 발생했나?	버스가 끼어드는 차를 피하기 위해 갑자기 멈춰 섰다
(4) 어떤 부상을 입었나?	나는 넘어졌고 팔에 골절상을 입었다
(5) 어떤 교훈을 얻었나?	건강이 얼마나 중요한지와 교통법규를 지키는 것이 얼마나 중요한지를 배웠다.

저를 다치게 만든 사고에 대해 말씀드리겠습니다. 그 일은 지난 5월 어느 토요일 아침에 발생했습니다. 그날, 저는 도서관에서 내리기 위해 버스 문 앞에 서있었습니다. 버스가 끼어드는 차를 피하기 위해 갑자기 멈춰 섰습니다. 그 결과, 저는 넘어졌고 팔에 골절상을 입었습니다. 그 사고로, 저는 건강이 얼마나 중요한지와 교통법규를 지키는 것이 얼마나 중요한지를 배웠습니다.

B

My Favorite School Subject	
(1) the name of the subject	English
(2) when you started learning the subject	seven years old
(3) a description of the subject	a foreign language that all students learn because it is the most international language in the world
(4) the reason for liking the subject	it has contributed to my overall intellectual growth as it has shown me many different opinions, ideas, and beliefs of people around the world

My favorite school subject is (1)English, which I have learned since (2)I was seven years old. It is (3)a foreign language that all students learn because it is the most international language in the world. The reason I chose the subject is that (4)it has contributed to my overall intellectual growth as it has shown me many different opinions, ideas, and beliefs of people

around the world.

내가 가장 좋아하는 과목	
(1) 과목 이름	영어
(2) 그 과목을 배우기 시작한 때	일곱 살 때
(3) 과목 설명	가장 국제적인 언어이므로 모든 학생들이 배우는 외국어
(4) 좋아하는 이유	전세계 사람들의 다른 견해. 사상. 신념을 보여주므로 내 지적 성장에 기여함

내가 가장 좋아하는 학교 과목은 영어인데, 나는 그것을 일곱 살 이후로 공부해왔다. 그것은 세계에서 가장 국제적인 언어이기 때문에 모든 학생들이 배우는 외국어이다. 내가 그 과목을 선택한 이유는 영어는 나에게 전세계 사람들의 다른 관점. 이념. 종교를 보여줌으로써 나의 전반적 지적 성장에 기여했기 때문이다.

05 Listening Test 정답

p. 50

01 ①	02 ②	03 ③	04 ③	05 ①
06 ③	07 ③	08 ⑤	09 ②	10 ⑤
11 ②	12 ⑤	13 ①	14 ③	15 ④
16 ⑤	17 ⑤	18 ①	19 ③	20 ④

01

M Mommy, I don't feel very good.

W What's the matter, sweetheart?

M I have a stomachache.

W Maybe you've caught the flu.

M I feel like I'm going to vomit.

W What did you eat for lunch?

M Not much.

W Really? What did you have today?

M Let's see. I had a bagel, a can of tuna fish, potato wedges, cookies, soda, and some bacon for lunch.

That's all I had for today.

W No wonder your stomach hurts! It's all that junk food.

남 엄마, 저 기분이 좋지 않아요.
여 무슨 일이니, 아가?
남 복통이 있어요.
여 아마도 독감에 걸린 것 같구나.
남 토할 것 같아요.
여 점심으로 뭘 먹었니?
남 별로 많이 먹지 않았어요.
여 정말이니? 오늘 뭘 먹었니?
남 잠시 생각해 볼게요. 베이글, 캔 참치, 웨지 감자, 쿠키, 소다와 약간의 베이컨을 점심으로 먹었어요. 그게 오늘 먹은 거 다예요.
여 배가 아플 만도 하구나! 모두가 쓰레기 같은 음식이잖니.

stomachache 복통 **catch the flu** 독감에 걸리다 **vomit** 토하다

02

M I'd like to reserve a campsite for next weekend.
W We don't take reservations. It's first come, first served.
M Do you fill up on the weekends?
W Only on holidays.
M What do you charge for an overnight stay?
W 35 dollars per night.
M When do we have to leave the campsite the next day?
W By 2 p.m.
M Can we build a fire?
W You can do that only in the designated area to avoid forest fires.
M Thank you. You've been most helpful.

남 다음 주말에 캠핑장을 예약하고 싶습니다.
여 예약을 받지 않습니다. 선착순입니다.
남 주말에는 붐비나요?
여 휴일에만요.
남 하룻밤 머무르는 비용이 얼마인가요?
여 하루에 35달러입니다.
남 다음 날 언제 캠핑장을 떠나야 하나요?
여 오후 2시까지입니다.
남 캠프파이어를 해도 되나요?

여 산불방지를 위해 지정된 장소에 한해서만 할 수 있습니다.
남 감사합니다. 많은 도움이 되었습니다.

campsite 캠핑장 **first come, first served** 선착순인 **fill up** 가득차다
overnight stay 1박 **designated** 지정된

03

M Attention, please! Sometime between May 10 and June 1 a fire drill will occur at Central Plaza between the hours of 1:30 p.m. and 2:30 p.m. The drill will occur on a Monday through to a Friday. No other prior notice will be given as to what day the drill will take place on. You have to evacuate the building during the fire drill. Please follow all safety procedures appropriately. We do apologize for the inconvenience this may cause you as a result. Thank you for your understanding.

남 주목해주세요. 5월 10일과 6월 1일 사이 어느 때에 소방훈련이 오후 1시30분에서 2시30분 사이에 센트럴 플라자에서 있을 예정입니다. 훈련은 월요일에서 금요일 중 하루에 있을 것입니다. 무슨 요일에 있을지는 사전 공지되지 않을 것입니다. 소방 훈련하는 동안 여러분은 본 건물에서 대피해야 합니다. 모든 안전 절차를 잘 따라 주십시오. 이 소방훈련의 결과로 일어날 수 있는 불편에 대해 사과드립니다. 이해해주셔서 감사 드립니다.

fire drill 소방훈련 **prior notice** 사전 공지 **evacuate** 떠나다. 대피하다
apologize 사과하다 **inconvenience** 불편

04

W Excuse me. Could you help me to find the book 'Introduction to Functional Grammar'?
M Okay. Let me check our computer database. Do you know who the writer is?
W It is written by Michael Holliday.
M Are you looking for the second edition?
W Yes, I am.
M Sorry, we don't have it in stock at the moment. Do you want me to order one?
W How long will it take before it arrives?
M Probably, it will take five days to a week because it

comes <u>from overseas</u>.

W Oh, dear! I'm <u>in trouble</u>. I need it tomorrow.

....

여 실례합니다. 'Introduction to Functional Grammar'라는 책을 찾는 걸 좀 도와 주시겠어요?

남 네, 컴퓨터 데이터베이스를 확인해 보겠습니다. 저자가 누구인지 아세요?

여 Michael Holliday에 의해 쓰여졌어요.

남 2판을 찾고 계신가요?

여 네 그렇습니다.

남 죄송합니다. 현재 재고가 없네요. 제가 주문해드릴까요?

여 그 책이 도착하는데 얼마나 걸릴까요?

남 해외에서 오니까 아마도 5일에서 일주일 걸릴 거예요.

여 오, 이런. 큰일 났네. 내일 필요한데.

① 안심한   ② 겁먹은   ③ 걱정하는
④ 만족하는   ⑤ 무관심한

●●
second edition 2판 **in stock** 재고가 있는 **overseas** 해외 **in trouble** 난처한, 곤경에 빠진

05

[Telephone rings.]

W Star Cable, this is Jenny.

M I'd like to report my cable isn't <u>working properly</u>.

W What's your <u>area code</u> and phone number?

M 02-3769-5824.

W Mr. Brown?

M That's right.

W What seems to be the trouble?

M The low-end <u>channels are</u> fuzzy or blurry.

W The <u>first opening</u> we have is on <u>Friday</u> between <u>9</u> a.m. and <u>1</u> p.m. or between 3 p.m. and 6 p.m.

M Oh, please send your <u>technician</u> between <u>9</u> and <u>1</u>. Thank you.

....

[전화가 울린다.]

여 스타 케이블. Jenny 입니다.

남 제 유선TV 고장 신고를 하려고 합니다.

여 지역번호와 전화번호가 어떻게 되시나요?

남 02-3769- 5824 예요.

여 Brown 씨 되시나요?

남 맞습니다.

여 무엇이 문제인 것 같은가요?

남 낮은 번호 채널이 흐릿하게 나와요.

여 가장 빠른 시간은 금요일 오전 9시에서 오후 1시 사이이거나 오후 3시에서 오후 6시 사이입니다.

남 오, 9시에서 1시 사이에 기술자를 보내주세요. 감사합니다.

●●
area code 지역번호 **low-end channels** (1, 2, 3 등) 낮은 번호 채널 **fuzzy** (모습, 소리가) 흐릿한 **blurry** 흐릿한 **first opening** 가장 빠른 시간 **technician** 기술자

06

W Could you <u>pick me up</u> at the airport next Sunday?

M No problem. When is your <u>flight arriving</u>?

W I am coming in <u>around</u> 2:00 in the afternoon.

M I think that by the time you clear <u>customs</u>, I will be able to meet you in the arrival area around 2:30.

W Okay. But the plane <u>might</u> be <u>delayed</u>.

M Don't worry. I can <u>track your flight</u> on my smartphone using an app I have.

W I want to be able to call you on my cell phone if there is a problem.

M I'll make sure to <u>keep</u> my cell phone with me and <u>turned on</u>.

W Don't wait for me for <u>more than half an hour</u>. If there is a problem, I can take a <u>shuttle</u>.

M You won't need to. I will be there.

....

여 다음 주 일요일에 날 공항에서 태워줄 수 있겠니?

남 물론이지. 네 비행기가 언제 도착하니?

여 오후 2시 경에 들어올 거야.

남 내 생각엔 네가 세관을 통과하는 시간 때문에 2시 30분 경에 입국장에서 너를 만날 수 있을 것 같아.

여 그래. 그런데 비행기가 지연될지도 몰라.

남 걱정 마. 내가 갖고 있는 앱을 이용해서 스마트폰으로 네 비행기를 추적할 수 있어.

여 문제가 있으면 내 휴대전화로 네게 전화할 수 있으면 좋겠어.

남 전화기 꼭 가지고 있으면서 켜놓을게.

여 날 30분 이상 기다리지 마. 만약 문제가 있으면, 셔틀타면 돼.

남 그럴 필요 없을 거야. 거기 있을게.

●●
customs 세관 **arrival** 도착 **delay** 지연되다 **track** 추적하다

07

M Hello, do you have anything <u>metal</u> on you? Any <u>change</u> in your wallet, <u>watches</u>, <u>jewellery</u>?

W No.

M Do you have any <u>liquids</u> or gels?

W I have this <u>water</u> bottle.

M Is it less than <u>100</u> milliliters?

W No, it is <u>500</u>.

M I'm sorry, you will have to <u>throw</u> <u>it</u> <u>away</u>.

W Oh, alright.

M Please place your <u>jacket</u> and carry-on in the <u>tray</u> and proceed through the <u>metal</u> <u>detector</u>.

남 안녕하세요, 금속물질을 가지고 있으신가요? 지갑에 동전이나, 시계, 보석류는요?

여 없습니다.

남 액체류나 젤류를 소지하고 계신가요?

여 이 물병을 가지고 있습니다.

남 100 밀리리터 미만인가요?

여 아뇨, 500 이에요.

남 죄송하지만 버리셔야 합니다.

여 오, 알겠습니다.

남 자켓과 짐을 바구니에 놓고 금속 탐지기를 통과해 지나가 주세요.

●●
jewellery 보석류, 장신구   **carry-on** 휴대용 짐   **tray** 바구니, 쟁반
proceed 진행하다   **metal detector** 금속탐지기

08

M Do you like <u>volunteering</u> here?

W I'm very happy to help <u>the elderly</u>. How about you?

M Me too. I learn a lot about life from them. They also seem to be happy <u>spending</u> <u>time</u> with me.

W <u>How</u> <u>often</u> do you come here?

M I used to come <u>twice</u> <u>a</u> <u>week</u>, every <u>Wednesday</u> and <u>Saturday</u> but now I come on Saturday only. How about you?

W Every weekend. <u>What</u> <u>made</u> <u>you</u> <u>start</u> coming here?

M When my grandfather <u>passed</u> <u>away</u> three years ago, I missed him so much. In order to <u>make</u> <u>up</u> the <u>enormous</u> <u>gap</u> caused by his death, I decided

to come here.

W Oh, I have to go now, but let's have tea together another time.

M Okay.

남 이 곳에서 봉사하는 것 좋니?

여 어르신들을 도와드리는 것이 기뻐. 너는?

남 나도 그래. 그 분들께 삶에 대해 많이 배워. 어르신들께서도 나와 함께 시간을 보내는 것이 행복해 보이셔.

여 여기 얼마나 자주 와?

남 전에는 일주일에 두 번, 수요일과 토요일마다 왔었는데 지금은 토요일에만 와. 너는?

여 매 주말마다 와. 이 곳에 오게 된 계기가 뭐야?

남 3년 전에 할아버지가 돌아가셨을 때 할아버지가 너무 그리웠어. 할아버지의 죽음으로 인한 큰 허전함을 메우기 위해 오기로 결심했어.

여 어머, 지금 가야만 해. 다른 때 함께 차나 마시자.

남 좋아.

●●
elderly 연장자, 노인   **pass away** 죽다, 사망하다   **enormous** 엄청난,
매우 큰   **gap** 간격, 빈 곳

09

M Did you decide which club you are <u>going</u> <u>to</u> <u>join</u>?

W <u>Not</u> <u>yet</u>. Can you help me decide? There are so many <u>interesting</u> <u>clubs</u> in my school. So I'm still thinking about which one is best for me.

M What are you interested in?

W I'm into tennis, <u>choir</u>, <u>photography</u>, <u>broadcasting</u>, and debating.

M Wow! You <u>can't</u> <u>join</u> all of them. It sounds <u>tough</u> to pick one.

W Hmmm... Well, I think I've just decided not to join either the tennis or photography clubs. And I'm going to <u>remove</u> the English debate club from my list, too.

M Do you mean you <u>narrowed</u> <u>down</u> the list to two?

W Actually, I have decided. Since I am planning to <u>major</u> <u>in</u> <u>voice</u> at university, I will join the one that is <u>related</u> <u>to</u> it.

M That is a great choice.

남 너 어떤 동아리에 가입할 건지 정했어?

여 아니 아직. 결정하는 데 도움 좀 줄래? 우리 학교에 정말 흥미로운

동아리들이 많이 있어. 그래서 어느 것이 나에게 제일 좋을지 아직도 생각 중이야.

남 너는 무엇에 관심이 있는데?

여 나는 테니스, 합창단, 사진, 방송, 그리고 토론 동아리에 관심이 있어.

남 우와! 그것들을 다 가입할 순 없잖아. 하나를 고르기는 힘들 것 같네.

여 음... 방금 테니스와 사진 동아리는 들지 않기로 결심했어. 그리고 영어 토론 클럽도 목록에서 지울거야.

남 목록을 두 개로 줄였다는 얘기야?

여 실은 결정했어. 나는 대학에서 성악을 전공 할 계획이라서 그것과 관련된 동아리를 들거야.

남 훌륭한 선택이네.

●● **choir** 합창단 **broadcasting** 방송 **debate** 토론(하다) **tough** 힘든, 어려운 **narrow down** 줄여나가다 **major in voice** 성악을 전공하다

10

M Please turn on channel 9.

W Why? I'm watching this soap opera. Today is the final episode so I have to see it.

M It won't take so long, please turn it on just for a while.

W Come on. What are you going to watch?

M I'll just check the winning lottery numbers.

W What? What would you do if you won the lottery?

M Well. First, I would give half of it to my parents to thank them. And I would donate some to my elementary school. I also would like to buy a sports car and a vacation home in Jeju Island.

W You seem to be building castles in the air, but who knows. Good luck.

M Thank you.

남 9번 틀어요.

여 왜요? 드라마 보고 있어요. 오늘이 마지막 회라 봐야 해요.

남 오래 안 걸릴 거니 잠시 틀어봐요.

여 왜 그래요. 뭐 보려고 그래요?

남 복권 당첨번호 확인하려구요.

여 뭐라고요? 복권에 당첨되면 무엇을 할건데요?

남 음. 먼저 부모님께 감사를 표시하기 위해 절반을 드릴 거예요. 그리고 초등학교에 기부를 할거예요. 또 스포츠카도 사고 제주도에 별장도 구입할 거예요.

여 허황된 꿈을 꾸고 있는 것처럼 들리지만 누가 알겠어요. 행운을 빌어요.

남 고마워요.

●● **soap opera** 드라마, 연속극 **final episode** 마지막 회 **win the lottery** 복권에 당첨되다 **donate** 기부하다 **elementary school** 초등학교 **build castles in the air** 허황된 꿈을 꾸다

11

M Mina, are you ready for your presentation tomorrow?

W Yes, except for one thing.

M What's that one thing? What is the problem?

W When I present, I am going to use a laser pointer to point at the stressed words or sentences and to scroll down the screen.

M So? Don't you have a pointer? I can lend you mine.

W No, it's not that. I already bought one. I don't know how to use it.

M Oh, it's simple. Did you read the manual?

W I did, but... If you don't mind, please teach me how to use it.

M Sure. Look.

남 Mina, 내일 발표 준비 다됐어?

여 응. 한가지 빼고.

남 그 한가지가 뭔데? 뭐가 문제야?

여 발표할 때, 강조되는 단어나 문장을 가리키거나 화면을 내릴 때 레이저 포인터를 사용할거야.

남 그래서? 포인터가 없어? 내 것 빌려줄게.

여 아니. 그게 아니야. 이미 샀어. 그것을 어떻게 사용하는 지 몰라.

남 오. 간단해. 사용설명서는 읽었어?

여 응. 그런데… 괜찮으면 어떻게 사용하는지 가르쳐줘.

남 물론이지. 봐봐.

●● **except** 제외하고 **laser pointer** 레이저 포인터 **stress** 강조하다 **lend** 빌려주다 **manual** 사용설명서

12

M Ladies and gentlemen! This is Vincent Brown from the property management office. May I have your attention, please? As we informed you last week, we are going to clean the water tank today from 9 a.m. to 1 p.m. So the water supply will be cut off during that time. It is to supply clean and safe water to you so please understand the situation. We will try our best to finish as soon as possible. Sorry for the inconvenience. Thank you for your cooperation.

남 신사숙녀 여러분! 저는 관리사무소의 Vincent Brown입니다. 잠시 주목해 주시겠습니까? 지난 주에 공고해드린 것처럼, 오늘 오전 9시부터 오후 1시까지 물탱크 청소를 할 것입니다. 따라서 그 시간 동안에는 수도 공급이 중단됩니다. 깨끗하고 안전한 물을 제공하기 위함이오니 상황을 이해해 주시기 바랍니다. 가능한 빨리 끝날 수 있도록 최선을 다할 것입니다. 불편을 드려 죄송합니다. 협조해 주셔서 감사합니다.

●● **property management office** 아파트 관리사무소 **water supply** 수도공급 **cut off** 중단하다 **try one's best** 최선을 다하다 **cooperation** 협조

13

M Let's organize these magazines on the shelf and arrange the stock appropriately.

W Okay. If any of them are in short supply or out of stock, we need to reorder them.

M That's right. Let's check the monthly magazines first. We have 50 copies of *Muscle Mania* left in stock, but we don't have any copies of *Stars*. We need to order some.

W And we have 10 copies of the weekly magazine *Golf Lovers*, so we don't need to order any more.

M We have two copies of Beauty magazine left, right?

W Beauty magazine? Are you talking about *Gorgeous Hair*? And we only have one copy of it.

M Oh, sorry. Yes, I am. I made a mistake. I confused it with Beauty magazine. And we should order some more copies of the quarterly magazine *Street Fashion* because there aren't any left.

W OK. I think we are done now.

잡지				
	제목	분류	발간	재고
①	Muscle Mania	휘트니스	월간	15
②	Golf Lovers	스포츠	주간	10
③	Stars	연예	월간	0
④	Gorgeous Hair	미용	연간	1
⑤	Street Fashion	패션	분기별	0

남 진열대에 있는 이 잡지들을 정리하고 재고를 적절하게 조정합시다.

여 좋아요. 재고가 별로 없거나 아예 없으면 재주문을 해야 합니다.

남 맞아요. 먼저 월간지부터 확인해 봅시다. 〈Muscle Mania〉는 50권이 재고가 남아있지만 〈Stars〉는 하나도 없네요. 주문을 해야겠어요.

여 그리고 주간지 〈Golf Lovers〉는 10권이 남아있으니 주문할 필요가 없겠어요.

남 미용 잡지는 두 권 남았네요. 그렇죠?

여 미용 잡지요? 〈Gorgeous Hair〉 말씀하시는 건가요? 한 권 밖에 없는데요.

남 오, 미안해요. 맞아요. 제가 실수했네요. 그것과 미용 잡지를 혼동했어요. 분기별 잡지 〈Street Fashion〉은 하나도 없으니 몇 권 더 주문해야 겠어요.

여 좋아요. 이제 다한 것 같네요.

●● **organize** 정리하다 **on the shelf** 선반에, 진열대에 **arrange** 조정하다 **in short supply** 공급이 딸리는 **out of stock** 재고가 없는 **reorder** 재주문하다 **confuse with** ~와 혼동하다 **quarterly** 분기별

14

M What are all these colorful baskets?

W They are recycling bins. Look at the words and pictures printed on them.

M Ah! I can see the little pictures of paper, cans, plastic, and bottles. Why did you buy them? You have always separated and taken the recyclables to the recycling area, haven't you?

W Yes, I have. However, I used to put all of them in the same big box or a single plastic bag, and then I had to separate them in the recycling area.

M If you have these, it will be easier to recycle, won't it?

W Yes. That's what I mean.

M Where are you going to place them?

W I will put them next to the garbage can. I will do it now.

M Good idea.

남 이 색깔 있는 바구니들은 뭐니?
여 재활용 쓰레기통들이야. 거기에 새겨있는 글씨랑 그림들을 봐.
남 아! 종이, 캔, 플라스틱, 병의 작은 그림들이 보이네. 그것들을 왜 샀어? 너는 항상 재활용할 수 있는 것들을 분리해서 재활용장에 가져가잖아. 안 그래?
여 그래. 그런데 나는 큰 상자나 비닐봉투에 한꺼번에 넣고는 재활용장에서 분류해서 버리곤 했었어.
남 이것들이 있으면 재활용하기가 조금 수월하겠네. 그렇지?
여 응. 내 말이 그 말이야.
남 그것들을 어디에 놓아둘 거야?
여 쓰레기통 옆에 놓아두려고. 지금 가서 해야겠다.
남 좋은 생각이네.

recycling bin 재활용 쓰레기통 **separate** 분리하다 **recyclable** 재활용 가능한 **recycling area** 재활용장 **That's what I mean.** 내 말이 그 말이야.

15

W Welcome to the university library. Undergraduate students can check out up to five books for two weeks. Graduate students can check out ten books for two months. Books can be renewed up to two times. There is a 50 cent late fee per day for each overdue book up to a maximum of $15. Periodicals and reference books cannot be checked out. The library is open weekdays, 8:00 a.m. to 10:00 p.m., and on Saturdays from 9:00 a.m. to 8:30 p.m. The library is closed on Sundays.

여 대학교 도서관에 오신 것을 환영합니다. 학부생들은 다섯 권까지 이주일 동안 대출할 수 있습니다. 대학원생은 책 열 권을 두 달 동안 대출할 수 있습니다. 책은 두 번까지 갱신될 수 있습니다. 기한이 지난 각각의 책은 하루에 50센트씩 연체료가 부과되고 최고 15달러까지 부과될 수 있습니다. 정기간행물과 참고도서는 대출할 수 없습니다. 도서관은 주중에는 오전 8시부터 오후 10시까지, 토요일에는 오전 9시부터 오후 8시 30분까지 문을 엽니다. 일요일에는 문을 열지 않습니다.

undergraduate 학부의 **graduate student** 대학원생 **renew** 갱신하다, 재개하다 **overdue** 기한이 지난 **periodical** 정기간행물

16

W Thank you for taking some time off from your busy schedule to answer a few questions.
M It's my pleasure.
W Could you tell us about an average day in your life?
M Sure, I get up early at 7 in the morning. Then I have breakfast. After breakfast, I go to the gym.
W Are you studying anything now?
M Yes, I'm learning French for the new movie that I'm appearing in.
W Can you tell me about the story in the movie?
M It's about a funny French family. It can make you laugh and cry at the same time. You should watch it.
W Which scene are you shooting today?
M I'm shooting a scene about driving down a highway.

여 질문에 답해주시기 위해서 바쁜 일정 중에 시간을 내어주셔서 감사합니다.
남 천만에요.
여 평범한 하루 일과를 말씀해주시겠어요?
남 네. 아침 7시에 일어납니다. 그리고 아침을 먹죠. 아침을 먹은 후에는 체육관에 갑니다.
여 지금 공부하고 있는 것 있으세요?
남 네. 촬영하고 있는 새 영화를 위해서 불어를 배우고 있어요.
여 그 영화의 줄거리를 말씀해주시겠어요?
남 재미있는 프랑스 가족이야기입니다. 그것은 당신을 눈물 흘리게도 하고 웃게도 할 겁니다. 꼭 보셔야 해요.
여 오늘은 어떤 장면을 촬영하세요?
남 고속도로에서 운전하는 장면을 찍습니다.

① 나도 그 장면이 마음에 안 듭니다.
② 액션영화를 보고 싶습니다.
③ 나는 조연으로 발탁되었습니다.
④ 이 영화에서 주연을 맡고 있습니다.

average 평범한, 보통의 **shoot** 촬영하다

17

M Honey, what do you think of homeschooling Tom?
W Homeschooling him?

M Yes. I think you and I are able to teach him at home.

W But do we have time to do that?

M We each have flexible work schedules, so we can adjust our work schedules to help him.

W Okay. But why? What is good about homeschooling?

M It offers a great deal of educational freedom. He can focus on the subject matter that gets him excited.

W Sounds good, but how can he make friends?

M He can make friends by belonging to sports teams.

· ·

남 여보, Tom을 홈스쿨링하는 거 어떻게 생각해요?

여 그를 홈스쿨링한다고요?

남 네. 나는 당신과 내가 그를 집에서 가르칠 수 있다고 생각해요.

여 하지만 우리가 그렇게 할 시간이 있을까요?

남 우리는 각자 탄력적인 근무 일정을 갖고 있으니 그애를 돕기 위해 근무 일정을 조정할 수 있어요.

여 좋아요. 하지만 왜요? 홈스쿨링의 좋은 점이 뭐예요?

남 그것은 교육의 자유를 많이 줘요. 그는 자신이 흥미로워하는 주제에 중점을 둘 수 있어요.

여 좋은 것 같긴 한데, 하지만 그는 어떻게 친구를 사귀어요?

남 그는 스포츠 팀에 소속해서 친구를 사귈 수 있어요.

① 나는 그에게 고급수학을 가르칠 수 없어요.
② 나는 십대 때 친구들이 많았어요.
③ 나는 이번 주말에 학교 친구들을 방문하고 싶어요.
④ 모든 사람들은 18세까지 학교에 다녀야 해요.

•• flexible 탄력적인, 유동적인 adjust 조정하다 a great deal of 많은
subject matter 주제

18

M I heard that you went to the hospital yesterday.

W Yes I did. I had a high fever. I demanded that the doctor give me some antibiotics.

M That's not right.

W What do you mean?

M If you have the flu, antibiotics won't help. The flu is a viral infection. The doctor shouldn't prescribe something that won't help.

W But I need some medicine to get better.

M No, you don't. And haven't you heard that the prescription of too many antibiotics has led to a rise in antibiotic-resistant infections.

W Really?

M Yes, we have no medicines to fight them. So what will you do next time?

W I won't demand that I get antibiotics.

· ·

남 너 어제 병원에 갔다고 들었어.

여 응. 고열이 났었거든. 의사선생님께 항생제를 처방해 달라고 요구했어.

남 그건 옳지 않아

여 무슨 뜻이니?

남 독감에 걸리면 항생제는 효과가 없어. 독감은 바이러스성 감염이야. 의사는 효과가 없는 것을 처방해선 안 돼.

여 하지만 나으려면 약이 필요해.

남 아니, 그렇지 않아. 그리고 너무 많은 항생제 처방이 항생제 내성 감염의 증가를 일으켰다는 것 들어본 적 없어?

여 정말?

남 그래. 그것에 대항할 약은 없어. 그러니 다음엔 너 어떻게 할거야?

여 항생제를 달라고 요구하지 않을거야.

② 난 항생제를 먹기 때문에 건강해.
③ 나는 효과가 있는 더 강한 항생제를 먹을거야.
④ 의사에게 가서 항생제를 얻을 거야.
⑤ 집에서 더 가까운 다른 의사를 찾아갈 거야.

•• antibiotics 항생제 viral infection 바이러스성 감염 prescribe 처방하다 antibiotic-resistant 항생제 내성의

19

M Sarah. You look terrible. What's wrong?

W My grandmother just passed away.

M I'm so sorry to hear that. When did this happen?

W A couple of days ago. I just came back from the funeral.

M Is there anything I can do?

W No, not really. The sad thing is that I wasn't there when she died.

M I'm sure she knew you loved her. Did she pass away in the hospital?

W Yes, she died in her sleep.

· ·

남 Sarah. 많이 안좋아 보여. 무슨일이니?

여	우리 할머니가 돌아가셨어.
남	유감이야. 언제 돌아가신거야?
여	엊그제 돌아가셨어. 막 장례식장에 갔다왔어.
남	내가 해 줄 일이 있을까?
여	아니, 없어. 슬픈 일은 할머니가 돌아가실 때 내가 거기에 없었다는 거야.
남	할머니는 네가 당신을 사랑한다는 걸 아셨을 거야. 할머니는 병원에서 돌아가셨니?
여	응, 주무시다가 돌아가셨어.

① 그녀는 병원을 지나갔어.
② 아니, 그녀는 돌아가시지 않았어.
④ 그녀와 함께 갈 수 없어서 슬퍼.
⑤ 그녀는 어제 병원에 갔어.

●●
look terrible 기분이 안 좋아 보이다 **pass away** 돌아가시다 **funeral** 장례식

20

M	Today Abby is excited to start a new job. She wants to get to work early this morning in order to make a good impression on her new boss. So she leaves home early for work. However, traffic is backed up for kilometers because of a car accident. Furthermore, the road traffic shows no sign of getting better. She decides to call her boss to tell him that she is going to be late. In this situation, what would Abby probably say to her boss?

남	오늘 Abby는 새로운 직장에 출근해서 들떠있다. 그녀는 새로운 사장님께 좋은 인상을 주기 위해서 오늘 아침 일찍 출근하기를 원한다. 그래서 출근하기 위해 일찍 집에서 나왔다. 하지만, 자동차 사고 때문에 몇 킬로미터에 걸쳐서 차량이 정체되고 있다. 게다가 교통정체가 풀릴 기미가 보이지 않는다. 그녀는 사장님에게 전화해서 그녀가 늦을 거라고 말하기로 결심한다. 이런 상황에서 Abby는 그녀의 사장님에게 뭐라고 말할 것 같은가?

① 10시에 사무실에 있을 예정입니다.
② 걱정하지 마세요. 제시간에 거기에 갈 거에요.
③ 5번가에 차 사고가 났음을 알려드립니다.
④ 죄송하지만 교통정체 때문에 늦을 것 같습니다.
⑤ 죄송하지만 과속 때문에 경찰이 길가에 차를 세웠어요.

●●
make a good impression 좋은 인상을 주다 **be backed up** 차가 정체 되다 **furthermore** 더욱이, 게다가

1 She thinks that the man's stomach hurts because he had too much junk food.
2 I have to pay 70 dollars for two nights.
3 He thinks that it takes about half an hour to clear customs.
4 He used to come twice a week, every Wednesday and Saturday.
5 She wants to major in voice.
6 She will use it to point at the stressed words and sentences and to scroll down the screen.
7 They can check out ten books for two months and the books can be renewed up to two times.
8 It has led to a rise in antibiotic-resistant infections.

On **Y**our **O**wn 모범답안   p. 55

A

My Opinion on Using Antibiotics	
(1) What are antibiotics?	important medicines which help fight infections that are caused by bacteria
(2) My opinion	We should not use them too much.
(3) The reason for my opinion	Overusing antibiotics causes antibiotic resistance so they are no longer effective. And this is one of the most significant threats to patients' safety.

Antibiotics are (1)important medicines which help fight infections that are caused by bacteria. However, I think (2)we should not use them too much. The reason is that (3)overusing antibiotics causes antibiotic resistance so they are no longer effective. And this is one of the most significant threats to patients' safety. Therefore, I think (2)we must not overuse them and use them it the right way.

항생제 사용에 대한 나의 의견	
(1) 항생제는 무엇인가?	박테리아에 의해서 감염이 되었을 때 치료를 도와주는 중요한 약
(2) 나의 의견	우리는 그것들을 너무 많이 사용해서는 안된다.
(3) 나의 의견에 대한 이유	항생제 과다 사용은 항생제 내성을 일으켜, 그것이 더 이상 효과적이지 않게 된다. 그리고 이것은 환자들의 안전에 가장 중대한 위협들 중의 하나이다.

항생제는 박테리아에 의해서 감염이 되었을 때 치료를 도와주는 약이다. 그러나 나는 그것들을 너무 많이 사용해서는 안 된다고 생각한다. 그 이유는 항생제 내성을 일으켜 그것이 더 이상 효과적이지 않게 되기 때문이다. 그리고 이것은 환자들의 안전에 대해서 가장 중대한 위협들 중의 하나이다. 그러므로, 나는 항생제를 과다 사용해서는 안되며 올바른 방법으로 이용해야 한다고 생각한다.

B

Recycling	
Do you recycle every day?	(1) Yes
Do you think recycling is necessary or not? Why?	(2) necessary, prevents environmental pollution, saves resources
What are the things that you recycle?	(3) cans, paper, bottles, and plastic
Please think about two items which you can make with recyclable materials.	(4) a piggy bank from an empty milk carton (5) soap from used cooking oil

I am going to talk about recycling today. I (1)do recycle every day. I think recycling is (2)necessary because it (2)prevents environmental pollution and saves resources. I recycle (3)cans, paper, bottles, and plastic. I will tell you two items which I can make with recyclable materials. First, I can make (4)a piggy bank from an empty milk carton. Second, I can make (5) soap from used cooking oil.

재활용	
당신은 매일 재활용을 하십니까?	(1) 네
당신은 재활용이 필요하다고 생각하십니까 혹은 그렇지 않다고 생각하십니까? 왜인가요?	(2) 필요함, 환경 오염을 막음, 자원을 절약함
당신이 재활용하는 것들은 무엇입니까?	(3) 캔, 종이, 병, 플라스틱
재활용품을 가지고 만들 수 있는 것들을 2가지만 생각해 보세요.	(4) 빈 우유팩으로 만든 저금통 (5) 폐식용유로 만든 비누

오늘 저는 재활용에 대하여 이야기 할 것입니다. 저는 매일 재활용을 합니다. 저는 재활용이 꼭 필요하다고 생각합니다. 왜냐하면 환경오염을 방지할 수 있고 자원을 절약할 수 있기 때문입니다. 저는 매일 캔, 종이, 병, 그리고 플라스틱을 재활용합니다. 재활용품을 가지고 만들 수 있는 두 가지 물품을 말씀 드리겠습니다. 첫 번째로 저는 빈 우유상자로 돼지 저금통을 만들 수 있습니다. 두 번째로 폐식용유로 비누를 만들 수 있습니다.

06 Listening Test 정답   p. 60

01 ②	02 ③	03 ③	04 ②	05 ⑤
06 ②	07 ①	08 ①	09 ②	10 ⑤
11 ③	12 ④	13 ④	14 ①	15 ③
16 ③	17 ①	18 ③	19 ④	20 ④

01

M Come on. It's five o'clock. I want to be out of here by five thirty.

W It's still dark out.

M I guess we've done everything. Our two puppies are in the pet carrier on the back seat.

W Did you stop the newspaper delivery?

M Yes.

W I'm tired. I want to stay home.

M You can sleep in the camper. Let's double check everything. Have you got the map? What about the suitcases, the camcorder and some food?

W Yes. We're all set.

M Then, let's hit the road.

- - - - - - - - - -

남 어서. 5시야. 5시 30분까지는 여기를 나가고 싶어.

여 밖이 여전히 깜깜해.

남 난 다 챙긴 것 같은데. 우리 강아지 두 마리는 뒷좌석 개 집에 있고.

여 신문 배달은 중지시켰니?

남 응.

여 피곤해. 집에 있고 싶어.

남 캠핑카에서 자면 돼. 모든 걸 다시 확인해보자. 지도 챙겼니? 여행 가방, 캠코더, 약간의 식량은?

여 응. 우린 모두 다 준비됐어.

남 그럼, 길을 나서자.

delivery 배달 **camper** 캠핑카 **suitcase** 여행가방 **hit the road** 길을 나서다

02

W That meal was delicious. We should eat out more often.

M How about at least once every two week?

W Great. Let's do that. Where's my jacket?

M I have no idea.

W Oh, no! I must have left it at the restaurant.

M Where else could you have left it?

W Nowhere. I'm sorry.

M It's no big deal. We'll go back. Let me turn around. I hope it's there.

- - - - - - - - - -

여 식사 맛있었어. 우린 좀더 자주 외식해야 해.

남 적어도 두 주마다 한 번 어때?

여 좋아. 그러자. 내 자켓 어디 있니?

남 난 모르겠는데.

여 오, 안돼! 식당에 두고 온 게 틀림없어.

남 다른 어딘가에 둔 건 아닐까?

여 아무데도 없어. 미안.

남 별 일도 아닌데 뭐. 되돌아 가야지. 차를 돌릴게. 거기에 있길 바래.

eat out 외식하다 **must have p.p.** ~임에 틀림없다 **nowhere** 아무데도 없는 **big deal** 큰 거래. 중대 사건 **turn around** 차를 돌리다

03

W Do you want to improve the functioning of your brain? Making walnuts part of your diet could be a good way. The human brain needs high-quality fats like omega-3s to function properly. Walnuts have plentiful omega-3s, which make them the ultimate "brain food." Are you tired of counting sheep at night? Maybe a pre-bedtime snack of walnuts would help you get some shuteye. Walnuts also contain manganese, copper, iron, magnesium, and calcium — all nutrients which are important for good health. Walnuts, like most nuts, can help lower cholesterol and improve heart health.

- - - - - - - - - -

여 두뇌 기능을 향상시키고 싶으세요? 호두를 식단의 일부로 만드는 것이 한 가지 좋은 방법입니다. 인간의 두뇌는 알맞게 기능하기 위해 오메가-3 같은 양질의 지방을 필요로 합니다. 호두는 오메가-3가 풍부한데, 이것이 호두를 궁극의 "두뇌음식"으로 만들어 줍니다. 밤에 양을 세는 것에 지쳤나요? 잠자리 들기 전 간식으로 호두는 당신이 잠드는 데 도움을 줄 수 있습니다. 호두는 또한 망간, 구리, 철, 마그네슘, 칼슘을 포함하고 있는데 이들은 모두 건강에 중요한 영양소입니다. 대부분의 견과류들처럼 호두는 콜레스테롤을 낮추고 심장건강을 향상시키는데 도움을 줄 수 있습니다.

function 기능. 기능하다 **plentiful** 풍부한 **ultimate** 최종적인. 궁극의 **pre-bedtime** 잠자리 들기 전 **shuteye** 잠 **manganese** 망간 **copper** 구리 **nutrient** 영양소

04

W How may I help you?

M I came here to pick up the prize for the winner of the giveaway event this month.

W Oh, congratulations!

M Thank you. This is the first time I am a winner of an event. I feel like I'm walking on air.

W Could you show me your ID card and the message we've sent?

M Here's my ID card and the message.

W Alright. You won the third prize in this event.

M What is the prize?

W It's a dining voucher worth 100 dollars. Your tax and

utility <u>charges</u> are <u>33</u> percent of the surface value.

M Oh, no! I can buy the voucher at a <u>discount</u> of <u>70</u> percent through an Internet group purchase program.

여 어떻게 도와 드릴까요?

남 이번 달 경품행사 당첨자를 위한 상품을 받으러 왔어요.

여 오, 축하드립니다!

남 감사합니다. 어떤 행사의 당첨자가 된 건 이번이 처음이에요. 하늘을 나는 기분이에요.

여 신분증과 저희가 보낸 당첨 메시지를 보여주시겠어요?

남 여기 신분증과 메세지예요.

여 좋습니다. 이번 행사에서 3등에 당첨되셨습니다.

남 상품이 뭔가요?

여 100 달러 상당의 가치가 있는 외식상품권입니다. 제세공과금은 액면가의 33% 입니다.

남 오, 이런! 그 상품권을 인터넷 공동구매 프로그램을 통해 70% 할인가로 살수 있어요.

① 미안한 → 감사한
② 흥분된 → 실망한
③ 지루한 → 궁금한
④ 좌절한 → 신나는
⑤ 당황한 → 질투나는

••
giveaway event 경품행사 **dining voucher** 외식상품권 **tax and utility charge** 제세공과금 **surface value** 액면가 **group purchase** 공동구매

05

W Surprise! I didn't expect to see you here. What are you reading?

M I'm reading a book on the history of Rome.

W Oh, are you taking a <u>world</u> <u>history</u> <u>class</u> this <u>semester</u>?

M No. You know what? I'm planning to <u>backpack</u> <u>through Italy</u> this summer. I believe this book will help me appreciate what I see. Anyway, <u>what brings</u> <u>you</u> <u>here</u>?

W I was searching for some <u>articles</u> for my <u>report</u>.

M What's that about?

W It's about <u>the brain</u>. I'm writing a research paper that argues that we only use 10 percent of our

brain.

M That sounds interesting. Are you going to <u>check</u> some books <u>out</u> now?

W No, the books with the articles I wanted have already been checked out.

여 놀랐지! 널 여기서 볼 줄은 몰랐어. 뭐 읽고 있니?

남 로마의 역사에 관한 책을 읽고 있어.

여 이번 학기에 세계 역사 수업 듣니?

남 아니. 너 그거 아니? 이번 방학에 이탈리아를 배낭여행할 계획이야. 이 책이 내가 보는 것을 이해하는 데 도움이 될 거라 믿어. 아무튼, 넌 무엇 때문에 여기 왔어?

여 리포트를 위해 기사를 찾고 있었어.

남 무엇에 관한 거니?

여 뇌에 관한 거야. 우리가 뇌의 10%만을 사용한다고 주장하는 논문을 쓰고 있어.

남 그거 흥미로운데. 이제 책을 대출할 거니?

여 아니. 그러고 싶은데 내가 원하는 글이 있는 책들이 이미 대출되었어.

••
semester 학기 **backpack** 배낭을 지고 걷다 **appreciate** 이해하다 **article** 기사, 글

06

M I'm looking for a suit that isn't <u>too</u> <u>expensive</u> <u>to</u> <u>wear</u> on a <u>job</u> <u>interview</u>. Can you help me find <u>something</u> <u>nice</u>?

W Okay. I think this <u>black</u> <u>suit</u> will <u>look</u> <u>good</u> <u>on</u> you. Would you like to <u>try</u> <u>it</u> <u>on</u>?

M Oh, that's great. How much is it?

W It's <u>165</u> dollars. Don't you need a shirt <u>that</u> <u>matches</u> <u>this</u> <u>suit</u>?

M Yes, I need one. Could you show me <u>the</u> <u>blue</u> <u>shirt</u> over there? It's really nice!

W You <u>have</u> <u>an</u> <u>eye</u> <u>for</u> the latest fashion! That will make you look <u>more</u> <u>stylish</u>. It's <u>35</u> dollars.

M Oh, <u>I</u> <u>wish</u> <u>it</u> <u>were</u> a bit cheaper.

W Hmm… here's <u>a</u> <u>deal</u>. If you buy those two items, I'll give you a 10% discount <u>on</u> <u>the</u> <u>total</u>.

M Okay, then I'll buy <u>both</u> <u>of</u> <u>them</u>. Thank you.

남 구직 면접에 입을 너무 비싸지 않은 정장을 찾고 있어요. 멋진 걸로 찾는 걸 도와 주시겠어요?

여 네. 이 검은 정장이 손님께 잘 어울릴 것 같네요. 한번 입어보시겠어요?

남 오, 그거 멋진데요. 얼마인가요?

여 165달러 입니다. 이 정장과 어울리는 셔츠는 필요하지 않으세요?

남 네, 필요합니다. 저기 있는 파란 셔츠를 보여주시겠어요? 정말 근사한데요!

여 최신패션을 보는 안목이 있군요! 저것이 손님을 좀더 멋지게 보이게 해 줄 거예요. 35달러 입니다.

남 오, 그게 좀더 싸길 바랬는데.

여 음… 제안을 드리죠. 저 두 아이템을 사시면, 총액에서 10% 할인해 드리겠습니다.

남 좋습니다. 그럼 둘 다 살게요. 감사합니다.

••
suit 정장 **look good on** ~에 잘 어울리다 **have an eye for** ~을 보는 안목이 있다 **stylish** 유행을 따른, 멋진

07

M Excuse me. I <u>enrolled</u> in Science 307, but I don't know which classroom it is in.

W Well, there's a room <u>assignment</u> <u>sheet</u> on the <u>bulletin</u> <u>board</u> outside this office.

M Yeah, I know. But Science 307 isn't <u>listed</u> there. There <u>must</u> <u>be</u> some kind of <u>mistake</u>. Could you check for me, please?

W Hmmm… ok, let me check on the computer. I'm sorry, but it says here that it was <u>cancelled</u>. You should have gotten a text message about this.

M What? I didn't get one.

W It says on the computer that an SMS was sent out to students <u>three</u> <u>days</u> <u>ago</u>.

M Oh, I haven't changed my cell phone number. And how can you <u>cancel</u> <u>a</u> <u>class</u> after offering it?

W I know it's really <u>inconvenient</u> for you, but if enough students don't <u>sign</u> <u>up</u> for a course, we <u>can't</u> <u>offer</u> it.

- -

남 실례합니다. 과학 307 수업을 등록했는데, 어떤 강의실에서 하는지 모르겠어요.

여 음. 이 사무실 밖 게시판에 방배정표가 붙어있어요.

남 네, 압니다. 하지만 과학 307은 거기에 실려있지 않아요. 뭔가 착오가 있는 게 틀림없어요. 살펴봐 주시겠어요?

여 음… 알겠습니다. 컴퓨터로 확인해 보겠습니다. 죄송합니다만. 취소되었다고 하네요. 이것에 대해 문자 메시지를 받으셨어야 하는데요.

남 뭐라고요? 받지 못했는데요.

여 컴퓨터 상으로는 3일전에 학생들에게 SMS가 발송되었다고 하거든요.

남 오, 제 전화번호를 변경하지 않았어요. 그런데 수업을 개설한 후 어떻게 취소를 할 수 있죠?

여 불편하시다는 걸 압니다만, 과정에 등록생이 충분치 않으면 저희는 그걸 개설해드릴 수가 없답니다.

••
enroll 등록하다 **room assignment sheet** 방배정표 **bulletin board** 게시판 **listed** 표[명단]에 실린

08

M Hello, what can I do for you?

W Hello. Please <u>fill</u> <u>it</u> <u>up</u>.

M Which one? Diesel, unleaded, or super-unleaded?

W <u>Unleaded</u>, please. It's <u>nearly</u> <u>empty</u> now and I have to fill it up because I'm going to drive all day.

M Why? Are you a <u>salesman</u> or <u>going</u> <u>far</u> <u>away</u>?

W I'm going to Busan now and <u>coming</u> <u>back</u> late at night.

M That's a long drive for one day. Pretty tiring!

W It is, but I have no choice. Is it finished? Here is my card.

M [Pause] Here is the receipt. <u>Drive</u> <u>safely</u>.

- -

남 안녕하세요. 무엇을 도와드릴까요?

여 안녕하세요. 가득 채워주세요.

남 경유, 무연, 고급휘발유 어떤 거요?

여 무연이면 됩니다. 지금 거의 비어서요. 하루 종일 운전해야 해서 가득 채워야 합니다.

남 왜요? 판매원이세요 아니면 멀리 가시나요?

여 지금 부산 가서 밤 늦게 돌아올 거예요.

남 하루 동안의 장거리 운전이네요. 지치시겠어요!

여 선택의 여지가 없죠 뭐. 다 되었나요? 여기 카드 있습니다.

남 여기 영수증 있습니다. 운전 조심하세요.

① 주유소   ② 자동차 운전 학원 ③ 자동차 정비소
④ 고속도로 휴게소   ⑤ 카드 회사

••
Please fill it up. (주유소에서) 가득 채워주세요. **empty** 텅 빈 **unleaded** (휘발유가) 무연의

09

① M I'd like to <u>enroll</u> in the Barista course. <u>What</u> <u>should</u> <u>I</u> <u>do</u>?

W Please <u>fill</u> <u>out</u> <u>this</u> <u>form</u> first and <u>pay</u> <u>the</u> <u>tuition</u> <u>fee</u>.

② M May I help you?

W I'd like to have <u>a</u> <u>cup</u> <u>of</u> coffee without <u>sugar</u> and <u>cream</u>.

③ M Did you make these <u>sandwiches</u>?

W Yes. Would you like to try some? <u>Help</u> <u>yourself</u>.

④ M I'd like to have hot chocolate with <u>whipping</u> <u>cream</u> on top.

W Okay. It will be $2.50.

⑤ M Look at the <u>menu</u> and choose what you'd like to have.

W I will have <u>spaghetti</u> and a diet Coke.

··

① 남 바리스타 과정을 등록하고 싶습니다. 어떻게 하면 될까요?
　여 이 양식 작성해 주시고 수업료를 내시면 됩니다.
② 남 무엇을 도와드릴까요?
　여 설탕과 크림 없는 커피 한 잔 주세요.
③ 남 이 샌드위치들을 만드셨나요?
　여 네. 한 번 드셔 보실래요? 마음껏 드세요.
④ 남 휘핑 크림이 올려진 핫쵸콜릿 주세요.
　여 네. 2.5달러 입니다.
⑤ 남 메뉴 보시고 드시고 싶으신 것 고르세요.
　여 스파게티와 다이어트 콜라 주세요.

form 양식, 형식   **pay the tuition fee** 수강료를 납부하다   **Help yourself.** (음식을) 마음껏 드세요.   **whipping cream** 휘핑 크림

10

W How was your weekend? Did you have fun?

M Fun? <u>Not</u> <u>at</u> <u>all</u>. It was very <u>tiring</u> and <u>exhausting</u>.

W Ha, ha. What did you do? Last Friday you said you were excited about the <u>approaching</u> weekend.

M Yeah, at that time I didn't know that I'd have to do <u>spring-cleaning</u> over the weekend.

W At least you got it done. I'm planning to do it this weekend.

M Are you? Don't <u>ask</u> <u>me</u> <u>to</u> <u>help</u>.

W I won't, I promise. What are you going to do this weekend then?

M I will go to see a movie and <u>catch</u> <u>up</u> <u>on</u> my sleep. I need a good rest.

W That's right. I hope to see you <u>full</u> <u>of</u> <u>energy</u> on Monday.

··

여 주말 어땠어? 재미있었어?
남 재미? 전혀. 피곤하고 지쳤어.
여 하하. 뭐 했는데? 지난 금요일에 너 주말 다가온다고 신나 했잖아.
남 응. 그때는 주말에 봄맞이 대청소를 해야 하는지 몰랐을 때고.
여 적어도 너는 끝냈잖아. 난 이번 주말에 할 계획이야.
남 그래? 도와 달라고 하지마.
여 안 해. 약속해. 그럼 이번 주말에 뭐할 꺼야?
남 영화 보러 가고 부족한 잠을 좀 자야지. 푹 쉬는 게 필요해.
여 맞아. 월요일에 에너지 가득한 모습으로 볼 수 있기 바래.

approach 다가오다   **spring-cleaning** 봄맞이 대청소   **catch up on** ~을 따라잡다. 만회하다

11

M Thank you for everything, Mrs. Cha. Here's a <u>bouquet</u> <u>for</u> <u>you</u>.

W What a beautiful <u>flower</u> <u>bouquet</u> it is!

M You were such a great teacher who will <u>remain</u> <u>in</u> <u>my</u> <u>mind</u> forever.

W Oh, thank you for saying so. I won't forget you, either.

M Let's <u>take</u> <u>a</u> <u>picture</u> so we can keep this beautiful moment <u>forever</u>.

W Sure. Your <u>gratitude</u> makes me thankful that I chose to be a teacher.

M What are you going to do now? Do you have a <u>specific</u> <u>plan</u> after you <u>retire</u>?

W Well, I haven't thought a lot about it. But if I have a chance, I'd like to <u>publish</u> <u>a</u> <u>collection</u> of essays <u>based</u> <u>on</u> my teaching experiences.

M That would be wonderful.

··

남 차 선생님, 모든 것에 감사 드립니다. 여기 선생님을 위한 꽃다발입니다.
여 정말 아름다운 꽃다발이구나.
남 제 마음 속에 영원히 남아계실 정말 훌륭한 선생님이셨습니다.
여 오, 그렇게 말해주니 고맙네. 나도 너를 잊지 못할 거야.
남 이 아름다운 순간을 영원히 간직할 수 있게 사진 찍어요.
여 좋아. 네 감사 덕분에 교사가 되길 선택한 것에 감사하게 되는구나.
남 이제부터 무엇을 하실 계획이세요? 은퇴 후 특별한 계획이라도

여 있으세요?

여 음. 아직은 그것에 대해 많이 생각해보지 않았어. 그렇지만 기회가 된다면 내 교육 경험을 바탕으로 한 수필집을 출간해보고 싶어.

남 멋지겠는데요.

●●
flower bouquet 꽃다발 **remain in one's mind** ～의 기억에 남다
gratitude 감사 **chance** 기회 **publish** 출판하다 **based on** ～을 바탕으로 한

12

M What are you thinking about so <u>seriously</u>, Soyoon?

W I've been <u>offered</u> a <u>chance</u> to go to the States as an <u>exchange</u> <u>student</u>.

M Congratulations! That's what you've always wanted. Why do you have a <u>long face</u>?

W I can't decide <u>whether</u> I should <u>accept</u> this offer <u>or not</u>.

M What? What are you talking about? You should go.

W Do you really think so? Now that my dream actually has <u>taken place</u>, I am <u>afraid</u>.

M <u>If</u> <u>I</u> <u>were</u> <u>in</u> <u>your</u> <u>shoes</u>, I wouldn't think about doing anything else, I'd just go. You know what? An <u>opportunity</u> like this doesn't come very often.

W Thank you for your <u>advice</u>. I guess I'll have to take this chance right now.

M Good.

………………………………………………………

남 소윤아, 무슨 생각을 그렇게 골똘히 하고 있니?

여 미국에 교환학생으로 갈 수 있는 기회를 제공받았어.

남 축하해! 네가 항상 원했던 것이잖아. 왜 시무룩해 있어?

여 이 제안을 받아들여야 할지 말아야 할지 결정을 못하겠어.

남 뭐라고? 무슨 이야기를 하는 거야? 가야지.

여 정말 그렇게 생각해? 막상 꿈꿨던 일이 실제로 벌어지니 두려워.

남 내가 만일 너라면, 나는 다른 것들은 생각하지 않을 거야. 그냥 갈 거야. 너 그거 알아? 이런 기회는 자주 오지 않는 법이야.

여 충고해주어 고마워. 이 기회를 잡아야 할 것 같아.

남 그래.

① 백지장도 맞들면 낫다.
② 돌다리도 두들겨 보고 건너라.
③ 어려울 때 돕는 친구가 진정한 친구다.
④ 쇠뿔도 단김에 빼라.
⑤ 좋은 약은 입에 쓰다.

●●
seriously 심각하게 **exchange student** 교환학생 **have a long face** 우울한 표정을 짓다 **accept** 받아들이다 **if I were in your shoes** 내가 만일 네 입장이라면 **opportunity** 기회

13

M Can I help you? Are you looking for anything <u>in particular</u>?

W I'd like to buy flowers for Parents' Day.

M I see. Do you want a <u>bouquet</u> or a <u>basket</u>? Or maybe you want to buy them by the piece. We have a <u>wide</u> <u>selection</u>.

W Well. I haven't thought about that yet. What's most <u>popular</u>?

M It <u>depends</u> <u>on</u> the <u>customer's</u> <u>taste</u> but people usually choose a bouquet or a basket <u>rather</u> <u>than</u> by the piece.

W I see. Can you show some to me then?

M These small ones on the <u>left</u> <u>side</u> are $17 and these larger ones on the <u>right</u> side cost between $25 and $30.

W Oh, I like this one <u>on</u> <u>the</u> <u>right</u>. It has a blue basket.

M Good choice.

………………………………………………………

카네이션 판매			
가격	송이	꽃다발 스타일	바구니 스타일
$10 이하	①		
$10 – $20		②	③
$20 – $30			④
$30 이상		⑤	

남 무엇을 도와드릴까요? 특별히 찾는 것이 있으세요?

여 어버이 날을 위한 꽃을 사고 싶습니다.

남 그렇군요. 꽃다발, 혹은 바구니를 사시겠어요? 아니면 송이로도 사실 수 있어요. 다양하게 선택하실 수 있답니다.

여 음. 아직 생각해보지 않았는데요. 가장 잘나가는 것이 무엇인가요?

남 고객의 취향에 따라 다르긴 하지만, 사람들은 대개 송이보다는 꽃다발이나 바구니를 선택합니다.

여 그렇군요. 그럼 그것들을 보여주시겠어요?

남 여기 왼편에 작은 것들은 17달러이고, 오른 쪽에 큰 것들은 25달러에서 30달러입니다.

여 오, 오른쪽에 있는 게 좋네요. 파란 바구니요.

남 좋은 선택입니다.

in particular 특히   **piece** (꽃의) 한 송이   **wide selection** 폭 넓은 선택
depend on ~에 달려있다   **taste** 취향, 입맛

14

M Lauren, are you done with your homework? It's 2 o'clock now.

W Sorry, dad. I need one more hour to be finished.

M Okay. I will wait for you. Take your time.

W Thanks. Are you done with reading your novel already?

M Yes. I will turn on the news to check the weather. It looks like it's going to rain soon because the sky is covered with black clouds.

W Oh, no. If it is, we can't mow the lawn as we had planned. I hope it won't rain.

M We can do it next time. Don't worry.

W I will finish my homework as soon as possible so we don't have to change our plan.

남 Lauren, 숙제 다했어? 지금 2시야.

여 아빠 죄송해요. 끝내려면 한 시간 더 필요해요.

남 알았어. 기다리게. 천천히 하렴.

여 고마워요. 소설책은 다 읽으셨어요?

남 응. 날씨를 확인하려 뉴스를 켜야 겠구나. 하늘에 먹구름이 낀 것 보면 곧 비가 올 것 같아.

여 오, 안 되는데. 만일 그렇다면 우리 계획대로 잔디를 깎을 수 없잖아요. 비가 안 오길 바래요.

남 다음에 하면 되지. 걱정마.

여 가능한 한 숙제를 빨리 끝내서 계획에 차질이 없도록 할게요.

Take your time. 천천히 해.   **be covered with** ~로 뒤덮이다   **mow the lawn** 잔디를 깎다

15

W Thanksgiving Day is the fourth Thursday in November. It is a U.S. federal holiday, so schools, banks, post offices, and government offices are closed. Thanksgiving was the first holiday celebrated in America. It was first celebrated in the autumn of 1621 when the Wampanoag Indians and the Pilgrims got together for a three-day feast and festival of fun. Today, families celebrate Thanksgiving by eating turkey, mashed potatoes, gravy, yams, corn, cranberry sauce, and pumpkin pie. Macy's Thanksgiving Day Parade and an NFL football game are special Thanksgiving Day events.

여 추수감사절은 11월 4번째 주 목요일입니다. 그것은 미국 연방정부 공휴일이어서 학교, 은행, 우체국 그리고 관공서는 문을 닫습니다. 추수감사절은 미국에서 기념한 첫 번째 공휴일입니다. 그것은 Wampanoag 인디언과 순례자들이 모여서 삼일 동안 만찬과 재미난 축제를 한 1621년 가을에 처음으로 기념되었습니다. 오늘날, 가정에서는 칠면조, 으깬 감자, 그레이비, 얌, 옥수수, 크랜베리 소스 그리고 호박파이를 먹으면서 추수감사절을 기념합니다. Macy의 추수감사절 퍼레이드와 NFL 미식축구 경기는 추수감사절의 특별한 행사입니다.

federal 연방정부의   **pilgrim** 순례자   **mashed** 으깬

16

W Hey, Bill. What are you doing?

M Nothing much. What are you up to?

W I am just concerned about Sam. He hasn't been himself lately. He failed the final interview for the company he really wanted to work for.

M That's too bad. He must feel depressed.

W Yeah. He's been sitting in his room all day for the last 3 days.

M Why don't we take him out? We can try to take his mind off of it.

W That's a great idea. Why don't you call him? I already talked to him a couple of times and it might be good for him to hear from you.

M Ok. I'll call you back after I've done that.

여 안녕. Bill. 뭐 하는 중이니?

남 별 거 없어. 어떻게 지내?

여 Sam이 걱정돼. 요즘 그는 평소의 그가 아니야. 그는 정말 일하고 싶어하던 회사의 최종 면접에서 떨어졌어.

남 안됐네. 우울하겠구나.

여 응. 지난 3일동안 하루 종일 자기 방 안에서 앉아만 있어.

남 그를 밖으로 나오게 하자. 그가 그것을 잊도록 노력해 보는 거야.

여 좋은 생각이야. 네가 그에게 전화해보는 게 어때? 나는 이미 그에게

여러 차례 이야기해서 그가 너에게 연락을 받는 게 좋을 것 같아.

남　그래. 그렇게 하고 나서 너에게 다시 전화 할게.

① 네가 그에게 지금 연락해야 해.
② 그는 그것을 잊는 중이야.
④ 이번 금요일에 너를 불러낼게. 좋지?
⑤ 너의 연락을 간절히 기다리고 있어

··
concerned 걱정하는　**lately** 최근에　**take one's mind off**
(걱정거리를) 잊게 하다

17

W　Good morning, can I help you?

M　Good morning. I want to buy a <u>motorcycle</u>.

W　What kind of motorcycle are you looking for?

M　I want to purchase an <u>automatic</u> motorcycle.

W　Please have a look! We have many <u>automatic</u> motorcycles by a variety of <u>manufacturers</u>.

M　How much is this one?

W　It is $200.

M　That's a little <u>expensive</u>. Is there any way you can offer me a discount?

W　If you pay <u>by cash</u>, you can get a <u>15%</u> discount. If you use a <u>credit card</u>, you can purchase it on an <u>installment basis</u>. Which way do you prefer?

M　<u>Cash. I'd like to get the discount.</u>

여　안녕하세요. 도와드릴까요?
남　안녕하세요. 오토바이를 사고 싶어요.
여　어떤 종류의 오토바이를 찾고 계신가요?
남　자동 변속 오토바이를 사고 싶어요.
여　보세요. 여기 자동으로 변속하는 여러 제조사 오토바이들이 있어요.
남　이것은 얼마인가요?
여　200달러에요.
남　좀 비싸네요. 할인해 주는 방법이 있나요?
여　현금으로 지불하시면, 15% 할인을 받으실 수 있어요. 신용카드를 이용하실 경우에는, 할부로 구매 가능하시구요. 어느 것이 더 좋으세요?
남　<u>현금이요. 할인을 받고 싶어요.</u>

② 200달러를 빌리러 은행으로 갈거예요.
③ 저 오토바이 제조사를 모르겠어요.
④ 자동 변속 오토바이를 운전하는 게 더 좋아요.
⑤ 다른 종류의 오토바이를 보여주시겠어요?

··
automatic 자동의　**on an installment basis** 할부로　**prefer** 더 좋아하다

18

W　Thank you for coming to the meeting today, Mr. Kim.

M　My pleasure, Ms Lee. Now, <u>what problems</u> are we having around here?

W　Well, unfortunately, we're having a serious problem with <u>our clients in Canada</u>.

M　Haven't they paid yet?

W　Yes, they've paid on time. The problem is they <u>aren't satisfied</u> with the goods we've sent them.

M　How can that be? We always <u>provide</u> the best <u>quality products</u>.

W　But they aren't happy. They say they are meeting with a <u>new manufacturer</u> next week.

M　No way! What are we doing to <u>change things</u>?

W　<u>That's the reason for our meeting today.</u>

여　Mr. Kim, 오늘 회의에 참석해주셔서 감사합니다.
남　천만에요. Ms. Lee. 어떤 문제가 있나요?
여　음, 불행히도 캐나다에 있는 고객분들에게 심각한 문제가 발생했어요.
남　아직도 대금을 지불하지 않으셨어요?
여　아뇨, 제 시간에 지불하셨어요. 문제는 그들이 우리가 보낸 제품에 만족하지 않는다는 거에요.
남　어떻게 그럴 수 있나요? 우리는 항상 최고품질의 상품만 제공하잖아요.
여　그러나 그들은 만족하지 않아요. 그들이 다음주에 새로운 제조업자와 회의를 할거라고 말하네요.
남　절대 안돼요! 상황을 바꾸기 위해서 우리는 무엇을 할 건가요?
여　<u>그것이 오늘 회의의 이유입니다.</u>

① 그들에게 제 시간에 돈을 지불하라고 요청할 겁니다.
② 그것에 대해서 걱정할 필요 없어요.
④ 우리의 선적 회사를 바꾸어야만 해요.
⑤ 다음 주에 휴가차 캐나다에 갈 거예요.

··
unfortunately 불행히도　**client** 고객　**provide** 제공하다　**product** 제품　**manufacturer** 제조업자

19

W I can honestly say this is the <u>last time</u> I'll come here.

M I have the <u>same opinion</u>. I don't like this place, either.

W The service was <u>too slow</u> and the food was <u>terrible</u>.

M This steak is as <u>tough</u> as leather and it is even quite <u>smelly</u>.

W It <u>used to be</u> a good restaurant. I wonder why everything has changed.

M Well, I heard that <u>the owner</u> of this restaurant <u>changed</u> and he hired a <u>new chef</u>.

W I think the new owner has reduced the quality of the ingredients in the dishes and the new chef is <u>not good at</u> cooking.

M I'm going to <u>find out where</u> the old chef is working.

W <u>Wherever it is, let's go there next time.</u>

....

여 나는 다시는 여기 안 올 거야.
남 나도 같은 생각이야. 나 역시 여기는 별로 안 좋아.
여 서비스도 느렸고 음식도 형편없었어.
남 이 스테이크는 가죽만큼이나 질기고 심지어 냄새도 나.
여 전에는 좋은 음식점이었는데. 왜 모든 것이 바뀌었는지 궁금해.
남 음, 이 음식점 주인이 바뀌었고 그가 새로운 주방장을 고용했다고 들었어.
여 내 생각에 그 새 주인은 요리 재료의 품질을 낮추었고 새로운 주방장은 요리를 못해.
남 예전 주방장이 어디서 일하는지 찾아봐야겠어.
여 그곳이 어디든 다음 번엔 거기로 가자.

① 그 얘길 들어서 유감이야.
② 오늘 여기서 만나서 반가워.
③ 내일 오후에 나는 일할거야.
⑤ 예전 주방장은 새로운 주방장보다 더 별로야.

•• **smelly** (역겨운)냄새가 나는 **leather** 가죽 **chef** 주방장 **ingredient** 재료

20

M Mrs. Wilson takes her seven-year old son and five-year old daughter <u>to the park</u> on <u>Saturday</u> <u>mornings</u>. The park has quite a large playground for young children. Her children like to play on the swings, slides and teeter-tooters. They spend <u>several hours</u> at the park. Today her neighbor <u>asks</u> <u>her</u> to <u>take her children</u> to the park, too. But Mrs. Wilson <u>doesn't want</u> to take other people's children to the park. Also she doesn't want to <u>hurt her</u> <u>neighbor's feelings</u>, either. In this situation, what would Mrs. Wilson probably say to her neighbor?

....

남 Mrs. Wilson은 그녀의 일곱 살짜리 아들과 다섯 살짜리 딸을 토요일 아침마다 공원에 데려간다. 그 공원에는 어린아이들이 놀 수 있는 꽤 큰 놀이터가 있다. 그녀의 아이들은 그네, 미끄럼틀, 시소 타는 것을 좋아한다. 그들은 공원에서 몇 시간을 보낸다. 오늘 그녀의 이웃이 그녀에게 자신의 아이들도 공원에 데려가 달라고 부탁한다. 하지만 그녀는 다른 사람들의 아이들을 공원에 데려가고 싶지 않다. 또한, 그녀는 그녀의 이웃의 감정도 상하게 하고 싶지 않다. 이런 상황에서, Mrs. Wilson은 그녀의 이웃사람에게 뭐라고 말할 것 같은가?

① 두 시간 동안 거기에 있을 거에요.
② 좋아요. 감사합니다.
③ 죄송하지만, 당신과 함께 갈 수 없어요.
④ 미안하지만 저는 아이 네 명을 감당할 수 없어요.
⑤ 네. 집에서 그들을 보살필게요.

•• **swing** 그네 **slide** 미끄럼틀 **teeter-tooter** 시소 **handle** 다루다

Further Study 정답

p. 64

1 They put their two puppies <u>in the pet carrier on the back seat</u>.

2 They will eat out at least <u>once every two weeks</u>.

3 He has to show her his <u>ID card</u> and <u>the message</u> which the company sent to him.

4 He is going to <u>go to see a movie</u> and <u>catch up on his sleep</u>.

5 The reason was that the woman has been offered <u>a chance to go to the States</u> as an <u>exchange student</u>.

6 The reason is that it looks like <u>it's going to rain soon</u>.

7 Wampanoag <u>Indians</u> and the <u>Pilgrims</u> first

celebrated it in <u>the autumn of 1621</u>.

8 The reason is that Sam failed the <u>final interview</u> for the company he really <u>wanted to work for</u>.

On Your Own 모범답안

p. 65

A

My Favorite Type of Vacation	
What type of vacation do you prefer?	(1) backpacking
What is the main reason?	(2) It is cheap so I can travel for a longer period of time.
What are other reasons?	(3) go any place and at any time I want (4) like meeting the locals as well as seeing the sights using public transportation
Which country would you like to travel in?	(5) Spain

I prefer (1)<u>backpacking</u> for a vacation. The main reason is that (2)<u>it is cheap so I can travel for a longer period of time</u>. There are other reasons. (3)<u>I can go any place and at any time I want</u>. Moreover, (4)<u>I like meeting the locals as well as seeing the sights using public transportation</u>. If I have a chance, I would like to travel (5)<u>in Spain</u>.

내가 좋아하는 휴가 형태	
선호하는 휴가 형태는?	(1) 배낭여행
주된 이유는?	(2) 저렴해서 더 오랜 기간 여행할 수 있어서
다른 이유들은?	(3) 내가 원할 때 언제 어디든 갈 수 있음. (4) 대중교통을 이용하며 관광을 하는 것뿐만 아니라 현지인들을 만나는 것을 좋아함.
어느 나라를 여행하고 싶은가?	(5) 스페인

저는 배낭여행을 선호합니다. 주된 이유는 저렴해서 더 오랜 기간 여행할 수 있기 때문입니다. 다른 이유들도 있습니다. 제가 원할 때 언제 어디든 갈 수 있다는 것입니다. 게다가 저는 대중교통을 이용해 볼 것들을 보는 것뿐만 아니라 현지인들을 만나는 것을 좋아합니다. 만약 제게 기회가 있다면, 저는 스페인을 여행하고 싶습니다.

B

The Most Important Traditional Holiday in Korea	
(1) the name of the traditional holiday	Seolnal, which is the first day of the Korean lunar calendar
(2) what people do on the holiday	People return to their hometowns to visit their parents and other relatives and perform a memorial ceremony for their ancestors. Many people wear traditional Korean clothing called Hanbok and eat tteokguk (rice cake soup).
(3) the reason for it being the most important one	We pay respect to our parents, relatives and ancestors on that day. We wish one another a Happy New Year.

I think that the most important Korean traditional holiday is (1)<u>Seolnal, which is the first day of the Korean lunar calendar</u>. During (1)the <u>Seolnal</u> holidays, (2)<u>people return to their hometowns to visit their parents and other relatives and perform a memorial ceremony for their ancestors. Many people wear traditional Korean clothing called Hanbok and eat tteokguk (rice cake soup)</u>. I think (1)<u>Seolnal</u> is the most important traditional holiday in Korea because (3) <u>we pay respect to our parents, relatives and ancestors on that day</u>. Also, <u>we wish one another a Happy New Year</u>.

가장 중요한 한국 명절	
(1) 명절의 이름	설날, 음력 1월 1일
(2) 명절을 지내는 방법	사람들은 부모님과 다른 친척들을 뵙기 위해서 고향으로 내려가고, 조상에게 차례를 지낸다. 많은 사람들은 한국 전통의상인 한복을 입고 떡국을 먹는다.
(3) 그 명절이 가장 중요한 이유	그날 부모님, 친척들, 그리고 조상에게 존경을 표한다. 서로서로의 행복한 한 해를 기원한다.

나는 한국에서 가장 중요한 명절은 음력 1월 1일인 설날이라고 생각한다. 설날 연휴동안에 사람들은 부모님과 다른 친척들을 뵙기 위해서 고향으로 내려가고, 조상에게 차례를 지낸다. 많은 사람들은 한국 전통의상인 한복을 입고 떡국을 먹는다. 내가 설날을 가장 중요한 명절이라고 생각하는 이유는 그날 부모님, 친척들, 그리고 조상에게 존경을 표하기 때문이다. 또한, 서로서로의 행복한 한 해를 기원한다.

01 ⑤	02 ①	03 ④	04 ⑤	05 ①
06 ③	07 ⑤	08 ④	09 ③	10 ⑤
11 ②	12 ②	13 ①	14 ④	15 ④
16 ⑤	17 ①	18 ④	19 ②	20 ④

01

M   Wow, look at these <u>musical</u> <u>posters</u> on the wall. Can you guess <u>how</u> <u>many</u> <u>there</u> <u>are</u>?

W   It looks like <u>more</u> <u>than</u> <u>fifty</u>. I can't believe that all these musicals are now playing in the city.

M   I heard that some shows have <u>eight</u> <u>performances</u> <u>a</u> <u>week</u>.

W   Oh, that might be the reason why it's so easy for people <u>to</u> <u>watch</u> a <u>musical</u> on Broadway when they travel to New York.

M   I can see <u>some</u> <u>familiar</u> ones. *The Phantom of the Opera, Chicago, Jesus Christ Superstar, Les Miserables, Mamma Mia*, the *Lion King*, and *Wicked*.

W   As we are in New York we can't <u>miss</u> <u>this</u> <u>chance</u>. Which one would you like to see among these?

M   Why don't we watch *Mamma Mia*?

W   Sorry. I saw it last year. How about *The Phantom of the Opera*? It has <u>been</u> <u>running</u> for <u>20</u> <u>years</u>.

M   Oh, that sounds great. There must be <u>something</u> <u>which</u> <u>attracts</u> <u>people</u> to it.

남   와, 벽에 붙은 이 많은 뮤지컬 포스터 좀 봐. 몇 개나 될까?

여   50개는 더 되어 보이는데. 이 뮤지컬들 모두가 지금 이 도시에서 상연되고 있다니 믿을 수가 없다.

남   이들 가운데 일부는 일주일에 8번 공연을 한다는군.

여   오, 그게 아마도 사람들이 뉴욕을 여행할 때 브로드웨이에서 뮤지컬을 쉽게 볼 수 있는 이유인 것 같아.

남   몇몇 친숙한 것들이 보여. 〈오페라의 유령〉, 〈시카고〉, 〈지져스크라이스트 수퍼스타〉, 〈레미제라블〉, 〈맘마미아〉, 〈라이온킹〉, 〈위키드〉.

여   우리가 여기 뉴욕에 있으니 이 기회 놓칠 수 없지. 이것들 중 뭘 보고 싶니?

남   〈맘마미아〉 보는 거 어때?

여   미안. 나 그거 작년에 봤어. 〈오페라의 유령〉은 어때? 20년째 공연되고 있어.

남   오, 그거 좋은데. 사람을 끄는 뭔가가 분명히 있을거야.

•• **performance** 공연   **familiar** 친숙한, 익숙한   **phantom** 유령   **wicked** 사악한   **run** 상연되다, 공연되다

02

M   Mom, I've got a problem.

W   What's up?

M   I have <u>a</u> <u>soccer</u> <u>match</u> this afternoon. All my friends are <u>riding</u> <u>their</u> <u>bikes</u> to the playground.

W   What's your problem, then?

M   You know Mike, my friend, don't you? I <u>let</u> <u>him</u> <u>borrow</u> <u>mine</u>. His bike needs to be repaired.

W   Well, I don't know what I can do.

M   Could you please tell Jenny to <u>let</u> <u>me</u> <u>use</u> <u>hers</u>? She <u>won't</u> <u>let</u> <u>me</u> <u>use</u> it because I <u>got</u> <u>a</u> <u>flat</u> <u>tire</u> the last time I used it.

W   Oh, I remember that. You didn't <u>repair</u> the tire. So your sister couldn't use it when she needed to.

남   엄마, 제게 문제가 하나 있어요.

여   무슨 일이니?

남   오늘 오후에 축구경기가 있는데요. 제 친구들 모두 운동장까지 자전거를 타고 갈 거에요.

여   그럼, 너한테 문제 될게 뭐니?

남   제 친구 Mike 아시죠? 제 걸 그애에게 빌려줬어요. 그애 자전거는 수리해야 해서요.

여   글쎄, 내가 무엇을 해줄 수 있는지 모르겠구나.

남   Jenny에게 그애 것을 제가 쓸 수 있게 해주라고 말해 주실 수 있으세요? 제가 지난번에 그애 자전거를 쓸 때 펑크를 냈기 때문에 제게 안 빌려줄 거에요.

여   오, 기억이 나는구나. 네가 타이어를 수리하지 않았지. 그래서 네 동생이 필요한 제 때 자전거를 사용할 수 없었지.

•• **borrow** 빌리다   **repair** 수리하다   **flat tire** 펑크 난 타이어

03

M   Good morning, students! My name is Michael Woods and I am running for <u>president</u> of the student council. I am running for this position because I want to be the voice for all the students in this school. 'Dedicated, Responsible and Enthusiastic,' these are the three words that describe me, and three reasons why you should vote for me. Some ideas I have to improve the school are more fundraisers, better food in the cafeteria, more lighting in classrooms, and more electives. I want students to know they can come to me with suggestions and I will listen to them and try to make a difference. I look forward to your votes on November 8th. Thank you.

남 안녕하세요, 학생 여러분! 제 이름은 Michael Woods이고 학생회 회장에 출마했습니다. 제가 이 보직에 출마한 이유는 이 학교의 모든 학생들을 위한 목소리를 내고 싶기 때문입니다. '헌신적이고, 책임감 있고 열정적인', 이것이 저를 묘사한 세 단어이고 여러분이 저를 뽑아야 할 세 가지 이유입니다. 제가 학교를 향상 시키기 위해 갖고 있는 몇 가지 아이디어는 더 많은 모금행사, 구내식당의 더 나은 음식, 교실에 더 많은 조명 설치 그리고 더 많은 선택과목 입니다. 저는 학생들이 제안을 가지고 제게 다가 올 수 있고 저는 그것을 듣고 변화를 만들기 위해 노력할 것이라는 점을 학생들이 알아주시길 바랍니다. 11월 8일 여러분의 투표를 기대합니다. 감사합니다.

••
run for ~에 출마하다 **president** 회장 **student council** 학생회 **position** 위치, 지위 **dedicated** 헌신적인 **responsible** 책임감 있는 **enthusiastic** 열정적인 **vote** 투표하다 **fundraiser** 모금행사 **elective** 선택과목

04

W It's 9 o'clock at night. Tom should have been home hours ago.

M Did you call Jason's house?

W Yes. I called Steve's house and Paul's house, too. I'm worried sick.

M He should have called us by now.

W Let's call the police.

M I heard that they won't do anything until a person has been missing for twenty-four hours.

W I can't take this.

M I'm sure he's all right.

W If he is all right, he's going to be punished.

여 밤 9시예요. Tom이 집에 올 시간이 벌써 몇 시간이나 지났어요.

남 Jason의 집에 전화해 봤소?

여 네. Steve와 Paul의 집에도 걸어 봤어요. 너무 걱정되네요.

남 지금쯤은 집에 전화라도 걸었어야지.

여 경찰에 신고해요.

남 경찰은 사람이 실종된 지 24시간까지는 아무 것도 안 한다고 들었소.

여 이 상황을 받아들일 수가 없군요.

남 그 애는 틀림없이 괜찮을 거요.

여 그렇다면, 그 애는 혼이 나야 해요.

① 안심한   ② 무관심한   ③ 놀란
④ 의심하는   ⑤ 속상한

••
by now 지금쯤은 **worried sick** 매우 걱정되는 **missing** 실종된 **punished** 벌받는, 혼나는

05

M Oh, is it raining outside? You're all wet!

W It is raining cats and dogs. I got caught in the rain when I was on the way back home from the grocery store.

M According to the weather forecast this morning, it is supposed to be sunny today.

W The weather is really unpredictable these days. I don't think the rain will stop soon.

M Really? I am going to play soccer with my friends this afternoon.

W I think you'd better not do that. You should wait till the rain stops.

M Yeah, you're right. I am going to text everyone right now.

W I hope you'll have the game tomorrow.

남 오, 밖에 비 오나요? 완전히 다 젖었어요!

여 비가 억수같이 퍼붓고 있어. 식료품점에서 집으로 돌아오는 길에 비를 만났어.

남 오늘 아침 일기예보에선 오늘 날씨는 맑을 거라고 했어요.

여 요즘 날씨는 너무 예측할 수가 없어. 내 생각엔 비가 금방 멈출 것 같지 않아.

남 정말요? 오늘 오후에 친구들과 축구할 예정인데요.

여 내 생각엔 안 하는게 낫겠어. 비가 멈출 때까지 기다려야 해.

남 네, 알았어요. 지금 당장 모두에게 문자 보내야겠어요.

여 내일은 게임 할 수 있길 바래.

rain cats and dogs 비가 억수같이 쏟아지다 **be[get] caught in the rain** 비를 만나다 **be supposed to-V** ~하기로 되어 있다 **unpredictable** 예측 불가능한

06

M Where's the bill? [Pause] Oh, it's here.

W Oh, let me get it this time.

M No. I'll get it.

W Come on. It's my turn. I insist!

M Don't worry, we'll split it then.

W All right. Let's do that this time.

M Let's see... the pasta is 16 dollars and chicken tender salad is 18 dollars. Then the total will be 34 dollars. How should we split it?

W Well, I ate the chicken tender salad so I'll pay for it. Here's the money.

M OK, I'll take it to the counter. I'll be back in a minute.

남 계산서 어디 있지? 아, 여기 있네.

여 오, 이번엔 내가 낼게.

남 아니야, 내가 낼게.

여 이봐, 이번엔 내 차례야. 내가 낸다구!

남 걱정 마. 그럼 나누어서 내자.

여 좋아. 이번엔 그렇게 하자.

남 어디 보자, 파스타 16 달러, 닭살 샐러드 18 달러야. 그럼 총 34 달러네. 어떻게 나눌까?.

여 음, 내가 닭살 샐러드를 먹었으니까 그건 내가 낼게. 여기 돈 있어.

남 좋아. 내가 카운터게 가서 낼게. 금방 올게.

turn 차례 **insist** 주장하다 **tender** (고기 등이) 부드러운, 연한 **total** 합계, 총액 **split** 쪼개다

07

M What are your qualifications?

W Well, I have an MBA from Yale Graduate School, not to mention a law degree from Harvard University.

M That's impressive. Do you have any experience?

W Yes. During my college years, I interned at a trading company.

M I see. And why do you want to work for us?

W I think your company has a large potential for growth.

M What section do you want to work in?

W I'd like to work in the overseas department.

남 자격요건이 어떻게 되시나요?

여 저는 하버드 대학교에서 받은 법학 학위 말고도 예일대 대학원의 경영학석사 학위를 소지하고 있습니다.

남 놀랍군요. 경험은 있으신지요?

여 네. 대학 재학 시절, 한 무역회사에서 인턴으로 근무했습니다.

남 네 알겠습니다. 왜 저희 회사에서 일하고 싶으신 거죠?

여 제 생각엔 이 회사가 성장가능성이 큰 것 같습니다.

남 어떤 부서에서 근무하고 싶으신가요?

여 해외부서에서 일하고 싶습니다.

qualification 자격요건 **not to mention** ~은 말할 것도 없고 **MBA** 경영학 석사학위 **impressive** 인상적인 **intern at** ~에서 인턴으로 근무하다

08

M It's been a long time, Sally.

W How have you been, Brian? We have the same day off, so it has been quite hard to make an appointment with you.

M Sorry for the inconvenience. How would you like it to be done this time?

W I brought a picture showing what I would like done. Here it is.

M Oh, this is called a pin curl perm. It is the in style this spring.

W Do you think it will look good on me?

M Of course. But I'll need to cut off the damaged ends first before I begin perming your hair.

W Okay. Please don't make it too short though.

M Don't worry.

남 오랜만이네요, Sally.

여 Biran, 어떻게 지내셨어요? 우리가 쉬는 날이 같아서 예약을 하기가 꽤 어려웠습니다.

남 불편을 드려 죄송합니다. 이번에는 어떻게 해드릴까요?

여 제가 원하는 걸 보여주는 사진을 가져왔어요. 여기 있습니다.

남 오, 이것은 핀컬펌이라고 불러요. 올 봄 유행하는 스타일입니다.

여 저에게 어울릴까요?

남 물론이요, 하지만 펌을 하기 전에 먼저 상한 머리를 잘라내야 해요.

여 네. 너무 짧게 하진 말아주세요.

남 걱정 마세요.

••
day off 쉬는 날, 비번 **inconvenience** 불편 **in style** 유행하는 **look good on** ~에 잘 어울리다 **cut off** 잘라내다 **damaged** 손상된

09

① M Welcome to the Zoo, Zoo, Zoo.

W Where can I see the giraffes?

② M How long will it take to get to the zoo?

W It will take about an hour by public transportation.

③ M Look at the sign over there. You can't feed the animals.

W I'm sorry. I didn't see it.

④ M What do you think of this uniform?

W It looks good on you.

⑤ M I wonder what's wrong with you.

W I left my lunch box on the bus.

....

① 남 Zoo, Zoo, Zoo에 오신 것을 환영합니다.

여 기린은 어디에서 볼 수 있나요?

② 남 동물원에 가는 데 얼마나 걸리나요?

여 대중교통으로 대략 한 시간 걸립니다.

③ 남 저 쪽에 있는 표지판을 보세요. 동물에게 먹이를 주시면 안됩니다.

여 죄송합니다. 못 봤어요.

④ 남 이 유니폼 어때?

여 잘 어울리는데.

⑤ 남 너 무슨 일인지 궁금해.

여 버스에 점심도시락을 놓고 왔어.

••
giraffe 기린 **get to** ~에 도착하다 **feed** 먹이를 주다

10

W Did you have a chance to look it over for me?

M Yes, I did. I just finished reading it.

W What do you think about it? Do you think it is okay?

M In my opinion, you'd better rewrite the conclusion. It is too weak. It doesn't summarize the main points well. In other words, it is not clear enough.

W What do you recommend I do?

M Well. You have to read your paper again and highlight the sentences that are important.

W And then?

M Try to summarize and restate what you highlighted in the conclusion. Your main point should be clearly understood.

W I will try. If it's okay with you, can you please review it again before I turn it in?

M No problem. Send it to me by Saturday.

....

여 그것 검토해 볼 기회가 있었니?

남 응. 방금 읽는 걸 끝냈어.

여 어떻게 생각해? 괜찮을까?

남 내 생각에는 결론 부분을 다시 쓰는 게 더 나을 것 같아. 너무 약해. 요지를 잘 요약하지 못하고 있어. 다시 말해서, 명확하지가 않아.

여 내가 어떻게 했으면 하니?

남 음. 네 리포트를 다시 읽고 중요한 문장에 강조 표시를 해.

여 그런 다음에는?

남 결론에서 네가 강조한 것을 요약하고 재서술해봐. 너의 요지가 명확하게 이해되어야 해.

여 해볼게. 만일 괜찮으면 내가 제출하기 전에 다시 봐줄 수 있겠니?

남 문제없어. 토요일까지 보내줘.

••
in my opinion 내 의견으로는 **rewrite** 고쳐 쓰다 **conclusion** 결론 **summarize** 요약하다 **in other words** 다시 말해서 **restate** 고쳐 말하다 **turn in** 제출하다

11

[Telephone rings.]

M Hello, Fastro Customer Service. Can I help you?

W Hello. I'd like to extend the contract on my Internet connection.

M May I have your name and phone number?

W This is Kate Smith. My number is 02-100-0207.

M Confirmed. How long do you want to extend the contract for?

W For a year. Do you have any special offers for customers renewing their contract?

M Well, since you've been with us for three years now, we can upgrade your connection speed and give you one month's free service.

W Great. I will take that offer.

M　A serviceman will visit your house to upgrade the connection next week. He will call you. Please sign the contract at that time. Thank you.

....

[전화벨이 울린다.]

남　여보세요. Fastro 고객서비스 입니다. 무엇을 도와드릴까요?

여　여보세요. 인터넷 연결 계약을 연장하고 싶은데요.

남　이름과 정화번호를 알려주시겠어요?

여　제 이름은 Kate Smith입니다. 번호는 02-100-0207입니다.

남　확인되셨습니다. 얼마나 연장하실 건가요?

여　1년이요. 계약 갱신하는 고객을 위한 특별 혜택이 있나요?

남　음, 삼년 째 우리와 함께 하셨으니 연결 속도를 업그레이드 해드리고, 한달 무료서비스를 드릴 수 있습니다.

여　좋네요. 제안을 받아들일게요.

남　다음 주에 서비스맨이 댁에 방문해서 연결을 업그레이드 시켜드릴 것입니다. 전화를 드릴 테니 그때 계약서에 사인하시면 됩니다. 감사합니다.

●●
customer service 고객서비스　**extend** 연장하다　**contract** 계약
Internet connection 인터넷 연결　**confirmed** 확인된　**renew** 갱신하다, 연장하다　**offer** 제안

12

M　Please come in. How can I help you?

W　I am not sure which one would be a good pet for my son.

M　Do you want to give him a pet he can play with or one which he has to take care of inside its cage?

W　I haven't thought about that. Which type is better for a five-year-old boy?

M　Well, it depends. If your son is active, I recommend a puppy or a cat to play with. But if he is not active, a hamster is a good choice.

W　Any exotic animals?

M　Some children like to raise iguanas or lizards.

W　Thank you for your helpful information.

M　You're welcome. I'll give you some time to think about it.

....

남　들어오세요. 무엇을 도와드릴까요?

여　애완동물로 제 아들에게 무엇이 좋은지 모르겠습니다.

남　아드님께 함께 놀 수 있는 것을 주고 싶으세요 아니면 우리 안에서 돌보는 것을 주고 싶으세요?

여　그건 생각해보지 않았습니다. 5살 남자 아이에겐 어떤 것이 좋을까요?

남　음, 경우에 따라 다릅니다. 만일 아드님이 활동적이라면, 함께 놀 수 있는 강아지나 고양이를 추천합니다. 하지만 활동적이지 않다면 햄스터가 좋은 선택입니다.

여　이국적인 동물은요?

남　어떤 아이들은 이구아나나 도마뱀 기르는 것을 좋아합니다.

여　도움되는 정보 감사해요.

남　천만에요. 생각해 볼 시간을 좀 드리지요.

●●
cage 우리　**It depends.** 경우에 따라 다르다　**recommend** 추천하다
exotic 외래의, 이국적인　**iguana** 이구아나　**lizard** 도마뱀

13

① M　It is about the life saving.

② M　It is a month-long contest throughout March.

③ M　You can only apply online.

④ M　The difference in winnings between second and third is 800 dollars.

⑤ M　You can ask for further information over the phone or by email.

....

┌───┐
아이디어 콘테스트

① 부문: 삶을 더 쉽게 만들어주는 아무것이나

② 기간: 3월 1일 부터 3월 31일

③ 신청 방법: 온라인

④ 시상내역: 1등 2,000달러
　　　　　　　2등 1,500달러
　　　　　　　3등 700달러

⑤ 기타문의: 080-8080-1234 또는 ideacontest@contest.com
└───┘

① 남　그것은 인명구조에 관한 것이다.

② 남　3월 한달 동안 치러지는 대회이다.

③ 남　온라인으로만 지원할 수 있다.

④ 남　2등과 3등 사이의 상금의 차이는 800달러이다.

⑤ 남　기타 문의는 전화나 이메일로 할 수 있다.

●●
life saving 인명구조　**apply** 지원하다　**difference** 차이　**winnings** 상금　**further information** 기타문의

14

M　Are you done with your social studies report?

W　Yes. I just finished it. How about you?

M　I need some more time to finish it. I will continue

working on it over the weekend.

W That's too bad. You know what? I'm planning to do something special this weekend.

M What's that? Going somewhere?

W Yes. I will visit an orphanage with my church friends. We go there the second Saturday of every month.

M Really? That sounds great. Can I join you next time?

W Why not? Why don't you go to the senior center with us next weekend?

M Ok, I will. Please remind me the day before.

남 너 사회 리포트 끝냈니?

여 응. 방금 끝냈어. 너는?

남 끝내려면 시간이 조금 더 필요해. 아무래도 주말 동안에 계속해야 할 것 같아.

여 안됐구나. 너 그거 알아? 나 이번 주말에 특별한 것 할 계획이야.

남 뭔데? 어디 가?

여 응. 교회 친구들이랑 고아원 갈 거야. 우리는 매월 둘째 토요일에 가.

남 정말? 멋지다. 다음 번에 나도 가도 돼?

여 당연하지. 다음 주에 우리와 양로원에 가는 건 어때?

남 그럴게. 하루 전에 나에게 알려줘.

•• **social studies** 사회 **continue** 계속하다, 유지하다 **orphanage** 고아원 **senior center** 양로원 **remind** 생각나게 하다

15

W Hello, passengers of flight 705 bound for Chicago, with a stop in L.A. The departure gate has been changed to 30B. Also, there will be a slight departure delay due to the heavy snowstorm outside. The ground crew is clearing the snow on the runway in preparation for departure. It also looks like the flight is slightly overbooked, so we are offering free round-trip tickets to a few passengers willing to take a later flight. We should be boarding in a quarter of an hour. Thank you for your patience.

여 LA를 경유하는 시카고 행 705항공편 승객 여러분 안녕하세요. 출발 탑승구가 30B로 변경되었습니다. 또한, 폭설 때문에 출발이 다소

지연될 예정입니다. 지상근무 단이 출발준비로 활주로에 있는 눈을 치우고 있는 중입니다. 또한 예약이 조금 초과되어서 다음 비행편을 이용해주실 승객님께는 무료 왕복권을 제공해드리고 있습니다. 대략 15분 후에 탑승을 시작하겠습니다. 기다려 주셔서 감사합니다.

•• **bound for** ~행의 **departure gate** 출발 탑승구 **heavy snowstorm** 폭설 **runway** 활주로 **board** 탑승하다

16

W Congratulations on your new job, Chris!

M Thanks, Angie. To tell you the truth, I'm not so sure I like to work.

W Why do you say that? Last year you wanted to get out of university!

M I know, but that was last year. Now, it's just that I only work. I work hard all day, every day.

W Oh, come on. Don't complain. You're making a good salary now.

M Right. Now, I have money and a nice car. But I don't have any time to enjoy either of them.

W It can't be all that bad.

M No, of course it isn't. I still have my weekends.

W So tell me, what do you miss about university?

M Going to parties and staying up late talking with friends.

여 Chris, 새 직장 축하해.

남 고마워, Angie. 사실, 내가 일하는 걸 좋아하는지 정말 확신이 없어.

여 왜 그런 말을 하니? 작년에는 대학교에서 벗어나고 싶어했잖아.

남 나도 알아, 하지만 그건 작년 일이지. 지금은 오직 일 뿐이야. 하루 종일 매일 열심히 일만 해.

여 이봐. 불평하지마. 너는 지금 돈 잘 벌잖아.

남 맞아. 지금은 돈도 있고, 멋진 차도 있지. 하지만 그것들 전부를 누릴 수 있는 시간이 없어.

여 전부 그렇게 나쁘지는 않아.

남 응, 다 나쁜 건 아니지. 여전히 주말이 있으니까.

여 그럼 말해봐. 대학생활에서 어떤 게 그립니?

남 파티에 가고 친구들과 이야기하면서 늦게까지 자지 않는 것.

① 이번 주말에 산에 갈 거야.

② 나의 동료들과 함께 휴가를 가고 싶어.

③ 가능한 한 많은 친구를 만들었어야 했는데.

④ 화학시험을 치르지 못해서 추가 시험을 봐야 해.

to tell the truth 사실을 말하자면 **get out of** ~에서 벗어나다 **all day**
하루 종일 **make a good salary** 돈을 잘 벌다

17

W Hello. BestStay Hotel. May I help you?

M Yes, I'd like to reserve a room for two on the 21st
of August.

W Okay. Let me check our computer here for a
moment. August 21st, right?

M Yes, are you all booked that night?

W Well, we have one suite available, complete with a
kitchenette and a sauna bath. And the view of the
city is great, too.

M How much is that?

W It's only $300, plus a 10% room tax.

M That's a little too expensive for me.

여 안녕하세요. BestStay Hotel입니다. 도와드릴까요?

남 네. 8월 21에 두 명이 묵을 방을 예약하고 싶습니다.

여 네. 잠깐 여기에 있는 컴퓨터로 확인해 볼게요. 8월 21일 맞죠?

남 네. 그 날은 예약이 다 찼나요?

여 음. 작은 부엌과 사우나탕이 완비된 스위트룸이 하나 있습니다. 그리고
도시 전망도 멋집니다.

남 얼마인가요?

여 300달러에 세금 10%가 붙습니다.

남 저에게는 좀 많이 비싸네요.

② 이용 가능한 스위트룸 있나요?

③ 조부모님을 뵐 계획이에요.

④ 아뇨, 저는 다른 방을 추천하고 싶어요.

⑤ 사탕을 많이 산다면, 할인을 받을 수 있나요?

suite 스위트룸 (연결된 몇 개의 방으로 이루어진 공간) **complete with**
~이 완비된 **kitchenette** 작은 부엌

18

M I have to give a presentation on international
relations on Friday, and I am so nervous.

W There are a lot of things you can do to make
yourself feel more confident and less nervous.

M What should I do, Mary?

W First of all, you need to understand the subject
matter thoroughly.

M I have done a lot of research on the subject, and
I believe I can answer any questions I will receive
from the audience.

W Then you're ready to write your presentation. And
after you write it, make a brief outline which you'll
use to practice speaking.

M You mean I shouldn't read everything I wrote
down.

W That's right. Look at the outline when you speak.

남 국제관계에 대해서 금요일에 발표를 해야 하는데 너무 긴장돼.

여 더 자신감을 가지고 덜 긴장하도록 네가 할 수 있는 많은 방법들이
있어.

남 나 어떻게 해야 할까, Mary?

여 먼저, 너는 주제를 완전히 이해해야 해.

남 나는 주제에 대해서 많은 연구를 했고, 청중으로부터 받게 될 어떤
질문에도 대답할 수 있다고 생각해.

여 그런 다음엔 네 발표를 쓸 준비가 되어 있어야 해. 그것을 쓴 다음 발표
연습에 사용할 간단한 개요를 만들어야 해.

남 내가 쓴 모든 것을 읽어선 안 된다는 거구나.

여 맞아, 말할 때는 개요를 봐.

① 좋아, 나는 내 연설의 개요를 만들었어.

② 나는 연설문을 쓰는 법에 대해 많이 읽었어.

③ 그래, 너는 주제부터 먼저 결정해야 해.

⑤ 아니, 너는 혼자 20분 이상 말해야 할 거야.

give a presentation 발표하다 **confident** 자신감 있는 **thoroughly**
완전히, 철저히 **do research on** ~을 연구하다 **audience** 청중
outline 윤곽, 개요

19

M My uncle was hospitalized yesterday.

W What seems to be the problem?

M He has got lung cancer. The doctor said that it was
probably caused by his bad habit of smoking.

W I'm sorry to hear that. So how long has he been
smoking?

M I'm not really sure, but it might be about 20 years.

W Oh, that's too long. He must stop smoking now or
the cancer will get worse.

M I think so, too. Smoking just makes matters worse. Hopefully he can stop smoking.

W Shall we visit him today?

M Yes, if you don't mind.

W No problem. Let's go buy some fruit first.

....

남 삼촌이 어제 병원에 입원하셨어.

여 어디가 안 좋으셔?

남 그는 폐암에 걸리셨어. 의사선생님이 그의 나쁜 흡연습관에 의해서 발병된 것 같다고 하셨어.

여 안됐다. 그래서 얼마나 오랫동안 담배를 피우신 거야?

남 정확하지는 않지만, 20년 정도 될 거야.

여 오, 너무 오래되셨다. 금연하시지 않으면 병이 더 악화될 거야.

남 나도 그렇게 생각해. 흡연은 문제를 더 악화시켜. 바라건대, 그는 금연을 하실 거야.

여 우리 오늘 병문안 갈까?

남 응, 네가 싫어하지 않는다면.

여 괜찮아. 먼저 과일 좀 사고 가자.

① 응, 내일은 너를 방문하기 힘들어.

③ 좋아, 그의 검사 결과가 내일 나올 거야.

④ 그러면 네가 그를 병원에 데려가야 한다고 생각해.

⑤ 괜찮아. 내일은 그를 방문하기 좋은 때야.

be hospitalized 입원하다 **lung** 폐 **mind** 꺼려하다

20

W Bomi's family is on vacation. They are staying in Hawaii for five days. Everyone in her family is excited. She and her brother want to go on a submarine tour and see fish underwater. Her mother wants to go shopping and her father wants the family to go hiking in the morning and have a barbecue on the beach in the evening. However, he is worried about spending too much money. Her mother thinks he worries too much about money and wants him to relax and forget about money while they are on vacation. In this situation, what would Bomi's mother probably say to her husband?

....

여 보미 가족은 휴가 중이다. 그들은 하와이에서 5일 동안 머무르고 있다. 가족 모두는 들떠있다. 보미와 보미의 동생은 잠수함 투어를 가서 바다속 물고기를 보고 싶어 한다. 그녀의 엄마는 쇼핑을 하고 싶어하고

그녀의 아빠는 아침에 가족이 함께 하이킹을 하고 저녁에 해변에서 바비큐를 먹기를 원한다. 하지만, 그는 돈을 너무 많이 쓰는 것을 걱정한다. 그녀의 엄마는 그가 돈 걱정을 너무 많이 한다고 생각하고 그들이 휴가를 보내는 동안은 그가 돈을 잊어버리고 휴식을 취하기를 원한다. 이런 상황에서 보미의 엄마는 그녀의 남편에게 뭐라고 말할 것 같은가?

① 여보, 우리 심각한 자금 문제가 생긴 것 같아요.

② 너무 재미있으니 매년 여기로 여행 오자.

③ 그것에 대해서 계속 생각하면 답을 구할 수 있을 거에요.

④ 여보, 걱정 그만하고 휴가를 즐겨봐요.

⑤ 돈을 좀 구하려고 은행에 가야할 것 같아요.

be on vacation 휴가중이다 **submarine** 잠수함

p. 74

Further Study 정답

1 It has been running for 20 years.

2 He does not have it because he let Mike borrow his bike.

3 According to what she said, I expect her to punish him.

4 She has to read her paper again and highlight the sentences that are important.

5 She'd like to extend the contract for her Internet connection.

6 She goes there the second Saturday of every month.

7 He works hard all day and doesn't have any time to enjoy his money and car.

8 It's $300, plus a 10% room tax.

A

A Speech for the Election	
(1) Position	the president of the student council
(2) Why are you running for this position?	I want to be the voice for all the students in this school.
(3) Why should students vote for you?	I am dedicated, responsible and enthusiastic.
(4) What ideas do you have to improve the school?	more fundraisers, better food in the cafeteria, more lighting in classrooms, and more electives

Good morning, students! My name is Michael Woods and I am running for (1)president of the student council. I am running for this position because (2)I want to be the voice for all the students in this school. You should vote for me because I am (3)dedicated, responsible and enthusiastic. Some ideas I have to improve the school are (4)more fundraisers, better food in the cafeteria, more lighting in classrooms, and more electives. Thank you.

선거 연설	
(1) 보직	학생회 회장
(2) 왜 이 보직에 출마했나?	이 학교의 모든 학생들을 위한 신문고가 되고 싶기 때문
(3) 왜 학생들이 당신을 뽑아야 하는가?	나는 헌신적이고, 책임감 있고 열정적이기 때문에
(4) 학교를 개선시키기 위해 갖고 있는 아이디어는?	더 많은 모금행사, 구내식당의 더 나은 음식, 교실 안에 더 많은 조명설치와 더 많은 선택과목

안녕하세요. 학생 여러분! 제 이름은 Michael Woods이고 저는 학생회 회장에 출마했습니다. 제가 이 보직에 출마한 이유는 이 학교의 모든 학생들을 위한 신문고가 되고 싶기 때문입니다. 저는 헌신적이고, 책임감 있고 열정적이기 때문에 저에게 투표하셔야 합니다. 제가 학교를 개선하기 위해 갖고 있는 몇 가지 아이디어는 더 많은 모금행사, 구내식당의 더 나은 음식, 교실 내 더 많은 조명설치와 더 많은 선택과목 입니다. 감사합니다.

B

My New Hairstyle	
(1) How long would your hair be?	waist-length
(2) What color would it be?	either blond or chocolate brown
(3) Would you have bangs? Why? Why not?	No. They bother me a lot when they keep falling down in my face.
(4) Would you prefer straight hair or wavy hair? Why?	wavy hair / It looks more fashionable and feminine.

I'm going to talk about the hairstyle I would have if my school lifted restrictions on hairstyles. My hair would be (1)waist-length. I would have (2)either blond or chocolate brown hair. I wouldn't have bangs because (3)they bother me a lot when they keep falling down in my face. I would prefer to have (4)wavy hair because it looks more fashionable and feminine.

나의 새 헤어스타일	
(1) 얼마나 깁니까?	허리 길이
(2) 무슨 색입니까?	금발 혹은 짙은 밤색
(3) 앞머리가 있나요? 이유는?	없음. 얼굴을 계속 가려서 성가심
(4) 생머리가 좋나요 아니면 웨이브 머리가 좋나요? 이유는?	웨이브 머리/ 유행에 앞서 보이고 여성스러워 보여서

저는 두발에 대한 학교 규제가 풀렸을 때 제가 하고 싶은 헤어스타일에 대해 이야기 할 것입니다. 저는 제 머리가 허리까지 길 것입니다. 저는 금발이나 초콜릿 브라운 색깔 머리를 할 것입니다. 앞머리는 내리지 않을 것인데 계속 얼굴에 흘러내리면 귀찮기 때문입니다. 저는 더 멋스럽고 여성스러워 보이기 때문에 웨이브 머리를 선호합니다.

L istening T est 정답

중학영어듣기 모의고사 08화

p. 80

01 ①	02 ⑤	03 ⑤	04 ②	05 ③
06 ④	07 ⑤	08 ④	09 ⑤	10 ④
11 ①	12 ③	13 ②	14 ③	15 ④
16 ①	17 ⑤	18 ④	19 ④	20 ②

01

M I'm looking for a television to <u>install</u> in my living room. Can you recommend one?

W The <u>45</u> and 50-inch <u>screens</u> are the most popular sizes for the living room. How about a 50-inch Smart TV?

M I've heard a lot about Smart TVs, but I don't know anything about them. Could you tell me <u>about them</u>?

W Okay. A Smart TV is a <u>hybrid</u> TV <u>device</u>. It includes various functions such as a <u>digital</u> television system, a set-top box, <u>digital</u> <u>media</u> <u>players</u> and game consoles <u>as</u> <u>well</u>.

M Oh, fantastic. Well, I have some Blu-Ray movies. Can I play them with it?

W Of course. It also <u>functions</u> as a Blu-Ray player.

M Sound perfect. But I think a 50-inch screen is <u>too big</u> for my <u>cozy</u> <u>living</u> <u>room</u>. Do you have a <u>40</u> or <u>42</u>-inch <u>one</u>?

W We have <u>both</u>.

M Okay, then I'll take a <u>40</u>-inch one.

· ·

M 거실에 설치할 텔레비전을 찾고 있어요. 추천해 주시겠어요?

W 거실용으로는 45인치와 50인치 화면이 인기 있습니다. 50인치 스마트 TV가 어떠세요?

M 스마트 TV에 대해 들어본 적은 많은데 그것에 대해 아는 것이 하나도 없네요. 그것에 대해 말씀 좀 해 주시겠어요?

W 네. 스마트 TV는 혼합 TV 장치입니다. 그것은 다양한 기능을 갖고 있는데요. 예를 들면 디지털 텔레비전 시스템, 셋톱박스, 디지털미디어 플레이어, 게임기 등의 역할을 포함합니다.

M 오, 환상적이네요. 그런데, 제가 블루레이 영화를 몇 편 가지고 있는데요. TV에 그걸 틀 수 있을까요?

W 물론이죠. 블루레이 작동장치로도 기능을 합니다.

M 완벽해요. 하지만 50인치는 제 아담한 거실에는 너무 큰 것 같아요. 40인치 혹은 42인치가 있나요?

W 네, 둘 다 있습니다.

M 좋아요. 그럼 전 40인치로 하겠습니다.

··
hybrid 혼성체, 혼합물   **device** 장치   **function** 기능하다   **Blu-Ray** 광디스크 저장 매체

02

W Hey, Chris! This is my brother's <u>present</u> for you.

M What's this <u>present</u> for? My birthday is <u>three</u> <u>months</u> <u>off</u>.

W He knows that. Just open it.

M Wow, this shirt is <u>the style</u> that I really like. By the way, could you tell me why he is giving this to me?

W This morning, my brother said it isn't <u>his</u> <u>style</u>. He bought it yesterday <u>on impulse</u> as it was 50% <u>off</u>. Unfortunately, it's <u>nonrefundable</u>.

M I'm sorry to hear that.

W He said you are <u>the</u> <u>right</u> <u>person</u> to wear this style.

M It's my good luck I guess. How do I look?

W Oh, he was right! It <u>looks</u> really <u>good</u> <u>on</u> you. You look very <u>stylish</u>.

M Yeah, I'm <u>on the same page</u> with you. Say thanks to him.

· ·

여 이봐, Chris! 이건 널 위한 우리 오빠의 선물이야.

남 무엇 때문에 주는 선물이야? 내 생일은 3개월이나 남았는데.

여 그도 그걸 알아. 그냥 열어봐.

남 와, 이 셔츠는 내가 정말 좋아하는 스타일이야. 그런데 그가 왜 내게 이걸 주는지 이유를 말해줄래?

여 아침에 오빠가 이 옷이 자기 스타일이 아니라고 했어. 오빠 이걸 어제 50% 할인이라 충동구매 했거든. 불행하게도, 환불이 안돼.

남 유감이구나.

여 오빠가 이 스타일을 입을 딱 맞는 사람이 바로 너래.

남 내가 운이 좋은 것 같아. 나 어떠니?

여 오, 오빠가 맞았네! 너한테 정말 잘 어울려. 너 정말 스타일 좋아 보여.

남 그래, 나도 네 말에 동의해. 그에게 고맙다고 전해줘.

··
on impulse 충동적으로   **nonrefundable** 환불되지 않는   **on the same page** 같은 생각을 하고 있는, 동의하는

03

M Please return items by their due date as someone else is waiting for them. If items are not returned by their due date, other users, who have recalled or placed holds on these items, are inconvenienced. To discourage this, the library levies fines. If you have outstanding fines on your record, you will not be allowed to borrow until these are cleared. Students in their final year will not be able to graduate until all debts to the library have been cleared. Remember that you need never pay a library fine if you return your loans on time!

남 다른 누군가가 기다리고 있으니 주어진 기일까지 품목들을 반환해주세요. 만약 마감일까지 품목들이 반환되지 않는다면, 재요청자 혹은 이 품목에 예약을 걸어놓은 다른 사용자들이 불편을 겪게 됩니다. 이것을 막기 위해, 도서관은 벌금을 부과합니다. 여러분의 기록에 체납 벌금이 있다면, 이것이 정리될 때까지 대출이 허용되지 않을 것입니다. 졸업학년의 학생들은 도서관 부채가 정리되기 전까지 졸업하실 수 없을 것입니다. 제때에 대출을 상환하신다면 도서관 벌금을 물어야 할 필요가 없다는 것을 기억하세요!

•• **due date** 마감일, 기한 **recall** 다시 불러들이다, 회수하다 **inconvenienced** 불편한 **discourage** 막다, 말리다 **levy fines** 벌금을 부과하다 **outstanding** 뛰어난, 두드러진 **debt** 빚 **loan** 대출

04

M Hi, Cindy. It's me, Tom. I'm here in front of the theater. Where are you now?

W Hi, Tom. I'm terribly sorry. I'm still on the way there. I left the office early, but I've been stuck in traffic for over half an hour.

M When do you expect to be here?

W I'm not sure. I shouldn't have taken this route. It's completely backed up.

M Oh, according to the traffic report, there is a bad accident on the road near the concert hall.

W I thought as much.

M I booked a table for a light dinner in a restaurant near the concert hall where we're going to watch the musical, I'll have to cancel it.

W Sorry, I can't help it. The traffic is terrible. Anyway I'll do my best to get there as fast as possible.

M I hope we won't miss this musical due to the traffic jam.

남 안녕, Cindy. 나야, Tom. 여기 극장 앞인데. 너 지금 어디니?
여 안녕, Tom. 정말 미안해. 나 여전히 거기로 가고 있어. 일찍 사무실을 떠났는데, 30분 넘게 교통체증에 갇혀 있어.
남 여기 언제쯤 도착할 것 같니?
여 잘 모르겠어. 이 길로 오지 말았어야 하는 건데. 완전히 막히네.
남 오, 교통 방송 안내에 따르면, 콘서트 홀 근처 도로에서 사고가 났대.
여 내 그럴 줄 알았어.
남 뮤지컬 볼 콘서트홀 근처 레스토랑에서 간단한 저녁 먹으려고 좌석을 예약했는데. 취소해야겠다.
여 미안해, 나도 어쩔 수 없어. 교통체증이 너무 심해. 어쨌든, 빨리 도착하도록 최선을 다할게.
남 교통체증 때문에 우리가 이 뮤지컬을 놓치지 않길 바래.

① 기분 좋은　　② 걱정하는
③ 편안한　　　④ 외로운
⑤ 자신만만한

•• **stuck in traffic** 교통이 막힌[정체된] **be backed up** 밀려있다, 꽉 막히다 **traffic report** 교통 방송 안내 **cancel** 취소하다

05

M Good morning. Could you do me a favor?

W What can I do for you?

M I have to deliver this package to one of your residents. Unfortunately, there's no unit number on it.

W Have you tried to contact the receiver?

M Of course, I did. But she didn't pick up her cell phone. There's no reply to my text message as well.

W Alright, let me check the name on the box, and then I'll check the residents' list.

M Okay, have a look at this. Her name is Martha Jones.

W Oh, she lives in Unit 321. Just leave the box here and let her know her package is here.

M Thank you so much.

남 안녕하세요. 부탁 좀 드릴 수 있을까요?

여 무엇을 도와 드릴까요?

남 이 소포를 여기 주민 중 한 분께 배송해야 하는데요. 불행하게도 그것에 세대 동호수가 없습니다.

여 받으실 분에게 연락해보셨나요?

남 물론 해봤습니다. 하지만 그녀는 전화를 받지 않았어요. 제 문자에도 답변이 없고요.

여 알겠습니다. 상자 위에 이름을 확인해 본 후 거주자 명단을 확인하겠습니다.

남 네. 여기를 보세요. 이름이 Martha Jones입니다.

여 오, 그녀는 321호에 살아요. 상자를 여기에 두시고 그녀에게 소포가 여기 있다는 것을 알려주세요.

남 정말 감사합니다.

•• **deliver** 배달하다, 배송하다 **resident** 거주자 **unit** (공동주택내의) 한 가구 **receiver** 수신자, 받는 사람 **reply to** ~에 답변하다. 대응하다

06

W May I help you?

M Yes, I'd like to reserve <u>four seats for</u> tonight's Mozart concert.

W What section would you like? We have seats in the <u>general section</u> and seats in the <u>front circle</u> available.

M How much is each section?

W A ticket in the <u>general section</u> is <u>30</u> dollars, and a ticket in the <u>front circle</u> is <u>40</u> dollars.

M Do <u>students</u> and <u>seniors</u> get a discount?

W Yes, they do. Students and seniors receive a 10% <u>discount</u> with proper ID.

M I'd like 1 seat for a <u>student</u>, 2 seats for <u>adults</u>, and 1 seat for a <u>senior</u> in the <u>front circle</u>.

W How would you like to pay, sir?

M With this debit card, please.

여 무엇을 도와드릴까요?

남 오늘밤 모차르트 콘서트 네 자리를 예약하고 싶습니다.

여 무슨 자리를 원하세요? 가능한 좌석은 일반석과 정면석입니다.

남 각각 얼마인가요?

여 일반석은 30달러, 정면석은 40달러입니다.

남 학생과 노인은 할인이 되나요?

여 네. 학생과 노인은 신분증을 제시하시면 10% 할인을 받습니다.

남 정면석으로 학생표 1장, 성인표 2장, 경로우대표 1장 주세요.

여 지불은 어떻게 하시겠습니까, 손님?

남 이 체크카드로 부탁드립니다.

•• **general section** 일반구역 **available** 이용가능한 **senior** 연장자, 노인

07

M Excuse me, how do I get to Hoyts' Theater?

W I'll <u>show you the way</u>. I'm going there myself <u>as a matter of fact</u>.

M I'm rather <u>pressed</u> for time. Do you know a <u>shortcut</u>?

W Sure. <u>Follow me</u>.

M You really know <u>this area</u> well. Have you lived here long?

W Yes. I've lived here all my life.

M By the way, <u>how far is it</u>?

W It's <u>just across the street</u>. Can you see <u>the sign</u> over there?

M Yes, I can. You are very <u>hospitable</u> to strangers. Without you, I would have <u>gotten lost</u> and <u>wandered around</u> for hours. Thank you very much.

남 실례합니다. Hoyts 극장에 어떻게 가면 되나요?

여 제가 길을 안내해 드릴게요. 실은 저도 거기에 가는 길이에요.

남 제가 시간이 좀 촉박한데요. 지름길을 아시나요?

여 물론이죠. 따라오세요.

남 이 지역을 정말 잘 아시는 군요. 여기 오래 사셨어요?

여 네. 평생을 여기에서 살았어요.

남 그건 그렇고, 얼마나 먼가요?

여 바로 길 건너편에 있어요. 저기 간판 보이시죠?

남 네, 보여요. 낯선 사람에게 정말 친절하시군요. 당신이 아니었으면, 길을 잃고 몇 시간을 헤매 다녔을 거예요. 정말 감사합니다.

•• **as a matter of fact** 사실은 **pressed** 압박을 받고 있는 **shortcut** 지름길 **hospitable** 환대하는, 친절한 **stranger** 이방인 **wander around** 헤매다

08

M How do you feel today?

W Not bad. What's the <u>training schedule</u> for today?

M Since this is your first day, you will <u>exercise lightly</u>. First, you'll do some running to warm up.

W Good. I like running. I can run 10 kilometers without taking a rest.

M That's good. What's your fastest time to run 10 kilometers?

W About an hour and a half.

M In a month from now, you will be able to do it in under an hour.

W But the Hangang Marathon is three weeks from now. I'm going to run the 10km course and I want to be faster by then.

M Don't expect magic. Just try to do your best this time and try again next year.

남 오늘 기분이 어떠세요?
여 나쁘지 않습니다. 오늘 훈련 일정이 어떻게 되나요?
남 오늘이 처음이시니 가볍게 운동하겠습니다. 먼저 몸을 풀기 위해 달리기를 하겠습니다.
여 좋네요. 저는 달리는 것을 좋아합니다. 저는 쉬지 않고 10킬로미터를 달릴 수 있습니다.
남 좋군요. 10킬로미터 달리기 최고 기록이 어떻게 되세요?
여 한 시간 반이요.
남 한 달 후에는 한 시간 안에 달리실 수 있을 것입니다.
여 하지만 지금부터 3주 후에 한강 마라톤이 있는데요. 10키로 코스를 달릴 예정이니 그 때까지는 더 빨라지고 싶어요.
남 마술을 기대하지 마세요. 이번에는 최선을 다하시고 내년에 다시 시도해보세요.

••
training schedule 훈련 일정 **exercise lightly** 가볍게 운동하다 **expect** 기대하다 **do one's best** 최선을 다하다

09

① M Where can I rent a formal suit or tuxedo for my graduation ceremony?
   W Here is the number of a shop downtown.
② M Do you know to whom the award is to be presented?
   W No. Do you?
③ M I'm very happy that you are getting this prize.
   W Thank you. I owe it all to you.
④ M Let's go to the auditorium now or we will be late.
   W Okay.

⑤ M Thank you for your praise and encouragement.
   W You deserve it.

① 남 졸업식에 입을 정장이나 턱시도는 어디에서 빌릴 수 있나요?
   여 여기에 시내 상점의 연락처가 있습니다.
② 남 당신은 누구에게 상이 수여될지 아십니까?
   여 아니요. 당신은요?
③ 남 당신이 이 상을 받게되어 기뻐요.
   여 고마워요. 다 당신 덕분이예요.
④ 남 지금 강당에 가요. 그렇지 않으면 늦을거예요.
   여 알았어요.
⑤ 남 칭찬과 격려 감사합니다.
   여 넌 그럴 자격이 있어.

••
graduation ceremony 졸업식 **award** 상 **present** 주다. 제시하다 **auditorium** 강당 **praise** 칭찬, 찬양 **encouragement** 격려 **You deserve it**. 너는 그럴만한 자격이 있다.

10

M How is the organizing for the English Speech Contest going?

W You mean the one for first year students on Thursday, don't you?

M Yes. I'd like to double check all the arrangements.

W Here is a list of everything that I have planned. What do you think about the lunch menu?

M Are sandwiches and fruit going to be enough?

W I think so. And we will serve coffee, fresh fruit juice and mineral water for drinks.

M Good. What about the tables and chairs? Do we have enough of them?

W We will prepare 10% more than the expected number of people.

M And please check the microphone and the speakers at least a day ahead.

W I will, sir. Don't worry. Everything will go fine without any incidents.

남 영어 말하기 대회 준비는 어떻게 되고 있죠?
여 목요일에 있을 일학년 학생들 대회 말이지요?
남 네. 모든 준비상황을 다시 확인해보고 싶어서요.
여 여기 제가 계획해 놓은 모든 목록이 있어요. 점심 메뉴에 대해 어떻게 생각하세요?

남 샌드위치와 과일이면 충분할까요?

여 네. 그럴 것 같아요. 그리고 마실 것으로는 커피, 신선한 과일주스, 그리고 생수를 제공할 것입니다.

남 좋네요. 테이블과 의자는요? 그것들은 충분한가요?

여 예상인원보다 10% 더 준비할 것입니다.

남 최소 하루 전에 마이크와 스피커를 확인하세요.

여 네. 걱정하지 마세요. 모든 것이 아무 일 없이 잘 될 것입니다.

••
organize 조직하다. 준비하다 **arrangement** 배열. 준비 **expected number** 예상 인원 **a day ahead** 하루 전 **without any incidents** 별일 없이

11

W Why are you <u>pulling</u> the car over?

M Can't you hear the <u>ambulance</u> <u>siren</u>? We have to pull over to the <u>side</u> <u>of</u> <u>the</u> <u>road</u>.

W Oh, sorry. Now I can hear it.

M My goodness. Look at the cars! They are not <u>clearing</u> <u>the</u> <u>way</u>.

W Oh, no! I can't <u>believe</u> my <u>eyes</u>. I saw it on TV the other day. Many people don't <u>get</u> <u>out</u> <u>of</u> the way when they see the <u>emergency</u> <u>vehicles</u>.

M <u>How</u> <u>selfish</u> they are! What would they think it were them who needed help?

W I know. What should we do? We can't just sit and do nothing here.

M How about helping to <u>direct</u> <u>traffic</u> so the ambulance can <u>get</u> <u>past</u>?

W Great idea.

⋯⋯⋯⋯⋯⋯⋯⋯⋯⋯⋯⋯⋯⋯⋯⋯⋯⋯

여 왜 차를 갓길에 세우는 거야?

남 앰뷸런스 사이렌 소리 안 들려? 차를 길옆에 세워야 해.

여 오, 미안. 이제 들리네.

남 이런. 차들 좀 봐. 길을 안 비켜 주고 있어.

여 오, 이런! 내 눈을 믿을 수가 없어. 지난 번에 TV에서 봤어. 많은 사람들이 응급차를 보고도 길을 비켜주지 않아.

남 정말 이기적이야! 도움이 필요한 게 자신들이면 뭐라고 생각할까?

여 그러게 말이야. 우리 어떻게 해야 하지? 여기에 그냥 가만히 앉아서 아무것도 안 할 수는 없는데.

남 앰뷸런스가 지나갈 수 있게 차량들을 지도하는 걸 돕는 게 어때?

여 좋은 생각이야.

••
pull over 차를 갓길에 세우다 **emergency** 응급 상황 **vehicle** 차량 **the other day** 며칠 전에 **selfish** 이기적인 **direct** 지도하다

12

W Honey! I'm so <u>proud</u> <u>of</u> our son, Jimmy. Don't be so <u>surprised</u>, but listen to this!

M What is it? Please stop <u>beating</u> <u>around</u> <u>the</u> <u>bush</u> and tell me.

W I got a call from his <u>homeroom</u> <u>teacher</u> this morning and she said Jimmy is going to <u>graduate</u> the top of his class.

M Oh, really? I graduated the top of my class when I was in grade 8, too.

W <u>Like</u> <u>father</u>, <u>like</u> <u>son</u>.

M Ha, ha. Right. I hope Sally will be like him, but I think she is more interested in <u>singing</u> and <u>dancing</u> than studying.

W But she is really good at them. I think having <u>passion</u> and <u>talent</u> for doing something is <u>important</u>, too. Studying isn't everything.

M That's a reasonable explanation. Let's try to encourage her to develop her <u>natural</u> <u>talent</u>.

⋯⋯⋯⋯⋯⋯⋯⋯⋯⋯⋯⋯⋯⋯⋯⋯⋯⋯

여 여보! 우리 아들 Jimmy가 정말 자랑스러워요. 놀라지 말아요. 들을 준비 되었어요?

남 뭔데요? 뜸들이지 말고 말해요.

여 오늘 아침에 담임선생님께 전화를 받았는데 Jimmy가 반 수석으로 졸업을 한데요.

남 오, 정말이요? 나도 8학년 때 반 수석으로 졸업했어요.

여 부전자전이네요.

남 하하. 맞아요. 나는 Sally도 그 애와 같았으면 좋겠어요. 그녀는 공부하고는 노래하고 춤추는 것에 더 흥미가 있어요.

여 하지만 그것들을 정말 잘 하잖아요. 나는 무엇인가에 열정과 재능을 가지는 것 또한 중요하다고 생각해요. 공부가 전부는 아니잖아요.

남 수긍이 가는 설명이네요. 그애의 타고난 재능을 살리도록 격려해 줍시다.

••
beat around the bush 뜸을 들이다 **Like father, like son** 부전자전 **passion** 열정 **talent** 재능 **reasonable** 분별있는. 이치에 맞는 **encourage** 격려하다

13

① M It is a <u>wedding</u> <u>invitation</u> <u>card</u> for the marriage of Donna and Vincent.

② M The wedding will be <u>on</u> <u>September</u> <u>30</u>, <u>2015</u>.

③ **M** The <u>ceremony</u> will be at 12 o'clock.

④ **M** The venue <u>is located on</u> Elizabeth Street, Brooklyn.

⑤ **M** You can <u>have lunch</u> after the ceremony.

청첩장

Donna 와 Vincent
신랑 신부가 결혼 서약을 하오니
결혼식에 참석해주셔서 자리를 빛내주시기 바랍니다.
2015년 9월 13일
정오
Grand 빌딩
123 Elizabeth 길 Brooklyn, New York
점심식사와 유쾌한 떠들썩함이 이어집니다.

① 남 Donna와 Vincent의 청첩장이다.

② 남 결혼식은 2015년 9월 30일에 열린다.

③ 남 결혼식은 12시 예정이다.

④ 남 장소는 Brooklyn의 Elizabeth길에 있다.

⑤ 남 예식 후에 점심을 먹을 수 있다.

•• **wedding invitation card** 결혼식 청첩장 **ceremony** 예식 **venue** 개최지 **presence** 참석 **vow** 서약 **merriment** (격식) 유쾌하게 떠들기

14

M Welcome to Seoul Culture Center. May I help you?

W I'd like to see a list of the various courses for <u>local residents</u>. Do you have a timetable of the courses?

M Here it is. You'd better decide which types of courses you <u>are interested in</u>. We offer <u>various</u> and <u>exciting</u> courses in art, music, <u>foreign languages</u> and sports.

W I see. The Chinese conversation class sounds interesting to me.

M What do you think about your Chinese-speaking <u>proficiency</u>? Are you a beginner, intermediate, or advanced speaker?

W I'm definitely a beginner. What should I do in order to <u>enroll in the class</u>?

M Please fill out this <u>application form</u> and make a <u>payment</u> at the <u>reception desk</u>.

W Okay. Thank you for your kind <u>explanation</u>.

남 서울문화센터에 오신 것을 환영합니다. 무엇을 도와드릴까요?

여 지역 주민을 위한 다양한 프로그램 목록을 보고 싶습니다. 시간표 있으세요?

남 여기 있습니다. 먼저 어느 영역에 흥미를 가지고 계신지 결정하셔야 합니다. 저희는 미술, 음악, 외국어, 또는 스포츠 분야에서 다양하고 흥미 있는 프로그램들을 제공합니다.

여 그렇군요. 중국어회화 수업이 재미있을 것 같은데요.

남 중국어 말하기 수준이 어느 정도 된다고 생각하세요? 초급, 중급, 혹은 고급이요?

여 저는 당연히 초보입니다. 수업에 등록하려면 어떻게 하면 되죠?

남 이 지원서를 작성하시고 접수처에서 수강료를 내시면 됩니다.

여 알겠습니다. 친절한 설명 감사드립니다.

•• **culture center** 문화센터 **timetable** 시간표 **proficiency** 능숙, 숙달 **intermediate** 중급의 **advanced** 상급의 **enroll in a class** 수업에 등록하다 **application form** 지원서 **make a payment** 납부하다 **reception desk** 접수처

15

W Whales are large, magnificent, intelligent, aquatic mammals. They <u>breathe in air</u> through a blowhole and then it goes into their <u>lungs</u>. They are the only <u>mammals</u> that live their entire lives in the water, and the only mammals that have <u>adapted to life</u> in the <u>oceans</u>. They are the biggest animals in the world, even bigger than any of the <u>dinosaurs</u> were. Many whales <u>migrate</u> over <u>long distances</u> every year, sometimes in groups, from cold water feeding grounds to warm water breeding grounds. Some whale species are <u>endangered</u> because of <u>hunting</u> that still exists in countries such as <u>Japan</u>.

여 고래는 크고, 웅장하고, 총명한 수생 포유류이다. 그들은 공기를 분수공을 통해서 폐로 불어넣는다. 그들은 물에서 평생을 사는 유일한 포유류이고, 바다에서의 삶에 적응한 유일한 포유류이다. 그들은 세상에서 가장 큰 동물이고 심지어는 어떠한 공룡보다도 더 크다. 많은 고래들은 때때로 무리지어, 먹이가 풍부한 찬 바다 에서부터 번식지인 따뜻한 바다까지 매년 긴 거리를 이동한다. 몇몇 고래 종들은 일본과 같은 나라에서 여전히 존재하는 사냥 때문에 멸종위기에 처해있다.

•• **magnificent** 웅장한 **aquatic** 수생의 **breathe** 불어넣다, 숨쉬다 **blowhole** 분수공 **entire life** 평생 **adapt to** ~에 적응하다 **migrate** 이주하다 **endangered** 멸종위기에 처한

16

W Bill, where are you going?

M I'm going to my taekwondo school to take a
   lesson.

W I didn't know you took taekwondo lessons. Which
   belt do you have now?

M I have a poom belt which is a red and black belt.

W Wow, you must be good at taekwondo. I started to
   learn it two months ago, too.

M You did? Great. It is really helpful in training your
   body and mind. Practice it every day to be healthy.

W Okay, I will. I have a yellow belt test tomorrow.

M Don't be nervous and you can succeed.

W Thanks. What about your next belt test?

M Mine is on October 10th.

여 Bill, 어디에 가니?

남 태권도 도장에 수업 들으러 가는 중이야.

여 네가 태권도 배우는지 몰랐었어. 지금 무슨 띠니?

남 붉은색과 검은색 띠인 품띠야.

여 와, 너 태권도 잘 하겠는데. 나도 두 달 전에 태권도 배우기 시작했어.

남 그래? 잘됐다. 태권도는 몸과 정신을 단련시키는 데 정말 도움이 돼.
   건강해 지도록 매일 연습해.

여 응, 그렇게 할게. 내일 노란띠 승급시험이 있어.

남 긴장하지 않으면 성공할 수 있을 거야.

여 고마워. 네 승급시험은 언제?

남 내 시험은 10월 10일에 있어.

② 격려해줘서 고마워.

③ 내일 잘 하길 바래.

④ 품띠를 또 못땄어.

⑤ 너 오늘 태권도 평가 시험 있었구나.

••
belt 띠 **be good at** ~을 잘 하다 **train** 단련시키다 **succeed** 성공하다

17

W Hello. I'm Doctor Smith. What's the matter with
   you today?

M I have some pain right here, in my back and
   shoulders.

W How much does it hurt?

M It's pretty bad. Both my back and shoulders really

hurt.

W How would you rate the pain out of ten?

M I can't say. I don't have a lot of experience with
   pain. It's really hard to say.

W Well, ten would be unbearable and a five means
   somewhere in the middle, a moderate kind of pain.

M I'd say an eight out of ten.

W Okay. That's pretty severe. Does it stay for a long
   time or does it come and go?

M The pain has been constant for three days.

여 안녕하세요. 닥터 Smith입니다. 오늘은 어디가 문제이신가요?

남 여기, 등과 어깨가 아파요.

여 얼마나 아프세요?

남 많이 아파요. 등과 어깨가 다 아파요.

여 통증의 등급은 10중에서 얼마인 거 같나요?

남 말할 수가 없네요. 통증에 대한 경험이 별로 없어서요. 정말 말하기
   어려워요.

여 음, 10은 참을 수 없는 정도이고 5는 중간 정의 통증이에요.

남 10중에서 8정도인거 같아요.

여 네. 꽤 심각하네요. 통증이 오랫동안 머물러 있나요. 있다가 없다가
   한가요?

남 통증이 사흘 동안 계속되고 있어요.

① 미안하지만 거기에 갈 수 없어요.

② 기다려서 그것이 작동하는 방법을 봐요.

③ 물론이죠. 저는 여기 오래 머무를 수 있어요.

④ 네, 밤 동안에는 정말 아파요.

••
pain 고통 **rate** 등급을 매기다 **out of** ~중에서 **unbearable** 참을 수
없는 **moderate** 중간의, 적당한 **severe** 심한

18

M My brother's graduation ceremony will be held
   tomorrow. He will finally have finished his four
   years of studies.

W That's great. Congratulate him for me.

M Ok, I will. I think he'll be very excited.

W What does he plan to do after graduation?

M He plans to find a job first, and then he will go back
   to school for his master's degree.

W You mean he will quit his job to go back to school
   full time?

M No, he needs to work to support himself. He will work full-time and go to school part-time at night.

W It will be hard to hold a full-time job while going to school, won't it?

M It won't be easy, but he says many people have done it. So he can, too.

W With that attitude, I'm sure he'll succeed.

남 우리 형의 졸업식이 내일이야. 그는 드디어 4년 동안의 공부를 마쳐.

여 잘됐다. 그에게 축하한다고 말해줘.

남 응. 형은 매우 신날 것 같아.

여 졸업 후에 그는 무엇을 할 계획이니?

남 그는 직장부터 구할 계획이고 그리고 나서 석사과정을 위해서 학교에 다시 갈 거야.

여 전일제 학생으로 학교에 돌아가기 위해서 일을 그만둔다는 말이니?

남 아니, 그는 스스로 학비를 내기 위해서 일 해야 해. 그는 정규직으로 일하면서 밤에 시간제 학생으로 학교를 다닐 거야.

여 학교를 다니면서 정규직을 유지한다는 건 어려울 거야.

남 쉽지 않겠지만 많은 사람들이 그렇게 했다고 그는 말해. 그래서 그 역시 할 수 있을 거야.

여 그런 태도라면 그는 분명 성공할 거야.

① 그는 정말 너를 좋아하는 게 틀림없어.
② 물론이지, 그는 나를 위해서 그것을 할 수 있어.
③ 많은 사람이 실패했고 그도 그럴 거야.
⑤ 그는 전업으로 일하려고 학교를 그만둬선 안 돼.

•• **master's degree** 석사 학위 **quit** 그만두다 **support** 부양하다. 지탱하다
attitude 태도, 자세

19

M How are you feeling these days?

W I have been waiting for the result of my exam. So I'm anxious and nervous.

M When is the result going to be announced?

W In a week. I have so much time on my hands and I have nothing to do.

M Good luck to you. How about reading books? That's always a good way to spend time.

W That's true. How about you? How are you these days?

M I'm pretty good these days. My kid just finished kindergarten.

W That's great to hear. He must be big now. It's been a year since I saw your son.

M Yeah. He has grown a lot this year. And he's reading storybooks all by himself these days.

W I bet you're very proud of your son.

남 요즘 기분이 어때요?

여 시험 결과를 기다리는 중이에요. 그래서 걱정되고 긴장돼요.

남 결과는 언제 발표 나나요?

여 일주일 후에요. 시간은 많은데 할 일이 없네요.

남 행운을 빌어요. 책을 읽는 건 어때요? 시간을 보내기에는 좋은 방법이에요.

여 맞아요. 당신은 어때요? 요즘 어떻게 지내세요?

남 잘 지내요. 제 아이가 유치원 과정을 마쳤어요.

여 잘 됐네요. 이제 많이 자랐겠네요. 당신의 아들을 본 지 벌써 일년이 지났네요.

남 네, 그는 올해 많이 자랐어요. 그리고 요즘엔 혼자 동화책도 읽어요.

여 아들이 매우 자랑스러우시겠어요.

① 유감이에요.
② 외롭게 있다니 그는 정말 불쌍해요.
③ 당신은 이 상을 받을 자격이 있어요.
⑤ 그와 대화하는 게 즐거웠죠, 그렇죠?

•• **anxious** 걱정스러운 **nervous** 긴장되는 **kindergarten** 유치원

20

M Today is Arbor Day. Maria and her daddy are planting a tree in their garden. Her mom is preparing lunch and doesn't know what they are doing. Her daddy tells her trees are important for the environment as they create oxygen and provide a home for birds and other small animals. Maria decides to plant a tree for her mom in the middle of the garden. After planting it, she wants to show it to her mom. In this situation, what would Maria probably say to her mom?

남 오늘은 식목일이다. Maria와 그녀의 아빠는 정원에 나무를 심고 있다. 그녀의 엄마는 점심식사를 준비하고 있고 그들이 무엇을 하는 중인지 모른다. 그녀의 아빠는 그녀에게 나무들이 산소를 만들고 새와 작은 동물들의 보금자리를 제공해주기 때문에 환경에 얼마나 중요한지를 이야기 한다. 이제, Maria는 정원 중앙에 엄마를 위해 나무를 심기로 결심한다. 그것을 심은 다음 엄마에게 보여주고 싶어 한다. 이런 상황에서 Maria는 그녀의 엄마에게 뭐라고 할 것 같은가?

① 엄마, 배고파요. 언제 점심 먹어요?

② 엄마, 정원에 있는 엄마를 위한 선물을 보세요.

③ 엄마, 제가 엄마대신에 화초에 물을 줄게요.

④ 엄마, 정원이 있는 집에서 살고 싶어요.

⑤ 엄마, 이 특별한 선물을 주셔서 감사합니다.

••
Arbor Day 식목일 **environment** 환경 **oxygen** 산소 **provide**
제공하다 **create** 만들다

Further **S**tudy 정답

p. 84

1 The reason is that a 50-inch screen is <u>too big for
his cozy living room</u>.

2 He bought the shirt <u>on impulse</u> as it was <u>50% off</u>.

3 He planned to have <u>a light dinner</u> in a <u>restaurant
near the concert hall</u> with the woman.

4 She will <u>exercise lightly</u> and do some <u>running to
warm up</u>.

5 She is interested in <u>singing and dancing</u>.

6 The center offers various courses in <u>art, music,
foreign languages and sports</u>.

7 They breathe in air <u>through a blowhole</u> and it goes
into their <u>lungs</u>.

8 He plans to <u>find a job</u> first, and then he will <u>go back
to school</u> for his <u>master's degree</u>.

On **Y**our **O**wn 모범답안

p. 85

A

What I Bought Impulsively	
(1) A useful item	a trench coat
(2) When and why did you get it?	3 years ago as it was displayed really well
(3) A useless item	a shirt with black stripes
(4) When and why did you get it?	last weekend as it was 50% off
(5) Why was it useless?	it wasn't my style
(6) So what did you do with it?	I gave it to my sister's friend who I thought would look good wearing it.

I'd like to contrast two items I bought on impulse. First of all, one of the useful items I bought on impulse was (1)<u>a trench coat</u>. I bought it (2)<u>3 years ago as it was displayed really well</u>. I'm still happy about buying it. On the contrary, one useless item I have bought on impulse was (3)<u>a shirt with black stripes</u>. I bought it (4)<u>last weekend as it was 50% off</u>. It was useless for me because (5)<u>it wasn't my style</u>. So (6)<u>I gave it to my sister's friend who I thought would look good wearing it</u>.

내가 충동적으로 산 것	
(1) 유용한 물품	트렌치 코트
(2) 어디서, 왜 구입했나?	3년 전 정말 근사하게 진열되어 있었기 때문에
(3) 쓸모 없는 물품	검정 줄무늬 셔츠
(4) 어디서, 왜 구입했나?	지난 주말 50% 할인이어서
(5) 왜 쓸모없었나?	내 스타일이 아니기 때문에
(6) 그래서, 그것을 어떻게 했나?	그것이 잘 어울릴 거라 생각되는 여동생의 친구에게 주었다

저는 제가 충동적으로 구입했었던 두 물건을 대조해 보고 싶습니다. 우선, 제가 충동적으로 구매했던 유용한 물품 중 하나는 트렌치 코트였습니다. 저는 그것을 3년 전에 정말 근사하게 진열되어 있었기 때문에 구입했습니다. 그렇지만 전 여전히 그것에 만족합니다. 대조적으로, 충동적으로 구매했던 쓸모 없는 물품은 검은 줄무늬 셔츠였습니다. 저는 그것을 지난 주말에 50% 할인이어서 샀습니다. 그것은 제 스타일이 아니었기 때문에 제겐 쓸모가 없었습니다. 그래서 저는 그것을 그것이 잘 어울릴 거라 생각되는 제 여동생의 친구에게 주었습니다.

B

The Most Memorable Award	
(1) What was the title of the award?	the Perfect Attendance Award
(2) When did you receive it?	when I graduated from elementary school
(3) Why did you get the award?	I hadn't missed a day during six years of elementary school.
(4) How did you feel when you received it?	very glad / proud of myself
(5) Why is it the most memorable award to you?	It shows how diligent and sincere I am.

I'm going to talk about the most memorable award I have ever received. The award is (1)"the Perfect Attendance Award." I received it when (2)I graduated from elementary school. The award is presented to any student who (3)didn't miss a day during six years of elementary school. I was (4)very glad and proud of myself when I received it. It is my most memorable award because (5)it shows how diligent and sincere I am.

가장 기억에 남는 상	
(1) 상의 이름은 무엇이었습니까?	개근상
(2) 그것을 언제 받았습니까?	초등학교 졸업때
(3) 그 상은 왜 받았습니까?	초등학교 6년 동안 하루도 빠지지 않아서
(4) 당신은 그것을 받았을 때 어떤 느낌이었습니까?	매우 기쁘고 내가 자랑스러웠음
(5) 왜 그 상이 당신에게 가장 기억에 남습니까?	내가 얼마나 근면하고 성실한지 보여주므로

저는 제가 받은 것 중 가장 기억에 남는 상에 대해 이야기 할 것입니다. 그 상은 "개근상"입니다. 저는 그것을 초등학교 졸업 때 받았습니다. 그 상은 초등학교 6년 동안 단 하루의 결석도 없는 학생에게 수여됩니다. 저는 그 상을 받았을 때 매우 기쁘고 제 자신이 자랑스러웠습니다. 그것이 나에게 가장 기억에 남는 상인 이유는 그것이 제가 얼마나 근면하고 성실한지 보여주기 때문입니다.

01 ②	02 ④	03 ④	04 ③	05 ④
06 ④	07 ③	08 ②	09 ①	10 ⑤
11 ③	12 ④	13 ④	14 ④	15 ②
16 ①	17 ④	18 ③	19 ⑤	20 ⑤

01

W Hi. I saw the sign 'Display Models on Sale.' Among them, are there any computers?

M Yes, there are some. Which type do you want, a desktop or a laptop?

W Could you show me both of them?

M Okay. How about this all-in-one desktop computer? It is a really popular model because it has the processor and monitor together, so you can save space. The discounted price is 600 dollars.

W Wow, it looks very neat and tidy. It's quite attractive. Could you recommend a laptop?

M Okay. The most popular one is this ultra book.

W How thin it is! And it's very light. How much is it?

M It's 850 dollars.

W Oh, that's too much for me. I'll take the former one.

여 안녕하세요. '진열상품 세일' 간판을 봤어요. 그것들 중에 컴퓨터도 있나요?

남 네, 있습니다. 책상용 컴퓨터와 노트북 중, 어느 것을 더 원하세요?

여 둘 다 보여 주실 수 있나요?

남 좋습니다. 이 일체형 책상용 컴퓨터 어떠세요? 프로세서와 모니터가 함께 있어 공간을 절약할 수 있어서 굉장히 인기 있습니다. 할인가는 600달러 입니다.

여 와, 굉장히 깔끔해 보이네요. 아주 매력적이예요. 노트북도 추천해 주시겠어요?

남 네. 가장 인기 있는 것은 이 울트라 북 입니다.

여 정말 얇군요! 그리고 정말 가볍고요. 이건 얼마예요?

남 850달러입니다.

여 오, 저에겐 너무 과하네요. 앞의 것을 할게요.

display 진열, 전시 **all-in-one** 둘(이상)을 하나로 만든, 일체형의 **ultra book** 울트라북 (태블릿PC의 장점과 노트북의 장점을 결합한 신개념 노트북) **former** 이전의, 앞서의

02

M How are the <u>tropical fish</u> you bought last month doing?

W Of the ones I bought there are only <u>two left</u>, but they are doing great, I guess.

M How come there are only 2 left? As I remember, you bought <u>2 male</u> fish and <u>6 female</u> fish. Isn't it correct?

W You're right. Unfortunately, <u>on the day</u> I bought them, 1 male fish died. Then the next day 5 female fish died as they <u>jumped out of</u> the fish tank onto the floor.

M It's <u>incredible</u>. Do you know why they did that?

W They <u>jump out of</u> the fish tank when they <u>get stressed</u>. Especially, when they have to <u>adapt to</u> a new tank, I've heard that it happens a lot.

M Oh, I see. Then, are you going to buy more fish and put them into the fish tank?

W No. I <u>won't do</u> that. You know what? My female goofy fish <u>gave birth</u> to <u>7</u> baby fish last week.

M Wow! <u>Congratulations</u>!

남 지난 달에 산 네 열대어들은 잘 있니?

여 거기서 산 것들 중 두 마리만 남았는데 둘 다 잘 지내는 것 같아.

남 어째서 두 마리만 남았어? 내가 기억하기론, 넌 수컷 2마리와 암컷 6마리를 샀는데. 그렇지 않니?

여 맞아. 불행하게도, 내가 구입했던 날 수컷 한 마리가 죽었어. 그리고 그 다음 날 암컷 5마리가 점프해서 수조를 나와 바닥으로 떨어져 죽었어.

남 믿을 수가 없어. 물고기들이 왜 그러는지 너 아니?

여 물고기들이 스트레스를 받으면 수조 밖으로 뛰어 나와. 특히 물고기들이 새 탱크에 적응해야만 할 때 그런 일이 많이 일어난다고 들었어.

남 아, 그렇구나. 그럼, 물고기를 좀 더 사서 수조에 넣을 거니?

여 아니. 안 살 거야. 너 그거 아니? 내 암컷 구피 물고기가 지난주에 7마리 치어를 낳았어.

남 와! 축하해!

tropical fish 열대어 **fish tank** 어항 **incredible** 믿을 수 없는 **give birth to** ~을 출산하다. 낳다

03

W Do you want <u>super cheap tickets</u> to great shows? Well, it's possible if you're a full-time student. Guard that <u>student card</u> like <u>gold</u>, because it's <u>worth its weight</u> in it. You can buy a student ticket for most shows at the Opera House for <u>as little as</u> $20. If you are a full time student, you have to <u>type</u> 'STUDENT' into the <u>promotion code window</u> when you book a ticket online. These online tickets can be picked up from the box office <u>one hour prior</u> to the performance. That's when you'll need to show your <u>valid</u> student ID. If you cannot book online, you can buy student tickets on the day of a show for as little as <u>25</u> dollars.

여 훌륭한 공연을 가장 저렴한 가격에 사고 싶으세요? 당신이 전일제 학생이라면 가능합니다. 학생증을 황금처럼 지키세요. 왜냐하면 그것은 아주 유용하기 때문입니다. 오페라 하우스의 대부분의 공연에 대해 겨우 20달러에 학생 티켓을 사실 수 있습니다. 전일제 학생이라면 온라인 예약 시 판촉 코드 입력창에 '학생'이라고 입력해야 합니다. 이 온라인 티켓은 매표소에서 공연 1시간 전부터 수령하실 수 있습니다. 바로 그 때 여러분의 유효한 학생증을 보여줘야 하는 것입니다. 온라인 예약이 어렵다면, 공연 당일 25달러에 학생 티켓을 구매하실 수 있습니다.

guard 지키다 보호하다 **worth its weight** 아주 유용한. 대단히 귀중한 **promotion code** 판촉용 부호 **type** 입력하다 **valid** 유효한, 정당한

04

W Wow! Finally, the <u>final exams are over</u>.

M I guess you did very well.

W No! Believe it or not, I <u>messed up</u> this time. I am just happy because my <u>final exams</u> are <u>finished</u>. How about you?

M I think I <u>flunked my math test</u>.

W I can't believe it. You told me you studied hard for the test.

M Yeah. I wanted to do well so I <u>crammed</u> the <u>whole night</u> before taking the math exam.

W You were <u>too tired to concentrate</u> on your test, weren't you? I had the same experience once before.

M I <u>should have listened</u> to my mom. I <u>should have reviewed</u> what I had learned that day at the end of each day. What should I tell her?

W Just tell her the truth. If you try to hide it, you won't be able to hide it for very long.

여 와! 마침내 기말고사가 끝났다.

남 넌 아주 잘 한 것 같구나.

여 아니야! 믿거나 말거나 이번엔 망쳤어. 난 단지 기말고사가 끝나서 기쁠 뿐이야. 넌 어떠니?

남 나 수학시험에서 낙제할지도 몰라.

여 믿을 수 없는데. 시험 공부를 열심히 했다고 했잖아.

남 응. 잘하고 싶어서 시험치기 전 밤새워 벼락치기로 공부했어.

여 너무 피곤해서 시험에 집중할 수 없었겠구나. 나도 전에 같은 경험을 한 적이 있어.

남 엄마 말씀을 들었어야 했어. 그날 배운 것들을 그날 늦게 복습했어야 했어. 엄마께 뭐라고 말씀 드리지?

여 그냥 사실을 말씀 드려. 그걸 숨기려고 하면 오래 동안 감출 수 없을 거야.

① 기쁜   ② 신난   ③ 걱정되는
④ 짜증나는   ⑤ 당황한

··
mess up 망치다   **flunk a test** 시험에 떨어지다, 낙제하다   **cram** 벼락치기로 공부하다   **concentrate on** ~에 집중하다   **review** 복습하다

05

[Telephone rings.]

M Townsville Community Center. How can I help you?

W I want to hold a workshop. Can I book one of your seminar rooms?

M It depends on the date. For example, all the Saturdays in July have already been booked. What day are you thinking of?

W Oh, I was thinking of Saturday July the 19th. Then, is Sunday July the 20th available?

M I'm afraid that day has already been reserved as well.

W Can you tell me the available days?

M Sunday July the 27th is still available.

W That sounds great! Then, could you please book a seminar room on that day under the name of Jane Smith?

M Okay. We have equipment such as projectors,

---

screens and special lights which can be used for a small surcharge. Are you going to need to use some of these?

W Oh, I think I'll need a projector and screen.

[전화벨이 울린다.]

남 Townsville 주민센터입니다. 어떻게 도와 드릴까요?

여 강습을 열고 싶은데요. 세미나실 중 하나를 빌릴 수 있을까요?

남 날짜에 따라 다릅니다. 예를 들면, 7월의 모든 토요일은 예약이 찼습니다. 언제를 생각하고 계신가요?

여 오, 7월 19일 토요일을 생각하고 있었는데. 그럼 7월 20일 일요일은 가능한가요?

남 그날도 이미 예약이 된 것 같군요.

여 가능한 날을 말씀해 주시겠어요?

남 7월 27일 일요일은 이용 가능합니다.

여 잘됐군요! 그럼, Jane Smith 이름으로 그 날로 세미나실을 예약해 주시겠어요?

남 좋습니다. 프로젝터, 스크린, 특수 조명과 같은 장치들을 적은 추가요금으로 이용하실 수 있습니다. 이 가운데 일부를 사용하시겠어요?

여 오, 프로젝터와 스크린을 사용해야 할 것 같군요.

··
workshop 강습   **under one's name** ~의 이름으로   **equipment** 장치, 설비   **special lights** 특수 조명   **surcharge** 추가요금

06

W Hi, I'd like to enroll in the Pilates beginners class.

M Okay. We have two classes for beginners: a regular one and an intensive one.

W How much is the tuition fee for each?

M For the regular one, it costs 100 dollars, and the intensive one is 160 dollars.

W What's the difference between the two classes?

M There is a difference in the number times it meets per week. The regular class meets twice a week, but the intensive class meets five times a week.

W Then I'll take the intensive class.

M I got it. If you pay three months' tuition at one time, you can get a 10% discount off the total price.

W Okay, I'll pay by credit card for three months now. Could you make it in three monthly installments? It's interest-free, so it's easier for me.

여 안녕하세요. 필라테스 과정의 초급반 수업을 등록하고 싶습니다.

남 네. 저희는 정규과정과 집중과정 두 개의 초급 강좌가 있습니다.

여 각각 수강료가 얼마인가요?

남 정규과정은 100달러이고, 집중과정은 160달러입니다.

여 두 과정의 차이점은 무엇인가요?

남 주당 수업 횟수가 다릅니다. 정규과정은 일주일에 2회 수업이지만 집중과정은 일주일에 5회 수업입니다.

여 그럼 집중과정으로 할게요.

남 알겠습니다. 3개월 비용을 한꺼번에 내시면, 전체 금액의 10%를 할인 받으실 수 있습니다.

여 좋아요. 지금 3개월 분을 신용카드로 계산할게요. 3개월 할부로 해주시겠어요? 무이자 혜택이 있어서 더 낫거든요.

●●
regular 정규의 **Pilates** 필라테스 (동양의 요가와 서양의 스트레칭을 합친 운동법) **intensive course** 집중 코스 **in monthly installments** 할부로 **interest-free** 무이자의

07

M I'd like a ticket for Blacktown, please.

W There are no more direct buses to Blacktown today. We run four nonstop buses per day, but the last bus left 30 minutes ago.

M What should I do then?

W You can get a bus to Burwood and transfer there onto a bus for Blacktown.

M That's fine. Then give me a ticket to Burwood, please.

W Okay. The next Burwood bus leaves in ten minutes, but since you need to transfer you are better off waiting for another 10 minutes for the express bus.

M Oh, thanks for the information. I'll get that one. How much is the ticket?

W It's 18 dollars.

M Okay, here you are.

- - - - - - - - - - - - - - - - - -

남 Blacktown 표 한 장 주세요.

여 오늘 Blacktown 행 직행은 더 이상 없습니다. 하루에 네 번 직행을 운행하는데 30분전에 마지막 버스가 떠났습니다.

남 그럼 전 어떡해야 하나요?

여 Burwood 행 버스를 타셔서 거기서 Blacktown 행으로 갈아타세요.

남 좋습니다. 그럼 Burwood 표 한 장 주세요.

여 네. 10분 뒤에 출발하는 버스가 한 대 있지만 갈아타셔야 하니까 10분 더 기다렸다가 직행버스를 타는 편이 나을 거예요.

남 오. 정보 감사합니다. 그걸 탈게요. 표는 얼마인가요?

여 18 달러입니다.

남 네. 여기 있습니다.

●●
direct 직행의 **transfer** 갈아타다 **express** 직행의

08

M I feel so relaxed. What about you? Do you feel the same as me?

W Yeah, I do. My work has been stressing me out so much these days, but all the negative feelings are gone now.

M I feel peaceful. When was the last time we walked barefoot on the sand together?

W Probably 5 years ago. Before coming here, we hadn't gone on a trip since I got pregnant with Laura.

M I'm so sorry.

W Don't say so. We were just busy working and raising our children. We are here now anyway.

M Look at Laura and Ralph. They are enjoying making a sandcastle.

W They are waving their hands at us. Let's go to them.

- - - - - - - - - - - - - - - - - -

남 정말 편안하네요. 당신은요? 저와 같은 느낌 인가요?

여 네, 그래요. 요즘에 일 때문에 정말 스트레스 많이 받았었는데 이제 모든 부정적인 감정들이 다 사라졌어요.

남 평화롭네요. 우리가 함께 마지막으로 모래 위를 맨발로 걸은 게 언제였지요?

여 아마도 5년 전 일거예요. 여기 오기 전에 Laura를 임신한 이후로 여행을 안 갔으니까요.

남 정말 미안해요.

여 그렇게 말하지 말아요. 우리는 단지 일과 아이들 키우는 것으로 인해 바빴던 것이니까요. 어쨌든 현재는 이 곳에 있잖아요.

남 Laura와 Ralph를 봐요. 모래성을 만들고 있네요.

여 아이들이 우리를 향해 손을 흔들고 있네요. 아이들에게 가요.

●●
relaxed 편안한 **stress out** 스트레스를 주다 **negative** 부정적인
peaceful 평화로운 **walk barefoot** 맨발로 걷다 **pregnant** 임신한

09

① M How would you like to send the parcel? By plane or ship?

W By plane, please.

② M How much does it weigh?

W It weighs 13kg. Can you help me move it?

③ M What's your weight?

W It is not good manners to ask a woman her weight.

④ M How can I get to the post office?

W Sorry, I'm a stranger here.

⑤ M How much is this?

W It's $25. It's on sale.

....

① 남 소포를 어떻게 보내실 것입니까? 항공편이요 혹은 배편이요?

여 항공편이요.

② 남 무게가 얼마나 나갑니까?

여 13키로입니다. 옮기는 것을 도와주시겠습니까?

③ 남 너 몸무게가 몇이니?

여 여자에게 몸무게를 묻는 것은 예의가 아니야.

④ 남 우체국에 어떻게 갑니까?

여 죄송합니다. 저는 이곳이 처음입니다.

⑤ 남 이것은 얼마입니까?

여 25달러입니다. 세일 중이에요.

••
send the parcel 소포를 보내다 **by plane** 항공편으로 **weigh** 무게가 나가다 **weight** 무게 **stranger** 낯선 사람

10

M Amy! I heard that you are going to run in the school presidential election. Is it right?

W I haven't decided yet, but I'm thinking positively about doing it.

M Don't hesitate. Just go for it. You are the right person for the position. I will help you as much as I can.

W You give me the courage to be a candidate.

M Let's go to a photo shop and get some pictures taken for a poster and pamphlet. I will help you make both of them. Let's think about a catchphrase.

W Thank you.

M Before you take the picture, let's go to a dress shop and buy a nice dress. And then let's go to a beauty salon to get your hair and makeup done for the photo.

W I don't know how to repay you for all this.

M What are friends for? I'm sure you will be elected president of the student council.

....

남 Amy야! 네가 학생회장 선거에 출마할 거라고 들었어. 맞아?

여 아직 결정 못했는데 긍정적으로 생각하고 있어.

남 망설이지마. 그냥 출마해. 네가 적임자야. 내가 도와줄 수 있는 한 많이 도와줄게.

여 후보자가 되도록 내게 용기를 주는구나.

남 사진관에 가서 포스터와 팜플렛용 사진을 찍자. 내가 둘 다 만드는 것 도와줄게. 선전 구호를 생각해 보자.

여 고마워.

남 사진 찍기 전에, 옷가게에 가서 괜찮은 옷 한 벌 사자. 그런 다음 미용실에 가서 사진 위한 머리하고 메이크업도 하자.

여 이 모든 것을 어떻게 되갚아야 할 지 모르겠네.

남 친구 좋다는 게 뭐니? 나는 네가 학생회장으로 뽑힐 것이라 확신해.

••
run in the election 선거에 출마하다 **hesitate** 망설이다 **right person** 적임자 **candidate** 후보 **catchphrase** 선전 구호 **repay for** 은혜를 갚다 **What are friends for?** 친구 좋다는 게 뭐니?

11

M Were you looking for me?

W Yes. I really need your help. Do you have some free time for a little while?

M What do you want me to do for you?

W I will give a presentation in my sociology class the day after tomorrow, so I want to practice presenting in front of you.

M Okay. So do you want me to give you some tips on how to improve your presentation right now?

W YES! Can you?

M No problem. I strongly recommend you rehearse your presentation as often as you can.

W Thank you so much. When can I meet you?

M See you right after school.

....

남 너 나 찾고 있었어?

여 응. 나 정말 네 도움이 필요해. 잠깐 시간 있어?

남 무얼 도와줬으면 좋겠니?

여 내일 모레 사회학 시간에 발표를 해야 해서. 네 앞에서 발표 연습을 해보고 싶어.

남 좋아. 지금 어떻게 개선해야 하는지 조언을 해달라는 거야?

여 응! 그래 줄 수 있어?

남 문제없어. 나는 네가 발표를 가능한 한 자주 예행 연습해볼 것을 강력히 추천해.

여 정말 고마워. 언제 만날 수 있어?

남 방과 후에 보자.

for a while 잠시 동안 **sociology** 사회학 **the day after tomorrow** 내일 모레 **improve** 향상시키다 **rehearse** 예행연습을 하다

12

M Mom. What's that <u>smell</u>? What are you making?

W I'm making <u>vegetable</u> <u>soup</u> for lunch.

M Vegetable soup? Oh, mom! You know how much I <u>hate</u> <u>to</u> <u>eat</u> <u>vegetables</u>. Why are you making that? I'm not going to eat it.

W Tim, listen! Vegetables are good for your health. You have to eat a <u>balanced</u> <u>diet</u>. Don't be so <u>picky</u>.

M But they are <u>not</u> <u>delicious</u> <u>at</u> <u>all</u>. I <u>prefer</u> <u>to</u> eat pizza or hamburgers.

W You'd better <u>correct</u> your <u>eating</u> <u>habit</u>. Stop eating fast food from now on and try to eat proper meals.

M Mom, please…

W <u>Stop</u> <u>whining</u>! I want you to <u>grow</u> <u>up</u> and be <u>healthy</u> <u>without</u> any <u>illnesses</u>.

남 엄마. 이거 무슨 냄새예요? 무얼 만들고 계세요?

여 점심에 먹을 야채 수프 만들고 있어.

남 야채 수프요? 오, 엄마! 저 야채 먹는 것 싫어하는 거 알잖아요. 그걸 왜 만드세요? 전 안 먹을 거예요.

여 Tim, 들어봐. 야채는 네 몸에 좋아. 균형 잡힌 식단을 먹어야 해. 까다롭게 굴지 마.

남 하지만 그것들은 맛이 없어요. 저는 피자나 햄버거를 먹는 게 더 좋아요.

여 너는 식습관을 바로 잡아야 해. 이제부터 패스트푸드 먹는 것을 그만두고 올바른 식사를 하도록 노력하렴.

남 엄마, 제발요…

여 징징거리지 마. 나는 네가 병 없이 건강하게 자라기를 바래.

balanced diet 균형 잡힌 식단 **picky** 까다로운 **not at all** 전혀 ~가 아닌 **correct** 바로 잡다 **from now on** 이제부터 **whining** 징징거리는, 투덜거리는 **illness** 병

13

M I lost my pet dog. It is <u>male</u> and the <u>breed</u> of the dog is Cocker Spaniel. Its hair is <u>mostly</u> <u>white</u>, but its ears are <u>covered</u> <u>with</u> light brown hair. I saw him for the last time in April Park <u>standing</u> <u>by</u> a <u>large</u> <u>tree</u>. If you have seen him around your neighborhood or have any <u>information</u>, please <u>contact</u> me at 010-100-8282. There is a small <u>reward</u> of $50 for information that results in finding him. Please don't just <u>walk</u> <u>by</u>. I <u>look</u> <u>forward</u> <u>to</u> <u>hearing</u> from you.

분실

① 애완견:

② 수컷/ 코커스파니엘/ ③ 흰 털에 귀에 밝은 갈색 털

④ 마지막으로 본 곳:

April 공원의 잔디 위에서 뛰고 있었음

⑤ 어떤 정보라도 가지고 계시면:

아래 번호로 전화주세요

010-100-8282

보상!!

남 저는 애완견을 잃어버렸습니다. 그것은 수컷이고 품종은 코커스파니엘입니다. 그것의 털은 대부분 흰 색이나 귀는 밝은 갈색으로 덮여있습니다. 저는 그것이 April 공원에서 큰 나무 옆에 서있는 것을 마지막으로 봤습니다. 주위에서 그것을 보셨거나 정보를 가지고 계시면 010-100-8282로 제게 연락주세요. 그를 찾게 되는 정보를 주시면 50달러의 작은 사례금도 있습니다. 그냥 지나치지 마세요. 당신의 연락을 기다리겠습니다.

pet dog 애완견 **male** 수컷 **breed** (개의)품종 **contact** 연락하다 **reward** 보상, 사례 **walk by** 지나치다 **look forward to -ing** ~을 학수고대하다

14

M <u>How</u> <u>do</u> <u>you</u> <u>find</u> this apartment?

W I like it. I like its <u>interior</u>, <u>location</u> and the <u>view</u>. And especially, the price is <u>reasonable</u>.

M Why don't you sign the contract now then?

W I will. When can I move in?

M When do you want to? Anytime is fine because nobody is living here now.

W Then I will move into this place this coming weekend.

M You will be busy packing throughout the week. If you need a recommendation for a moving company just let me know.

W Okay, I will. Thank you.

··········

남 이 아파트 어때요?

여 좋아요. 저는 인테리어, 위치, 그리고 전망이 좋아요. 그리고 특히 가격이 적당하군요.

남 그러면 계약서에 사인하시는 게 어때요?

여 그럴게요. 언제 이사할 수 있어요?

남 언제를 원하세요? 여기에 아무도 살고 있지 않아 언제든지 좋습니다.

여 그러면 이번 주말에 이사할게요.

남 주중 내내 짐 싸시느라 바쁘시겠네요. 이삿짐 센터 추천이 필요하시면 이야기 하세요.

여 네, 그럴게요. 감사합니다.

··
location 위치 **view** 전망 **especially** 특히 **reasonable** 타당한, 합리적인 **contract** 계약서 **pack** 짐을 싸다

15

W The ancient Egyptians believed in many gods. They also believed that their kings, called pharaohs, were gods. They believed that there was a life after death and the pharaoh could take care of them even after he had died. Because of this, they wanted the pharaoh to have a good afterlife. One way to give the pharaoh a good afterlife was to preserve his body. Egyptians believed it was important for the pharaoh's spirit to recognize his body. This is the reason the Egyptians made mummies.

··········

여 고대 이집트인들은 많은 신들을 믿었다. 그들은 또한 파라오라고 불려지는 그들의 왕도 신이라고 믿었다. 그들은 죽은 후에도 삶이 있고 파라오가 죽고 난 후에도 그들을 보살펴 준다고 믿었다. 이것 때문에 그들은 파라오가 좋은 사후 세계를 살기를 바랐다. 파라오에게 좋은 사후세계를 줄 수 있는 한 가지 방법은 그의 몸을 보존하는 것이었다.

이집트인들은 파라오의 영혼이 자신의 몸을 알아보는 것이 중요하다고 믿었다. 이것이 바로 이집트인들이 미라를 만들었던 이유이다.

··
ancient 고대의 **afterlife** 사후 세계 **preserve** 보존하다 **spirit** 영혼 **recognize** 알아보다 **mummy** 미라

16

W Hey, Max. I just got hired to work as a cook at the buffet restaurant in the Rideau Hotel.

M Congratulations. That's great!

W I'm so happy. To work there has always been my dream and it has finally come true.

M When do you start?

W I start next Monday.

M You're going to have to put in a lot of hours you know.

W I know. I'm a little nervous, but just the thought of working there makes my heart flutter.

M I bet you'll do a good job.

W Thanks. I'm going to celebrate tonight. Can you join me?

M Sure. It's on you, right?

··········

여 안녕, Max. 나 Rideau 호텔 뷔페 식당에 요리사로 취직됐어.

남 축하해. 잘됐다.

여 너무 기뻐. 거기에서 일하는 것이 나의 꿈이었고 마침내 내 꿈이 실현되었어.

남 언제 일 시작해?

여 다음주 월요일부터 시작해.

남 너도 알겠지만 많은 시간을 근무해야 할거야.

여 알고 있어. 조금 긴장되긴 하지만 거기서 일한다는 생각만 해도 가슴이 설레.

남 너는 틀림없이 잘 할거야.

여 고마워. 오늘밤 축하를 하려고 해. 너도 어울릴래?

남 물론이지. 네가 사는 거지, 그렇지?

② 응, 내가 내일 그 호텔로 갈게.

③ 걱정하지마. 제시간에 거기로 갈게.

④ 오늘밤엔 왜 일하지 않니?

⑤ 아니, 나는 그와 시간을 보내고 싶지 않아.

··
hire 고용하다 **come true** 실현되다 **flutter** 두근거리다 **hang out** 친하게 지내다, 어울려 시간을 보내다

17

M What's that?

W It's a bigger and better tomato. It's been genetically modified.

M You're not going to eat that, are you?

W Yes. I'm making a salad. Want one?

M No way. I don't want to eat it. Who knows what kind of strange gene it has?

W It's perfectly safe. It's been modified to grow faster, have more nutrients, and be resistant to disease and pests.

M And it may contain strange mutations as part of its genetic makeup that they didn't tell you about.

W Farmers use selective breeding with animals and crops to bring us bigger and better food. This tomato is no different.

M It is different because scientist modified its genes.

W Oh, it's still safe to eat!

M Well, I'll never eat genetically modified foods.

남 그게 뭐야?

여 더 크고 더 좋은 토마토야. 유전자가 조작된 거지.

남 너 그거 안 먹을 거지, 그렇지?

여 아니 먹을 거야. 샐러드 만드는 중이야. 너도 먹을래?

남 절대 안 먹어. 나는 먹고 싶지 않아. 어떤 이상한 종류의 유전자를 갖고 있는지 누가 알겠어?

여 완벽하게 안전해. 그것은 더 빠르게 자라고, 더 많은 영양물질을 가지게 하려고, 그리고 병이나 해충에 저항력을 주려고 조작된 거야.

남 그리고 그것은 유전자 조작의 부분으로 너에게는 말하지 않은 이상한 돌연변이를 포함하고 있을 지도 몰라.

여 농부들은 더 크고 더 좋은 음식을 사람들에게 주려고 동물과 농작물에 선발번식을 사용해. 이 토마토도 다르지 않아.

남 과학자들이 유전자를 조작했으니 다르지.

여 오, 그래도 먹기엔 안전해!

남 음, 난 절대로 유전자 조작 식품은 먹지 않을 거야.

① 네가 옳아. 이 음식은 먹기에 안전해.

② 너는 요즘 안전에 대해 많이 생각하고 있구나.

③ 그럼 나는 더 크고 좋은 토마토를 키워야겠어.

⑤ 나는 맛이 없어서 토마토 먹는 것을 싫어해.

●●
genetically modified 유전자가 변이된 **gene** 유전자 **nutrient** 영양분 **pest** 해충 **mutation** 돌연변이 **selective breeding** 선발번식 **crop** 농작물

18

W Finally, it's break time. I'm going to the vending machines. Do you want something, John?

M No, thanks, Sara.

W Don't you like snacks or chocolate bars?

M I like them, but I don't get them from these vending machines.

W Why not?

M Last week, that machine swallowed my coins. Nothing came out; no snack, no money back.

W That's terrible. So, what did you do?

M I kicked the machine a few times, but nothing happened.

W Well, I really hope it works today.

여 마침내, 휴식시간이야. 나 자동판매기에 갈 꺼야. 필요한 거 있니, John?

남 아니, Sara.

여 너는 과자나 초콜렛바 안 좋아하니?

남 좋아하는데, 이 자동판매기에서는 안 사.

여 왜 안 사?

남 지난주에 저 자동판매기가 내 동전을 삼켜버렸어. 과자도 돈도 아무것도 나오지 않았어.

여 안됐다. 그래서 넌 뭘 했니?

남 그 기계를 몇 차례 발로 찼지만, 아무 일도 없었어.

여 음, 오늘은 잘 작동하면 정말 좋겠어.

① 재미있겠다.

② 나는 초콜렛바를 정말 많이 좋아해.

④ 이 기계엔 과자가 없어.

⑤ 다음 번엔 공을 더 세게 차.

●●
break time 쉬는 시간, 휴식 시간 **vending machine** 자동판매기 **swallow** 삼키다

19

M Mom, can we take one of these puppies?

W I would love to raise a puppy, but we can't take one. We live in an apartment. A dog in an apartment is not a good idea.

M But my friend who lives in an apartment has a dog.

W Yes, I know many people raise dogs in their

apartments, but I think it's <u>not</u> good for <u>either</u> <u>us</u> <u>or</u> the dog.

M If we <u>move</u> <u>into</u> <u>a</u> <u>house</u>, can we have a dog?

W Yes, of course. Someday you can have a dog, if we ever live in a house.

M Do we have a plan to live in a house?

W Not really. But it <u>might</u> <u>happen</u> <u>someday</u>.

M Then is there <u>any</u> <u>animal</u> we can take home today?

W <u>We can buy some fish in a small bowl.</u>

남 엄마, 이 강아지들 중에서 한 마리 데리고 가도 되요?

여 나도 강아지를 키우고 싶지만, 우리는 데려갈 수 없어. 우리는 아파트에 살잖아. 아파트에서 개를 기르는 건 좋은 생각이 아니야.

남 하지만, 아파트에 사는 내 친구는 개를 길러요.

여 응, 나도 많은 사람들이 아파트에서 개를 기르는 건 알아. 하지만 그것은 우리와 개 모두에게 좋은 생각이 아니라고 생각해.

남 우리가 주택으로 이사를 가면 개를 기를 수 있나요?

여 그럼, 물론이지. 언젠가 주택에서 살게 되면 개를 기를 수 있어.

남 주택에서 살 계획이 있나요?

여 그렇지는 않아. 하지만 아마도 언젠가는 그렇게 되겠지.

남 그러면 오늘 어떤 동물을 집에 데려갈 수 있어요?

여 <u>작은 어항에 담긴 물고기는 살 수 있어.</u>

① 이 귀여운 검은 강아지 데려가자.
② 내 친한 친구는 고양이를 키우고 있어.
③ 우리는 여기에 개와 고양이를 데려올 수 있어.
④ 응, 너는 어떤 동물이라도 데려갈 수 있어.

••
puppy 강아지 **someday** 언젠가

20

M Jamie is at the <u>dentist's</u> <u>office</u> today since he has a <u>toothache</u> on the right side of his mouth. He bought <u>some</u> <u>medicine</u> at the drugstore, but the <u>pain</u> <u>didn't</u> <u>stop</u>. As his last dental check-up was three years ago, he is <u>afraid</u> that he may have a serious problem. An x-ray technician took x-rays of his teeth. Fortunately, he has only <u>two</u> <u>cavities</u>. The dentist is <u>drilling</u> one of the cavities and filling it. However, he will have to <u>pull</u> <u>out</u> the other tooth which is <u>causing</u> <u>the pain</u>. In this situation, what would the dentist probably say to Jamie?

남 Jamie는 오른쪽 치아에 치통이 있어서 오늘 치과에서 진료를 받는 중이다. 그는 약국에서 약을 사서 복용했지만 치통이 멈추지 않았다. 그의 마지막 치아 검진이 삼 년 전이여서 그는 치아 상태가 나쁠까봐 걱정이다. 엑스레이 기사가 그의 치아 엑스레이를 찍었다. 다행히도, 그는 충치가 두 개만 있다. 치과의사는 충치 이빨들 중 하나에 구멍을 뚫고 때운다. 하지만 치통의 원인인 다른 이빨은 뽑아야만 할 것이다. 이런 상황에서 치과의사는 Jamie에게 뭐라고 말 할 것 같은가?

① 당신은 지금 바로 때울 충치가 두 개 있습니다.
② 제가 구멍을 뚫을 때 당신은 아플지도 몰라요.
③ 오른쪽에 있는 이 이빨 왜 뽑으셨어요?
④ 마지막으로 방문한 지 왜 3년이 되었죠?
⑤ 구멍이 너무 크기 때문에 이 치아는 뽑아야 겠어요.

••
have a toothache 치통이 있다   **pain** 고통, 아픔   **check-up** 검진
drill 구멍을 뚫다   **pull out** 뽑다

Further **S**tudy 정답   p. 94

1 You can <u>save space</u> because it has <u>the processor and monitor</u> together.

2 They get stressed when they have to <u>adapt to a new fish tank</u>.

3 They have to <u>type STUDENT</u> into the <u>promotion code window</u>.

4 The reason is that they were so <u>busy</u> working and <u>raising their children</u>.

5 They are going to go to <u>a photo shop</u>, <u>a dress shop</u>, and <u>a beauty salon</u>.

6 He prefers to eat <u>fast food</u> like <u>pizza or hamburgers</u>.

7 They made mummies for the pharaoh's <u>spirit</u> to <u>recognize</u> his <u>body</u>.

8 To grow <u>faster</u>, to have more <u>nutrients</u>, and to be <u>resistant</u> to <u>disease</u> and <u>pests</u>.

A

How to Prepare for Exams	
(1) What is the first thing you do?	make a study plan
(2) What subject do you spend more time on?	subjects which requires memorization such as history, sociology, geology, etc
(3) What subject did you cram for the night before the test?	math
(4) What was the result of your cramming?	I was so tired the next day that I flunked my math test.
(5) What will you do to prepare for your next exam?	follow my study plan and review what I have learned each day

I'd like to tell you about how I prepare for exams. The first thing I do is (1)make a study plan. I try to spend more time on (2)subjects which require memorization such as history, sociology, geology, etc. For my most recent exams, I crammed all night for the (3)math test. As a result, I (4)was so tired the next day that I flunked my math test. For my next exam, I will (5) follow my study plan and review what I have learned each day.

시험 공부 방법	
(1) 가장 먼저 하는 것은?	학습계획을 세우기
(2) 무슨 과목에 좀더 많은 시간을 쓰나?	역사, 사회, 지리 등 암기를 필요로 하는 과목들
(3) 시험 전 무슨 과목을 벼락치기 했나?	수학
(4) 결과는 어떠했나?	다음 날 너무 피곤해서 수학시험에서 낙제했다.
(5) 다음 시험을 위해 무엇을 할 것인가?	나의 학습계획을 따르고 그날 배운 것을 복습할 것이다

제가 시험 준비하는 방법에 대해 말씀 드리겠습니다. 가장 먼저 하는 것은 학습계획 세우기입니다. 저는 역사, 사회, 지리 등 암기를 필요로 하는 과목들에 좀 더 많은 시간을 쓰려고 노력합니다. 가장 최근 시험에서 저는 수학을 벼락치기로 공부했습니다. 그 결과 다음 날 너무 피곤해서 수학시험에서 낙제 했습니다. 다음 시험을 위해, 저는 제 학습계획을 따르고 매일 배운 것을 복습할 것입니다.

B

Genetically Modified Crops	
(1) What are genetically modified crops?	plants used in agriculture, the DNA of which has been modified using genetic engineering techniques
(2) My opinion of eating them	We should not eat these crops.
(3) The reason for my opinion	We still do not fully understand the effects that intentionally mutating an organism, at the genetic level, will have on the human body. Some researchers claim modified foods even cause cancer and disabilities.

Genetically modified crops are (1)plants used in agriculture, the DNA of which has been modified using genetic engineering techniques. In my opinion, I think (2)we should not eat these crops. The reason I think this is that (3)we still do not fully understand the effects that intentionally mutating an organism, at the genetic level, will have on the human body. Some researchers claim modified foods even cause cancer and disabilities. Therefore, I think we can say they aren't safe and (2)we should not eat them.

유전자 변이 농작물	
(1) 유전자 변이 농작물은 무엇인가?	유전공학 기술을 이용하여 DNA가 변이된, 농업에 사용되어지는 식물
(2) 그것을 먹는 것에 대한 나의 의견	이런 농작물들을 먹어서는 안된다
(3) 나의 의견에 대한 이유	우리는 생명체를 유전자 수준에서 의도적으로 변이한 것이 특히 사람 몸에 어떤 영향을 주는지에 대해서 완전히 모르고 있다. 몇몇 연구원들은 심지어 변이된 식품이 암과 장애의 원인이 된다고 주장한다.

유전자 변이 농작물은 유전공학 기술을 이용하여 DNA가 변이된, 농업에 사용되는 식물이다. 내 생각에 나는 이런 농작물들을 먹어서는 안 된다고 생각한다. 내가 이렇게 생각하는 이유는 우리는 생명체를 유전자 수준에서 의도적으로 변이한 것이 특히 사람 몸에 어떤 영향을 주는지에 대해서 완전히 모르고 있다. 몇몇 연구원은 심지어 변이된 식품이 암과 장애의 원인이 된다고 주장한다. 그러므로, 우리가 그것들이 안전하지 않다고 말할 수 있으며 그것들을 먹어서는 안 된다고 생각한다.

01 ②	02 ⑤	03 ⑤	04 ②	05 ②
06 ⑤	07 ①	08 ⑤	09 ②	10 ①
11 ④	12 ①	13 ③	14 ①	15 ④
16 ④	17 ③	18 ②	19 ②	20 ⑤

01

W　Excuse me. I'm looking for a bag I accidently left on subway line 5 last night. Could you check if anyone has turned it in?

M　I will check. [Pause] We have 3 bags that were turned in to the Lost and Found last night. Can you describe your bag for me?

W　It is a brown colored tote bag with a shoulder strap. It is a woven bag.

M　Is there anything special about it?

W　Well, the bag is woven from strips of dark brown leather and camel brown leather. So its color is two tones.

M　Can you describe the contents of your bag?

W　There is a wallet made of the same material as the bag inside it. I hope it wasn't stolen.

M　I think this is yours. Check it and if it is yours, sign this form, please.

W　Oh, I'm sure it's mine. I really appreciate your help.

여　실례합니다. 어젯밤 지하철 5호선에서 실수로 놓고 내린 제 가방을 찾고 있습니다. 누군가가 그것을 돌려주었는지 확인해주시겠어요?

남　확인해보겠습니다. 어젯밤 이 분실물센터로 건네진 가방이 3개가 있네요. 제게 가방을 묘사해주시겠어요?

여　어깨 끈이 달린 갈색 손가방입니다. 짜서 만든 가방이에요.

남　특별한 점은 없나요?

여　글쎄요, 그 가방은 짙은 갈색 가죽 줄과 카멜 갈색 가죽 줄을 엮어 만든 거에요. 그래서 가방 색이 두 가지예요.

남　가방 안에 들어 있는 것에 대해 말씀해주시겠어요?

여　가방과 같은 소재로 만들어진 지갑이 안에 있어요. 도둑맞지 않았길 바래요.

남　이게 당신 것인 것 같군요. 이걸 확인해 보시고, 맞으면 여기에 서명 부탁 드리겠습니다.

여　오, 제 것이 틀림없어요. 도움 주셔서 정말 감사합니다.

●●
turn in ~을 돌려주다, 반납하다　**Lost and Found** 분실물센터
shoulder strap 어깨끈　**woven** 엮은, 짠　**camel brown** 카멜 갈색
tone 색조　**contents** 내용물　**appreciate** 고마워하다, 감사하다

02

W　What's up, Mike? You look worried.

M　Well, Tom and I were shagging flies and he hit a ball over the fence and broke a window in Mr. Johnson's house.

W　Then what happened?

M　We both took off.

W　What a surprise!

M　I feel bad about running away, but…

W　I want you to go over to Mr. Johnson's house and tell him you broke the window and you'll pay for it.

M　Mom, I didn't break it, Tom did.

W　That's not the point. You were there, so you both are responsible. Don't shy away from your responsibility.

여　무슨 일이니, Mike? 너 걱정스러워 보이는 구나.

남　저, Tom 하고 제가 배팅 연습을 하다가 Tom이 친 공이 담장을 넘어 Johnson 아저씨네 유리창을 깼어요.

여　그래서 어떻게 했니?

남　저희 둘 다 도망갔어요.

여　뜻밖이구나!

남　제가 도망간 거 잘못했다고 느껴요. 하지만…

여　난 네가 Johnson씨에게 가서 유리창을 깼다고 말씀 드리고 변상해드리겠다고 했음 좋겠구나.

남　엄마, 제가 창문을 깬 게 아니고, Tom이 그랬어요.

여　그게 중요한 게 아니야. 네가 거기 있었고, 너희 둘 다에게 책임이 있어. 네 책임을 회피하려 하지마.

●●
shagging flies 배팅연습 (한 사람은 치고 다른 한 사람은 플라이볼을 잡는 연습 야구)　**take off** 도망가다　**responsible** 책임이 있는　**shy away** ~을 피하다　**responsibility** 책임

03

M　Attention, visitors! McKinley Mountain Maintenance Department has scheduled a closure of the South Eastern <u>trail</u> from <u>August</u> <u>1st</u> to <u>August 15th</u>. This trail will be <u>temporarily</u> closed due to the <u>presence</u> of <u>dead</u> <u>and</u> <u>diseased</u> <u>trees</u> in large numbers which pose a <u>safety</u> <u>hazard</u> to visitors. Efforts are underway to <u>remove</u> <u>hazardous</u> <u>trees</u> and to <u>protect</u> <u>wildlife</u> in this area. The trail will <u>reopen</u> after the work has been <u>completed</u>. For further information, please contact Robert Donovan at 360-856-5700. Thank you for your patience.

남 방문객 여러분, 주목해주세요! 맥킨리 산 관리실에서는 8월 1일부터 8월 15일까지 남동쪽 등산로를 폐쇄할 예정입니다. 이 등산로는 방문객들에게 안전위협요소로 문제가 제기된 많은 수의 죽거나 병든 나무들이 존재하고 있기 때문에 임시로 폐쇄됩니다. 이 지역에서 위험한 나무를 제거하고 야생동물들을 보호하기 위한 노력을 기울이고 있습니다. 이 등산로는 처치가 완료된 후 재개장 될 것입니다. 더 자세한 정보는 360-856-5700번 Robert Donovan에게 연락하세요. 끝까지 들어주셔서 감사합니다.

•• **closure** 폐쇄 **pose** (위협, 문제를) 제기하다 **safety hazard** 안전 위협 요소 **underway** 진행중인 **wildlife** 야생동물 **complete** 완성하다, 완수하다 **patience**. 인내, 기다림

04

W If you take Judy to the <u>shopping</u> <u>center</u> at <u>11</u> o'clock and keep her busy until <u>12:30</u>, her friends will all have <u>arrived</u> at our house by <u>then</u>. Do you think <u>20</u> <u>minutes</u> is enough for you two to <u>get</u> <u>home</u>?

M It will be alright. When she comes back, she'll be <u>so</u> <u>surprised</u>.

W I want her best friend Wendy to <u>keep</u> <u>her</u> <u>mouth</u> <u>shut</u>.

M I'm sure she won't <u>give</u> <u>it</u> <u>away</u>.

W <u>How</u> <u>many</u> <u>kids</u> will be coming?

M We've invited <u>twenty</u>.

W I hope there'll be a good <u>turnout</u>.

M Aren't you <u>as</u> <u>excited</u> <u>as</u> Judy's going to be?

W I am. Just make sure you <u>keep</u> her <u>at</u> <u>the</u> <u>mall</u> until 12:30.

M Don't worry. Trust me.

W Oh, here comes Judy. <u>Button</u> <u>your</u> <u>lip</u>.

여 네가 Judy를 11시에 쇼핑 센터에 데리고 가서 12시30분까지 그 애를 붙잡아 놓으면, 그때까지 그애 친구들이 우리 집에 모일 거야. 너희 둘이 집에 오는 데 20분이면 충분할 것 같니?

남 괜찮을 거야. 집에 오면, 그 애가 엄청 놀라겠지.

여 난 그 애 절친 Wendy가 함구해 주길 바래.

남 그 앤 발설하지 않을 거야.

여 애들이 몇 명이나 오니?

남 우리 20명 초대했잖아.

여 많이 나타나주길 바래.

남 Judy가 흥분할 것만큼 너도 흥분되지 않니?

여 응, 나도 그래. 12시 반까지 그 앨 꼭 쇼핑센터에 붙잡아 놓아야 해.

남 걱정 마. 날 믿어.

여 오, Judy가 와. 비밀 지켜.

① 깜짝 놀란　　② 신난　　③ 긴장한
④ 무관심한　　⑤ 질투나는

•• **keep one's mouth shut** 입을 닫다. 함구하다 **give away** ~을 폭로하다. 누설하다 **a good turnout** (모임에) 많이 나타남 **button one's lip** 함구하다. 비밀을 지키다

05

M How can I help you?

W I'm here to <u>reserve</u> a package <u>tour</u> to Bangkok.

M Are you traveling with anyone?

W No, I'm going to travel <u>alone</u>. Do I have to <u>share</u> <u>the</u> <u>room</u> with someone else if I get a <u>package</u> <u>tour</u>? I don't want to.

M Don't worry about it. You can have your <u>own</u> <u>room</u> for a small extra payment.

W Okay, I'll do that. Then, could you check flights? I would like to <u>depart</u> <u>next</u> <u>Saturday</u>.

M I'm afraid that no tickets are available for <u>Saturday</u>. <u>The</u> <u>soonest</u> <u>day</u> you can leave is <u>next</u> Sunday. Is that okay with you?

W It should be fine.

M Here are your tickets and <u>travel</u> <u>itinerary</u>. As soon as you arrive at the airport, find our <u>tour</u> <u>guide</u> at <u>the</u> <u>arrival</u> <u>gate</u>.

남 어떻게 도와 드릴까요?

여 방콕행 패키지 여행을 예약하려고 왔습니다.

남 누구와 함께 여행하실 예정이신가요?

여 아뇨, 혼자 여행하려고 합니다. 패키지 여행에 합류하면 다른 사람과

함께 방을 함께 써야 하나요? 그러고 싶지 않은데요.

남 걱정 마세요. 적은 추가 요금으로 자신만의 방을 가지실 수 있습니다.

여 네, 그렇게 할게요. 그럼 비행편을 확인해주시겠어요? 전 다음주 토요일에 출발하고 싶습니다.

남 애석하게도 토요일은 이용 가능한 좌석이 없습니다. 가장 빨리 출발하실 수 있는 날은 다음주 일요일입니다. 괜찮으신가요?

여 괜찮은 것 같습니다.

남 여기 표와 여행일정 입니다. 공항에 도착 즉시, 도착 게이트에서 저희 여행가이드를 찾으세요.

•• **extra** 추가의, 여분의 **depart** 출발하다 **travel itinerary** 여행일정 **arrival gate** 도착 게이트

06

W Welcome to Mount Cook Ski Resort! How can I help you?

M Hi, I would like to buy two day <u>passes</u> for <u>adults</u>.

W The regular price for a day pass is <u>50</u> dollars. And with that pass you can enjoy skiing and snowboarding from <u>8:30</u> a.m. to <u>5:30</u> p.m.

M Oh, can't I ski <u>at night</u>?

W No, with a day pass you can't. To do that, you should buy a <u>full-day</u> <u>pass</u>. It's 60 dollars.

M Do you have <u>full-day</u> passes for periods of several days? I'm going to stay at this resort for <u>3 nights</u>.

W Yes, we have them. It is <u>150</u> dollars for a full-day pass for three days.

M Okay. I'll have <u>two</u> <u>full-day</u> passes for three days. And my friend and I have to <u>rent</u> <u>clothing</u> and skiing gear for the three days.

W Renting clothing is 10 dollars <u>per</u> <u>person</u> per day and skiing gear is 20 dollars per person per day.

여 Mount Cook 스키 리조트에 오신 것을 환영합니다! 어떻게 도와드릴까요?

남 안녕하세요. 성인용 주간권 2장을 사고 싶습니다.

여 주간권의 정상가는 50달러입니다. 그것으로 오전 8시30분부터 오후 5시30분까지 스키와 보드를 즐기실 수 있습니다.

남 오, 밤에는 스키를 탈수 없나요?

여 주간권으로는 안됩니다. 그러시려면, 종일권을 구매하셔야 합니다. 그것은 60달러입니다.

남 며칠 기간의 종일권도 있나요? 3일간 이 리조트에 머무를 거예요.

여 네, 있습니다. 3일간 종일권은 150달러입니다.

남 네. 3일권 2장 하겠습니다. 그리고 제 친구와 제가 3일간 스키복과 장비를 대여해야 합니다.

여 의류대여는 하루에 인당 10달러, 장비는 하루에 인당 20달러입니다.

•• **period** 기간 **gear** 장비 **per person per day** 하루에 인당

07

M Where to, ma'am?

W The Canadian Embassy. It's behind City Hall. You can <u>drop me off</u> there if there is too much traffic around City Hall.

M All right, ma'am.

W Could you <u>step on it</u>? I'm <u>in a hurry</u>. I have to <u>submit</u> <u>my</u> <u>application</u> to renew my passport before they close at 5 pm.

M I'll do my best.

W Is it possible to <u>switch lanes</u>? This lane is <u>going nowhere</u>!

M Oh, you really are a <u>backseat</u> <u>driver</u>.

W Excuse me, but what did you say?

M No, nothing.

남 손님 어디로 가시나요?

여 캐나다 대사관이요. 시청 뒤에 있어요. 시청 근처가 막히면 거기서 내려주세요.

남 네, 알겠습니다. 손님

여 속도를 좀 내주시겠어요? 제가 좀 급해서요. 5시에 문닫기 전에 제 여권갱신을 위해 신청서를 접수해야 해서요.

남 최선을 다하겠습니다.

여 차선을 바꿀 수 있을까요? 이 차선은 진전이 없네요!

남 오, 당신은 뒤에서 이래라 저래라 하는 뒷좌석 운전자군요.

여 실례합니다만 뭐라고 하셨죠?

남 아뇨, 아무것도 아닙니다.

•• **drop off** (차에서) 내려주다. 떨어뜨리다 **step on it** 속도를 내다 **in a hurry** 급한, 서두르는 **switch** 바꾸다 **lane** 차선 **go nowhere** 아무 성과[진전]를 못보다 **backseat driver** 뒷좌석 운전자 (운전자 뒤에 앉아 이래라 저래라 하는 사람)

08

M Excuse me. This is my <u>first time</u> coming here. Can I ask you <u>for a hand</u>?

W Of course. What can I do to help?

M I don't know the best way to find a book I want.

W First, look up the book you want on the computer over there. It will show you where you can find it and whether it is in stock or out of stock.

M What should I do if it is out of stock?

W Then you can go to the customer service desk and get a copy ordered for you.

M If I want to order a book, do you know if I have to put some money down first?

W I'm sorry. I'm not sure about that.

M I see. Thank you very much for helping me.

· ·

남 실례합니다. 제가 여기 처음이라서요. 도움을 요청해도 될까요?

여 물론이죠. 무엇을 도와드릴까요?

남 제가 원하는 책을 찾는 좋은 방법을 몰라서요.

여 우선, 저 쪽에 있는 컴퓨터로 검색해보세요. 그것은 책이 어디에 있고 재고가 있는지 없는지를 보여줍니다.

남 재고가 없으면 어떻게 해야 하나요?

여 그러면 고객서비스 창구에 가서 당신을 위해 책을 주문하세요.

남 주문을 원하면 돈을 먼저 내야 하는지 아닌지 아시나요?

여 미안합니다. 그것은 잘 모르겠습니다.

남 그렇군요. 도와주셔서 정말 감사 드립니다.

••
ask for a hand 도움을 요청하다 **look up** 검색하다 **in stock** 재고가
있는 **out of stock** 재고가 없음

09

M Is there any specific item you'd like to buy, ma'am?

W I'm looking for a comforter for my daughter.

M There are a variety of designs for kids. What kind of design do you have in mind?

W Which one is popular with kids these days? Can you recommend one of them to me, please?

M This way, please. Take a look at these striped, floral, and animation character designs.

W Oh, the last one sounds great to me.

M Which one do you prefer: Mickey Mouse, Cinderella riding in a pumpkin coach or Snow White and the Seven Dwarfs?

W The last one, please.

· ·

남 구입하고 싶으신 특별한 물품이 있으신가요, 부인?

여 내 딸에게 줄 이불을 찾고 있습니다.

남 아이들을 위한 다양한 디자인이 있습니다. 어떤 디자인을 생각하고 계세요?

여 요즘 아이들에게는 어떤 것이 인기가 있나요? 그것들 중 몇 개만 추천해 주시겠습니까?

남 이쪽으로 오세요. 이 줄무늬, 꽃무늬, 애니메이션 캐릭터 디자인을 보세요.

여 오, 마지막 것이 좋은 것 같은데요.

남 어떤 것이 더 좋으세요. 미키마우스, 호박마차를 타고 있는 신데렐라 혹은 백설공주와 일곱 난장이 중에서요.

여 마지막 걸로 주세요.

••
have in mind 염두에 두다 **popular** 인기 있는 **striped** 줄무늬의
floral 꽃무늬의 **pumpkin coach** 호박 마차

10

W Why didn't you return my phone call this morning?

M I'm sorry, I was very busy so I had no time to call you back.

W What were you doing?

M I had to go to the airport to pick up my cousin from France. My uncle called me at dawn and asked me to do it. So I was late for work.

W Oh, that's too bad. You said your boss is very strict about getting to work on time.

M I explained my situation to him and he understood.

W Good. So where is your cousin now? In your house?

M Yes. He is probably preparing for his job interview tomorrow.

· ·

여 왜 오늘 아침에 내 전화 안 받았어?

남 미안해. 너무 바빠서 네게 전화할 시간이 없었어.

여 뭐했어?

남 프랑스에서 온 사촌을 데리러 공항에 가야 했어. 삼촌이 새벽에 전화하셔서 그렇게 해달라고 부탁하셨거든. 그래서 회사도 늦었어.

여 안 됐다. 상사가 정시에 출근하는 것에 매우 엄격하다고 말했잖아.

남 내 상황을 설명 드렸고 이해해 주셨어.

여 잘됐네. 네 사촌은 지금 어디 있어? 너희 집에 있어?

남 응. 내일 있을 면접 준비를 하고 있을 거야.

••
at dawn 새벽에 **strict** 엄격한 **on time** 정각에

11

W Honey, do you know what our son Jack is doing now?

M Isn't he doing his homework in his room?

W No! He read comic books right after finishing eating breakfast, and now he is playing computer games.

M How about leaving him alone? It's Sunday today. He needs some time to refresh his mind.

W What? Are you serious? But he has to do his homework for tomorrow.

M Honey, listen. I don't want to force my son to study hard. As you know, studying hard is not everything.

W You're right. Let's leave him for a while and trust him to act responsibly in the future. However, if he keeps on acting this way, I'll have to talk to him.

M Alright. That's a good idea.

여 여보, 우리 아들 Jack이 지금 뭐하고 있는지 아세요?

남 자기 방에서 숙제하고 있는 거 아녜요?

여 아뇨! 아침 먹은 직후에 만화책을 읽었는데 지금은 컴퓨터 게임을 하고 있어요.

남 그냥 놔두는 게 어때요? 오늘은 일요일이잖아요. 그 애도 정신을 맑게 할 시간이 필요해요.

여 뭐라고요? 진심이예요? 그렇지만 내일 숙제를 해야 해요.

남 여보, 들어봐요. 나는 우리 아들에게 공부를 열심히 하라고 강요하고 싶지 않아요. 당신도 알다시피, 공부 열심히 하는 게 전부는 아니잖아요.

여 맞아요. 잠시 그 애를 놔두고 앞으로 책임감 있게 행동하리라 믿읍시다. 하지만, 계속 이런 식으로 한다면 제가 말할 거예요.

남 좋아요. 좋은 생각 이예요.

•• **refresh one's mind** 정신을 맑게 하다 **force** 강요하다 **trust** 믿다
keep on -ing 계속 ~하다

12

M Grandma, is it that important to keep a promise you make with someone?

W You bet it is! It is one of the best ways to build a good reputation. Moreover, building trust is very important in your life.

M But you know it is hard to keep every promise you make. Haven't you ever broken a promise?

W I surely have.

M Then do you have a bad reputation among people?

W Ha, ha. Of course not. Whenever I broke a promise because of some unavoidable factor, I fully explained and deeply apologized to the person.

M Ok, I'll try to do that, too.

W There is a saying "A man dies but his name remains." So keeping a promise and having a good reputation are very important.

남 할머니, 누군가와 약속을 지키는 것이 그렇게 중요한가요?

여 당연하지! 좋은 평판을 쌓는 가장 중요한 방법들 중의 하나야. 게다가 신뢰를 쌓는 것은 너의 인생에서 매우 중요해.

남 하지만 모든 약속을 지키는 것은 어렵다는 걸 아시잖아요. 할머니는 약속을 깬 적이 없으세요?

여 물론 있지.

남 그러면 사람들에게서 나쁜 평판을 가지고 계세요?

여 하하. 당연히 아니지. 피할 수 없는 이유때문에 약속을 어겼을 때마다 그 사람에게 충분히 설명하고 깊이 사과했단다.

남 좋아요. 저도 그렇게 하려고 노력할게요.

여 "사람은 죽어서 이름을 남긴다."라는 말이 있어. 그러니 약속을 지키는 것과 좋은 평판을 남기는 것은 아주 중요해.

① 시작이 반이다.
② 반짝인다고 모두 금은 아니다.
③ 구르는 돌에는 이끼가 끼지 않는다.
④ 솜씨 없는 일꾼이 연장만 나무란다.
⑤ 호랑이는 죽어서 가죽을 남기고 사람은 죽어서 이름을 남긴다.

•• **keep a promise** 약속을 지키다 **a good reputation** 호평 **build trust** 신뢰를 쌓다 **unavoidable** 피치 못할 **apologize** 사과하다

13

W Are you still looking for a new USB, Ken?

M Yes, but I can't decide which one would be best for me. I have to consider the capacity, the inclusion of a cable, and the price.

W Let's take a look at each of them one by one. How large do you need it to be?

M Actually, I just realized that it doesn't really matter because it will only be for my in-class presentations. I will store just a few files on it.

W What about the price? What's your budget? It is usually the most important consideration.

M Less than 25 dollars. The cheaper, the better, though.

W There are two choices left. And they are the same price and capacity. The difference is only the inclusion of a cable.

M I don't need to think about it. I will pick the one with the cable.

모델	용량	가격	케이블
① Mega 3.0	32기가	55달러	○
② Mega 2.0	16기가	35달러	X
③ Mega 1.0	8기가	20달러	○
④ Vega 2.0	16기가	30달러	○
⑤ Vega 1.0	8기가	20달러	X

여 Ken, 너 아직도 새 USB 찾고 있니?

남 응. 어떤 것이 나에게 좋은 건지 결정을 못하겠어. 용량, 케이블 유무, 그리고 가격도 고려해야 해.

여 하나씩 보자. 용량은 얼마나 커야 해?

남 실은, 학교 발표 때만 쓸 거라서 크게 상관은 없다는 걸 방금 알았어. 거기에 파일만 몇 개 저장할거야.

여 가격은? 예산이 얼마인데? 가장 중요한 고려 사항이잖아.

남 25달러 이하야. 하지만 쌀수록 좋지 뭐.

여 두 개의 선택이 남았네. 가격이 같고 용량도 같아. 차이는 단지 케이블 유무야.

남 생각할 것도 없어. 케이블 있는 것으로 할게.

●●
consider 고려하다 **capacity** 용량 **inclusion** 포함 **cable** 케이블 **one by one** 하나씩 **store** 저장하다 **budget** 예산 **the** 비교급, **the** 비교급 더 ~할수록 더 …한

14

[Telephone rings.]

W Hello, Ted. Are you still at work?

M Hi, Jenny. Yes, I'm still in the office. Why?

W Please don't forget to stop by the wine shop and get a bottle of ice wine.

M I already bought it during the lunchtime. Don't worry about it.

W Good. I was about to go to the bakery to buy a cake, but the wine just came to my mind.

M Is there anything else you want me to get?

W Please get a new wine opener. The one in the house has a dull point so it is quite hard to open bottles.

M Alright. You have had a hard job preparing all the food and decorating the house. I will do the dishes and clean up after the party.

W Thank you. I'm going to buy a chocolate cake. Is it alright?

M Sure. It's really delicious.

W Okay. I'll go get it now

[전화벨이 울린다.]

여 여보세요, Ted. 아직 회사야?

남 안녕, Jenny. 응. 아직 사무실이야. 왜?

여 와인가게에 들러서 아이스 와인 한 병 사오는 것 잊지마.

남 점심시간에 이미 샀어. 걱정하지마.

여 잘 했어. 제과점에 가서 케이크를 사려던 참이었는데 와인이 갑자기 떠올랐어.

남 다른 것 사갈 것 있어?

여 새 와인따개 좀 사와. 집에 있는 것은 끝이 무뎌서 병을 따기가 좀 힘들어.

남 알았어. 음식 준비하고 집을 꾸미느라 힘들었겠다. 파티 후에 설거지는 내가 할게.

여 고마워. 초콜릿 케이크 사려고 하는데. 괜찮아?

남 물론이지. 그건 정말 맛있어.

여 좋아. 이제 사러 나가야겠다.

●●
stop by 들르다 **a bottle of** 한 병의 **come to one's mind** 떠오르다, 생각나다 **dull** 무딘

15

W The Mayan people of Mexico and Central America had the greatest civilization in the New World. These native Mesoamerican people developed one of the most sophisticated cultures before the arrival of the Spanish. Their religion was characterized by the worship of nature gods, especially the gods of sun, rain and corn. Other features were the existence of a priestly class, the importance of astronomy and astrology, rituals of human sacrifice, and the building of elaborate pyramidal temples.

여 멕시코와 중미의 마야인들은 신세계(과거에 남북아메리카를 가리키던 말)에서 가장 위대한 문명을 가지고 있었다. 토착 메소 아메리칸들은 스페인 사람들이 도착하기 전까지 가장 세련된 문화들 중 하나를 발전시켰다. 그들의 종교는 특히 태양, 비 그리고 옥수수의 신들과 같은 자연신 숭배로 특징지워졌다. 또한 다른 특징들을 살펴보면, 제사장 계급, 천문학과 점성술의 중요성, 사람을 제물로 바치는 의식 그리고 정교한 피라미드모양의 사원을 짓는 것 등이다.

··
civilization 문명 **native** 토착의, 원주민의 **sophisticated** 세련된 **arrival** 도착 **worship** 숭배 **priestly** 제사장의 **astrology** 점성술, 점성학 **ritual** 제사 **sacrifice** 희생, 제물 **elaborate** 정교한 **pyramidal** 피라미드 모양의, 거대한 **temple** 사원

16

W What is this sticker on your driver's license?

M It indicates that I've signed up for the organ donation program.

W You mean you're going to donate your organs?

M Yes. If anything bad happens to me, I want my organs to go to other people who need them.

W So you want somebody else to have your heart and liver?

M That's right. Also, my eyes, kidneys, or anything else that can be given to someone else. Don't you want to donate your organs?

W Me? No way. I'll never agree to doctors cutting up my body after I die.

M But you won't need those organs when you're dead.

W That might be true, but I can't imagine somebody else walking around with my heart.

M But you can save someone's life.

여 네 운전면허증에 있는 이 스티커 뭐야?
남 그것은 내가 장기기증 프로그램에 가입했다는 표시야.
여 네 장기를 기증할 거라는 거야?
남 응. 나에게 나쁜 일이 일어난다면, 나는 내 장기가 그것을 필요로 하는 다른 사람들에게 가기를 원해.
여 그럼 너는 다른 누군가가 너의 심장과 간을 가지기를 원한다는 거야?
남 맞아. 또한, 눈, 신장 등 다른 사람에게 줄 수 있는 것은 어떤 것이든. 넌 장기를 기증하고 싶지 않니?

여 나? 절대로 안 해. 나는 내가 죽은 후에 의사들이 내 몸을 절단하는 걸 동의하지 않을 거야.
남 하지만 네가 죽으면 그 장기들은 필요 없어.
여 그것은 사실이겠지만. 난 다른 누군가가 나의 심장을 가지고 걸어 다니는 상상을 할 수가 없어.
남 하지만, 네가 누군가의 생명을 구할 수 있어.

① 걷는 것은 너의 건강에 좋아.
② 심장 손상 위험이 있니?
③ 나는 그것에 익숙해 질 수도 없었어.
⑤ 네 건강 문제를 들으니 유감이다.

··
organ 장기, 기관 **donation** 기부 **liver** 간 **kidney** 신장 **save** 구하다

17

W It is beyond me how you and Henry can be roommates. You're very tidy and he's not.

M It's not always easy, but we're making it work.

W Isn't he really messy all the time? Whenever I see him, his clothes are not clean and his hair is untidy.

M His room is just as you would expect it to be.

W How can you live with him then?

M He keeps the common areas in passable condition. However, I often have to straighten up the living room, and sometimes have to pick up and put away his stuff.

W That's very tolerant of you.

M And he has just agreed to pay a fine sometimes.

W Pay a fine? You mean when he's really messy.

M Yes, when that happens, he has to pay me $1.

여 너와 Henry가 룸메이트가 되다니 상상할 수 없어. 너는 깔끔하고 그는 아니잖아.
남 항상 쉬운 건 아니지만, 우리는 나름 잘 지내고 있어.
여 그는 정말 항상 지저분하지 않니? 내가 그를 만날 때마다 그의 옷은 깨끗하지 않고 그의 머리는 단정하지 않아.
남 그의 방은 네가 예상하는 그대로야.
여 그럼 너는 그와 어떻게 같이 살 수 있어?
남 그는 공용공간은 그런대로 괜찮은 상태를 유지해. 하지만 종종 내가 거실 정리를 해야 하고 가끔은 그의 물건을 주워서 치워야 하지.
여 너 정말 아량이 넓구나.
남 그리고 그는 가끔 벌금을 내는 데 동의했어.
여 벌금을 낸다구? 그가 정말 지저분하게 어질렀을 때를 말하는구나.

남 응. 그런 일이 일어나면 그가 나에게 1달러를 내야 해.

① 그가 너에게 벌금을 내야 한다고 생각하지 않아.
② 아니, 기한이 넘지 않았으니 벌금은 없어.
④ 내 부모님은 나를 쫓아다니며 치워야 하지 않았어.
⑤ 아니, 나는 지저분한 사람과 함께 살고 싶지 않아.

●●
untidy 지저분한   **common area** 공용지역   **passable** 그런대로 괜찮은
tolerant 아량이 넓은, 관대한

18

W I'm really glad to ride a bike again. It's <u>been years</u>
   since I rode a bicycle last.

M This is the only way to travel. You get to really see
   the <u>scenery</u> and enjoy the <u>fresh air</u>.

W Hey, watch out! You <u>almost</u> rode into that huge
   pothole. Watch out or you might fall off your bike.

M Thanks for the warning.

W Not at all. This asphalt needs to be repaired.

M Oh, slow down! There's a <u>big dip ahead</u>.

W I didn't see that coming. I almost <u>lost control</u>
   on that slippery section of path. Sorry, I nearly
   swerved into you. Are you okay?

M Yes, I'm fine. I thought this would be an easy ride
   since it's <u>paved</u> all the way. I didn't <u>bargain</u> for
   these <u>bad road conditions</u>.

W <u>Be careful, and keep your eyes open.</u>

....

여 자전거 다시 타게 되어서 너무 좋아. 자전거를 마지막으로 탄 지가
    벌써 몇 년이 됐어.
남 이것이 여행을 하는 유일한 방법이야. 풍경을 보고 신선한 공기를 즐길
    수 있잖아.
여 어, 조심해! 너는 저기 크게 패인 곳에 거의 빠질 뻔 했어. 조심하지
    않으면 자전거에서 떨어질 거야.
남 알려줘서 고마워.
여 천만에. 이 아스팔트는 보수를 좀 해야겠어.
남 오, 천천히 가! 앞에 크게 움푹 패인 곳이 있어.
여 저게 있는지 보지 못했어. 길의 미끄러운 부분에서 거의 중심을 잃을
    뻔 했어. 네 쪽으로 방향을 틀어서 미안해. 괜찮아?
남 응. 난 괜찮아. 나는 도로가 내내 포장되어 있어서, 쉽게 자전거 탈 수
    있다고 생각했어 이런 안 좋은 길 상태를 예상하지 못했어.
여 <u>조심해, 그리고 눈을 크게 뜨고 살펴봐.</u>

① 자전거 타러 가기에 나쁜 날은 아니야.

③ 이 자전거를 살 때 저렴하게 샀어.
④ 더 빨리 가! 도로가 평탄하고 일직선이야.
⑤ 나는 배우는 중이라 자전거를 타고 균형을 유지할 수 없어.

●●
pothole 움푹 패인 곳   **dip** (도로의) 움푹 패인 부분   **swerve** 방향을 바꾸다
bargain for ~을 예상하다, 대비하다

19

W I want to live <u>close to downtown</u>. We can <u>walk</u> to
   most amenities.

M Downtown is always <u>bustling</u> and <u>noisy</u>. And the
   crime rate is really high as well.

W If we live downtown, we won't have to worry
   about the <u>commuting time</u> and the <u>traffic</u>. We can
   walk to work and take public transportation.

M I want to <u>settle down</u> somewhere for a while, not
   move every couple of years.

W Is that why you want to live in the suburbs? I think
   the suburbs have <u>no character</u>.

M That's not true.

W Downtown has a dynamic and interesting
   character.

M I want to live in a <u>quiet neighborhood</u>. I want to
   garden in the backyard and take a walk in the local
   park.

W <u>I'm sorry, but it sounds boring to me.</u>

....

여 나는 도심 가까이에 살고 싶어요. 대부분의 편의시설들을 다 걸어서 갈
    수 있잖아요
남 도심은 항상 혼잡하고 시끄러워요. 범죄율 또한 정말 높구요.
여 도심에 살면, 우리는 통근 시간과 교통을 걱정할 필요가 없어요.
    걸어서 출근할 수 있고 대중교통을 타면 되요.
남 나는 이 년마다 이사하는 게 아니라 어디든 한동안 정착하고 싶어요.
여 그게 당신이 교외에서 살고 싶어하는 이유인가요? 교외지역은 개성이
    없어요.
남 그건 사실이 아니에요.
여 도심은 동적이고 재미있는 특징이 있어요.
남 난 조용한 지역에 살고 싶어요. 뒷마당에 정원을 꾸미고 동네 공원에서
    산책하고 싶어요.
여 <u>미안하지만 나에겐 지루하게 들리네요.</u>

① 우리 둘이 마침내 의견이 일치해서 기뻐요.
③ 나도 매일 공원에서 산책하고 싶어요.

④ 우리 이웃은 진짜 재미있는 인물이예요.
⑤ 나는 우리 이웃들과 잘 지내고 싶어요.

amenity 편의시설　**bustling** 혼잡한　**commute time** 통근시간
settle down 정착하다　**suburb** 교외　**character** 개성, 특징
neighborhood 이웃, 동네

20

M　Ms. Adams is a real estate agent. Now, she is waiting for her clients to show them a decent apartment whose price is quite reasonable for the area. It is a newly built apartment with good transportation nearby and a nice view. Another real estate agent has another family that is interested in it, so Ms. Adams needs to work fast if her clients want it. However, her clients aren't showing up at the appointed time. She tries to call them several times and finally gets hold of them. In this situation, what would Ms. Adams probably say to her clients?

··

남　Ms. Adams은 부동산 중개인이다. 지금, 그녀는 그 지역에서 상당히 합리적인 가격으로 나온 괜찮은 아파트를 그녀의 고객들에게 보여주기 위해서 기다리고 있다. 그것은 교통이 편리하고 전망이 좋은 새로 지어진 아파트이다. 다른 중개인이 그 아파트에 관심을 보이는 다른 가족을 데리고 있어서 그녀의 고객이 그 아파트를 원한다면 Ms. Adams는 빨리 일 처리를 해야 한다. 하지만, 그녀의 고객들은 약속된 시간에 나타나지 않는다. 그녀는 통화를 하기 위해서 여러 번 전화를 하고 마침내 통화가 된다. 이런 상황에서 Ms. Adams는 그녀의 고객들에게 뭐라고 말 할 것 같은가?

① 늦어서 죄송합니다.
② 언제 만날까요?
③ 그것은 이미 다른 가족에게 팔렸어요.
④ 새 아파트에 살기를 바래요.
⑤ 빨리 오시지 않으면 다른 사람이 그것을 살 수 있어요.

real estate agent 부동산 중개인　**decent** 괜찮은　**show up** 나타나다
appointed 약속된, 지정된　**get hold of** ~와 연락하다

Further **S**tudy 정답　　　　　　　　　　p. 104

1　It is taking place at the Lost and Found for subway line 5.
2　She wants Mike to tell Mr. Johnson he broke the window and he will pay for it.
3　She can have her own room for a small extra payment.
4　He went to the airport to pick up his cousin from France.
5　He needs one to store a few files for his in-class presentations.
6　She asked the man to buy a wine opener because the one she has a dull point.
7　They were the worship of nature gods, the existence of a priestly class, the importance of astronomy and astrology, rituals of human sacrifice, and the building of elaborate pyramidal temples.
8　It indicates that he has signed up for the organ donation program.

On **Y**our **O**wn 모범답안　　　　　　　　p. 105

A

I Broke a Promise When...	
(1) When did you break a promise?	three years ago when I was 13 years old
(2) Who did you make it to?	my mom
(3) What was it about?	not playing computer games before finishing my homework
(4) What was the person's reaction when you broke it?	got angry, changed the password on the computer
(5) How did you resolve it and what was the result?	wrote a letter of apology, made another promise / decided to trust me once again

I'm going to talk about a moment when I broke a promise. It was (1)three years ago when I was 13 years old. I made the promise to (2)my mom. It was about (3)not playing computer games before finishing my homework but I didn't keep it. She (4)really got angry at me and changed the password on the computer so that I couldn't turn it on. I (5)wrote a letter of apology and made another promise. Fortunately, (5)she decided to trust me once again and I have never broken a promise since then.

....

나는 …할 때 약속을 어겼다	
(1) 당신은 언제 약속을 어겼나요?	3년 전 13살 때
(2) 누구와 한 것이었나요?	엄마
(3) 무엇에 관한 것이었나요?	숙제를 끝내기 전에 컴퓨터 게임을 하지 않는 것
(4) 당신이 약속을 어겼을 때 상대방의 반응은 어땠나요?	화를 내심 / 컴퓨터 암호를 바꾸었음
(5) 당신은 그 문제를 어떻게 해결했으며 결과는 어땠나요?	사과 편지를 씀, 다른 약속을 함/ 다시 한번 나를 믿기로 결정함

저는 제가 약속을 어긴 순간에 대해 이야기 할 것입니다. 그것은 3년 전 제가 13살 때입니다. 저는 엄마와 약속을 했습니다. 그것은 숙제를 끝내기 전에는 컴퓨터 게임을 하지 않는다는 것이었으나 저는 지키지 않았습니다. 엄마는 제게 무척 화를 내셨고, 내가 컴퓨터를 켜지 못하도록 비밀번호를 바꾸셨습니다. 저는 반성문을 쓰고 다시 약속을 했습니다. 다행스럽게도, 엄마는 저를 다시 믿기로 결심하셨고 저는 그때 이후로 약속을 어기지 않고 있습니다.

B

In a Big City or in the Country?	
The place	a big city
The 1st reason	facilities in a big city are more easily available so we don't need to go that far to find what we want to buy or do
The 2nd reason	We can find more opportunities for getting good jobs and a good education because a big city has more companies and a better educational system.
My conclusion	I have a better chance to live a more comfortable life as the city offers so many things.

When people talk about where they prefer to live, different people have different points of view. From my personal perspective, I prefer to live in a big city.

First, facilities in a big city are more easily available so we don't need to go that far to find what we want to buy or do. Second, we can find more opportunities for getting good jobs and a good education because a big city has more companies and a better educational system. In sum, I want to live in a big city because I have a better chance to live a more comfortable life as the city offers so many things.

....

대도시 또는 시골?	
장소	대도시
첫번째 이유	대도시에 있는 편의시설들을 더 쉽게 이용할 수 있어서 사거나 하려고 하는 것을 찾으러 멀리 갈 필요가 없다
두번째 이유	일자리 또는 교육의 기회가 더 많은데 왜냐하면 대도시는 더 많은 회사와 더 나은 교육제도가 갖춰져 있기 때문이다.
나의 결론	도시가 제공하는 많은 것들 때문에 더 편리한 삶을 살 더 많은 기회를 갖는다.

사람들이 어디에서 살기를 더 좋아하는지에 대해 말할 때 사람들은 각자 다른 견해를 갖고 있다. 내 개인적인 견해로 나는 대도시에 사는 것이 더 좋다. 우선 대도시에선 편의시설을 더 쉽게 이용할 수 있어서 사고자 하거나 하고 싶은 것을 찾기 위해 그리 멀리 갈 필요가 없다. 둘째로 대도시는 더 많은 회사와 더 좋은 교육 체계를 갖고 있기 때문에 좋은 직장과 교육을 얻을 더 많은 기회를 찾을 수 있다. 요약하면 도시는 많은 것들을 제공해주어 내가 더 안락한 삶을 살 수 있는 더 좋은 기회를 가질 수 있기 때문에 나는 대도시에서 살고 싶다.

01 ④	02 ③	03 ②	04 ②	05 ①
06 ⑤	07 ②	08 ④	09 ④	10 ③
11 ③	12 ⑤	13 ②	14 ②	15 ⑤
16 ④	17 ⑤	18 ⑤	19 ②	20 ①

01

M　I feel like my legs are <u>numb</u> because I have been <u>sitting</u> for a long time.

W　How about doing some <u>stretching</u> exercises? In my experience, they are easy but <u>effective</u>.

M　That's a good idea. Can you recommend something?

W　Okay. I'll <u>let you know</u> one of my favorites. First, plant your feet flat on the ground, about shoulder-width <u>apart</u>. Your feet should be slightly outward, not <u>straight</u> ahead.

M　Is it okay?

W　Right. Then, look straight ahead and <u>bend your knees</u> as if you were going to <u>sit back</u> in a chair, keeping your heels <u>on the floor</u>.

M　It is getting difficult.

W　Good, so far. Don't allow your knees to go <u>too far forward</u>. In a controlled manner, slowly <u>lower yourself</u> down and back so that your upper legs are nearly <u>parallel</u> with the floor.

M　Oh, it's really hard to <u>keep my balance</u>.

W　In that case, <u>extend</u> your arms for balance.

··

남　너무 오래 앉아 있어서 다리에 감각이 없는 느낌이야.

여　스트레칭을 해 보는 게 어때? 내 경험상으로는 쉽지만 효과적이야.

남　좋은 생각이야. 뭔가 추천해 줄 수 있어?

여　좋아. 내가 좋아하는 것 중 하나를 알려줄게. 우선, 발을 어깨 넓이만큼 벌려서 바닥에 둬. 발이 일자로 앞을 향해선 안되고 살짝 바깥쪽으로 향해야 해.

남　이거 괜찮아?

여　맞아. 그 다음, 뒤꿈치를 바닥에 계속 붙인 채로 마치 의자에 편안히 앉는 것처럼 똑바로 앞을 보고 무릎을 굽혀.

남　점점 어려워지는군.

여　여기까지 좋았어. 무릎이 너무 앞으로 나가지 않도록 해. 조심스럽게

천천히 몸을 아래와 뒤쪽으로 낮추어서 네 위쪽 다리가 거의 바닥과 평행하게 해.

남　오, 균형 잡기가 정말 어려운데.

여　그런 경우, 균형을 잡기 위해 팔을 뻗어봐.

•• **numb** 감각이 없는　**stretching exercises** 이완 운동　**plant** (특정 장소에 단단히) 놓다, 두다, 자리를 잡다　**shoulder-width** 어깨 넓이로　**sit back** 편안히 앉다　**in a controlled manner** 조심스럽게, 통제된 자세로　**heal** 발뒤꿈치　**parallel with** ~과 평행한

02

W　Tom, I'm sorry, but I'm afraid I have some bad news for you.

M　What's it? Haven't you finished making the PowerPoint for <u>our presentation</u>?

W　That's not it. Fortunately, I finished it <u>last night</u>. Do you remember that you <u>lent</u> me your science <u>encyclopedia</u> last week?

M　Of course I remember. Did you <u>lose</u> it?

W　No, that's not it. By mistake last night, I <u>knocked my</u> coffee mug <u>over</u> and <u>spilled coffee</u> on your book.

M　Oh, no! You <u>should have been</u> more <u>careful</u>.

W　I should have. I was too sleepy. I'm terribly sorry.

M　Do you think it will be <u>too stained to read</u> it?

W　I guess so. I have ordered a <u>replacement</u> from an Internet bookstore, but it won't arrive <u>until at the end</u> of this week.

M　That's Ok. I don't need it until then.

··

여　Tom, 미안하지만, 너에게 전할 나쁜 소식이 좀 있어.

남　그게 뭐니? 우리 발표에 쓸 PPT 만들기 아직 못 끝냈니?

여　아니. 다행스럽게도 그건 어젯밤 끝냈어. 너 지난주에 내게 과학 백과사전 빌려줬던 거 기억하지?

남　물론 기억하지. 너 그거 잃어버린 거니?

여　아니. 그게 아니야. 실수로 어젯밤, 커피 컵을 엎질러서 네 책에 커피를 쏟았어.

남　오, 이런! 좀 더 조심했어야지.

여　그랬어야 했는데. 너무 졸렸어. 정말 미안해.

남　너무 얼룩져서 읽기 어려울 것 같니?

여　그런 것 같아. 인터넷 서점에서 대체할 책을 주문했는데, 이번 주말이 끝날 때까지는 도착하지 않을 거야.

남　괜찮아. 그때까진 필요없어.

encyclopedia 백과사전 **knock something over** ~을 넘어뜨리다, 쓰러뜨리다 **stained** 얼룩진 **replacement** 대체물

03

M When planning your next holiday, make sure you do your <u>research</u> and that you have a <u>safety</u> <u>net</u> in case things <u>go</u> <u>wrong</u>. Take out appropriate <u>travel</u> <u>insurance</u> which should cover you for such things as <u>cancellations</u>, lost luggage, and <u>stolen</u> <u>travel</u> <u>documents</u>. Check your <u>level</u> <u>of</u> <u>coverage</u> as it may also depend on where you travel. Travel insurance should cover <u>medical</u> <u>expenses</u> incurred during <u>overseas</u> <u>travel</u>; however, your national health plan always covers medical expenses incurred when travelling in this country. And always <u>consult</u> <u>a</u> <u>doctor</u> for appropriate health advice before <u>travelling</u> <u>overseas</u>.

남 다음 휴가를 계획할 때 자신이 직접 조사를 해보고 일이 잘못될 것을 예상해 안전장치를 가져야 한다는 것을 명심하세요. 취소, 짐 분실, 여행관련 문서 도난 등을 보상해주는 알맞은 여행 보험을 가지고 가세요. 어디를 여행하는지에 따라 다를 수 있으니 보상수준을 확인하세요. 여행 보험은 해외여행 중에 발생하는 의료비를 보상해야 하지만 국민의료보험은 국내여행 중에 일어나는 의료비를 항상 보상합니다. 그리고 해외 여행을 하기 전 항상 의사에게 적절한 건강 관련 조언을 구하세요.

safety net 안전망, 안전장치 **insurance** 보험 **cancellation** 취소
medical expense 의료비 **overseas** 해외의 **incur** 비용을 발생시키다

04

W I got a letter from Grandma today. Well, it's not exactly a letter, but it doesn't <u>matter</u>.

M What do you mean? What did you get?

W She sent me a <u>birthday</u> <u>card</u>.

M Good for you.

W And she sent me a <u>gift</u> <u>card</u> for <u>fifty</u> <u>dollars</u>.

M Wow! Let me see it, you <u>lucky</u> <u>duck</u>. I wish I had fifty dollars. I need a new backpack.

W Well, you'll have to wait. I'm going to buy some

<u>clothes</u> for myself.

M Can I see the gift card?

W Why? It's not <u>yours</u>!

M I know. Hmm... My middle school <u>graduation</u> is <u>soon</u>. I'm sure I'll get some money then.

W I'm going to have so much fun shopping today.

M Hey, I don't want to hear that.

여 오늘 할머니한테서 편지를 받았어. 음, 정확히 편지는 아니지만 상관없어.

남 무슨 말이야? 뭘 받았는데?

여 생일카드를 보내셨어.

남 잘 됐네.

여 그리고 할머니가 내게 50달러 선물카드를 주셨어.

남 와! 어디 좀 봐. 행운아야. 나도 50달러가 있으면 좋겠다. 새 백팩이 필요한데.

여 음, 오빠 기다려야 할거야. 난 내 옷을 살거야. .

남 선물 카드 좀 보여줄래?

여 왜? 그건 오빠 것이 아니야!

남 알아. 음… 내 중학교 졸업이 곧 다가오는 걸. 나는 그때 돈을 좀 받게 될 거라고 확신해.

여 난 오늘 쇼핑하면서 즐겁게 보내야지.

남 이봐. 그런 소린 듣고 싶지 않아.

① 외로운   ② 질투나는
③ 걱정스러운   ④ 만족스러운
⑤ 유쾌한

matter 중요하다 **gift card** 선물 카드 **lucky duck** 행운아

05

[Telephone rings.]

W Hello, <u>emergency</u> services!

M We need an <u>ambulance</u> quick!

W What's the <u>exact</u> <u>address</u>?

M 45 Barton Street.

W What's the telephone number you're calling from?

M 02-9823–5698.

W What's the problem? Tell me exactly <u>what</u> <u>happened</u>.

M A man was drinking <u>a</u> <u>cup</u> <u>of</u> <u>tea</u> in an armchair and he suddenly <u>collapsed</u>.

W How old is he?

M He looks like he is in his <u>fifties</u>.

W Is he <u>conscious</u>?

M No.

W Is he <u>breathing</u>?

M Yes.

W I am sending the <u>paramedics</u> to help you now, <u>stay on the line</u> and I'll tell you <u>exactly</u> <u>what</u> <u>to</u> <u>do</u> <u>next</u>.

....

[전화벨이 울린다.]

여 여보세요, 구급차 비상서비스입니다.

남 구급차가 급히 필요합니다.

여 정확한 주소가 어떻게 되나요?

남 Barton가 45 번지입니다.

여 지금 전화하고 계신 전화번호는 무엇인가요?

남 02-9823 - 5698 입니다.

여 무엇이 문제입니까? 무슨 일이 일어났는지 정확하게 말씀해주세요.

남 한 남자가 흔들의자에서 차 한 잔을 마시고 있다가 갑자기 쓰러졌습니다.

여 그는 몇 살인가요?

남 그는 50대로 보입니다.

여 의식이 있나요?

남 아니요.

여 숨을 쉬고 있나요?

남 네.

여 저는 지금 당신을 도와 줄 긴급 의료진을 보내고 있습니다. 전화 끊지 마세요. 당신이 다음에 정확히 무엇을 해야 하는지 말씀 드리겠습니다.

••
emergency 비상사태 **collapse** 무너지다. 쓰러지다 **conscious** 의식이 있는, 깨어있는 **paramedics** 긴급 의료진 **stay on the line** 전화 끊지 마세요

06

W I <u>used</u> up my weekly allowance <u>in</u> <u>three</u> <u>days</u>.

M How can you <u>go</u> <u>through</u> your allowance so fast?

W I don't know. I think I didn't spend much, but all my money <u>has</u> <u>gone</u>.

M I think you'd better <u>keep</u> <u>track</u> <u>of</u> your spending. Do you know how I <u>manage</u> my weekly allowance?

W No, tell me. I'm listening.

M My allowance is <u>20</u> dollars <u>a</u> <u>week</u>. When I receive my allowance, the first thing I do is to put 5 dollars into my <u>bank</u> <u>account</u>.

W Wow! I always thought that my 20 dollars a week allowance <u>isn't</u> <u>enough</u>.

M Next thing I do is to put <u>11</u> dollars into a <u>separate</u> <u>section</u> in my wallet. That's for the <u>subway</u> tickets going to and from school for 5 days.

W Then what about <u>the</u> <u>rest</u> of your allowance?

M I can use it to do my own thing. For example, last week, I bought a <u>highlighter</u> for studying. That was 1 dollar. And I spend 2 dollars 50 cents on a movie ticket. Then, I put the <u>leftover</u> <u>money</u> in my piggy bank.

....

여 나 삼일 만에 일주일 용돈을 다 써버렸어.

남 어떻게 그렇게 빨리 용돈을 써버리니?

여 나도 모르겠어. 별로 쓰지도 않았는데, 내 돈이 모두 없어졌어.

남 내 생각에 너의 지출을 아는 것이 좋을 것 같아. 내가 어떻게 내 일주일 용돈을 관리하는지 아니?

여 아니, 말해줘. 귀 기울여 듣고 있어.

남 내 용돈은 일주일에 20달러야. 용돈을 받으면 제일 처음 하는 일이 5달러를 내 은행구좌에 저축하는 거야.

여 와! 난 항상 일주일에 20달러 용돈이 충분치 않다고 생각했는데.

남 그 다음 하는 일이 11달러를 내 지갑의 별도의 공간에 넣어두는 거야. 그건 5일간 학교를 오가는 지하철 표를 위한 거야.

여 그럼 나머지 용돈은?

남 내 마음대로 쓸 수 있지. 예를 들면, 지난주에 공부를 위해 형광펜 하나를 샀어. 그건 1달러였고, 그리고 영화표에 2달러 50센트를 썼어. 그런 다음 나머지를 내 돼지저금통에 저축했어.

••
use up 다 써버리다 **allowance** 용돈 **go through** 통과하다, 지나가다 **manage** 관리하다 **bank account** 은행 계좌 **separate section** 별도구역, 특별한 공간 **highlighter** 형광펜 **leftover** 남은 것

07

M Is this the <u>line</u> <u>to</u> <u>buy</u> <u>tickets</u>?

W No, it's <u>over</u> <u>there</u>.

M Oh, I see. Wow, it's really <u>crowded</u>. Is it always like this?

W Only during <u>rush</u> <u>hour</u>.

M <u>What</u> <u>a</u> <u>shame</u> I thought that <u>rush</u> <u>hour</u> was finished at around <u>8:30</u> in the morning. By the way, do you know <u>how</u> <u>often</u> the trains run?

W <u>Every</u> <u>five</u> <u>minutes</u>, I believe. They run <u>extra</u> <u>trains</u> during <u>the</u> <u>rush</u> <u>hour</u>.

M That's good to know. Well, I guess I'd better buy my ticket now and go down to the platform. Bye.

W Yes, take care.

남 이 줄이 표 구매를 위한 줄인가요?

여 아뇨, 그건 저쪽입니다. .

남 오, 알겠습니다. 와, 정말 붐비네요. 항상 이렇습니까?

여 혼잡 시간대에만 그래요.

남 창피하게도 저는 혼잡시간대가 오전 8시30분쯤에 끝났다고 생각했어요. 그건 그렇고, 기차가 얼마나 자주 운행되는지 아세요?

여 매 5분 마다 있는 걸로 알고 있습니다. 혼잡시간 때에는 기차를 추가로 운행해요.

남 좋은 정보네요. 이제 제 표 사서 플랫폼으로 내려가야겠어요. 안녕히 가세요.

여 네, 조심해 가세요.

●●
crowded 붐비는 **rush hour** 혼잡 시간대 **what a shame** 부끄러워라

08

M Please sit down on the chair over there and <u>stay</u> <u>still</u>. Is this for a <u>passport</u>?

W Yes. Do I have to <u>take</u> <u>off</u> the <u>earrings</u> and <u>necklace</u>?

M They are small. You don't need to. However your <u>bangs</u> are <u>covering</u> <u>your</u> <u>eyes</u>. Please put a hairpin in your hair so that your eyes are <u>visible</u>.

W Okay. What about the <u>eye</u> glasses? Are they fine, too?

M I'm afraid they aren't. Big horn-rimmed glasses are <u>banned</u>.

W The <u>policy</u> is quite <u>strict</u>. Anyway, I'm ready.

M Three! Two! One! Oh, wait! Don't show your <u>teeth</u>. Just make a <u>little</u> <u>smile</u>.

W Alright.

M That's <u>perfect</u>. Please come back <u>in</u> <u>30</u> <u>minutes</u>. I will <u>develop</u> them.

남 저 쪽에 있는 의자에 앉으시고 가만히 계세요. 여권용인가요?

여 네. 귀걸이와 목걸이를 뺄까요?

남 작은 것이네요. 안 그러셔도 됩니다. 하지만 앞머리가 눈을 덮네요. 머리에 핀을 꽂아 눈이 보이게 해주세요.

여 네. 안경은요? 괜찮나요?

남 안 될 것 같네요. 큰 뿔테 안경은 금지되어 있습니다.

여 정책이 꽤 엄격하네요. 어쨌든, 준비 되었습니다.

남 셋! 둘! 하나! 오, 잠시만요! 치아를 보이지 마세요. 그냥 살짝 미소만 지으세요.

여 알겠어요.

남 완벽해요. 30분 후에 오세요. 현상해 놓을게요.

●●
stay still 가만히 있다 **passport** 여권 **take off** 벗다, 빼다 **bangs** 앞머리 **visible** 볼 수 있는 **banned** 금지된 **policy** 정책 **strict** 엄격한 **develop** 현상하다

09

① M May I help you?

　 W I am <u>looking</u> <u>for</u> this sweater in a medium.

② M Can I <u>get</u> <u>a</u> <u>refund</u> on this sweater?

　 W Sure. Do you <u>have</u> <u>the</u> <u>receipt</u> with you?

③ M Why don't you <u>try</u> <u>it</u> <u>on</u>?

　 W Okay. Where is the <u>fitting</u> <u>room</u>?

④ M Do you have this in a medium?

　 W I'll check if we have it <u>in</u> <u>stock</u> <u>or</u> <u>not</u>.

⑤ M Where can I buy a sweater nearby here?

　 W There's one clothing shop <u>at</u> <u>the</u> <u>end</u> <u>of</u> this street.

---

① 남 무엇을 도와드릴까요?

　 여 이 스웨터 중간 사이즈를 찾고 있습니다.

② 남 이 스웨터 반품할 수 있을까요?

　 여 물론입니다. 영수증 있으세요?

③ 남 한 번 입어보시지 그러세요?

　 여 네. 탈의실이 어디 있나요?

④ 남 이거 중간 사이즈 있나요?

　 여 재고가 있는지 없는지 확인해보겠습니다.

⑤ 남 이 근처에서 스웨터를 어디에서 살 수 있습니까?

　 여 이 길 끝에 있습니다.

●●
get a refund 환불 받다 **try on** 입어보다 **fitting room** 탈의실 **in stock** 재고가 있는 **nearby** 가까이에

10

W Dokdo is in the <u>southeast</u> of the East Sea. Dokdo <u>consists</u> of 91 small <u>islets</u> including two main islets called Seodo (Western Island) and Dongdo (Eastern Island). The weather is <u>mostly</u> <u>foggy</u> and cloudy.

There are only about 45 clear days throughout the year. About 126 bird species have been found to inhabit the islets. The islets lie in rich fishing grounds which may also contain large deposits, about 600 million tons of natural gas. It has great potential to become a main source of clean energy in the future. The island chain is claimed by both South Korea and Japan. However, Dokdo is Korean territory without a shadow of a doubt.

여: 독도는 동해의 남동쪽에 있습니다. 독도는 서도(서쪽 섬)와 동도(동쪽 섬)라고 불리는 두 개의 주요 섬을 포함하여 91개의 작은 섬들로 구성되어 있습니다. 날씨는 대부분 안개와 구름이 끼어있습니다. 1년 내내 단 45일만 맑습니다. 약 126 품종의 새가 섬에 서식하고 있는 것으로 발견되었습니다. 섬들은 천연가스가 6억 톤 가량 대량으로 매장되어 있는 풍부한 어장에 자리잡고 있습니다. 그것은 미래 클린 에너지의 중요한 자원이 될 높은 가능성을 가지고 있습니다. 독도는 한국과 일본 모두 소유를 주장하고 있습니다. 하지만 독도는 추호의 의심의 여지가 없이 한국 영토입니다.

① 지리　　　　② 기후와 생태　　　③ 인구
④ 천연 자원　　⑤ 영토 분쟁

●●
southeast 남동쪽　**consist of** ~로 구성되다　**islet** 섬　**throughout the year** 1년 내내　**species** 품종　**inhabit** 서식하다　**fishing ground** 어장　**natural gas** 천연가스　**potential** 잠재력　**claim** (제 것이라고) 주장하다　**territory** 영토

11

W　Sunuk, what did you get in English conversation class?

M　I got a C. Mrs. Francisco gave me a lower grade than I expected.

W　What happened to your score? Didn't you say you made a good speech last week?

M　Yeah, I did. She even told me to take part in the speech contest in October.

W　Why did she give you a low grade then?

M　I actually went to her and asked her. She said I missed one assignment. If I submit it by tomorrow, she will change my grade.

W　Good! What is the assignment?

M　I need to interview a friend and write a report about the interview. So if you don't mind, I want you to be the interviewee.

W　No problem. Let's start now.

여　선욱아, 영어 회화수업에서 몇 점 받았어?
남　C 받았어. Francisco 선생님께서 내가 기대했던 것 보다 낮게 주셨어.
여　네 점수에 무슨 일이 일어난 거야? 너 지난 주에 말하기도 잘했다고 하지 않았어?
남　응. 맞아. 선생님께서는 내게 10월에 있을 말하기 대회에 나가라고 하시기도 했어.
여　그럼 왜 낮은 점수를 주셨을까?
남　사실 선생님을 찾아가서 여쭤봤어. 보고서를 하나 제출하지 않았다고 하시더라고. 만일 내가 내일까지 제출하면 내 성적을 수정해 주신데.
여　잘됐다! 그 숙제가 뭐야?
남　친구를 인터뷰해서 그 인터뷰에 대해 보고서를 쓰는 거야. 그래서 너만 괜찮으면 나는 네가 인터뷰 받는 사람이 되어주면 좋겠어.
여　문제 없어. 지금 시작하자.

●●
speech contest 말하기 대회　**mark** 점수　**interviewee** 인터뷰 받는 사람

12

M　Long time no see. How have you been?

W　I've been doing well. How about you?

M　My daily schedule is just repeating the same thing endlessly. I heard you went on a blind date yesterday. How was it?

W　People are talking about it already? Who told you?

M　Come on. It's not important. Tell me about it.

W　To be honest, considering his appearance, he is my ideal type. He is tall, gorgeous, and well-built.

M　Sounds like you really like him. Did he ask you out again?

W　[Sighing] No. I'm waiting for his call.

M　I hope your relationship with him develops.

남　오랜만이야. 잘 지냈어?
여　잘 지냈지. 너는?
남　내 하루 일정은 같은 일을 끝없이 반복하는 거야. 너 어제 소개팅 했다고 들었는데. 어땠어?
여　사람들이 벌써 그것에 대해 이야기하고 있어? 누가 말해줬어?
남　왜 그래. 그건 중요하지 않아. 그것에 대해 얘기해줘.

여　솔직히 말하면, 그의 외모를 보면 내 이상형이야. 키 크고, 멋있고, 몸도 좋아.

남　너 그 사람을 정말 좋아하는 것 같아. 그가 다시 만나자고 말했어?

여　(한숨 쉬며) 아니. 그 사람 전화 기다리고 있어.

남　그 사람과의 관계가 발전되길 바래.

repeat 반복하다　**blind date** 소개팅　**to be honest** 솔직히 말하자면 **appearance** 외모　**ideal type** 이상형　**gorgeous** 아주 멋진　**well-built** 체격이 좋은

13

M　Look at the horses. It is <u>strange</u> to see horses <u>in the heart</u> of downtown.

W　You're right. Why don't we <u>go for a ride</u>? We can <u>tour the city</u> riding horses on such a fine day.

M　Let's go to the <u>ticket booth</u> and check the <u>schedule</u>.

W　It takes an hour and visits several <u>tourist spots</u> around here. What time is it, now?

M　It's exactly 9:00. There's one tour in thirty minutes, but it's <u>sold out</u>.

W　What about the next one? <u>Is there room</u> for us?

M　<u>Fortunately</u>, yes. Let's go on it and <u>have lunch</u> after that.

W　Hooray! I'm so excited.

말 타기 시내투어	
광화문 출발	광화문 도착
① 오전 8:00	오전 9:00
② 오전 9:30	오전 10:30
③ 오전 11:00	오후 12:00
점심 시간	
④ 오후 2:00	오후 3:00
⑤ 오후 3:30	오후 4:30

남　말들 좀 봐. 도심 한 복판에서 말들을 보니 낯설네.

여　맞아. 우리 타볼까? 이렇게 좋은 날에 말을 타고 도시를 구경할 수 있잖아.

남　매표소에 가서 일정을 확인해보자.

여　한 시간 걸리고 이 근처의 관광명소를 몇 군데 가네. 지금 몇 시지?

남　정확히 9시야. 30분 후에 있긴 한데 매진이야.

여　다음 꺼는? 자리 있어?

남　다행스럽게도, 있어. 그거 타고 끝난 후에 점심 먹자.

여　야호! 흥분된다.

strange 낯선　**in the heart of downtown** 도심 한 복판에 **tourist spot** 관광명소　**sold out** 매진된　**room** (빈) 공간, 자리

14

W　Why do you have <u>such a long face</u>, Carter?

M　I had a <u>quarrel with</u> my girlfriend last night over the phone so I couldn't <u>sleep a wink</u>.

W　Really? Why?

M　She got mad at me because she sent me 5 <u>text messages</u>, but I didn't <u>reply to</u> any of them.

W　Why not? What were you doing?

M　I was in the <u>library</u> so my cell phone was <u>in vibration mode</u>. I didn't know about them. Then I saw the messages as I was going to bed.

W　Did you <u>explain</u> that to her?

M　Yes, but her <u>anger</u> didn't <u>go away</u>.

W　Don't worry. She just needs some time. If you are so <u>worried</u>, go to her and say sorry. <u>Face to face</u> is the best way.

M　Okay, I will. Thanks for the <u>advice</u>.

여　Carter, 왜 그렇게 시무룩해 보이는 거야?

남　나 어젯밤에 전화로 여자친구랑 싸워서 한 숨도 못 잤어.

여　정말? 왜?

남　여자친구가 화가 났어. 그녀가 문자를 5개나 보냈는데 내가 답장을 안 했거든.

여　왜 안 했어? 뭐하고 있었는데?

남　도서관에 있어서 내 핸드폰이 진동으로 되어 있었거든. 문자가 왔는지 몰랐어. 그런 다음 잠자리에 들려고 할 때 그 메시지를 봤어.

여　여자친구에게 설명했어?

남　응. 그런데 화가 안 풀리네.

여　걱정 마. 그녀는 시간이 좀 필요할 거야. 만일 너무 걱정되면, 그녀에게 가서 미안하다고 이야기해. 직접 보고 이야기하는 것이 가장 좋은 방법이야.

남　알았어. 그렇게. 충고 고마워.

have a long face 시무룩해 보이다　**have a quarrel with** ~와 말다툼을 하다　**sleep a wink** 한숨 자다　**in vibration mode** 진동 모드 **face to face** 직접

15

W The polar bear is one of the most unique animals in the world. It has a beautiful white coat of fur which is partly for protection but also it allows it to sneak up on its prey. Their typical prey are seals. The polar bear's coat also has special hairs that are water repellent and a dense underfur for warmth. But under their fur, polar bears have black skin to soak up the warming rays of the sun. A full grown adult male polar bear will weigh approximately 650kg while a female will weigh about half as much. The polar bear can only be found in the Northern Hemisphere.

여 북극곰은 세상에서 가장 독특한 동물들 중 하나이다. 그것은 아름다운 하얀색 털을 가지고 있는데, 때로는 보호용이지만 그것은 또한 먹이에 몰래 다가갈 수 있게 해준다. 북극곰의 전형적인 먹이는 물개이다. 북극곰의 털은 또한 방수가 되는 특수한 털과 보온을 위한 고밀도의 잔털로 이루어져있다. 그러나 그들의 털 밑에는 태양의 따뜻한 광선을 흡수하는 검은색 피부가 있다. 다 자란 수컷 북극곰은 약 650킬로그램 정도 무게가 나가는 반면 암컷은 그 절반 정도 무게가 나간다. 북극곰은 오직 북반구에서만 발견된다.

unique 독특한, 유일한 **sneak up** ~에게 몰래 다가가다 **prey** 먹이 **seal** 물개 **water repellent** 방수의 **soak up** 흡수하다 **full grown** 다 자란 **hemisphere** 반구

16

W Were you excited today? It was your first day of work.

M Yes. I was. Last night I was really looking forward to going to work for the first time.

W What was more exciting, starting university or starting work?

M It's difficult to choose one over the other. How about you?

W For me, I think starting school was more exciting.

M Does that mean work isn't that great now?

W It's different for everyone, but because I knew school was going to be so much fun, I really got excited about it.

M But work is a huge portion of our lives. I'm looking forward to making sure I have fun at my job.

W That's a great attitude to have. I think you won't have any problems at your work.

M I hope you're right.

여 오늘 재밌었어? 너의 첫 출근날이었잖아.
남 응. 어제 밤엔 난생 처음 출근하는 것이 몹시 기대되었어.
여 대학교 시작하는 것과 근무를 시작하는 것 중 어떤 것이 더 신났어?
남 하나를 선택하기가 어려워. 너는 어때?
여 내 경우에는 학교를 다니기 시작한 게 더 신났었어.
남 그 말은 근무는 그렇게 좋지는 않다는 의미니?
여 사람마다 다르겠지만 난 학교가 정말 재미있을 거라는 걸 알았기 때문에 학교에 다닌다는 것에 신이 났어.
남 하지만 직장은 우리 삶의 큰 일 부분이야. 나는 직장에서 꼭 즐겁게 지내게 되길 고대하고 있어.
여 좋은 자세네. 나는 네가 직장에서 아무런 문제가 없을 거라고 생각해.
남 네 말이 옳으면 좋겠어.

① 괜찮아.
② 나는 네 말에 동의해.
③ 좋은 생각이야.
⑤ 너는 그렇게 생각하지 않니?

look forward to ~을 기대하다 **huge** 거대한, 큰 **portion** 부분 **attitude** 태도

17

W Your passports, please. What is your final destination?

M We're going to Los Angeles.

W How long is your stay?

M We'll be there for a week.

W What is the purpose of your trip?

M I'm going there on business and my family is accompanying me on vacation.

W Whom are you traveling with?

M I'm with my wife and children.

W Are you bringing in any restricted items? Any plants, fruits and vegetables, meats, or animals?

M No. I am not bringing anything illegal.

W Do you have anything to declare?

M Here's the receipt for some duty-free items we

<u>bought.</u>

··

여 여권주세요. 최종 목적지가 어디인가요?

남 로스엔젤레스로 갑니다.

여 체류기간은 얼마입니까?

남 거기에서 일주일 동안 있을 겁니다.

여 여행의 목적이 무엇입니까?

남 저는 사업차 왔고 제 가족은 휴가차 저와 함께 왔습니다.

여 누구와 함께 여행 중이세요?

남 제 아내와 아이들과 함께입니다.

여 제한된 물품을 가지고 계십니까? 식물, 과일과 채소, 고기 또는 동물 있으세요?

남 아니요. 저는 불법적인 건 하나도 가져오지 않았습니다.

여 신고하실 물품이 있으신가요?

남 <u>여기 우리가 구입한 면세품의 영수증이 있습니다.</u>

① 사실 저는 부자가 아닙니다.

② 저는 잘못한 것이 없다고 공언합니다.

③ 아뇨, 당신에게 어떤 것도 말하기 싫습니다.

④ 우리는 모두 이 여행에 유효한 여권을 갖고 있습니다.

•• **accompany** ~와 동행하다 **restricted** 제한된 **illegal** 불법의 **declare** 신고하다

18

M This is the <u>second</u> <u>time</u> I've been <u>turned</u> <u>down</u> for a credit card in a month. I don't know what I'm doing wrong.

W Have you checked your <u>credit</u> <u>report</u> recently? Maybe your credit is bad.

M I have a <u>full-time</u> job with a <u>good</u> <u>salary</u>, which they can easily check, and I don't have any <u>debt</u>, so what could be the problem?

W Have you had a credit card <u>before</u>?

M Yes.

W Did you always make your payments on time?

M Well, no. I <u>easily</u> <u>forget</u> to pay the <u>bills</u>.

W Then that may be <u>your</u> <u>answer</u>.

M What do you mean by that?

W <u>Not paying bills on time can make your credit bad.</u>

··

남 한 달 동안 두 번이나 신용카드 만드는 데 거절 당했어. 내가 뭘 잘못했는지 모르겠어.

여 최근에 신용 평가 보고서 확인해봤니? 아마도 너의 신용은 나쁠 거야.

남 나는 좋은 월급에 정규직인데다 그것은 쉽게 확인 가능해. 나는 빚도 없는데 뭐가 문제 일까?

여 전에 신용카드를 가진 적 있니?

남 응.

여 돈은 항상 제때에 지불했니?

남 글쎄, 아니. 나는 청구서 내는 것을 잘 잊어버려.

여 그럼 그게 이유일거야.

남 무슨 말이야?

여 <u>돈을 제때에 지불하지 않는 것은 너의 신용을 나쁘게 만들 수 있어.</u>

① 너는 더 높은 월급의 더 좋은 직장이 필요해.

② 우리는 청구서를 지불할 충분한 돈이 없어.

③ 돈을 빌리기 위해선 좋은 신용등급이 있어야 한다.

④ 난 평생 기한을 넘겨 돈을 낸 적이 없다.

•• **be turned down** 거절당하다 **credit** 신용 **debt** 빚 **pay the bills** 청구서를 지불하다

19

M I'm surprised at the <u>variety</u> of <u>people</u> on this tour.

W Oh, really? I hadn't noticed.

M Well, we'll be spending the next <u>two</u> <u>weeks</u> with these people so I think I should <u>get</u> <u>to</u> <u>know</u> some of them.

W That's nice.

M Did you see that thirty-something couple with <u>two</u> <u>toddlers</u>? I'm really <u>surprised</u> they're on this tour.

W <u>So</u> <u>am</u> I. They will spend all their time taking care of their kids.

M And how about that group of <u>seniors</u>? Some of them look like they're in their <u>late</u> <u>seventies</u>.

W Yes, I see them. They may be old, but they seem <u>pretty</u> <u>healthy</u>.

M But what really <u>surprises</u> <u>me</u> is those middle-aged couples travelling with their <u>teenage</u> children. They are at an age when they can act out and <u>rebel</u>.

W <u>They seemed pretty well-behaved to me.</u>

··

남 나는 다양한 사람들이 이 여행에 참가해서 놀랐어.

여 오, 정말? 나는 알아채지 못했었는데.

남 음, 앞으로 2주를 이 사람들과 함께 보낼 예정이라서 몇몇 사람들은 알고 지내야 한다고 생각해.

여 좋아.

남 걸음마를 배우는 두 아이를 데리고 온 30대 부부 봤어? 나는 그들이 이 여행에 참가해서 정말 놀랐어.

여 나도 그래. 그들은 아이들을 돌보는 데 시간을 다 보낼 거야.

남 그리고 노인 분들은 어때? 몇몇 분들은 70대 후반으로 보이시더라.

여 응. 보여. 연세가 드셨지만 건강해 보이셔.

남 하지만 나를 정말 놀라게 만든 건 10대 자녀들과 함께 여행하는 저 중년 부부들이야. 그들은 돌출 행동을 하고 반항할 수 있는 나이잖아.

여 내가 보기엔 그들은 매우 예의 바른 것 같았어.

① 걱정하지마 그리고 괜찮아질 거야.
③ 너와 즐거운 시간을 보내게 되어서 행복해.
④ 응, 네가 예의 바른 청소년이 아니었다는 것을 알아.
⑤ 맞아. 그들은 이제 걷는 것을 배우고 있는 중이야.

••
variety 각양각색, 다양성　**get to know** 알게 되다　**toddler** 걸음마를 배우는 아기　**rebel** 반항하다　**well-behaved** 예의 바른

20

M Jack is a single man living alone. Every morning on his way to work, he drops by a donut shop and purchases a chocolate donut and a cup of coffee. He likes this morning routine because it is quick and easy. He doesn't have to cook breakfast or wash the dishes. Today Jack goes to the doctor for a regular check-up. His doctor tells him that his cholesterol level is so high that he has to take medicine. He is also told that he has to stop eating foods that are high in fat. So he asks his doctor what kind of food he should eat. In this situation, what would his doctor probably say to him?

· ·

남 Jack은 혼자 사는 독신남이다. 매일 아침 직장에 가는 길에 그는 도넛 가게에 들러서 초콜릿도넛과 커피 한잔을 산다. 그는 빠르고 쉬워서 이런 아침 일과를 좋아한다. 그는 아침식사를 요리하거나 설거지를 할 필요가 없다. 오늘 Jack은 정기검진을 받기 위해서 병원에 간다. 그의 의사는 그의 콜레스테롤 수치가 너무 높아서 약을 복용해야 한다고 말한다. 그는 또한 지방이 많은 음식은 그만 먹어야 한다는 이야기를 듣는다. 그래서 그는 의사에게 어떤 종류의 음식을 먹어야 하는지 묻는다. 이런 상황에서, 그의 의사는 그에게 뭐라고 말할 것 같은가?

① 당신은 과일과 야채를 더 많이 먹어야만 합니다.
② 식사를 거르지 마세요. 하루에 세 번 드세요.
③ 당신은 바쁘니까 패스트푸드를 많이 먹어야만 합니다.
④ 프라이드 치킨은 배고플 때 정말 맛있어요.
⑤ 규칙적인 운동을 하는 것은 당신이 해야 할 유일한 거예요.

••
regular 정기적인, 규칙적인　**level** 수치　**fat** 지방　**be told** 듣다

Further Study 정답 p. 114

1 In order to keep my balance, I have to extend my arms.

2 She has ordered a replacement from an Internet bookstore.

3 He spends $11 on subway tickets for five days.

4 It is mostly foggy and cloudy. There are only about 45 clear days throughout the year.

5 She says that he is tall, gorgeous, and well-built.

6 The reason was that he had a quarrel with his girlfriend over the phone.

7 The role of it is to soak up the warming rays of the sun.

8 She thinks the reason is that his credit is bad because he didn't pay his bills on time.

On Your Own 모범답안 p. 115

A

Using Credit Cards	
(1) The advantage(s)	Credit cards reduce our need to carry cash so we don't need to go to a bank or an ATM to get money.
(2) The disadvantage(s)	They can make cardholders spend more money that they don't really have. When we borrow money with a credit card, we pay a lot of interest.
(3) Your suggestion	Think carefully before applying for a credit card and use it wisely.

Credit cards (1)reduce our need to carry cash so we don't need to go to a bank or an ATM to get money. On the other hand, they (2)can make cardholders spend more money that they don't really have. And (2) when we borrow money with a credit card, we pay a lot of interest. Therefore, it is strongly recommended that (3)we should think carefully before applying for a credit card and use it wisely.

신용카드 사용하기	
(1) 장점	신용카드는 현금을 가지고 다닐 필요를 줄여주어서 돈을 찾으러 은행이나 현금입출금기에 갈 필요가 없다.
(2) 단점	신용카드는 카드 소지자가 자신들이 실제 가지고 있지도 않은 더 많은 돈을 사용할 수 있게 한다. 신용카드로 돈을 빌릴 때 우리는 많은 이자를 지불한다.
(3) 당신의 제안	카드를 만들기 전에 신중히 생각해보고, 그것을 현명하게 이용한다.

신용카드는 현금을 가지고 다닐 필요를 줄여주어서 우리가 돈을 찾으러 은행이나 현금입출금기에 갈 필요가 없어진다. 반면에 그것은 카드 소지자가 자신들이 실제 가지고 있지도 않은 더 많은 돈을 사용할 수 있게 한다. 그리고 신용카드로 돈을 빌릴 때 우리는 많은 이자를 지불한다. 그러므로 카드를 만들기 전에 신중히 생각해보고 그것을 현명하게 사용해야 한다.

B

My Ideal Man / Woman	
(1) Name and job	Jason Hopkins / my English teacher
(2) Appearance	tall, well-built, good-looking, wears eye glasses
(3) Personality	very generous, understanding, humorous
(4) Ability	playing soccer and speaking foreign languages like Korean and Japanese
(5) Why the person is your ideal type	a perfect man who has everything / an admirable man / passion and patience

I am going to talk about my ideal man. His name is (1) Jason Hopkins. He is (1)my English teacher. He (2)is tall, well-built, good-looking, and wears eye glasses. People say that he (3)is very generous, understanding, and humorous. He is good at (4)playing soccer and speaking foreign languages like Korean and Japanese. He is my ideal man because (5)he is such a perfect man who has everything. In addition, (5)he is an admirable man who has a lot of passion and patience.

내 이상형의 남자 / 여자	
(1) 이름과 직업	Jason Hopkins, 나의 영어 선생님
(2) 외모	키가 크고 건장하며 잘생겼음. 안경을 씀
(3) 성격	매우 관대하고 이해심이 많고 유머러스함
(4) 능력	축구를 하며 한국어와 일본어 같은 외국어를 함
(5) 그 사람이 당신의 이상형인 이유	모든 것을 가진 완벽한 사람/ 놀라운 사람/ 열정과 인내

저는 저의 이상형의 남자에 대해 이야기 할 것입니다. 그의 이름은 Jason Hopkins 입니다. 그는 나의 영어 선생님입니다. 그는 키가 크고, 몸이 좋고, 잘생기고 안경을 썼습니다. 사람들은 그가 매우 관대하고, 이해심 많고 유머러스 하다고 말합니다. 그는 축구를 잘하고 한국어와 일본어 같은 외국어에 능숙합니다. 그는 모든 것을 가진 완벽한 사람이기 때문에 저의 이상형입니다. 게다가 그는 강한 열정과 인내를 가진 훌륭한 사람입니다.

12 Listening Test 정답   p. 120

01 ⑤	02 ①	03 ②	04 ①	05 ⑤
06 ②	07 ⑤	08 ①	09 ③	10 ③
11 ①	12 ⑤	13 ④	14 ③	15 ④
16 ⑤	17 ③	18 ②	19 ②	20 ⑤

01

M Have you been to the Four Seasons Restaurant before?

W Yes, I went there with my sister about a month ago.

M What did you have?

W I was going to have a steak, but my sister is a vegetarian and she wouldn't let me have a steak. I had a strawberry pancake and my sister had tomato spaghetti. They were both really delicious.

M What is the specialty of the restaurant? Is it pizza?

W No, it's marinated barbequed pork ribs with grilled

potatoes.

M Sound delicious. Do they grill the ribs <u>over</u> <u>charcoal</u> to get a real barbequed <u>flavor</u>?

W Yes, they do. I saw them doing that <u>behind</u> the restaurant in a huge barbeque pit. The next time I go, I will try it.

M How about trying it today for lunch? It's <u>my</u> <u>treat</u>.

W Great. I'd love to go there for lunch.

....

남 너 Four Seasons 레스토랑에 가본적 있니?

여 응, 한 달쯤 전에 우리 언니랑 가봤어.

남 뭘 먹었니?

여 스테이크를 먹으려고 했지만 언니가 채식주의자여서 내가 스테이크 먹는 걸 허락하지 않았어. 난 딸기 팬케익을 먹었고 언니는 토마토 스파게티를 먹었어. 둘다 아주 맛있었어.

남 그 식당 특별 음식이 뭐야? 피자야?

여 아니, 구운 감자를 곁들인 양념 바비큐 돼지 갈비야.

남 맛있을 것 같다. 진정한 바베큐 맛을 내기 위해 숯불 위에서 갈비를 굽니?

여 맞아. 식당 뒤 큰 바비큐장에서 그렇게 하는 것을 봤어. 다음 번에 거기 가면 그걸 먹어볼 거야.

남 오늘 점심으로 그거 먹어보는 거 어때? 내가 낼게.

여 좋아. 점심 먹으러 거기 가고 싶어.

vegetarian 채식주의자　**marinated** 양념에 재운　**barbequed** 바베큐한　**ribs** 갈비　**grill** (석쇠에) 굽다　**charcoal** 숯　**flavor** 맛, 풍미　**treat** 대접, 한턱

02

M Hi. Are you ready to <u>check</u> <u>out</u>?

W Yes, please. Here's my <u>library</u> <u>card</u> and the books and DVDs I want to <u>check</u> <u>out</u>.

M Ok. You can return these books in <u>two</u> <u>weeks</u>, but you have to return these DVDs in <u>a</u> <u>week</u>. And you are only allowed to borrow two DVDs at a time. So which two DVDs do you want?

W Why can't I borrow all of them?

M There's <u>too</u> <u>big</u> a <u>demand</u> for our DVDs. So we <u>limit</u> the number of <u>loans</u> to two and we don't allow DVD loans to be <u>renewed</u>.

W Then it means <u>whether</u> I have watched them <u>or</u> <u>not</u>, I have to return them <u>after</u> <u>7</u> <u>days</u>, right?

M <u>I'm</u> <u>afraid</u> <u>so</u>.

W I see. I'll take these two.

....

남 안녕하세요. 대출하실 준비가 되셨나요?

여 네. 도서관 카드와 대출하고 싶은 책과 DVD 여기 있습니다.

남 네. 이 책들은 2주 내에 반납하시면 됩니다만 DVD들은 일주일 내에 반납하셔야 합니다. 그리고 DVD는 한번에 두 개까지만 대출이 허용됩니다. 그러니 어떤 DVD 두 개를 원하시나요?

여 왜 그걸 다 빌릴 수 없나요?

남 DVD 수요가 많기 때문입니다. 그래서 2개로 대여 숫자를 제한하고 있고 또한 대출 갱신도 허가하지 않고 있습니다.

여 그럼 그건 제가 그걸 보든 안보든 7일후엔 반드시 반납해야 한다는 거죠, 그렇죠?

남 유감이지만 그렇습니다.

여 알겠습니다. 이 두 개로 할게요.

check out 대출하다　**demand** 요구, 수요　**loan** 대여　**renew** 갱신하다　**whether ~ or not** ~이든 아니든

03

M <u>Have</u> <u>you</u> <u>ever</u> <u>heard</u> of TV Parental Guidelines? TV programs fall into one of <u>six</u> <u>ratings</u> <u>categories</u>: TV-Y, TV-Y7, TV-G, TV-PG, TV-14 or TV-MA. Then, content descriptors of D, L, S, V, and FV are added to the ratings. Each alphabetic letter <u>lets</u> <u>parents</u> <u>know</u> if a show contains suggestive dialogue, coarse language, sexual content, violence, or fantasy violence. For example, a program rated TV-Y7-FV is designed to be <u>appropriate</u> <u>for</u> children of all ages. The program is <u>not</u> <u>expected</u> <u>to</u> frighten younger children, but is generally more <u>intense</u> as it has some fantasy violence.

....

남 TV 보호자 지침에 대해 들어보셨나요? TV 프로그램은 TV-Y, TV-Y7, TV-G, TV-PG, TV-14 혹은 TV-MA의 여섯 등급 중의 하나로 나뉩니다. 그런 다음 D, L, S, V와 FV의 내용설명어가 등급에 덧붙여집니다. 각각의 알파벳 글자들은 부모님께 상영물이 외설적인 대화, 거친 말투, 선정적 내용, 폭력, 공상 폭력을 포함하는지를 알려드립니다. 예를 들면, TV-Y7-FV로 등급이 매겨진 프로그램은 모든 연령층의 어린이들에게 적절하도록 설계되었습니다. 그 프로그램은 어린아이들을 놀라게 하지는 않을 것으로 예상되지만 약간의 공상 폭력을 포함하고 있어서 일반적으로 좀더 강렬합니다.

Parental Guidelines 보호자 지침서　**rating** 순위, 등급　**fall into** ~으로 나뉘다　**content descriptor** 내용설명어　**suggestive**

dialogue 외설적인 대화 **coarse language** 거친 말투 **sexual content** 선정적 내용 **violence** 폭력 **intense** 극심한, 강렬한

04

M Did you watch Yuna Kim's retirement performance on TV last night? It was so wonderful.

W Oh, I went to the ice rink to see it in person with my family.

M I feel terrible about missing the last chance to see her perform live. Last week when I tried to buy tickets online, they were sold out.

W I was just lucky. My mom and dad are huge fans of hers, so they booked tickets quickly after they went on sale a month ago.

M I should have done that. I always leave things until the last minute.

W I think she proved her real worth as the queen of figure skating with last night's performance. My whole family cried when she gave her final remarks saying that she was happy but also sad to leave the sport.

M Maybe we will never see perfect jumps like the ones we saw last night again.

남 어젯밤에 TV에서 김연아의 은퇴공연 봤니? 너무 멋졌어.

여 오, 난 우리 가족과 함께 그거 보러 직접 아이스 링크에 갔었어.

남 그녀의 공연을 실제로 볼 마지막 기회를 놓쳐서 아쉬워. 지난 주 온라인으로 표를 사려고 했을 땐, 매진이었어.

여 난 운이 좋았어. 엄마와 아빠가 그녀의 열렬한 팬이어서 한달 전에 표가 판매된 후 재빨리 예약을 해놓으셨어.

남 나도 그랬어야 했는데. 난 항상 마지막까지 일을 남겨두거든.

여 어젯밤의 공연에서 그녀는 피겨의 여왕으로서의 그녀의 진가를 보여줬다고 생각해. 그녀가 행복하지만 운동을 그만두게 되어 슬프기도 하다는 마지막 말을 했을 때 우리 가족 전부 울었어.

남 우리가 어젯밤 보았던 것과 같은 완벽한 점프는 아마 다시는 볼 수 없을 거야.

① 감동한   ② 걱정하는
③ 실망한   ④ 무서운
⑤ 신난

retirement performance 은퇴 공연 **in person** 직접, 몸소 **sold out** 매진인 **remark** 말

05

W Hey, Tom. What are you making?

M I'm making leaflets to advertise my new small business. I will take care of people's dogs when they go on holidays.

W I guess that is your part-time job during this vacation.

M Yes. It's a perfect idea, isn't it? I know about dogs better than anyone and I love dogs.

W I can't agree with you more. Oh, I heard that my aunt has to go on a business trip next week. I'll call and ask her about using your service. [Pause]

M What did she say?

W She said she would like to use your service.

M Thanks a lot. As she is my first customer, I'll take care of her dog one day free of charge.

W Great. She will be happy about that.

여 이봐, Tom. 너 뭘 만들고 있니?

남 나의 작은 새 사업을 홍보할 전단지를 만들고 있어. 사람들이 휴가 가 있는 동안 그들의 애완견을 돌볼거야.

여 그게 이번 방학 동안 아르바이트로 할 일이구나.

남 응. 훌륭한 생각이지, 그렇지 않니? 난 누구보다도 개에 대해서 잘 알고 개를 사랑하잖아.

여 네 말에 전적으로 동의해. 오, 우리 이모가 다음 주에 출장가야 한다고 들었는데. 이모한테 전화해서 네 서비스를 이용할지 물어볼게.

남 이모가 뭐라고 하셔?

여 네 서비스를 받고 싶다고 하셨어.

남 정말 고마워. 그녀가 내 첫 고객이니까, 그녀의 개를 하루 무료로 돌봐줄게.

여 좋아. 이모가 좋아하실 거야.

leaflet 전단지, 광고지, 안내지 **better than anyone** 누구보다도 더 나은 **go on a business trip** 출장 가다 **customer** 고객 **free of charge** 무료로

06

W I can't wait! Gold Coast Water Park will be open tomorrow! And we're both going. I guess another hot summer is just around the corner.

M When it's hot, nothing can beat a water park.

W I was lucky to only spend $50 on two tickets

because of their special deal for early birds. You know I got more than 50% off.

M You did a good job! I can't wait to enjoy all the water activities there.

W What time shall we meet tomorrow?

M Did you look up the opening times on the website?

W Yes. Operating hours are from 9:30 a.m. to 9:30 p.m. on weekdays and from 9 a.m. to 11 p.m. on weekends and holidays. It will take about an hour to get there by car. Let's meet at 8:00 am.

M 8:00? I think it'll take longer to drive there than an hour. Why don't we meet thirty minutes earlier because we have to factor in the traffic?

W Oh, I didn't think of it. I'll see you then.

· ·

여 기다리지 못하겠어. Gold Coast Water Park가 내일 개장한대! 그래서 우리 둘이 갈거야. 무더운 여름이 정말 코 앞이잖아.

남 더울 땐, 워터파크 만한 게 없지.

여 조기예약자를 위한 특가로 표 2장에 50달러 밖에 쓰지 않았으니 난 참 운이 좋았어. 있잖아 50% 이상 할인을 받았어.

남 잘했어! 빨리 거기서 모든 수상활동을 즐기고 싶어.

여 내일 몇 시에 만날까?

남 웹사이트에서 개장시간을 살펴봤니?

여 응. 개장시간은 평일은 오전 9시 30분에서 밤 9시 30분이고 주말과 휴일은 오전 9시에서 밤 11시까지야. 차로 거기 도착하는 데 한 시간 정도 걸릴 거야. 오전 8시에 만나자.

남 8시? 운전해서 가려면 한 시간 이상 걸릴거야. 교통체증까지 고려해야 하니까 그보다 30분 전에 만나는 게 어때?

여 오, 그건 생각지 못했어. 그때 보자.

· ·

around the corner 아주 가까운 **operating hours** 개장시간 **factor in** 고려하다

07

M Oh, you're traveling with an infant today.

W Yes, my daughter Mia. She's 14 months.

M Okay. I'll need to see your daughter's birth certificate to prove that she is under two years of age.

W Here you are. Say, would we be able to get an aisle seat? I may have to walk around with her if she gets fussy.

M Sure. I'll put you near the lavatory too.

W Thanks. Can I take my stroller to the gate?

M Yes, we'll check it in as over-sized luggage after you board. Are you just checking these two bags today?

W Yes, I'll take my knapsack as my carry-on.

M Okay. Here is your boarding pass. Be at the gate one hour prior to the boarding time. You will be able to preboard because you are traveling with an infant.

· ·

남 오, 오늘 유아와 함께 여행하시는군요.

여 네, 제 딸 Mia입니다. 14개월이에요.

남 네. 연령이 2세 미만인지 확인을 위해 따님의 출생확인서를 봐야 합니다.

여 여기 있습니다. 저기요, 통로 석에 앉을 수 있을까요? 얘가 투정을 부리면 함께 걸어다녀야 할 것 같아서요.

남 물론이죠. 화장실도 가까이 있는 곳으로 드리겠습니다.

여 감사합니다. 게이트까지 유모차를 가져갈 수 있나요?

남 네. 탑승 후 부피가 큰 짐으로 부쳐드리겠습니다 오늘 이 가방 두 개를 부치시겠습니까?

여 네, 배낭은 제가 가지고 탈게요.

남 네. 여기 탑승권 있습니다. 탑승시간 1시간 전에 게이트에 계세요. 영아와 함께 여행하시기 때문에 우선탑승이 가능하십니다.

① 안전요원 – 여행 가이드
② 이민국 직원 – 경찰
③ 조종사 – 승무원
④ 여행사 직원 – 여행객
⑤ 항공사 직원 – 승객

· ·

infant 유아 **birth certificate** 출생증명서 **aisle seat** 통로석 **fussy** 까다로운, 야단스런 **lavatory** 화장실 **stroller** 유모차 **over-sized luggage** 부피가 큰 짐 **knapsack** (작은) 배낭 **carry-on** 가지고 타는 짐 **boarding pass** 탑승권

08

W Can I help you?

M I would like to exchange Korean won into Japanese yen. What's the exchange rate for today?

W It is 10.50 won per 1 yen. How much would you like to exchange?

M I'd like to exchange 300,000 won. Here are the bills.

W Do you <u>have an account</u> with us?

M Why? Is there a <u>benefit</u>?

W Yes. I can give you a slightly better exchange rate <u>than</u> the <u>going rate</u>.

M Really? How nice. I do have an account here. Do you need the number?

W Yes, and please show me either your <u>identification</u> card or driver's <u>license</u>.

- -

여 무엇을 도와드릴까요?

남 한국 원을 일본 엔으로 바꾸고 싶은데요. 오늘의 환율이 어떻게 되나요?

여 1엔에 10.50원입니다. 얼마나 바꿔드릴까요?

남 30만원 바꿔주세요. 여기 지폐가 있습니다.

여 저희 은행 계좌가 있으신가요?

남 왜요? 혜택이 있나요?

여 네, 현행 환율보다 약간 더 좋은 환율로 해드릴 수 있습니다.

남 정말요? 잘됐네요. 여기 계좌를 갖고 있어요. 번호가 필요한가요?

여 네, 그리고 주민등록증이나 운전 면허증 보여 주세요.

① 은행 　　　② 관리사무소 　　　③ 백화점
④ 운전 학원 　　　⑤ 출입국 사무소

●●
exchange A into B A를 B로 바꾸다　**have an account** 계좌가 있다
benefit 혜택　**going rate** 현행 율　**identification card** 주민등록증
driver's license 운전면허증

09

① M I like your <u>laptop</u> computer. How much is it?
　W It is $<u>150</u>.

② M I'm so sorry. My hand just <u>slipped</u>.
　W Oh, no! I <u>might have lost</u> the file that I was working on.

③ M Would you like to drink <u>a cup of coffee</u>?
　W I'd love to. Thank you.

④ M Do you know how to <u>back up</u> all your files?
　W I don't know how. Can you teach me?

⑤ M What's up? You <u>look upset</u>.
　W My computer <u>just crashed</u>. What should I do?

- -

① 남 나는 네 노트북 컴퓨터가 마음에 들어. 얼마야?
　여 150달러야.
② 남 정말 미안해. 손이 미끄러졌어.

여 오, 이런! 일하고 있었던 데이터를 다 잃어버렸을지 몰라.

③ 남 커피 한 잔 마실래?
　여 좋아. 고마워.
④ 남 네 파일을 전부 백업하는 법 아니?
　여 어떻게 하는지 몰라. 나에게 가르쳐 줄래?
⑤ 남 무슨 일이야? 화나 보여.
　여 컴퓨터가 망가졌어. 어떻게 해야 하지?

●●
laptop computer 노트북 컴퓨터　**slip** 미끄러지다　**lose a file** 화일을 잃다　**crash** (컴퓨터가) 기능을 멈추다

10

M Honey. It is very <u>shocking to review</u> Jenny's report card.

W Why? Are there any serious problems?

M Look at this <u>evaluation</u> that shows her <u>scores</u> from the beginning of the year. They have been decreasing <u>since last semester</u>.

W Really? What do you think is the <u>main reason</u>? She always studies in her room, doesn't she?

M In my <u>opinion</u>, she doesn't focus on her studies. We never <u>checked</u> up on her. We don't know whether she is really studying or not.

W Do you mean she is telling us a <u>lie</u> and doing <u>something else</u>?

M I'm not sure, but there is a <u>possibility</u>.

W Why don't we just call Jenny and ask her <u>directly</u>? I don't want to <u>doubt</u> our <u>lovely</u> daughter.

M That's good. Let's ask her if anything is <u>wrong</u>. She might have a problem that we don't know about.

- -

남 여보. Jenny의 성적표를 검토하니 충격적이군요.

여 왜요? 심각한 문제라도 있나요?

남 올초부터 그애의 점수를 보여주는 이 평가표를 봐요. 지난 학기 이후로 계속 떨어지고 있어요.

여 정말요? 주된 이유가 무엇이라고 생각하세요? 그앤 항상 방에서 공부를 하잖아요, 안 그래요?

남 내 생각에는 공부에 집중을 하지 않는 것 같아요. 우리는 그 애를 확인하지 않았잖아요. 우리는 그 애가 실제 공부를 하는지 몰라요.

여 당신 말은 우리에게 거짓말을 하고 다른 것을 한다는 이야기예요?

남 확실하지는 않지만 가능성은 있다는 거죠.

여 Jenny를 불러서 직접 물어보는 것은 어때요? 저는 우리의 사랑스런 딸을 의심하고 싶지 않아요.

남 좋아요. 그녀에게 어떤 문제가 있는지 물어봐요. 우리가 모르는 문제를 가지고 있을 수도 있으니까요.

●●
report card 성적표 **evaluation** 평가 **semester** 학기 **possibility** 가능성 **directly** 직접적으로 **doubt** 의심하다

11

M Have you decided what you're going to buy Rose for Children's Day?

W No. Have you?

M I have already bought her a Barbie doll.

W Wow! She will love it. Can you recommend a good present for me to get her?

M Well. How about buying some clothes or a house for the doll I bought?

W That sounds great. Thanks for the information.

M One more thing, the Tim's Toy Store on Guil Street is having a sale. You can get either of those at the cheapest possible price there.

W Sounds wonderful. I will go there right away.

남 당신 어린이 날에 Rose에게 무엇을 사줄 지 결정했어?

여 아뇨. 당신은요?

남 난 이미 Barbie인형을 샀어.

여 우왜! 정말 좋아하겠네요. 나에게도 무슨 선물을 사줄 지 추천해 줄래요?

남 음. 옷이나 내가 산 인형의 집은 어때?

여 좋네요. 정보 고마워요.

남 한가지 더, Guil로에 있는 Tim's 장난감 가게가 세일 중이야. 거기서 그것 둘다 가장 저렴한 가격에 구입 할 수 있어.

여 멋진데. 지금 당장 가야겠어요.

●●
information 정보 **cheap** 저렴한

12

M Rebecca, what are you doing?

W I'm inserting these invitation cards into envelopes.

M Will you send them by mail or deliver them in person?

W It depends. If they live nearby, I'll give them in person. And if they live far away, I'll send them by mail.

M I see. Do you want me to write down the people's names on the each envelope?

W Oh, thank you. But please write in tiny lettering at the bottom.

M No problem.

W Because of your help, I can finish much earlier than I thought. Thanks.

남 Rebecca, 너 뭐하고 있니?

여 이 초대장들을 봉투에 넣고 있어.

남 우편으로 보낼 거야 아니면 직접 배달할 거야?

여 상황에 따라 달라. 가까이에 살면 직접 줄 거야. 만일 멀리 살면, 우편으로 보낼 거야.

남 그렇구나. 내가 각각의 봉투에 사람들 이름을 쓸까?

여 오, 고마워. 그렇지만 아래쪽에 아주 작게 써줘.

남 알겠어.

여 네 도움 덕분에 내가 생각했던 것 보다 훨씬 더 빨리 끝나겠다. 고마워.

① 시작이 반이다.
② 피는 물보다 진하다.
③ 뜻이 있는 곳에 길이 있다.
④ 부전자전.
⑤ 백지장도 맞들면 낫다.

●●
insert into ~에 집어 넣다 **invitation card** 초대장 **envelope** 봉투 **deliver** 배달하다 **tiny lettering** 작은 글씨 **at the bottom** 아래쪽에

13

M Attention, prospective students! Hana College is offering a campus tour on Sunday, April 17th from 10 a.m. to 5 p.m. Senior students are volunteering to guide you and answer your questions about our school. Anyone who is interested in applying to our school is welcomed to go on the tour. You can fill out the application form and submit it online. A free lunch will be provided during the tour! For further information, please visit our website at www.hanacollege.com.

```
캠퍼스 개방 투어
① 언제? 4월 17일, 일요일 오전 10시부터 오후 5시
② 어디서? Hana 대학교
③ 무엇을? 2학년 학생들이 안내하며 학교에 대한 질문에 답해 줌
④ 누구에게? 저희 학교 지원에 관심이 있는 고등학교 3학년생들만
⑤ 어떻게? 지원서 작성 후 온라인에 제출
www.hanacollege.com 웹사이트 방문
```

남 주목해주세요, 미래의 학생 여러분! Hana 대학은 4월 17일, 일요일에 오전 10시부터 오후 5시까지 캠퍼스 투어를 제공합니다. 2학년 학생들이 여러분을 안내해주고 학교에 대한 질문에 대답해 줄 자원봉사를 할 것입니다. 저희 학교 지원에 관심이 있는 사람은 누구나 투어에 참여하기를 환영합니다. 지원서를 작성하시고 온라인으로 제출해 주시기 바랍니다. 투어 동안에 무료 점심이 제공됩니다! 자세한 정보는 우리 웹사이트 www.hanacollege.com을 방문해 주세요.

•• **attention** 주목 **prospective** 장래의, 곧 있을 **senior students** 2학년 학생들 **fill out** 작성하다 **application form** 지원서 **submit** 제출하다

14

W Please show me the tickets. What are our <u>seat numbers</u>?

M They are J55 and J56. You sit in J55, I'll <u>sit in</u> J56.

W Okay. Uh-oh. I can't see the <u>screen</u> well. The man <u>wearing</u> a <u>cap</u> in front of me is <u>blocking</u> <u>my</u> <u>view</u>. He is tall and he is sitting very straight.

M Then let's <u>switch</u> places. You sit in mine, I'll sit in yours.

W Great idea. That's very kind of you. But it might be a little <u>uncomfortable</u> for you, too. I don't want to cause you too much trouble.

M It's okay. I will ask him to <u>take off</u> his cap.

W Ask him <u>politely</u>, or he might be <u>annoyed</u>.

M Don't worry. I will.

···

여 티켓을 보여줘. 우리 자리 번호가 뭐야?

남 J55랑 J56이야. 네가 J55에 앉아. 내가 J56에 앉을게.

여 좋아. 이런. 스크린을 잘 볼 수가 없어. 내 앞의 모자를 쓰고 있는 남자가 내 시야를 가려. 키가 너무 크고 똑바로 앉아 있어.

남 자리 바꾸자. 네가 내 자리에 앉고 내가 네 자리에 앉을게.

여 좋은 생각이야. 너 정말 친절하다. 하지만 너도 불편할 텐데. 네게 피해를 주고 싶지 않아.

남 괜찮아. 모자를 벗어달라고 말 할거야.

여 정중히 얘기해. 안 그러면 짜증낼 거야.

남 걱정 마. 그렇게.

•• **block one's view** 시야를 막다 **switch** 바꾸다 **uncomfortable** 불편한 **take off** 벗다 **politely** 예의 바르게 **annoyed** 짜증내는, 화난

15

W The Nobel Prizes were <u>named after</u> Alfred Nobel, the Swedish chemist and <u>inventor</u> of dynamite. The prizes were first awarded in <u>1901</u>, five years after Alfred Nobel's <u>death</u>. They were awarded in <u>five</u> <u>subjects</u>: chemistry, physics, physiology or medicine, literature, and peace. And the <u>sixth</u> <u>subject</u>, <u>economics</u>, was added in <u>1969</u>. The prizes can only be awarded to <u>individuals</u>, except the Peace Prize. Each award can be given to a maximum of three people per year. Each prize constitutes a gold medal, a <u>diploma</u>, and a sum of money. If there are <u>multiple</u> winners for one subject, the award money is <u>split</u> <u>equally</u> among the winners.

···

여 노벨상은 스웨덴의 화학자이자 다이너마이트를 발명한 Alfred Nobel의 이름을 따서 지어졌다. 그 상은 Alfred Nobel의 사망 5년 후인 1901년에 처음으로 수여되었다. 5개 분야인 화학, 물리학, 생리학 또는 의학, 문학 그리고 평화 분야에 시상되었다. 그리고 6번째 분야인 경제학은 1969년에 추가되었다. 노벨 평화상을 제외하고 노벨상은 오직 개인에게만 시상될 수 있다. 각각의 상은 매년 최대 3명까지 수여될 수 있다. 각 상은 금메달, 증서 그리고 상금으로 이루어진다. 한 분야에 다수의 수상자가 있다면, 상금은 수상자들 사이에서 균등하게 나눠진다.

•• **be named after** ~의 이름을 따서 짓다 **chemist** 화학자 **dynamite** 다이너마이트 **award** 수여하다 **physiology** 생리학 **economics** 경제학 **individual** 개인 **maximum** 최대 **diploma** 증서 **be split** 나눠지다

16

M Who were you talking to on the phone?

W My mother. We were talking about my dad's <u>retirement</u>.

M Your father retired a couple of <u>months ago</u>. That

was a good thing, right?

W Well, it's good that he doesn't have to work anymore, but he hasn't found a useful way to spend his time yet.

M Why doesn't he take up a hobby? That would give him something interesting to occupy his time.

W My mother has tried to interest him in various things, but nothing has worked.

M How about encouraging him to take up golf or bowling?

W He wouldn't be interested in those hobbies. I think he needs something more challenging like playing a musical instrument.

M Maybe he needs time to find out what interests him.

남 누구와 전화로 이야기 했어?
여 우리 엄마. 아빠의 은퇴에 대해서 이야기했어.
남 너의 아버지는 두 달 전에 퇴직하셨잖아. 잘 되신 일이지, 그렇지?
여 음, 아빠가 더 이상 일할 필요가 없다는 건 좋아, 하지만 아빠는 아직 시간을 보내는 유용한 방법을 못 찾으셨나봐.
남 취미를 가져보시는 건 어때? 시간을 쏟을 재미난 뭔가를 그에게 줄 거야.
여 엄마가 다양한 것들로 그에게 흥미를 불러일으키게 해 봤지만 아무것도 효과가 없었대.
남 골프나 볼링을 하시게 하는 건 어때?
여 그런 취미들에는 흥미가 없으실 거야. 내 생각에는 악기 연주처럼 뭔가 더 도전적인 게 필요하신 것 같아.
남 아마도 그는 흥미를 끄는 것을 찾을 시간이 필요한 거 같아.

① 내 취미는 첼로를 연주하는 거야.
② 그는 틀림없이 기분이 정말 좋을 거야.
③ 내 아버지는 골프에 흥미가 있으셔.
④ 멋져. 그가 악기를 시작해서 기뻐.

occupy one's time ~의 시간을 쏟다 **challenging** 도전적인 **interest** 흥미를 끌다 **musical instrument** 악기

W We do have a free airport shuttle service.

M That sounds great, but will it get me to the airport on time?

W Yes, it should. The next shuttle leaves in 15 minutes, and it takes approximately 25 minutes to get to the airport.

M Fantastic. I'll just wait in the lounge area. Will you please let me know when it is leaving?

W Of course, sir. If you like, you can leave your baggage with the porter and he can load your bags onto the shuttle for you when it arrives.

M That would be great, thank you.

W Would you like to sign the hotel guestbook while you wait?

M Sure, I'll tell other people to come here.

여 편안히 묵으셨어요?
남 네, 아주 좋았어요. 하지만 약 두 시간 후에 떠나는 비행기를 타야 하는데 공항에 가는 가장 빠른 방법이 뭔가요?
여 저희 호텔에는 무료 공항 셔틀 서비스가 있어요.
남 좋군요, 하지만 그게 제 시간에 공항에 데려다 주나요?
여 네, 그럴 겁니다. 다음 셔틀은 15분 후에 떠나고 공항에 도착하는데 약 25분 걸려요.
남 좋아요. 라운지에서 기다릴게요. 출발할 때 저한테 말씀해주시겠어요?
여 물론이죠. 원하신다면, 가방을 포터에게 맡기시고 셔틀이 오면 포터가 가방을 실어드릴 거예요.
남 좋아요. 감사합니다.
여 기다리시는 동안 호텔 방명록에 서명하시겠어요?
남 물론이죠. 다른 사람들에게 여기에 오라고 말해야겠어요.

① 네, 얼마에요?
② 감사하지만 사양할게요. 저는 책을 읽고 싶지 않아요.
④ 가격이 합리적이면 제가 살게요.
⑤ 미안하지만 그것을 살만큼 충분한 돈이 없어요.

approximately 대략, 약 **load** 짐을 싣다 **baggage** 짐 **guestbook** 방명록

17

W Did you enjoy your stay with us?

M Yes, very much. However, I have a flight that leaves in about two hours, so what is the quickest way to get to the airport?

18

W Any plans for this weekend?

M I'm thinking of going skiing.

W But you won't have fun because the ski resorts haven't got much snow yet.

M Maybe you're right. Do you know what the weather is supposed to be like on Saturday?

W The report says that it will be windy and dry with little chance of snow.

M Okay. Then I'd better not go skiing this weekend. How about you? Do you have any plans?

W Saturday is my sister's birthday, and we are throwing her a party. Can you come?

M Sure, I can come to her party. Will it be at your house?

W No. My aunt has a larger house with a big basement room where everyone can play. So we're having the party there.

M Oh, good! Where is it?

W I'll text you the address.

······································

여 이번 주말에 계획 있니?

남 스키를 타러 갈까 생각 중이야.

여 하지만 스키장에 아직 눈이 많이 없어서 재미있지 않을 거야.

남 아마 네 말이 맞을 거야. 토요일에 날씨가 어떤지 아니?

여 일기예보에선 눈이 올 확률은 거의 없고 바람불고 건조할거라고 말하더라.

남 응. 그러면 이번 주말에는 스키 타러 안가는 게 낫겠다. 너는 어때? 계획 있니?

여 토요일이 내 여동생의 생일이어서 그녀에게 파티를 열어 줄 거야. 너도 올래?

남 물론이지. 파티에 갈 수 있을 거야. 너의 집에서 파티 여는 거야?

여 아니. 이모가 모두가 놀 수 있는 큰 지하실이 있는 더 큰집을 갖고 있어. 그래서 거기서 파티를 열거야.

남 오. 잘됐네. 거긴 어디야?

여 문자로 주소 보내줄게.

① 그래. 택시타자.

③ 캐주얼하게 옷을 입으면 돼.

④ 우리집은 A-Mart 근처야.

⑤ 스키장까지 한 시간이야.

••
with little chance of snow 눈이 올 확률이 없는 **throw a party** 파티를 열어주다 **basement** 지하실

19

M Have you decided where to go for your honeymoon?

W We've decided on Guam.

M I've been there before. It's a fantastic place.

W What did you do there?

M There is an amazing variety of leisure activities in Guam. I went scuba diving and snorkeling.

W That's good. I'm looking forward to our honeymoon.

M How long are you planning to stay there?

W We decided on 8 days. We are leaving on Saturday and returning on Sunday.

M That should be long enough. Do you have all your travel plans in order?

W Yes, everything is set.

······································

남 신혼여행 어디로 갈지 결정했어요?

여 괌으로 결정했어요.

남 전에 거기에 가 본 적이 있어요. 환상적인 곳이에요.

여 거기서 뭐했어요?

남 괌에는 놀랄만큼 다양한 종류의 레저활동이 있어요. 저는 스쿠버다이빙과 스노클링을 했어요.

여 훌륭하네요. 신혼여행이 기다려져요.

남 거기에서 얼마나 머물 계획이에요?

여 8일 정도 머무를 거예요. 토요일에 출발해서 일요일에 돌아올거예요.

남 충분히 긴 시간이네요. 여행계획은 다 정리되었어요?

여 네, 다 준비됐어요.

① 재미있겠네요.

③ 네. 완벽하게 청소했어요.

④ 아뇨. 보이는 것만큼 그렇게 지저분하지는 않아요.

⑤ 감사합니다만. 저 혼자 할 수 있어요.

••
have been there 거기에 가 본 적이 있다 **in order** 정리된

20

W Samantha has a favorite pair of white jeans that she wears only on special occasions. Yesterday her younger sister wore them without getting her permission. Her sister went to a movie theater with her boyfriend and he accidentally spilled Coke on the white jeans. Her sister put the jeans back in the drawer without saying anything to Samantha. Today, Samantha is invited to her friend's housewarming party and she decides that she wants to <u>wear</u> those white jeans with a blouse. Putting them on, she sees the <u>stain</u>. She knows the jeans were clean when she put them in the <u>drawer</u> a few days ago. In this situation, what would Samantha probably say to her sister?

··

여 Samantha는 특별한 행사에만 입는 가장 좋아하는 흰색 바지 한 벌이 있다. 어제 그녀의 여동생이 그녀의 허락 없이 그 바지를 입었다. 그녀의 동생은 그녀의 남자친구와 영화관에 갔고 그녀의 남자친구가 실수로 콜라를 그 바지에 엎질렀다. 그녀의 동생은 Samantha에게 아무 말도 하지 않은 채 다시 서랍에 바지를 넣어두었다. 오늘 Samantha는 친구의 집들이에 초대받아서 블라우스와 그 바지를 입기로 결정한다. 그 바지를 입으면서, 그녀는 얼룩을 발견한다. 그녀는 며칠 전 서랍에 그것을 넣을 때는 깨끗했다는 것을 안다. 이런 상황에서 Samantha는 그녀의 동생에게 뭐라고 말할 것 같은가?

① 말해줘서 고마워. 용서할게.
② 네 청바지를 입게 해줘서 고마워.
③ 내 대신 세탁소에 이걸 가져다 주겠니?
④ 내가 새 청바지를 어디서 살 수 있는지 아니?
⑤ 나한테 말도 않고 이 청바지 입었니?

•• **occasion** 행사 **permission** 허락 **spill** 쏟다 **put on** 입다

Further Study 정답   p. 124

1 Her sister, who <u>is a vegetarian</u>, wouldn't let her <u>order a steak</u>.

2 You can borrow only <u>2 DVDs</u> at a time, and you must return them <u>in a week</u> as they don't allow DVD loans <u>to be renewed</u>.

3 He is going to take care of <u>people's dogs</u> when they <u>go on holidays</u>.

4 He can get <u>a slightly better exchange rate</u> than the going rate.

5 The reason is that the store is <u>having a sale</u> so she can get items <u>at the cheapest possible price</u>.

6 It is on Sunday, <u>April 17th from 10 a.m. to 5 p.m.</u>

7 They were first awarded in <u>1901</u>, <u>five years</u> after Alfred Noble's <u>death</u>.

8 It leaves in <u>15 minutes</u> and it takes about <u>25 minutes</u> to get to the airport.

On Your Own 모범답안   p. 125

A

Watching Sporting Events	
(1) Which do you prefer, watching sports on TV or in person?	in person
(2) Why? (two reasons)	I can release my stress while I cheer for my team in the crowd. I can see my favorite players more often than on TV because they are not popular.
(3) What was the most memorable sporting event you have ever watched?	Yuna Kim's retirement performance which took place at the Seoul Olympic Park Gymnastics Stadium last month.
(4) Why can't you forget it?	I cried when Yuna Kim gave her final remarks saying she was happy but also sad to leave the sport.

I prefer watching sports (1) <u>in person</u>. The first reason is that (2)<u>I can release my stress while I cheer for my team in the crowd</u>. The second reason is that (2) <u>I can see my favorite players more often than on TV because they are not popular</u>. The most memorable sporting event I have ever watched <u>in person</u> is (3) <u>Yuna Kim's retirement performance which took place at the Seoul Olympic Park Gymnastics Stadium last month</u>. I can't forget it because (4)<u>I cried when Yuna Kim gave her final remarks saying that she was happy but also sad to leave the sport</u>.

운동 경기 보기	
(1) TV와 직접 관전 중 어느 것을 더 선호하나요?	직접
(2) 왜인가요?	군중 속에서 내 팀을 응원하면서 스트레스를 풀 수 있다 / 좋아하는 선수가 유명인이 아니기 때문에 TV에서 보다 더 자주 그들을 볼 수 있다
(3) 자신이 본 스포츠 이벤트 중 가장 기억에 남는 것은?	지난달 올림픽 공원에서 열렸던 김연아의 은퇴공연
(4) 왜 잊을 수 없는지?	김연아가 행복하지만 그만두게 되어 슬프다고 마지막 말을 했을 때 울었기 때문

저는 직접 스포츠를 관전하는 것을 좋아합니다. 그 첫 번째 이유는 군중 속에서 팀을 응원하면서 제 스트레스를 풀 수 있기 때문입니다. 두 번째 이유는 좋아하는 선수가 유명인이 아니기 때문에 TV에서 보다 더 많이 그들을 볼 수 있다는 것입니다. 직접 본 가장 기억에 남는 스포츠 이벤트는 지난달 올림픽 공원 체육관에서 열렸던 김연아의 은퇴공연이었습니다. 저는 잊을 수가 없는데 왜냐하면 김연아가 행복하지만 그만두게 되어 슬프다고 마지막 말을 했을 때 울었기 때문입니다.

B

Having a Hobby	
(1) What is a hobby?	An activity I enjoy doing
(2) My opinion	It is necessary for me to have a hobby.
(3) The 1st reason for my opinion	A hobby is the easiest way to restore my balance whenever I am overworked or stressed.
(4) The 2nd reason for my opinion	Since it is an activity I choose, it always gives me pleasure and helps me to unwind.

A hobby is (1)an activity I enjoy doing. And I think (2) it is necessary for me to have a hobby. The reason for my opinion is (3)a hobby is the easiest way to restore my balance whenever I am overworked or stressed. In addition, (4)since it is an activity I choose, it always gives me pleasure and helps me to unwind. Therefore, I think (2)having a hobby is important for my well-being.

취미 가지기	
(1) 취미는 무엇인가?	내가 즐기는 활동
(2) 나의 의견	내가 취미를 가지는 것은 꼭 필요하다.
(3) 내 의견에 대한 첫 번째 이유	취미는 내가 과로를 했거나 스트레스를 받을때마다 내 균형을 복구할 수 있는 가장 쉬운 방법이다.
(4) 내 의견에 대한 두 번째 이유	내가 선택한 활동이기 때문에 항상 나에게 기쁨을 주고, 긴장을 푸는 것을 도와준다.

취미는 내가 즐기는 활동이다. 그리고 나는 내가 취미를 가지는 것이 꼭 필요하다고 생각한다. 내 의견에 대한 이유는 취미는 내가 과로를 했거나 스트레스를 받을 때마다 내 균형을 복구할 수 있는 가장 쉬운 방법이기 때문이다. 또한, 내가 선택한 활동이기 때문에 항상 나에게 기쁨을 주고, 긴장을 푸는 것을 도와준다. 따라서, 나는 취미가 나의 건강한 삶을 위해서 중요하다고 생각한다.

01 Actual Test 정답

p. 132

01 ②	02 ④	03 ③	04 ③	05 ⑤
06 ②	07 ④	08 ②	09 ④	10 ②
11 ⑤	12 ②	13 ④	14 ⑤	15 ⑤
16 ⑤	17 ①	18 ④	19 ③	20 ②

01

W I have to write an article for our school newspaper.

M Oh, really? When do you have to finish it by?

W That's not the problem. I don't know what to write about.

M What about writing about sports?

W Good idea. I think many students like to read articles about sports.

M What sports do you like?

W I like all kinds of ball sports.

M So you like baseball, volleyball, basketball, and soccer, don't you?

W That's right. I love bowling, too. How about you?

M I don't like ball sports. I like swimming.

여 나는 학교 신문에 기사를 써야 해.

남 정말? 언제 그것을 끝마쳐야 하는데?

여 그게 문제가 아니야. 무엇에 대해서 써야 할 지 모르겠어.

남 스포츠에 대해서 쓰는 것은 어때?

여 좋은 생각이야. 내 생각에 많은 학생들이 스포츠에 대한 기사를 읽는 것을 좋아하는 것 같아.

남 넌 어떤 스포츠를 좋아하니?

여 나는 모든 종류의 구기 종목을 좋아해.

남 그럼 야구, 배구, 농구, 축구를 좋아하겠네, 그렇지 않니?

여 맞아. 나는 볼링도 좋아해. 너는 어떠니?

남 나는 구기 종목을 좋아하지 않아. 난 수영을 좋아해.

•• **all kinds of** 모든 종류의 ~ **ball sports** 구기 운동 **volleyball** 배구

02

W Mike, why are you so busy?

M I have to prepare a big party this evening.

W Is today your father's birthday?

M Yeah. All the things are ready, but …

W But what? You bought a book for your father the day before yesterday, didn't you?

M Yeah. I did it. But I found out that my brother had already bought the same thing.

W I'm sorry to hear that. You should have discussed it earlier with him.

M Yes, I should have.

W Did you buy another gift for your father yet?

M Not yet. I have to take the book back to the bookstore, but I don't know what I should buy instead.

W What about a music CD?

M That's a good idea. Thanks a lot.

여 Mike, 너 왜 이렇게 바빠?

남 오늘 저녁에 커다란 파티를 준비해야 해.

여 오늘이 너희 아빠 생일이시니?

남 응. 모든 것이 준비가 되어 있어, 하지만 …

여 하지만 뭐? 너는 그저께 아빠 선물로 책 샀지, 그렇지 않았어?

여 응. 그랬어. 근데 형이 이미 똑같은 걸 샀다는 것을 알게 되었어.

여 그 얘기 들으니 안타깝구나. 형하고 미리 상의해 보았어야 했는데.

남 응. 그랬어야 했어.

여 아빠 선물 다른 거 샀어?

남 아니 아직. 서점에 그 책을 도로 가져가야 해. 하지만 대신 무엇을 사야할 지 모르겠어. .

여 음악 CD 어때?

남 좋은 생각이다. 고마워.

•• **discuss** 의논하다 **the day before yesterday** 그저께 **instead** 대신

03

M Hello, listeners! This is Ben Simon from the Chipan Motor Corporation. First of all, we regret to inform you that our new model the NPE1 has some problems. We are issuing a recall notification for this model. If your car is this model, you can bring it to any Chipan Motor's service center and the recalled part will be replaced. Of course, this recall notification is bothersome for you. But you have to do it so that you can drive safely. For further information, you can contact either your car dealer or any of Chipan Motor's service centers.

남 청취자 여러분 안녕하세요! 저는 Chipan 자동차 회사의 Ben Simon입니다. 우선, 저희는 저희 신모델 NPE1에 몇 가지 문제점들이 있다는 것을 여러분께 알려드리게 되어 유감스럽게 생각합니다. 우리는 이 모델에 대해서 리콜을 공지하고 있습니다. 만약 여러분의 자동차가 그 모델이시라면, 여러분께서는 Chipan 자동차 서비스 센터로 가져오시면 리콜되는 부품을 교체받으실 수 있습니다. 물론, 이번 리콜 공지는 여러분께 성가실 수 있을 겁니다. 그렇지만 여러분은 안전하게 주행하기 위해 반드시 리콜받으셔야 합니다. 더 자세한 정보를 원하시면 자동차 영업 사원이나 저희 서비스 센터로 연락하시면 됩니다.

•• **motor corporation** 자동차 회사 **regret to-V** ~하게 되어 유감스럽다 **inform** ~을 알리다 **recall notification** 리콜 공지 **bothersome** 성가신

04

[Telephone rings.]

M Hello?

W Hello, it's me, Jenny. I have something to tell you.

M What is it?

W I can't <u>make it</u> this Friday night. I'm sorry, but I won't be there.

M Why? Is there a problem?

W I really want to come to the party for your parents' 30th wedding <u>anniversary</u>, but I forgot I had a <u>previous</u> <u>appointment</u>.

M Oh my goodness! I already told my parents that you <u>would</u> <u>be</u> <u>coming</u>.

W I'm so sorry. Can you tell them that I couldn't be with them <u>because</u> <u>of</u> a <u>bad</u> <u>cold</u>?

M I don't believe it. Do you really want me to <u>tell</u> <u>a</u> <u>lie</u> to them?

W Sorry again!

....

[전화벨이 울린다.]

남 여보세요?

여 여보세요, 나 Jenny야. 너에게 할 말이 있어.

남 뭔데?

여 이번 금요일 저녁약속을 못 지키겠어. 미안하지만 거기 못 갈 거야.

남 왜? 무슨 문제 있어?

여 네 부모님의 서른 번째 결혼기념일 파티에 꼭 가고 싶지만 선약이 있는 것을 깜빡 잊고 있었어.

남 아이구! 부모님께 네가 올 거라고 벌써 말씀드려 놓았는데.

여 정말 미안해. 심한 감기 때문에 함께 할 수 없다고 말해 줄 수 있겠니?

남 믿을 수가 없구나. 진짜 내가 거짓말을 하길 원하는 거야?

여 거듭 미안해.

① 지루한　　　② 궁금한　　　③ 실망한
④ 기쁜　　　　⑤ 질투하는

wedding anniversary 결혼 기념일　**previous appointment** 선약
tell a lie 거짓말하다

05

M Hi, Betty!

W Hi, Brian. How was your weekend?

M I <u>had</u> <u>a</u> <u>great</u> <u>time</u> with <u>my</u> <u>cousins</u>. Do you know my cousins, Brandon and James?

W Of course. How are they?

M They're fine. Brandon <u>received</u> a <u>scholarship</u> for this <u>semester</u>.

W Really? I <u>envy</u> <u>him</u> <u>a</u> <u>lot</u>. I really want to get a

scholarship so I don't have to work part time.

M If you talk to him, he will give you <u>some</u> <u>tips</u> about all the scholarship that students can <u>apply</u> <u>for</u>.

W Great. Can you tell me his phone number or his email address?

M Sure. His phone number is 010-6789-1234, and his <u>email</u> <u>address</u> is Brandon@email.ac.kr.

W Thanks a lot. I can't wait to hear his <u>tips</u> about how to get a scholarship.

....

남 안녕, Betty!

여 안녕, Brian. 주말은 어땠어?

남 나는 사촌들과 좋은 시간을 보냈어. 너 나의 사촌들, Brandon과 James를 알고 있니?

여 물론이야. 그들 어떻게 지내?

남 그들은 잘 지내. Brandon은 이번 학기에 장학금을 받았어.

여 정말? 그가 부럽다. 나도 파트타임으로 일하지 않아도 되게 장학금을 정말 받고 싶어.

남 그에게 물어보면, 학생들이 지원할 수 있는 모든 장학금에 대한 조언을 해줄 거야.

여 좋아. 그의 전화번호나 이메일 주소를 알려 줄 수 있니?

남 그럼. 그의 전화 번호는 010-6789-1234이고, 그의 이메일 주소는 Brandon@email.ac.kr이야.

여 정말 고마워. 어떻게 장학금을 받을 수 있는지에 대한 조언을 빨리 듣고 싶어.

have a great time with ~와 좋은 시간을 보내다　**receive** 받다
scholarship 장학금　**envy** 부러워하다

06

W Good morning. I'd like to get train tickets to Irvine, please.

M Good morning. When would you like to go?

W I'd like tickets for the <u>15th</u> of <u>March</u>, which is <u>next</u> <u>Thursday</u>.

M There are three trains <u>available</u> on that day. They are at <u>10:15</u> in the morning and <u>3:00</u> and <u>4:30</u> in the afternoon.

W I need four tickets, two <u>for</u> <u>adults</u> and two <u>for</u> <u>children</u>. How much are the tickets?

M It <u>depends</u> <u>on</u> the train. The 10:15 is $20, and both the 3:00 and 4:30 are $30. And children can get a 10% discount.

W   Why do the different trains have different prices?

M   The former is a regular train; the latter is an express one. The express is more expensive.

W   Both my husband and I have train membership cards. Can we get a discount?

M   Sure, we give our members a 10% discount on weekdays.

W   Okay, I want four tickets for the 10:15 train.

여   안녕하세요. Irvine행 열차표를 사고 싶습니다.

남   안녕하세요. 언제 가실 예정이세요?

여   3월 15일 열차표를 원합니다. 다음주 목요일입니다.

남   그 날은 3대의 열차가 있습니다. 오전 10시 15분, 오후 3시, 그리고 4시 30분요.

여   4장의 열차표가 필요합니다. 어른 2장, 그리고 아이 2장입니다. 얼마인가요?

남   열차에 따라 다릅니다. 10시 15분 열차는 20달러이고, 3시와 4시 30분 열차는 모두 30달러입니다. 그리고 아이들은 10% 할인을 받을 수 있습니다.

여   왜 기차마다 가격이 다르죠?

남   전자는 정기 열차이고, 후자는 고속 열차입니다. 고속 열차가 더 비쌉니다.

여   나와 남편은 모두 회원권이 있습니다. 할인이 되나요?

남   물론입니다. 저희는 회원님께 주중에 10% 할인을 제공해 드릴 수 있습니다.

여   좋아요. 10시 15분 열차로 4장 주세요.

••
available 이용가능한   **adult** 어른   **both A and B** A와 B 둘 다
regular train 정기열차   **express train** 고속열차

07

W   Good afternoon.

M   Good afternoon. How can I help you?

W   I am looking for a book for a birthday present.

M   What kind of book do you want?

W   Can you recommend some books for young adult readers?

M   Sure. This book, which was written by Sir. Arthur, is a bestseller in the young adult genre.

W   Unfortunately, the person who I will give the present to read that book last week.

M   Oh, really? Well, what about this other one by the same author?

W   Are you pointing at the book titled *After Twilight*?

M   Yes. That's right. This is the first book written by Sir Arthur.

여   안녕하세요.

남   안녕하세요. 어떻게 도와 드릴까요?

여   저는 생일 선물로 책을 찾고 있어요.

남   어떤 종류의 책을 원하시나요?

여   청년들을 위한 책을 추천해 주실 수 있어요?

남   물론입니다. 이 책은 Arthur 경이 쓴 책으로 청년 분야의 베스트셀러입니다.

여   안타깝네요. 제가 선물을 주게 될 사람이 지난 주에 그 책을 읽었어요.

남   아 정말요? 그럼, 같은 저자가 쓴 다른 책은 어떤가요?

여   After Twilight이라는 제목의 저 책을 가리키는 건가요?

남   네, 맞아요. 이 책은 Arthur 경의 첫 번째 책이예요.

① 사서 – 학생   ② 의사 – 환자   ③ 작가 – 독자
④ 고객 – 점원   ⑤ 고용인 – 직원

••
look for ~을 찾다   **genre** 분야   **author** 저자   **point out** ~을 가리키다

08

W   Excuse me? I have something to ask you.

M   Okay. You can ask me whatever you want to know.

W   I don't mean to be rude, but do you mind if I ask you the name of this painting?

M   Oh! I don't mind at all. This painting is called *Number 5*.

W   Could you tell me who painted it?

M   Sure. Jackson Pollack created this painting in 1950.

W   I think this painting is incredible. How did he paint this?

M   I know he used a creative method called the drip painting technique.

W   Really? It sounds difficult, but the result is very interesting.

M   Don't worry about it. Many visitors in here think it is difficult to understand.

여   실례합니다. 여쭐 것이 있습니다.

남   네. 알고 싶은 것이 무엇이든지 물어 보세요.

여   무례하고 싶지는 않지만, 이 그림의 이름을 여쭤어도 될런지요?

남 오! 괜찮습니다. 이 그림은 Number 5로 불립니다.

여 이 그림을 누가 그렸는지 말씀해 주실 수 있으세요?

남 네. Jackson Pollack이 이 그림을 1950년에 만들었어요.

여 이 그림은 믿기 힘들 정도예요. 그는 이것을 어떻게 그렸죠?

남 그는 드립 페인팅 기법으로 불리는 창의적인 수단을 이용했어요.

여 정말요? 어렵게 들리지만 결과물은 매우 흥미롭네요.

남 걱정마세요. 여기 많은 방문객들이 그것이 이해하기 어렵다고 생각해요.

① 콘서트장　　　② 미술관　　　③ 동물원
④ 실험실　　　⑤ 지하철역

••
whatever ~하는 것은 무엇이든지　**rude** 무례한　**create** 창조하다
incredible 믿기 힘들정도로 놀라운　**creative** 창의적인　**method** 수단
technique 기술, 기법

09

① W What are you doing there?
   M I am reading a book.
② W Are you reading a book now?
   M I am about to go out to buy scissors.
③ W Why are you holding a sharp knife?
   M I am making a paper boat.
④ W What are you doing with such dangerous scissors?
   M I am cutting this paper.
⑤ W What are you listening to?
   M I am making a paper boat while listening to music.

- - -

① 여 거기에서 뭐하고 있니?
   남 저는 책을 읽고 있어요.
② 여 너는 책을 읽고 있는 중이니?
   남 저는 가위를 사러 밖에 나가려고 하던 참이에요.
③ 여 너는 왜 날카로운 칼을 들고 있니?
   남 종이 배를 접으려구요.
④ 여 그렇게 위험한 가위를 가지고 뭐하고 있니?
   남 이 종이를 자르려고 하고 있었어요.
⑤ 여 뭘 듣고 있는 중이니?
   남 저는 음악을 들으면서 종이 배를 접고 있어요.

••
be about to-V 막 ~하려고 하다　**scissors** 가위

10

W Bulguksa is a very famous temple, which is located in Gyeongju, South Korea. The temple has several of Korea's national treasures. Inside the temple, Dabotap is located on the right side and Seokgatap is on the left side. Both of them are known as wonderful stone pagodas. In 1995, Bulguksa was included in the list of UNESCO World Heritage Sites. Bulguksa was constructed in 751 under King Gyeongdeok, the 35th ruler of the kingdom of Silla, but over the years it was partially destroyed because of invasions and wars. Restoration work beginning in the 1960s has brought Bulguksa to its current form.

- - -

여 불국사는 매우 유명한 절이며, 그것은 대한민국의 경주에 위치해 있습니다. 그 절은 몇 개의 한국의 국보들을 가지고 있습니다. 그 절 안에, 다보탑은 오른 편에 위치해 있고, 석가탑은 왼편에 있습니다. 그 둘 다 놀라운 석조탑으로 알려져 있습니다. 1995년, 불국사는 유네스코 세계 문화유산 목록에 포함되었습니다. 불국사는 751년 신라 35대왕 경덕왕 시대에 건설되었지만, 침략과 전쟁 때문에 오랜 기간에 걸쳐 부분적으로 파괴되었습니다. 1960년대에 시작된 복원 작업으로 불국사는 현재의 형태를 갖추게 되었습니다.

••
be located ~에 위치해 있다　**national treasure** 국보　**World Heritage List** 세계문화유산목록　**partially destroyed** 부분적으로 파괴된　**invasion** 침략　**restoration** 복원

11

M Hi, Mina. What did you do last weekend?
W I read the book *Freakonomics* all day long.
M *Freakonomics*? What is the book about?
W It's a non-fiction book which blends cultural topics with economics.
M Can you tell me about it more specifically?
W It applies economic theories to a variety of subjects in very interesting ways.
M Is it interesting to read?
W Yes. In fact, I used to think economics was a very difficult subject, but I don't any more thanks to this book.

M Really? I want to read the book right now. Can you lend me your book?

W Sorry, I can't. I'll read it again today. You can borrow it from our school library.

남 안녕 미나. 지난 주말에 뭐했어?

여 나는 하루 종일 Freakonomics(괴짜경제학)라는 책을 읽었어.

남 Freakonomics(괴짜경제학)? 뭐에 관한 책이야?

여 그것은 문화적 주제들과 경제학을 결합시킨 논픽션 책이야.

남 좀더 구체적으로 말해 줄래?

여 그것은 경제 이론을 다양한 주제에 매우 흥미롭게 적용하고 있어.

남 읽기에 재밌니?

여 응. 사실, 경제학을 매우 어려운 과목으로 생각하고 있었는데 이책 덕분에 더 이상 그렇지 않아.

남 정말? 지금 당장 그 책을 읽고 싶다. 나에게 책 빌려줄 수 있겠니?

여 미안하지만 안되겠어. 오늘 그것을 다시 읽을 거라서. 학교 도서관에서 그것을 빌릴 수 있을 거야.

blend A with B A와 B를 섞다 **specifically** 구체적으로 **theory** 이론
thanks to ~의 덕택으로 **lend** 빌려주다

12

W Michael, do you remember your flute lesson this evening?

M I almost forgot about the lesson. Thanks, mom!

W Did you finish your homework yesterday?

M Yes, mom. I also practiced a lot yesterday, so you don't have to worry about it.

W Do you think you will win the contest?

M Of course, mom. I'm the best flutist in my school.

W Michael, don't speak so boastfully.

M OK. I know there will be many other good competitors in the contest.

W You're right. You had better practice much more if you want to be the winner.

M I really appreciate your advice. After taking the lesson, I will practice for more than an hour.

여 Michael, 오늘 저녁 플루트 레슨 기억하고 있니?

남 그 레슨 거의 잊을 뻔 했어요. 고마워요 엄마!

여 어제 네 숙제는 끝냈구?

남 네 엄마. 저는 어제 많이 연습도 했으니까 걱정하지 않으셔도 되요.

여 대회에서 우승할거라고 생각해?

남 물론이죠. 우리 학교에서 제가 플루트를 제일 잘 연주해요.

여 Michael, 그렇게 자랑하듯 말하면 안돼.

남 좋아요. 대회에 훌륭한 경쟁자들이 많이 있을 거라는 것을 저도 알고 있어요.

여 네 말이 맞아. 승자가 되고 싶다면, 더 많은 연습을 하는 게 좋을 거야.

남 엄마 조언 정말 감사드려요. 레슨마치고 나서, 1시간 더 연습할 거예요.

boastfully 자랑하면서. 허풍떨면서 **competitor** 경쟁자 **appreciate**
감사하다

13

① W It is a construction notice put up by the Seoul Subway Public Works Department.

② W The construction will last for a month.

③ W The construction activities will include the removal and restoration of the asphalt.

④ W The construction activities will end in early October.

⑤ W Whoever wants to get more information can contact the Seoul Subway Public Works Department by phone.

> ### 건설 공사 공고
> 무엇을: 기존의 지하 시설 제거와 이전
> 언제: 2014년 10월 4일 토요일부터 2014년 11월 2일 일요일까지
> 작업 시간: 월~금: 오전 9:00 부터 오후 7 시
> 　　　　　토, 일: 오전 7:00부터 오후 6 시
> 어디서: 4호선 사당역 공사 현장
> 작업 내용: 기존 사당역 지하 시설 제거 및 이전
> 주된 작업 활동: 아스팔트 제거, 굴착 공사, 새로운 설비 이전과 아스팔트 복구
> 자세한 정보: 서울 지하철 공공 사업 부서 (070-1234-5678)

① 여 서울 지하철 공공사업부에 의한 공사 통보입니다.

② 여 그 공사는 한 달간 지속될 것입니다.

③ 여 공사 활동은 아스팔트 제거 및 복원을 포함합니다.

④ 여 공사활동은 10월 초에 끝날 것입니다.

⑤ 여 보다 많은 정보를 원하는 사람은 누구나 전화로 서울지하철 공공사업부에 연락을 취할 수 있습니다.

construction 건설 **notice** 통지. 공고 **last** 지속하다 **removal** 제거
asphalt 아스팔트

14

W Jeff, do you have a problem these days?

M I guess I do. I feel everything's not okay these days.

W I'm sorry to hear that. What is it that's bothering you?

M My problem is that I don't know what the problem is.

W Have you tried to relieve your stress? What about going to a concert?

M A concert? It sounds great. Is there a good concert coming up?

W Yes, a K-pop Star Concert will be held this Friday night.

M Really? What time does it start?

W Sorry. I don't remember when the concert starts exactly.

M I don't have my cell phone with me. So can you check the exact time for me?

....

여 Jeff, 요새 어떤 문제라도 있니?

남 그런 것 같아. 요즘 모든 게 좋지 않은 것 같아.

여 그런 얘길 들으니 안타깝구나. 너를 괴롭히는 게 뭐니?

남 내 문제는 무엇이 문제인지를 모르겠다는 것이야.

여 스트레스를 해소하려고 노력해봤니? 콘서트에 가는 것은 어때?

남 콘서트? 그게 좋을 거 같은데? 좋은 콘서트 하는 것 있니?

여 응. K-Pop 스타 콘서트가 이번 주 금요일 밤에 열릴 예정이야.

남 정말? 언제 시작하는데?

여 미안. 콘서트가 정확히 언제 시작하는지는 나도 기억이 안나.

남 내가 지금 휴대전화가 없어. 나 대신 정확한 시간을 확인해 줄 수 있겠니?

relieve one's stress 스트레스를 해소하다 **be held** 개최되다 **exactly** 정확히

15

M Online shopping is very popular today. It is a form of electronic commerce, and it is called e-shopping. Consumers can directly purchase goods or services from many sellers on the Internet. Now, through cell phones, consumers can easily shop online by using shopping apps. Online shoppers generally use their credit cards, electronic transfers and gift cards to pay for their purchases. In addition, online stores are usually open 24 hours a day, so many consumers can access online shopping whenever they want.

....

남 오늘날 온라인 쇼핑이 매우 인기가 있습니다. 그것은 전자 상거래의 일종이며, e-쇼핑이라고 불리기도 합니다. 소비자들은 인터넷의 많은 판매자들로부터 상품과 서비스를 직접 구입할 수 있습니다. 이제는 이동전화를 이용하여 소비자들은 쇼핑 앱을 사용함으로써 쉽게 온라인 쇼핑을 할 수 있습니다. 온라인 쇼핑을 하는 사람들은 구매한 것을 지불하기 위해 일반적으로 자신들의 신용카드, 온라인 이체, 기프트카드 등을 사용합니다. 게다가, 온라인 상점은 대개 하루에 24시간 열려 있어서 많은 소비자들은 그들이 원하는 언제든 온라인 쇼핑에 접속할 수 있습니다.

popular 인기있는 **electronic commerce** 전자상거래 **consumer** 소비자 **purchase** 구입하다. 구매 **electronic transfer** 온라인 이체 **access** 접속하다. 접근하다

16

W Hi, Brad.

M Hi, Vicky.

W How did you know to come here? Who told you to come here?

M Yesterday Bill told me to come here.

W Really? I kept calling you all day long yesterday. I was very upset because you didn't return my calls.

M Sorry, I couldn't return your calls because I was really busy helping my mom.

W By the way, did Bill tell you over the phone?

M No, I met Bill while shopping with my mom at the mall. Forgive me, Vicky.

W Okay. It is fortunate that we met each other here. But I don't want the same thing to ever happen again.

M OK, even if I'm busy, I'll return your call.

....

여 안녕, Brad

남 안녕, Vicky

여 여기에 오는 것 어떻게 알았어? 누가 너에게 여기 오라고 했어?

남 Bill이 어제 여기에 오라고 말해 줬어.

여 정말? 어제 하루 종일 너에게 전화했어. 네가 내 전화에 답을 안 해줘서 정말 기분이 나빴어.

남 미안, 엄마를 돕느라 너무 바빠서 너에게 전화를 할 수 없었어.

여 그런데, Bill은 너랑 전화로 얘기를 했니?

남 아니. 쇼핑몰에서 엄마와 쇼핑하는 동안 Bill을 만났어. 용서해줘 Vicky.

여 알았어. 우리가 여기에서 서로 만나서 다행이다. 하지만 이런 일이 또다시 일어나는 것은 원치 않아.

남 <u>좋아, 바쁘더라도 네 전화에 답할게.</u>

① 문제 없어. 나는 그녀를 전혀 그리워하지 않을 거야.
② 괜찮아. 나한테 전화하는 것 잊지마.
③ 맞아. 다음엔 Bill이 너에게 전화할 거야..
④ 좋아. 네 전화를 받지 않아야 한다는 것 알아.

keep -ing 계속해서 ~하다　**upset** 화가 난　**forget to-V** ~할 것을 잊다
be busy -ing ~하느라 바쁘다

17

[Telephone rings.]

W　Hello, this is HCM. How may I help you?

M　Yes, this is Andrew Rice from Pennsylvania. I'd like to talk to Ms. Parker.

W　I'm sorry. She can't talk to you because she is <u>at a</u> <u>conference</u> now.

M　Can I <u>leave</u> <u>a</u> <u>message</u>?

W　Sure. Could you <u>wait</u> <u>for</u> <u>a</u> <u>second</u> because I have to get a pen <u>to</u> <u>write</u> <u>with</u>?

M　Okay. When you're ready, let me know. [Pause]

W　Thank you. I'm ready.

M　I want to check <u>if</u> she can visit my office at <u>3</u> p.m. today.

W　Sorry, she isn't <u>able</u> to visit your office at that time because she already has <u>an</u> <u>appointment</u>.

M　<u>If so, I'm wondering when she can visit me today.</u>

- -

[전화벨이 울린다]

여 여보세요, HCM 입니다. 어떻게 도와드릴까요?

남 네. 저는 펜실베니아의 Andrew Rice입니다. Ms. Parker와 통화하고 싶습니다.

여 죄송합니다. 지금 설명회에 참석 중이어서 통화가 어려우세요.

남 제가 메시지를 남겨도 될까요?

여 물론이죠. 적을 펜을 찾아야해서 잠시동안 기다려 주실 수 있으세요?

남 네. 준비되시면, 말씀해 주세요.

여 고맙습니다. 준비가 되었어요.

남 저는 그녀가 오늘 오후 3시에 제 사무실에 방문하실 수 있는지를 확인하고 싶어요.

여 죄송하지만 그녀는 그 시간에 이미 선약이 있어서 당신 사무실에 방문하실 수 없어요.

남 <u>그렇다면 오늘 언제 그녀가 저를 방문하실 수 있는지 궁금하군요.</u>

② 그럼 그녀가 오후 3시에 저를 방문할 수 있는지 궁금하군요.
③ 오후 3시에 어디에서 그녀를 만나야 하는지 궁금하군요.
④ 당신이 내가 펜실베니아 출신이라는 것을 어떻게 아는지 궁금하군요.
⑤ 그녀가 늦는다면 얼마나 늦을지 궁금하군요.

conference 설명회, 회의　**leave a message** 메시지를 남기다
appointment 약속

18

M　Thank you for coming.

W　<u>Don't</u> <u>mention</u> <u>it</u>. What seems to be wrong with Bill?

M　Well, we are worried about Bill's failure <u>to</u> <u>concentrate</u>.

W　Please continue explaining Bill's situation to me.

M　He <u>hasn't</u> <u>read</u> any books since he became <u>addicted</u> <u>to</u> watching TV.

W　Well, you know spending a lot of time watching TV can make people <u>lose</u> <u>their</u> <u>ability</u> to <u>concentrate</u>.

M　We have just found out that he usually watches TV all afternoon after school.

W　How many hours does he watch TV every day?

M　Every day he <u>spends</u> <u>about</u> <u>6</u> <u>hours</u> watching TV.

W　<u>Spending six hours on TV is too long for a teenager.</u>

- -

남 와 줘서 고마워요.

여 별 말씀요. Bill에게 무슨 문제가 있는 것 같으신데요?

남 저. Bill이 집중을 하지 못하고 있는 것이 염려스러워요.

여 Bill의 상황에 대해서 계속 얘기해 주세요.

남 그애는 TV에 중독된 이후로 어떤 것도 읽지 않고 있어요.

여 음, 아시다시피 TV 시청에 너무 많은 시간을 소비하면 사람들은 집중력을 잃을 수 있어요.

남 방과 후 오후 내내 TV를 주로 보고 있다는 것을 알게 되었어요.

여 매일 얼마나 많은 시간 TV를 시청하고 있나요?

남 매일 6시간을 TV 보는 데 보내고 있어요.

여 <u>여섯 시간을 TV를 보며 보내는 것은 십대에게 너무 길어요.</u>

① TV를 보는 것은 방과 후에 휴식을 취하는 좋은 방법입니다.

② Bill은 오늘 오후에 독서로 여섯 시간을 보냈어요.

③ 매일 밤 숙제를 여섯 시간 하는 것은 너무 지나칩니다.

⑤ 당신은 잡지를 읽으면서 많은 시간을 보내야만 합니다.

●●
be wrong with ~에 문제가 있다   **failure** 실패   **concentrate** 집중하다
be addicted to -ing ~하는 것에 빠지다

19

M Hi, Betty! Richard and I are on the way to the movie theater.

W Really? Can I join you?

M Sure. The movie we are going to see is Mr. Brilliant.

W What? Mr. Brilliant? I saw it yesterday.

M Really? How is the movie? Is it interesting?

W Not at all. It is really boring. I was so bored I didn't concentrate on the movie.

M Really? I don't believe it. The reviews of the movie are really fantastic, aren't they?

W I read all the reviews, too, and then I decided to watch the movie. But it was terrible.

M Can you recommend another interesting movie?

W No. That is the only movie I've watched recently.

남 안녕, Betty! Richard와 나는 영화관에 가는 중이야.

여 정말? 나도 함께해도 될까?

남 그럼. 우리가 볼 영화는 Mr. Brilliant야.

여 뭐? Mr. Brilliant라구? 어제 그거 봤는데.

남 정말? 그 영화 어때? 재미있어?

여 전혀. 정말 지루해. 너무 지루해서 영화에 집중할 수 없었어.

남 정말? 믿지 못하겠어. 영화에 대한 평이 정말 끝내주는데, 그렇지 않아?

여 나도 영화평을 전부 읽었어. 그런 다음 그 영화를 보러 가기로 결정했지. 그러나 형편없었어.

남 다른 재미있는 영화 추천해 줄 수 있니?

여 아니. 그 영화가 최근에 내가 본 유일한 영화야.

① Mr. Brilliant는 재미있는 영화야.

② Richard를 위해서 좋은 영화를 추천해 주자.

④ 미안하지만 영화평 웹사이트를 모르겠어.

⑤ 인터넷에서 영화를 다운 받아서 보면 안 돼.

●●
on the way to ~로 가는 길에   **review** 비평, 논평   **fantastic** 환상적인

20

M The annual sports competition will be held at Henry's school next Friday. He has taken part in the soccer competition for 2 years. But he may not participate in this year's competition because he can't find his soccer shoes. Although he looked everywhere for them, he couldn't find them. He tried to borrow a pair from a few of his friends, but they don't have any extra shoes. All his classmates and homeroom teacher expect him to play and be captain of the soccer team, and it is certain that they will be disappointed if he can't. In this situation, what would Henry's mom probably say to Henry?

남 다음 주 금요일에 Henry의 학교에서 연례 체육대회가 열릴 것이다. 그는 2년 동안 축구 대회에 참가해 왔다. 그러나, 그는 축구화를 찾을 수 없어서 올해 대회에는 참가할 수 없을지도 모른다. 모든 곳을 찾아보았지만, 그것들을 찾을 수 없었다. 몇몇 친구들에게 빌리려고도 해보았지만, 그들은 여분의 축구화를 가지고 있지 않다. 모든 반 친구들과 담임 선생님은 그가 경기를 하고 팀의 주장이 될 것이라고 기대하고 있는데 그가 참가하지 못하면 실망할 것이 분명하다. 이런 상황에서, Henry의 엄마는 Henry에게 뭐라고 말할 것인가?

① 축구를 좀 더 연습하는 게 어때?

② 나가서 새로운 축구화를 사자.

③ 너의 아빠에게 그 비밀을 말하면 어떨까?

④ 너의 친구들에게 그것들을 너에게 빌려 주도록 부탁하면 어떨까?

⑤ 네가 경기를 하지 않아서 정말 실망스러워.

●●
annual 연례의   **captain** 주장

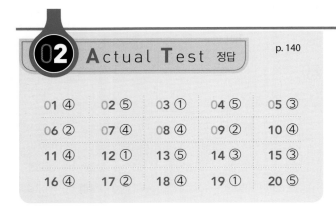

01 ④	02 ⑤	03 ①	04 ⑤	05 ③
06 ②	07 ④	08 ④	09 ②	10 ④
11 ④	12 ①	13 ⑤	14 ③	15 ③
16 ④	17 ②	18 ④	19 ①	20 ⑤

01

W How may I help you?

M I'm looking for a new house to move into. Could you show me some houses that are available?

W What kind of house do you have in mind?

M I want a two-story house with a front yard.

W I see. Do you prefer a house with a fence or without one?

M The latter.

W Anything else?

M It would be good if it is painted white rather than brown or blue.

W I'll show you some houses that have what you want. Let's go.

···

여 무엇을 도와드릴까요?

남 이사할 새 집을 찾고 있습니다. 제게 가능한 집을 좀 보여 주시겠습니까?

여 어떤 종류의 집을 생각해 두고 계세요?

남 앞뜰이 있는 이층집을 원합니다.

여 그렇군요. 울타리가 있는 것을 선호하세요, 아니면 없는 것을 선호하세요?

남 후자요.

여 다른 것은요?

남 갈색이나 파란색보다는 흰색으로 칠해져 있으면 좋겠습니다.

여 원하시는 것들을 가진 집을 보여드릴게요. 가시죠.

··

have in mind 염두에 두다   **two-story** 2층의   **yard** 뜰, 마당   **fence** 울타리   **latter** 후자

02

W What's up? You look stressed.

M I am really stressed. My school assignment is really late.

W Why? You never turn in late papers.

M Believe it or not, I was working on it for a week and had almost finished it, but…

W But what? What happened?

M My computer was infected with a virus a few days ago and I lost all my files.

W Oh, no! Were you able to remove the virus from the computer?

M Fortunately, yes. But I couldn't recover the lost files because I hadn't backed up my computer.

W Does it mean you had to write the paper all over again?

M Yes. I've taken the last 3 days to do it. I'm almost done.

W I'm very sorry to hear you've had so much trouble.

···

여 무슨 일이니? 스트레스 받아 보인다.

남 정말 스트레스 받아. 학교 과제가 아주 늦었어.

여 왜? 넌 한번도 보고서를 늦게 내지 않잖아.

남 믿거나 말거나, 일주일 동안 작업했고 거의 다 했어, 그런데…

여 그런데 뭐? 무슨 일이 일어났어?

남 내 컴퓨터가 며칠 전에 바이러스에 걸려서 내 파일을 모두 날렸어.

여 오, 이런! 컴퓨터에서 바이러스는 없앨 수 있었니?

남 다행스럽게도, 응. 하지만 내가 백업을 해놓지 않아서 잃어버린 파일은 복구하지 못했어.

여 보고서를 처음부터 모두 다시 써야 했다는 얘기니?

남 응. 그걸 하는 데 지난 3일이 걸렸어. 거의 다 됐어.

여 그런 문제를 겪었다니 안됐구나.

··

turn in 제출하다   **believe it or not** 믿거나 말거나   **be infected with a virus** 바이러스에 감염되다   **remove** 제거하다, 없애다   **recover** 회복하다

03

M Good morning, students. I'm Paula Hilton, the school principal. I will tell you about our school's renovation plan. As we announced before, we are planning to renovate the school cafeteria. It will take about 2 weeks starting next Monday. We will keep serving lunch, but as half the cafeteria is being renovated, there are fewer seats. The lunch times for every class will now be changed. Your homeroom teacher will tell you your new lunch time. Sorry for the inconvenience and thank you for understanding. I'm sure the cafeteria will serve you better after the renovations. Thank you.

....

남 학생 여러분, 좋은 아침입니다. Paula Hilton 교장입니다. 저는 학교의 수리 계획에 대해 여러분에게 이야기하겠습니다. 이전에 공고했듯이, 학교 구내식당을 수리할 예정입니다. 다음주 월요일부터 시작하여 약 2주가 걸릴 것입니다. 점심은 계속 판매하겠지만 식당 절반이 수리됨에 따라 좌석이 더 적을 것입니다. 이제 모든 학급의 점심 시간이 변경될 것입니다. 담임 선생님이 새 점심 시간을 알려줄 것입니다. 불편을 주어 죄송하고 이해해 주셔서 고마워요. 수리 후에는 더 잘 여러분을 맞을 수 있을 거라 확신합니다. 감사합니다.

••
principal 교장 **renovation** 수리 **announce** 공고하다 **seat** 좌석
inconvenience 불편함

04

W Excuse me. How much longer do I have to wait? I ordered about 20 minutes ago.

M Sorry, ma'am. I will go to the kitchen and check it out. I will be right back.

W Thank you.

M [Pause] It's coming up right away! Please wait a few more seconds.

W Okay. I'm so hungry. [Pause]

M Here's your order, ma'am.

W What's this? This is not what I asked for. I ordered seafood cream spaghetti, not tomato meatball spaghetti.

M Oh, I'm terribly sorry. I'll be right back with your order.

W Never mind. I'd like to cancel my order. I'm leaving!

....

여 실례합니다. 얼마나 더 오래 기다려야 할까요? 20분 전에 주문했는데요.

남 죄송합니다. 주방에 가서 확인해 보겠습니다. 바로 오겠습니다.

여 감사합니다.

남 이제 곧 나옵니다! 잠시만 더 기다려 주세요.

여 네. 배가 매우 고파서요.

남 여기 주문한 게 나왔습니다.

여 이게 뭐죠? 이것은 제가 요청한 것이 아닌데요. 저는 해산물 크림

스파게티를 주문했는데요. 토마토 미트볼 스파게티가 아니고요.

남 오, 정말 죄송합니다. 곧 주문한 것을 가져오겠습니다.

여 괜찮아요. 주문을 취소하고 싶어요. 난 갈거예요!

① 기쁜   ② 만족한   ③ 걱정하는
④ 부러운   ⑤ 화난

••
order 주문하다 **terribly** 끔찍한, 정말 **Never mind.** 신경 쓰지 마세요.
괜찮아요. **cancel one's order** ~의 주문을 취소하다

05

[Cell phone rings.]

W Hi, Taemin. What's up?

M I'd like to ask you about the English assignment. I accidently deleted the memo. What do I have to write about?

W You need to write about some of your favorite things such as your favorite food, season, or person.

M How long does it have to be?

W The teacher said 1,000 words. You have to include an introduction, a body, and a conclusion, too.

M I see. When is the due date, then?

W It is this Friday. You'd better start to write it now.

M Thank you very much.

....

[핸드폰이 울린다.]

여 안녕, 태민아. 무슨 일이니?

남 영어 과제에 대해 물어보고 싶어서. 내가 실수로 메모를 지웠거든. 무엇에 대해 써야해?

여 네가 좋아하는 음식, 계절, 혹은 사람과 같은 좋아하는 것들에 대해 써야 해.

남 얼마나 길어야 하니?

여 선생님은 1,000단어를 말씀하셨어. 도입, 본론, 결론을 포함해야 해.

남 그렇구나. 그러면 기한은 언제야?

여 이번 주 금요일이야. 지금 쓰기 시작하는 것이 좋을 거야.

남 정말 고마워.

••
assignment 과제 **accidently** 실수로 **delete** 지우다, 삭제하다
include 포함하다 **conclusion** 결론 **due date** 마감 날짜

06

W Excuse me. I'm looking for notebooks. How much

are they?

M It <u>depends</u>. <u>What kind of</u> notebooks do you want?

W Well. I have no idea. It is for my 10-year-old boy. Could you please <u>recommend</u> some to me?

M Sure. Come here. These are good ones for children that age. <u>Solid</u> ones are $1 and ones with <u>printed animation characters</u> on them are $1.50 each.

W I see. I will take 5 of each. Could you please <u>gift-wrap</u> them?

M Sure. But there is an <u>additional charge of</u> $2. Do you still want it done?

W Yes, please. Here is $20.

M Thank you. Here is your <u>change</u>.

⋯⋯⋯⋯⋯⋯⋯⋯⋯⋯⋯⋯⋯⋯⋯⋯⋯⋯⋯⋯

여 실례합니다. 공책을 찾고 있는데요. 얼마인가요?

남 다 달라요. 어떤 종류의 공책을 원하세요?

여 음. 잘 모르겠어요. 10살 남자 아이에게 줄 것이거든요. 제게 추천해 주시겠습니까?

남 물론이죠. 이쪽으로 오세요. 이것들이 그 나이 또래에 좋습니다. 단색들은 1달러씩이고요, 애니메이션 캐릭터가 인쇄되어 있는 것들은 1.5달러씩입니다.

여 그렇군요. 각각 5권씩 살게요. 그것들을 선물 포장 해 주시겠어요?

남 물론입니다. 하지만 2달러의 추가요금이 발생합니다. 그래도 하시겠습니까?

여 네, 그렇게 해주세요. 여기 20달러가 있습니다.

남 감사합니다. 여기 거스름돈이 있습니다.

•• **solid** 단색의 **additional charge** 추가 요금 **change** 거스름돈

07

W Dr. Flahive. Can I talk to you <u>for a while</u>?

M Yes. <u>Go ahead</u>.

W My brother in Seattle is in the hospital now, but there is no one to <u>take care of</u> him.

M Really? That's too bad. Do you need to <u>take</u> some <u>days off</u>?

W I'm sorry, but yes. Can I take a <u>week off</u>?

M Of course. We're not busy this week and I'm planning to <u>hire</u> the <u>part timer</u> who I <u>interviewed</u> yesterday.

W Thank you so much.

M But tell Mrs. White to take care of your work <u>while</u>

you're gone.

W Yes, I will. I hope she'll be understanding, too.

⋯⋯⋯⋯⋯⋯⋯⋯⋯⋯⋯⋯⋯⋯⋯⋯⋯⋯⋯⋯

여 Flahive 박사님. 잠시 이야기 할 수 있을까요?

남 물론이죠. 이야기 하세요.

여 Seattle에 있는 제 남동생이 지금 병원에 있는데 그를 돌봐줄 사람이 아무도 없습니다.

남 정말이요? 안됐군요. 며칠 휴가 내야 할 것 같나요?

여 죄송하지만, 그렇습니다. 한 주 쉬어도 될까요?

남 물론이죠. 이번 주에는 바쁘지 않고 어제 인터뷰한 파트타이머도 고용할 계획입니다.

여 정말 감사합니다.

남 그렇지만 White부인께 당신이 없을 동안 당신의 일을 봐달라고 이야기 하세요.

여 네, 그럴게요. 그녀도 이해해 주면 좋겠어요.

① 환자 – 의사　　② 학생 – 교사　　③ 영업사원 – 고객
④ 직원 – 상사　　⑤ 면접관 – 면접 응시자

•• **take days off** 며칠 쉬다, 휴가를 내다　**hire** 고용하다　**part timer** 파트타이머　**understanding** 이해심 있는

08

M Wow! She has beautiful <u>shiny hair</u> and ears.

W She sure does. Thanks for saying so.

M <u>What's wrong with</u> her?

W She used to be <u>active</u> and liked to play with me, but these days she just <u>sits on a couch</u> or <u>stays in</u> her house.

M What about her <u>appetite</u>? Does she <u>eat well</u>?

W Not really. She doesn't even take care of her little puppies.

M Hmm… Let's <u>take a blood test</u> and see the <u>result</u>.

W When will the result <u>come out</u>?

M It usually takes 3 days. Please come again on <u>Thursday</u>.

⋯⋯⋯⋯⋯⋯⋯⋯⋯⋯⋯⋯⋯⋯⋯⋯⋯⋯⋯⋯

남 우와! 정말 아름답고 빛나는 털과 귀를 가졌군요.

여 그렇죠. 그렇게 말해주니 고마워요.

남 무슨 문제가 있나요?

여 그녀는 활동적이었고 저와 함께 노는 것을 좋아했었는데 요즘에는 가만히 소파에만 앉아있거나 집 안에만 있어요.

남 식욕은 어떤가요? 잘 먹습니까?

여 꼭 그렇지는 않아요. 자기 강아지들 조차도 돌보지 않습니다.

남 음… 혈액검사 하고 결과를 봅시다.

여 결과는 언제 나오나요?

남 대략 3일 걸립니다. 목요일에 다시 오세요.

① 미용실　　　② 운동장　　　③ 거실

④ 동물 병원　　⑤ 학교

couch 소파　**stay in** ~에 머무르다　**appetite** 식욕　**take a blood test** 혈액 검사를 하다　**result** 결과

09

① W What do you want for a snack?

　M I want some fruit.

② W Oh, no. What are you doing?

　M I'm sorry, mom. I'll start studying hard.

③ W Aren't you hungry? Have a snack first.

　M No thanks, mom. I have to go out now.

④ W What are you doing, sweetie?

　M I'm playing a computer game. It's so much fun.

⑤ W Are you ready to go to school?

　M Almost. Please wait 5 more minutes.

① 여 간식으로 무얼 먹을래?
　남 과일이요.
② 여 오, 이런. 너 뭐하니?
　남 죄송해요. 엄마. 열심히 공부할게요.
③ 여 배고프지 않니? 간식 좀 먹으렴.
　남 괜찮아요. 엄마. 저 지금 나가야 해요.
④ 여 얘야 뭐하니?
　남 컴퓨터 게임하고 있어요. 정말 재미있어요.
⑤ 여 학교 갈 준비 다 됐니?
　남 거의 다 됐어요. 5분만 더 기다려 주세요.

sweetie 사랑하는 사람을 부를 때 쓰는 호칭　**Are you ready to-V?** ~할 준비가 되었니?　**minute** 분

10

W Hello, sir. Welcome to Oak Inn. How may I help you?

M Do you have a room available for tonight?

W Did you make a reservation?

M No. I didn't.

W Let me check first. Please wait for a while. [Pause] A single room is available. Is it okay for you?

M Yes, I'm by myself. How much is it?

W Do you have an A-1 Suites membership card? If you have it, you can get a 10 percent discount.

M No. This is my first time here.

W I see. If you'd like one, please fill in this form. You can get a card within a few minutes.

M Okay. I will.

여 안녕하세요. Oak Inn에 오신 것을 환영합니다. 무엇을 도와드릴까요?

남 오늘 밤에 빈 방이 있나요?

여 예약 하셨습니까?

남 아니오, 안 했어요.

여 일단 확인 해 볼게요. 잠시 기다려 주세요. 1인실은 가능합니다. 괜찮으시겠어요?

남 네. 저 혼자예요. 얼마입니까?

여 A1스위트 회원카드를 갖고 계세요? 만일 그러시면 10%할인 받으실 수 있습니다.

남 아니오. 이번이 처음입니다.

여 그렇군요. 만일 원하시면 이 양식을 작성해 주세요. 몇 분 안에 카드를 발급받으실 수 있습니다.

남 좋아요. 그렇게 할게요.

make a reservation 예약하다　**single room** 1인실　**membership card** 회원권　**fill in** (양식에) 기입하다

11

M Did you buy the tickets for the musical?

W Yes, I did. We are going to see Les Miserables. It is playing at the Sejong Center for the Performing Arts.

M Really? What time is it?

W It is at 1 p.m. tomorrow, Saturday.

M Hmm… To tell you the truth, I had a tough week finishing my project. I couldn't sleep enough all week.

W Do you mean you want me to cancel the reservation?

M No, no. It's not that. I just want to go in the evening not the afternoon. I want to sleep in really late and catch up on my sleep.

W I see. I will check <u>whether</u> we can go in the evening or not. I'll let you know.

M Thank you very much.

남 뮤지컬 표 샀니?

여 응. 우리 레미제라블 볼 거야. 세종문화회관에서 공연하고 있어.

남 정말? 몇 시인데?

여 내일 토요일 오후 한 시야.

남 음… 솔직히 말하자면, 난 과제를 끝내느라 힘든 한 주를 보냈어. 한 주 내내 잠도 충분히 못 잤어.

여 예약을 취소하기를 원하는 거니?

남 아니, 아니. 그게 아니야. 내 말은 단지 오후가 아니라 저녁에 가고 싶다고. 늦게까지 자고 부족한 잠도 보충하고 싶어서.

여 그렇구나. 저녁에 갈 수 있는지 한 번 보고 알려줄게.

남 정말 고마워.

••
tough 힘든 **cancel the reservation** 예약을 취소하다 **catch up on** ~을 따라잡다

12

M Terra! <u>Congratulations on</u> winning the Tennis Championship! How do you feel now?

W Thank you very much. I feel great! Fantastic!

M People didn't <u>expect</u> that you would <u>beat</u> last year's champion, Vera Chang. Were there any <u>special tips</u> or <u>strategies you used</u>?

W Well, I didn't think in a <u>negative way</u> and just tried to <u>focus on</u> the ball until the end of the match.

M You focused really well throughout the match. How do you learn to <u>concentrate</u> so well?

W Well, I usually <u>turn on</u> some rock music and play it very <u>loudly</u> while practicing. That way, I can <u>get used to</u> the noise of a real <u>competition</u>.

M That's <u>awesome</u>! What are you going to do now?

W I just want to go home and take a nap.

남 Terra! 테니스 챔피언십 우승을 축하해. 지금 기분이 어때?

여 정말 고마워. 기분 정말 좋아. 환상적이야!

남 사람들은 네가 작년 우승인 Vera Chang을 이길 것이라고 기대하지 않았어. 특별한 비법이나 전술이 있었니?

여 음, 나는 부정적인 쪽으로 생각하지 않고 경기가 끝날 때까지 공에 집중하려고 노력했어.

남 너는 경기 내내 정말 잘 집중했어. 어떻게 그렇게 잘 집중하는 걸

배우니?

여 음, 나는 대체로 연습할 때 록음악을 틀고 소리를 아주 크게 해. 그런 식으로 실제 경기의 소음에 익숙해질 수 있어.

남 멋지네! 이제 뭐 할거야?

여 그냥 집에 가서 낮잠 자고 싶어.

••
strategy 전술, 전략 **negative** 부정적인 **turn on** 켜다, 틀다 **loudly** 크게 **get used to** ~에 익숙해지다 **awesome** 멋진

13

[Telephone rings.]

W Hello. This is Dr. Tailor's <u>dental clinic</u>. How may I help you?

M Hello. This is Tony Romas. I'd like to <u>make an appointment</u> with Dr. Tailor.

W <u>Have you visited</u> our clinic before?

M Yes. I have a clinic card.

W Good. Can you describe your problem?

M I have a <u>toothache</u>. It's not too painful, but I want it checked out. And I'd like to get my teeth scaled after the doctor's <u>treatment</u>.

W No problem. Can you come in at 11 tomorrow morning? I mean <u>Wednesday</u>.

M I'm afraid I can't. I have an important meeting. Is it <u>possible</u> to make it the <u>following day</u>?

W That's fine. See you then.

메모
① 수신: Dr. Tailor
② 발신: Tony Romas
③ 증상: 치통, 스케일링
④ 병원카드: 있음 ☑ 없음 □
⑤ 약속시간: 수요일 오전 11시

[전화벨이 울린다.]

여 여보세요. Dr. Tailor 치과입니다. 무엇을 도와드릴까요?

남 여보세요. 저는 Tony Romas 입니다. Dr. Tailor와 예약을 하고 싶은데요.

여 이전에 저희 병원을 방문한 적이 있으세요?

남 네. 병원카드를 가지고 있습니다.

여 좋습니다. 문제점을 말씀해 주시겠어요?

남 치통이 있어요. 심하게 아프진 않지만 진료를 받고 싶습니다. 그리고 치료 후에 스케일링을 하고 싶습니다.

여 문제 없어요. 내일 오전 11시에 가능하세요? 제 말은 수요일이요.

남 안될 것 같은데요. 중요한 회의가 있어서요. 그 다음날은 가능할까요?

여 괜찮습니다. 그 때 뵐게요.

•• **dental clinic** 치과 **describe** 기술하다. 설명하다 **toothache** 치통 **treatment** 치료 **following day** 다음 날

14

W Hey, Dennis. What are you doing here?

M Oh, Gillian. I accidently dropped my cell phone in here, but it's locked.

W You mean in this recycling box? Oh, no. How did that happen?

M I was separating trash when the phone rang so I took the call. After the call I put it into this recycling bin by accident.

W I'm sorry to hear that. You'd better go to the apartment management office. They might have a key for this bin.

M I did. But the office isn't open now. The office hours are over.

W Did you ask the security guard, then? He might have one.

M That's a good idea. I'll go and ask him. Thank you very much.

....

여 Dennis야. 여기서 뭐해?

남 오, Gillian. 잘못해서 이곳에 핸드폰을 떨어뜨렸어. 그런데 잠겨있어.

여 여기 재활용 통에 말이야? 오, 저런. 어떻게 그런 일이 일어났니?

남 쓰레기를 분류하고 있는데 전화가 왔어. 그래서 통화를 했지. 통화 후에 그것을 실수로 이 쓰레기 통에 넣었어.

여 안됐구나. 아파트 관리실에 가는 게 좋겠어. 이 통 열쇠가 있을 거야.

남 갔었어. 하지만 지금 사무실이 안 열려 있어. 업무 시간이 끝났어

여 그러면 경비아저씨께 여쭤봤어? 가지고 있을 수도 있어.

남 좋은 생각이네. 가서 여쭤볼게. 정말 고마워.

•• **accidently** 잘못해서, 사고로 **recycling** 재활용 **separate trash** 쓰레기를 분류하다 **apartment management office** 아파트 관리실

15

W Listen well, everyone. Before I dismiss the class, I will make an announcement. Our school's student

union will offer a special lecture series every Wednesday for 5 weeks in a row. This Wednesday, June 4, HeavTec's CEO Rose Martin will give a lecture on Creative Thinking in room 101. You will be given a handout with a pen in the lecture hall on that day. I'm sure it will help you think in a creative way. Please come and join us for a wonderful time. Hope to see all of you there.

....

여 여러분, 잘 들으세요. 수업을 끝내기 전에 소식 하나 전할게요. 우리 학교의 학생회에서 5주 연속으로 매주 수요일에 특별 강좌를 제공합니다. 이번 주 수요일, 6월 4일에는 101호 에서 HeavTec의 CEO Rose Martin 께서 창의적인 생각에 대한 강연을 할 것입니다. 당일 강의실에서 인쇄물과 펜을 제공할 것입니다. 그 강의는 여러분이 창의적으로 생각하는 데 도움을 줄 것이라고 확신합니다. 와서 멋진 시간 함께 하도록 해요. 여러분 모두를 그 곳에서 보기를 바랍니다.

•• **dismiss the class** 수업을 해산하다, 마치다 **student union** 학생회 **lecture** 강의, 강연 **in a row** 연속으로 **handout** 배포 인쇄물, 유인물

16

M Good morning, Apple. Why have you come to school so early today?

W Hi, Jack. Didn't you know that I always come to school around this time every day? You are very early today.

M Every day? Are you serious?

W Of course I am.

M Why?

W I come early because my mom drives me to school on her way to work.

M What do you do before the class starts, then?

W It depends. I sometimes preview or review the lessons or listen to music.

M Wow! You're a really good student. What time do you usually get up?

W I usually get up at 6:30 in the morning.

....

남 좋은 아침이야, Apple. 오늘 왜 이렇게 학교에 빨리 왔어?

여 안녕, Jack. 너는 내가 매일 이 시간에 학교에 오는 것을 몰랐니? 너 오늘은 매우 이르구나.

남 매일? 정말이야?

여 물론이지.

남 왜?

여 내가 일찍 오는 이유는 엄마가 출근하시는 길에 나를 학교에 데려다 주시기 때문이야.

남 그러면 수업 시작하기 전에 뭐해?

여 때에 따라 달라. 나는 가끔 예습이나 복습을 하거나, 음악을 들어.

남 우와! 너는 정말 훌륭한 학생이구나. 너는 대체적으로 몇 시에 일어나?

여 <u>나는 대개 아침 6시 반에 일어나.</u>

① 우리 엄마도 운전을 잘 하셔.
② 나를 학교에 태워줄 수 있나요?
③ 나는 어젯밤 두 시에 잠자리에 들었어.
⑤ 여섯 시에 모닝콜을 좀 해주세요.

●●
around 대략 **serious** 심각한 **preview** 예습 **review** 복습

17

[Telephone rings.]

M Hello, this is Gold Star Electronics <u>customer service</u>. How may I help you?

W Hello. I had an <u>air conditioner installed</u> this morning. It was working quite well right after your <u>technician</u> had installed it.

M And?

W But when I turned it on with a <u>remote control</u> just a while ago, nothing happened. It is not working.

M I see. We're very sorry for the <u>inconvenience</u>. Let me ask you a few <u>questions</u> before sending someone.

W Okay. Go ahead.

M Did you check the <u>batteries</u> of the remote control?

W Of course I did. They are both new.

M Good. Could you please check the <u>power button</u> whether it is on? It is <u>at the back of</u> the air conditioner.

W <u>Okay, I will. Please wait for me for a while.</u>

. . . .

[전화 벨이 울린다.]

남 여보세요. Gold Star Electronics 고객 서비스 센터 입니다. 무엇을 도와드릴까요?

여 여보세요. 오늘 아침에 에어컨을 설치했습니다. 기술자가 설치를 한 직후에는 작동을 잘 했습니다.

남 그리고요?

여 하지만 조금 전 리모컨으로 켰을 때 아무 반응이 없었습니다. 작동을 하지 않아요.

남 알겠습니다. 불편을 드려 정말 죄송합니다. 누군가를 보내기 전에 몇 가지 질문을 하겠습니다.

여 네. 그렇게 하세요.

남 리모컨의 배터리는 잘 확인하셨나요?

여 물론이죠. 둘다 새 것들이에요.

남 네. 전원이 켜져 있는지 확인해 주시겠어요? 그것은 에어컨 뒤쪽에 있습니다.

여 <u>좋아요, 그럴게요. 잠시 기다려 주세요.</u>

① 에어컨을 어디에서 샀어요?
③ 오, 정말이요? 곧바로 배터리를 확인할게요.
④ 에어컨은 언제 배달되나요?
⑤ 걱정 마세요. 그 배터리는 용량이 남아 있어요.

●●
install 설치하다 **technician** 기술자 **remote control** 리모컨
inconvenience 불편

18

M May I help you?

W Yes, please. I have a question about this <u>scholarship application</u>.

M What is it?

W I actually <u>submitted</u> my application three days ago. However, I just <u>found out</u> that I <u>made a mistake</u> on the application form.

M Oh, no. Do you mean you put down the <u>wrong information</u>?

W Unfortunately, yes. If <u>possible</u>, I'd like to change the student ID number. Can I?

M Let me <u>check</u>. May I have your name, please?

W I'm Eva Rosa.

M Oh! Yours isn't in the <u>process</u> of being <u>evaluated</u> yet. Just <u>fill out</u> the <u>correct</u> information on this form.

W <u>Thank you very much. I was really worried about it.</u>

. . . .

남 무엇을 도와 드릴까요?

여 네. 장학금 신청에 대한 질문이 있습니다.

남 무슨 질문인가요?

여 저는 사실 3일 전에 신청서를 제출했습니다. 그런데 양식에 실수를 한 것을 알았습니다.

남 오, 이런. 잘못된 정보를 입력했다는 이야기인가요?

여 불행하게도 그렇습니다. 가능하다면 학생 ID 번호를 바꾸고 싶은데 괜찮나요?

남 확인해 볼게요. 이름이 무엇인가요?

여 Eva Rosa입니다.

남 오! 당신 것은 아직 심사 과정에 들어가지 않았네요. 이 양식에 정확한 정보를 써넣으세요.

여 정말 감사 드립니다. 저는 그것을 엄청 걱정했어요.

① 항상 밝은 쪽을 보려고 노력하세요.
② 학생 ID 번호를 알려주시겠어요?
③ 마감일은 3일 전이란 것 모르셨나요?
⑤ 장학금 신청의 자격이 무엇인가요?

●●
scholarship application 장학금 신청 **submit** 제출하다 **correct** 옳은 **process** 과정 **evaluate** 심사하다

19

M It is $57.50 in total. Are you going to pay in cash or by credit card?

W By credit card.

M Do you have a store membership card, too? You can get points for your purchase.

W Yes, here it is.

M Please sign on the screen. [Pause] Here is your receipt. Thank you.

W Wait! Wait! I was charged the wrong price for the three cans of soda. The sodas should be $2 not $6. They're on sale.

M Oh, really? Let me see it.

W Look! It says $6. It is not the discounted price.

M Oh, I am so sorry for that. I'll cancel this and recharge it. Can I have your credit card again?

W Okay. Here you are.

남 총 57.50달러 입니다. 현금으로 결제 하실 건가요, 아니면 카드로 결제하실 건가요?

여 카드로요.

남 상점 회원카드도 있으세요? 구매에 따른 포인트를 받으실 수 있어요.

여 네, 여기 있습니다.

남 화면에 사인해주세요. 여기 영수증이 있습니다. 고맙습니다.

여 잠깐! 잠시만요! 소다 캔 3개에 대해서 틀린 가격이 부과되었어요. 소다는 6달러가 아니라 2달러야 해요. 세일 중이거든요.

남 오, 정말요? 한 번 봅시다.

여 보세요! 6달러라고 써있지요. 이것은 할인된 가격이 아니예요.

남 오, 정말 죄송합니다. 취소하고 재결재 해드릴게요. 다시 카드를 주시겠어요?

여 네. 여기 있습니다.

② 세일은 언제 끝나나요?
③ 정말이요? 저는 그것들이 세일중인 줄 알았어요.
④ 불편을 드려 죄송합니다. 그것을 다시 결제할게요.
⑤ 어떤 종류의 카드를 발급받기 원하세요?

●●
in total 총, 합 **pay in cash** 현금으로 지불하다 **receipt** 영수증 **discounted price** 할인된 가격 **recharge** 재결제하다

20

M Teresa is going to give a presentation tomorrow in English class. She has been preparing and practicing for over a week. She even practiced in front of a mirror and recorded it one day. Today is the day of the presentation. She has breakfast and goes to school. However, she suddenly has a stomachache and breaks out in a cold sweat right before the English class starts. She is sick and knows it is impossible for her to give her presentation. So she decides to go to the staff room. In this situation, what would Teresa most likely say to her English teacher?

남 Teresa는 내일 영어시간에 발표를 할 예정이다. 그녀는 일주일 넘게 준비하고 연습해왔다. 그녀는 하루는 거울 앞에서 연습하고 녹화도 했다. 오늘은 발표 당일이다. 그녀는 아침밥을 먹고 학교에 간다. 그러나 영어 수업이 시작하기 직전에 갑자기 배가 아프고 식은땀이 난다. 그녀는 아파서 발표를 하는 것이 불가능하다는 것을 안다. 그래서 그녀는 교무실에 가기로 결심한다. 이 상황에서 Teresa는 영어 선생님께 무어라 말할까?

① 당신이 첫 번째 발표자가 될 수 있는지 모르겠네요.
② 힘내세요! 다음 번에 더 잘하실 수 있을 거예요.
③ 양호실이 어디에 있는지 아세요?
④ 당신이 발표를 할 수 있을 때 알려주세요.
⑤ 아파서 그런데 제 발표를 다음 수업 시간에 해도 될까요?

●●
record 녹화하다 **stomachache** 복통 **cold sweat** 식은 땀 **staff room** 교무실

MEMO

MEMO

MEMO

MEMO

MEMO

MEMO

MEMO